T0330386

Community Wealth Building and the
Reconstruction of American Democracy

JEPSON STUDIES IN LEADERSHIP

Series Editors: Kristin Bezio, George R. Goethals and Thad Williamson, *Jepson School of Leadership Studies, University of Richmond, USA*

Managing Editor: Cassie Price

Jepson Studies in Leadership is dedicated to the interdisciplinary pursuit of important questions related to leadership. The series aims to publish the best work on leadership from such fields as economics, English, history, philosophy, political science, psychology, religion, management, and organizational studies. In addition to monographs and edited collections on leadership, the series includes volumes that bring together influential scholars from multiple disciplines to think collectively about distinctive leadership themes in politics, science, civil society, and corporate life. The books in the series are of interest to humanists and social scientists, as well as organizational theorists and instructors teaching in business, leadership, and professional programs.

Titles in the series include:

Cultural Icons and Cultural Leadership
Edited by Peter Iver Kaufman and Kristin M.S. Bezio

Reconstruction and the Arc of Racial (in)Justice
Edited by Julian Maxwell Hayter and George R. Goethals

Leadership and Sexuality
Power, Principles and Processes
Edited by James K. Beggan and Scott T. Allison

Leadership, Populism, and Resistance
Edited by Kristin M.S. Bezio and George R. Goethals

Community Wealth Building and the Reconstruction of American Democracy
Can We Make American Democracy Work?
Edited by Melody C. Barnes, Corey D.B. Walker and Thad M. Williamson

Community Wealth Building and the Reconstruction of American Democracy

Can We Make American Democracy Work?

Edited by

Melody C. Barnes

Co-Director of the Democracy Initiative, Dorothy Danforth Compton Professor and Professor of Practice, Miller Center of Public Affairs, and a Distinguished Fellow, School of Law, University of Virginia, USA

Corey D.B. Walker

Wake Forest Professor of the Humanities, Wake Forest University, USA

Thad M. Williamson

Associate Professor of Leadership Studies and Philosophy, Politics, Economics and Law, University of Richmond, USA

JEPSON STUDIES IN LEADERSHIP

 Edward Elgar
PUBLISHING

Cheltenham, UK • Northampton, MA, USA

Published by
Edward Elgar Publishing Limited
The Lypiatts
15 Lansdown Road
Cheltenham
Glos GL50 2JA
UK

Edward Elgar Publishing, Inc.
William Pratt House
9 Dewey Court
Northampton
Massachusetts 01060
USA

A catalogue record for this book
is available from the British Library

Library of Congress Control Number: 2020944307

This book is available electronically in the **Elgar**online
Social and Political Science subject collection
http://dx.doi.org/10.4337/9781839108136

ISBN 978 1 83910 812 9 (cased)
ISBN 978 1 83910 813 6 (eBook)

Printed and bound by CPI Group (UK) Ltd, Croydon, CR0 4YY

Contents

Figures

Contributors

Lawrie Balfour is Professor of Politics at the University of Virginia and author of several books on race and American democracy, including *Democracy's Reconstruction: Thinking Politically with W.E.B. DuBois.*

Melody C. Barnes is Co-Director of the Democracy Initiative, Dorothy Danforth Compton Professor and Professor of Practice in the Miller Center of Public Affairs, and a Distinguished Fellow at the School of Law, University of Virginia. Her extensive career in public service includes serving as Assistant to the President and Director of the Domestic Policy Council during the first term of President Barack Obama.

Risha R. Berry is Assistant Professor at the Virginia Commonwealth University School of Education. She previously served as Project Management Analyst for the Office of Community Wealth Building and Acting Deputy Chief Administrative Officer for Human Services for the City of Richmond.

Richard Dagger is E. Claiborne Robins Distinguished Chair in the Liberal Arts and Professor and Chair of Political Science, University of Richmond. He is author of *Civic Virtues: Rights, Citizenship and Republican Liberalism* and *Playing Fair: Political Obligations and the Problems of Punishment.*

Meghan Z. Gough is Associate Professor and Chair of the Urban and Regional Studies and Planning Program at the L. Douglas Wilder School of Government and Public Affairs, Virginia Commonwealth University. She is author *of Public Gardens and Community Revitalization: Partnerships for Positive Social Change.*

Julian Maxwell Hayter is Associate Professor of Leadership Studies at the University of Richmond. He is author of *The Dream is Lost: Voting Rights and the Politics of Race in Richmond, Virginia.*

Margaret Kohn is Professor of Political Science at the University of Toronto. She is author of *Brave New Neighborhoods: The Privatization of Public Space* and *The Death and Life of the Urban Commonwealth.*

J.S. Maloy is Professor and Kaliste Saloom Endowed Chair in Political Science at the University of Louisiana-Lafayette. He is author of *The Colonial*

American Origins of Modern Democratic Thought and *Smarter Ballots: Electoral Realism and Reform.*

Ravi K. Perry is Professor and Chair of the Department of Political Science, Howard University. He is the author of *The Little Rock Crisis: What Desegregation Politics Says About Us* and *Black Mayors, White Majorities: The Balancing Act of Racial Politics.*

Kenneth P. Ruscio is Senior Distinguished Lecturer in Leadership Studies at the University of Richmond, and former President of Washington & Lee University. He is author of *The Leadership Dilemma in Modern Democracy.*

Isabel Sawhill is Senior Fellow in Economic Studies at the Brookings Institution. She is the author of, most recently, *The Forgotten Americans: An Economic Agenda for a Divided Nation.* She served as an Associate Director of the Office of Management and Budget under President Bill Clinton.

Corey D.B. Walker is Wake Forest Professor of the Humanities at Wake Forest University and former Dean of the Samuel Dewitt Proctor School of Theology at Virginia Union University. He is the author of *A Noble Fight: African American Freemasonry and the Struggle for Democracy in America.*

Thad M. Williamson is Associate Professor of Leadership Studies and Philosophy, Politics, Economics and Law at the University of Richmond. He is author of *Sprawl, Justice and Citizenship: The Civic Costs of the American Way of Life* and co-author of *Making a Place for Community: Local Democracy in a Global Era.* He served as the first Director of the Office of Community Wealth Building for the City of Richmond.

Barbara Brown Wilson is Assistant Professor of Urban & Environmental Planning at the University of Virginia. She is the author of *Resilience for All: Striving for Equity through Community-Driven Design.*

Nicholas J.G. Winter is Associate Professor of Politics at the University of Virginia. He is author of *Dangerous Frames: How Ideas About Race and Gender Shape Public Opinion.*

Acknowledgments

The editors would like to express their appreciation to each of the contributors to this book and the scholarly gathering on community wealth building and the future of American democracy hosted by the Jepson School of Leadership Studies at the University of Richmond in June 2019. They thank Dr. Allison Archer (formerly of the University of Richmond) for her help in planning this gathering as well as related events, Jepson School of Leadership Studies staff member Shannon Best for planning and logistical support, and Dean Sandra Peart of the Jepson School for overall support. They also thank Jepson School staff member Cassie Price for her assistance in copy-editing contributions to this book, and to Professors Kristin Bezio and George R. "Al" Goethals, series co-editors of the Jepson Series in Leadership published by Edward Elgar Publishing, of which this book is a part. They also express their appreciation to Senior Editor Alan Sturmer at Edward Elgar Publishing and to the Edward Elgar Publishing production staff for accepting their proposal and working diligently towards its timely publication.

Melody C. Barnes is deeply appreciative of those who supported this work so generously—engaging in robust and productive debate, and reading early drafts, including Tamar Bland, Sheri Brady, Marland Buckner, Chekemma Fulmore-Townsend, Olatunde Johnson, Sidney Milkis, Lara Putnam, Adria Scharf and Karen Zivi. She thanks her colleagues at the Aspen Institute Forum for Community Solutions whose equity-focused work at the local level serves as an inspiration and important lens. She is grateful for the support offered by the University of Richmond, and her partnership with co-editors Thad M. Williamson and Corey D.B. Walker. Thad and Corey brought their intellect as well as commitment to equity to this project. Without them, this book wouldn't be possible. She wishes to thank her parents, Frances and Charles Barnes who made all things possible. And finally, she thanks her biggest fan, most rigorous reviewer and favorite debate partner, her husband, Marland Buckner. His unwavering and constant support is a gift.

Corey D.B. Walker is truly grateful for the friendship of Greg Carr, Claudrena N. Harold, Keisha-Khan Y. Perry, James Pope, and Larry L. Rowley and the years of sustained and engaged conversations about race, religion, and democracy. Thanks also to the citizens of Charlottesville, Virginia, Providence, Rhode Island, Winston-Salem, North Carolina, and Richmond,

Virginia for allowing him to learn rewarding lessons about the rich textures of local politics and the promise of deep democracy.

Thad M. Williamson additionally expresses appreciation to his former City of Richmond colleagues who played integral roles in the formation, development and expansion of the Office of Community Wealth Building over the time period 2013–18, an experience that directly shaped this book, including especially Risha Berry, Selena Cuffee-Glenn, Nicholas Feucht, Reginald Gordon, Christina Mastroianni, Valaryee Mitchell, Councilwoman Ellen Robertson, and Evette Roots. Each of these individuals have been valued conversation partners, thought leaders, and practitioners in the work of bringing the community wealth building vision to life in Richmond, as well as treasured friends. He also thanks the Jepson School of Leadership Studies and the University of Richmond for its support of this important community work and in particular to colleagues and friends Julian Hayter, Amy Howard and Crystal Hoyt for countless conversations on topics related to this book. He thanks co-editors Melody C. Barnes and Corey D.B. Walker for many additional conversations fleshing out the meaning of "community wealth building" and its local and national application, as well as for their specific work on this book. Finally, he thanks his wife Adria L. Scharf and daughter Sahara Scharf Williamson for their unstinting and patient support of not only this specific book but also the years of practical work that informs it.

Melody C. Barnes, Corey D.B. Walker and Thad M. Williamson
Richmond, Virginia
February 2020

PART I

Community wealth building and the promise of democratic reconstruction

1. Introduction: can we make American democracy work?

Melody C. Barnes, Corey D.B. Walker and Thad M. Williamson

Historic levels of economic inequality. Deep partisan divides. Rising levels of intolerance and hate-fueled acts of violence. What started as an audacious experiment in political community now appears to be in crisis. And the current crisis is not a short-term one that can be "fixed" at the next election. Rather, the current crisis is historic and existential and calls into question the very legitimacy and future of American democracy. In many ways, American democracy stands in the wake of the probing question raised by Dr. Martin Luther King, Jr., "Where do we go from here?" (King, 1967).

Americans are frustrated by the inability of democracy to deliver. Viable and sustainable solutions to the litany of problems plaguing society seem to elude politicians, public officials, scholars, and citizens. To be sure, a healthy degree of frustration with the processes and outcomes of democratic institutions is not a defect but an essential institutional feature of democratic systems. However, in a democratic system of majority rule, democracy may succumb to what Alexis de Tocqueville termed "its prejudices and its passions" (Tocqueville, 1835 [2004], p. 15). A frustrated minority structurally out of power *and* a frustrated majority that holds power—each unable to fully respond to the real *and* felt needs of their respective constituency—precipitates a profound crisis.

While some aspects of the present political moment indeed take the familiar form of "normal" democratic politics, the election and the subsequent presidency of Donald J. Trump raises more fundamental questions about not only the present state of American democratic institutions but also the deeper flaws in the historic architecture of those institutions. Indeed, the election and presidency of Donald Trump have thrown new light on long-standing democratic deficits in the American republic—from the archaic Electoral College to the racial wealth gap to inequalities of political voice and influence. Thus, the election of Trump can be understood as the culmination of long-standing tendencies within American democracy and its inability to effectively respond to the demands of many of its citizens over a prolonged period of time.

Any political system that fails to deliver economic prosperity, expanded opportunity, effective problem-solving, and redress of historic injustices will lose legitimacy. America exhibits a unique inability to respond to centuries of chattel slavery and state-sanctioned racial discrimination. For nearly half a century, economic inequality in the U.S. has been widening, with incomes and social mobility stagnant for much of the population and the top 1 percent capturing the largest share of gains from economic growth. At the same time, a wide range of problems—from local public education to affordable housing to global climate change—simply have not been adequately addressed by policy-makers. Perceptions that the "system" is rigged in favor of special interests and the wealthy have risen along with distrust of public institutions and elected officials. Consequently, many millions of Americans are deeply dissatisfied with democracy and skeptical about the future.

Yet, America's democratic challenges are grounded in deeper structural issues:

- The fact that the U.S. is both an extremely diverse society and a nation with a history largely defined by white supremacy, chattel slavery, and state-sanctioned discrimination, and is largely defined by the historic and ongoing struggles to challenge structural racism in law, culture, and daily life. The exclusionary basis of the aspirations of the founding generation of American democracy and the history and present practice of America's racial democracy continue to expose the racialist and racist nature of disparities in well-being, health, income, and education that are constitutive of the U.S.
- The fact that U.S. democracy aspires to operate on a national scale while privileging localized decision-making through local and state governments. Part of American political history—and its future—involves the ongoing negotiation and rebalancing of federalism as a political arrangement; and part of American political and cultural history involves working through what it means to be a pluralist society marked by racial and ethnic diversity as well as profound regional, religious, and cultural differences.
- The fact that the U.S. has a consequential role in world affairs, variously described as either "global leadership" or "imperialist," characterized in part by the maintenance of an extraordinarily large military and near-continuous military conflicts over the past 20 years in the Middle East. The permanent "imperial presidency" is arguably both the consequence and cause of this fact, meaning that the presidency (understandably) occupies an outsized role in the American political system.

These structural issues expose the gap between our democratic aspirations and our current reality. In a moment of democratic disappointment and political anxiety, America comes perilously close to a legitimacy crisis. Such a crisis is distinguished by these characteristics:

- failure to develop a consensus and appropriate redress to the deeply racist and unjust legacy of its founding and subsequent history;
- failure to adequately address the economic needs of a substantial percentage of residents while inequalities of income, wealth, upward mobility, and political influence have expanded;
- failure to adequately address urgent long-standing and emergent problems, such as quality public education, equitable economic development, and ecological sustainability;
- declining faith in democracy as an institution and mode of governance and in democratic citizenship as an effective vehicle for self-rule and political community.

While it is plausible to portray these failures as a failure of political leadership, we believe there is a deeper, structural crisis afflicting American democracy. Indeed, it is not simply that political leaders have disappointed. It is that there is a lack of a compelling and coherent paradigm for addressing the most urgent, overlapping, and systemic challenges confronting American democracy in the 21st century.

Over the past half-century, political debate has been framed as a simplistic, left vs right dichotomy over the role and size of the federal government and the degree to which it should be used as a vehicle for promoting equity and progressive social change. In this configuration, liberal politics in the U.S. has been understood as an extension, restoration, or rejuvenation of the New Deal policy paradigm: bold action by the federal government to regulate capitalism, support social programs, redistribute resources, and provide a "safety net" for all citizens. Conservative politics aims at limiting, containing, and ultimately rolling back government's role in the interests of promoting liberty, free enterprise, and social policies that reinforce normative ideals of the family. With the ascendency of a dominant conservativism, democratic politics has been characterized by strengthening parts of government—such as the military–industrial complex, the prison–industrial complex, and numerous specific rules and regulations favoring politically connected corporate interests—while weakening government's regulatory and redistributive roles.

Certainly, any plausible or attractive vision for American democracy in the 21st century must go beyond a strong conservatism and a chastened liberalism. It is increasingly clear that the substantive limitations of the New Deal leave it wanting as a compelling 21st-century paradigm for democratic renewal. Equally important, returning to a New Deal vision no longer has the capacity to inspire the support of a robust majority of U.S. voters. The renewal of democratic life must begin (but not end) with a focus on promoting new ideas and practices that cultivate the capacities of citizens within a democratic framework that is accountable, responsive, just and equitable in meeting the shared needs and aspirations of communities. The operation of democratic institutions within local communities where highly consequential decisions are made that tangibly and visibly impact citizens' everyday life can provide a grounded, compelling, and sorely needed site for broad democratic renewal.

In the next chapter of this book, Chapter 2, Melody C. Barnes and Thad M. Williamson propose "community wealth building" as a fresh policy paradigm capable of invigorating the practice of American democracy. Barnes and Williamson assert that community wealth building—defined by the local practice of inclusive participation, setting bold equity goals, economic innovation to broaden wealth ownership, and a holistic understanding of wealth—provides a pathway by which communities can forge strategies for visible, tangible progress on urgent community priorities, even in circumstances where the federal government is absent or even hostile to such efforts. The peculiar and painful history of the authors' hometown of Richmond, Virginia, which launched the nation's first municipal Office of Community Wealth Building in 2014, is invoked to show how community wealth building fits within a long arc of struggle against white supremacy and racism in the former capital of the Confederacy. But Barnes and Williamson go beyond previous uses of the "community wealth building" terminology to describe its potential as a model of not just local governance but American democracy as a whole—connecting local, state, and federal institutions. The ambitious goal of community wealth building, on this account, is to simultaneously address long-standing and debilitating structures of racial inequity, redress massive disparities in wealth and influence, reinvigorate robust local democratic practice, and reconfigure progressive federalism in a manner that provides both more resources and responsibility to devolved localities without sacrificing (indeed, while strengthening) needed federal protections of civil rights, labor law, environmental protections, and other required national standards.

The purpose of this book is to both present this conception of community wealth building, and to interrogate it from a variety of perspectives. In June 2019, the contributors to this book, representing a variety of academic disciplines, gathered at the University of Richmond's Jepson School of Leadership Studies for a two-day discussion focused on community wealth building and the future of democracy. Contributors presented original papers relating to one or more of the themes raised in Barnes and Williamson's chapter; revised versions of those papers comprise the main body of the present book.

The proposed community wealth building paradigm necessarily touches on a range of topics and questions requiring greater scrutiny and critical reflection. The editors have grouped the remaining chapters into four main areas: race and

American democracy (Part II); the political economy of community wealth building (Part III); political institutions and the possibility of reform (Part IV); and the practical challenges and possibilities of implementing community wealth building initiatives "on the ground" in American communities (Part V).

Following Chapter 2 by Barnes and Williamson, Part II addresses the ethical underpinnings of the community wealth building approach—in particular, its challenge to white supremacy in the U.S. In Chapter 3, Lawrie Balfour provides an in-depth discussion of reparations as a paradigm potentially operating parallel to the community wealth building proposal; she argues for an understanding of reparations not as a one-time fix for historical injustice but as a deepened commitment to recognizing the depth of those historical injustices and the need for *ongoing* corrective action that may include but should not be limited to specific bold steps. In Chapter 4, Corey D.B. Walker explicates the epistemological and ethical foundations of a robust community wealth building approach. Engaging with social theorists like Habermas and Foucault, Walker first argues that community wealth building is consonant with a commitment to generating local knowledge as an alternative to dominant knowledge paradigms; he goes on to argue that it is also consistent with the ethic of public action expressed by Martin Luther King's conception of the "beloved community." This extension of the Barnes/Williamson proposal is significant because it underscores the fact that a successful community wealth building program must do much more than simply appeal to or draw upon citizens' self-interest; instead, it must also call upon a vision of *inclusive community* sufficiently robust to motivate collective action and indeed collective solutions to enduring community challenges.

Part III relates community wealth building to broader issues of political economy, capitalism, and economic inclusion. In Chapter 5, Isabel Sawhill diagnoses American capitalism's long-term trend of generating ever-greater inequality while undermining economic security for the majority of Americans, a trend she blames largely on the ascendancy of neo-liberal, free-market policy orientations in Washington. Sawhill provides an incisive critique of the flaws in "market fundamentalism," then goes on to discuss several alternative political-economic paradigms that "reject the primacy of markets." Sawhill's analysis complements and extends the discussion of political economy paradigms in Barnes and Williamson's chapter on community wealth building.

In Chapter 6, Margaret Kohn turns to the very different context of the Italian cooperative movement to argue that community wealth building is not a novel proposal, but in fact is a paradigm that exists in practice, at scale, in an established democratic country. Cooperatives represent a way to broaden the ownership of wealth and stabilize particular communities; while different kinds of cooperatives can be found within all capitalist societies, only in a few cases do they occupy a substantial share of the market. Italy is one such case. Kohn's chapter details not only the significant scale and long-term staying power of Italian cooperatives, but also elaborates its supporting legal structures. This success holds important lessons for future efforts to expand and institutionalize community wealth building in the U.S.

In Chapter 7, Richard Dagger takes up the issue of housing policy and homelessness as both a critical issue facing local governments and as a fundamental test of civic inclusion. Drawing on a republican understanding of the free, equal, and independent citizen, Dagger argues that "housing-first" social policy approaches are required both to treat homeless individuals with appropriate civic respect and to model the type of inclusive *community* envisioned by community wealth building. The chapter is a helpful and timely example of how clear thinking about fundamental issues of citizenship can inform social policy in general and community wealth building agendas in particular.

Part IV examines the role of formal political institutions and recent trends in American electoral politics in extending or blocking robust democratic practice. Accountability is a core value of the community wealth building paradigm, but what exactly does accountability mean? In Chapter 8, Kenneth P. Ruscio explores this question in the context of contemporary debates about impeachment. His wary conclusion is that while the framers of the U.S. Constitution wisely anticipated the potential for abuse of executive power within a republican system, it remains far from clear that impeachment (or other tools) are in fact adequate to the problem of holding reckless elected officials accountable. This finding suggests that advocates of community wealth building—or other approaches that seek to hold public officials accountable not just for abuses of power, but for delivering clear progress on public problems—must develop or resuscitate new tools for holding government accountable. The question of the need for institutional innovations to improve democratic practice is taken up by J.S. Maloy in Chapter 9. Maloy argues that the emergent practice of ranked-choice voting in local and state elections is a marked improvement as a method of both registering the aggregated preferences of voters and allowing new political voices to emerge and be heard. Drawing on recent experiences in Ireland, Maloy goes on to argue that *policy juries* offer a promising method for soliciting both democratic voice and meaningful deliberation for polities facing challenging and complex issues. Because localities, states, and nations seeking to implement community wealth building agendas will regularly wrestle with complex and controversial proposals, Maloy's explication of these institutional alternatives is a welcome contribution.

Chapters 10 and 11 turn to voting, electoral behavior, and voting rights law in the U.S. In Chapter 10, Nicholas J.G. Winter demonstrates how the increased political polarization of American national politics is connected to stronger connections over the past generation between partisan identification and feelings about the racial, gender, and class groups associated with the parties. This means that the stakes of national political debates transcend simple policy disagreements because they are deeply entwined with race, gender, and other components of personal identity. This finding reinforces Barnes and Williamson's contention that national politics is largely stuck in stalemate and that there may be more promise for building consensus starting (but not ending) at more local levels of politics. In Chapter 11, Julian Maxwell Hayter traces the long roll-back of the Voting Rights Act, culminating in the Supreme Court's removal of its key enforcement mechanisms in Southern states with a long history of hostility and exclusion towards African American voters. He shows how this decision resulted from a long-term, determined campaign by right-wing opponents of the law. Hayter's deeply troubling narrative is a potent reminder that the ever-increasing diversity of the American population will not necessarily translate into a more diverse *electorate* if governments are permitted to implement rules that restrict rather than promote equitable voter participation.

Part V turns to the work of implementing community wealth building agendas in practice, within cities and communities as we find them. In the American context, any compelling progressive agenda must not only "talk about" race but highlight racial disparities as an urgent matter of justice. In Chapter 12, Ravi K. Perry argues that the language of "targeted universalism" gives politicians—especially African American politicians—a framework for highlighting racial inequities while building broad, inclusive progressive coalitions for change, including in majority-white cities. Perry draws on numerous examples to show how targeted universalism has been deployed in practice by relatively successful mayors. Because one requirement of community wealth building is strong political support from local political leadership, Perry's analysis helpfully shows how mayors and other local leaders can knit together robust political coalitions while speaking with integrity about ongoing injustices and exclusions that harm the least well off.

Chapters 13 and 14 examine practical efforts at community wealth building in the Richmond context. In Chapter 13, Risha R. Berry details the challenges faced by Richmond's Office of Community Wealth Building (OCWB) in confronting multiple layers of structural racism and building a strategy to help residents (primarily African American) in Richmond achieve economic stability and eventually build wealth. Berry describes the workforce development component of OCWB as well as related efforts to advocate for structural policy change and increased resources so as to tear down barriers to economic thriving faced by thousands of Richmond residents. Her chapter makes clear that a robust and successful community wealth building approach is not a matter of implementing one or two new programs or low-cost interventions, but requires concerted systemic change at multiple levels of program and policy, simultaneously. In Chapter 14, Barbara Brown Wilson and Meghan Z. Gough critically consider how two prominent public universities—the University of Virginia and Virginia Commonwealth University—act as anchor institutions for the cities of Charlottesville and Richmond, respectively. Wilson and Gough illustrate the challenge and possibility of aligning internal university imperatives (and associated politics) with community-wide need on a larger, more intentional scale than has historically been the case in either institution.

Finally, in Chapter 15, Corey D.B. Walker and Thad M. Williamson reflect on key themes emerging from this book, as well as the many remaining questions concerning the community wealth building paradigm to be addressed in future work. Both the editors and contributors regard this book as but one critical conversation point in the development of community wealth building as a robust paradigm for reviving and reconstructing American democracy, on (at last) genuinely inclusive and equitable terms. That conversation necessarily will involve further academic analysis, but perhaps even more importantly must draw on accumulating knowledge from implementation efforts in the field and the experiences and perspectives of practitioners and citizens. Community wealth building is less a prescription for specific policies than an orientation and process aimed at delivering bold, community-driven change—a process that must always begin and end with the agency of situated democratic citizens.

REFERENCES

King, Martin Luther, Jr. (1967), *Where Do We Go from Here: Chaos or Community?* New York: Harper & Row.
Tocqueville, Alexis de (1835 [2004]), *Democracy in America*, translated by Arthur Goldhammer, New York: Library of America.

2. Becoming the American community we should be—but have never been

Melody C. Barnes and Thad M. Williamson

PROLOGUE

Richmond, Virginia, was in smoke and flames on April 3, 1865. The fire—intentionally set to destroy anything of value that might help Union troops—encouraged looting and bred chaos as the Confederate government escaped to Danville, Virginia, and citizens fled the city. Two hotels, three newspaper offices, rail depots, bridges, the Confederate post office, banks, tobacco factories, flour mills, and a paper mill were destroyed. Quoting Shakespeare, a *London Times* reporter wrote, "Hell is empty, and all the devils are here" (Ruane, 2015).

Yet, above the ruins of the city, for the first time in almost four years, the American flag was raised at 7:30 a.m., April 3, 1865, by Richard Gill Forrester, a young man of African American and Jewish descent. It was the same flag 14-year-old Forrester pulled from the trash, hid in his clothing, and concealed under his mattress on the day Virginia seceded from the Union four years earlier.

Richard, his parents, and his 19 siblings lived in Richmond as free people of color who were registered as slaves owned by their Jewish relatives, a strategy used to keep the family intact. They were affluent, and his father was an active participant in Reconstruction efforts, a member of elected Richmond City Council, and a member of the school board.

The Forresters were participants in Richmond's civic, economic, and political life. While unrepresentative of most African Americans, their lives were evidence of the promise of equality, a core democratic ideal, and what could be if all men and women had similar opportunities. Yet, they and others like them represented a threat to the old order and the countervailing principle of supremacy. That threat led Richmond's leaders to secession, to war, and to "burn the village to save it" from the Union army when the Confederate cause was lost. In the years that followed, it led their successors to do the same, using political and economic tools to sacrifice the city's residents—sometimes intentionally and sometimes with callous disregard—rather than build an integrated community (Belsches, 2015; Campbell, 2012, p. 129; Stokes, 2014).

To be sure, Richmond's story is one of Southern history, but it is also an American story and one that can help us understand why democracy has proven so frustrating today. It illuminates the earliest and most deep-seated defects in our founding DNA, including slavery and its legacy. It also demonstrates how those defects create persistent inequities that ensure that—even as we have made progress—the America of our essential and aspirational principles does not exist and has never existed. In Richmond, as throughout the nation, our frequently stated commitments to liberty, equality, and constitutional democracy collide full force with the realities of our history and the institutional legacy it has bequeathed.

So, the question for us today is, can we create and sustain the America that never was? Can we build a multicultural democracy in which everyone participates politically and economically and in which a new, inclusive American identity takes hold? We believe we can, but only if we acknowledge the truth and adopt a new paradigm to organize our communities as well as our political and economic life.

PART ONE: THE PRESENT

I.

It's tempting to ignore the deeper past and respond to America's frustrations with a recitation of recent political history, the promise and flaws of elected leaders, and the failure of leaders not only to provide a compelling vision but also to deliver the goods in support of that vision. Such analysis is helpful and necessary, but taken alone, badly incomplete. Donald Trump is a symptom, not a cause.

While we have made progress, we have *never* dismantled or undone the fundamental flaws of our founding.[1] A large gap remains between democratic norms—and our highest civic aspirations—and the realities of power and privilege in America. Well-off white men founded the country, and well-off white men still have vastly disproportionate wealth and political influence compared to other groups. The racial inequities that have defined American history, in turn have made it easier for those with wealth and influence to maintain political control and rewrite law and practice in ways—intentional or not—that reinforce disparities affecting people of color, women, and low- and moderate-income white Americans (Shapiro, 2004).

To be sure, there have been periods of major progress. The twentieth century was shaped by seismic social movements that struggled, and in important ways, succeeded in creating a more equitable and inclusive society: women's suffrage, civil rights movements, labor movements, feminism, LGBT movements, disability rights activism (Snow, Soule and Kriesi, 2007). The core ideas that all have the right to equal citizenship and equal treatment under the law have gained wider acceptance. In economic terms, too, much of the twentieth century is a story of greater and more broadly distributed prosperity, leading to dramatically higher literacy rates, life expectancies, and overall living standards for the population as a whole. Crucial reforms enacted in the New Deal and extended in the Great Society established a stronger safety net, and for a generation after World War II, the economy grew in a broadly equitable way that led to impressive gains in real living standards for even the poorest one-fifth of Americans (Gordon, 2017).

Recent decades, however, have placed the very real democratic gains of the twentieth century under threat, as well as undermined the legitimacy of democracy itself. Since the 1970s, income and wealth inequality have been rising not falling, and the disproportionate political influence of the very rich has grown rather than shrunk (Gordon, 2017; Stone et al., 2019). The past decade has shown that racial anxieties and resentments—historically stoked to divide those with common interests and allow the few to maintain wealth and power—have intensified rather than faded, despite the expectations of many after the election of Barack Obama.[2] Evidence of our continuing failure to treat women as fully equal participants in all arenas of life is all around us. The inability of governments to arrest these trends and enact more policies benefitting the majority of the population has predictably led to loss of faith in democracy itself.[3] The degraded, hyper-partisan nature of national politics leaves precious little room for effective governance and problem-solving to meet our deep challenges (Mansbridge, 2012). Even worse, our complex digital world and global economy compound these challenges and magnify old problems, while creating new ones (Tufekci, 2018).

Time is of the essence. There is little reason to believe that growing inequities will dissipate in the absence of bold action, and our constitutional republic will attenuate where grave power imbalances thrive. What is required is a bold new paradigm—community wealth building—to create the America that should be.[4]

Community wealth building is both a strategy for directly confronting entrenched inequalities of wealth, power, and opportunity and a method of community-driven problem-solving that aims at inclusivity and empowerment. Community wealth building seeks to harness the full range of resources available in a community and establish shared goals for sustained community change. While we do not contend that this process will or should be conflict free, in many cases it can be positive-sum (in which everyone benefits from improved community outcomes) rather than zero-sum.

Importantly, community wealth building also seeks to change the dominant logic of our existing politics and create a new political equation. Entrenched economic and political elites as well as many ordinary citizens are all but impervious to claims and arguments made from "the other side of the aisle," or the other side of the ideological spectrum. We contend, however, that *at the community level*, different groups have enough commonality of interest and shared concern for local public institutions that a serious and quite practical conversation about addressing entrenched community problems is *possible, desirable, and necessary*. At this level, it is possible to ask challenging but essential questions—do we always want to be a community marked by a 40 percent child poverty rate and counted among those with the lowest rates of upward mobility in the nation?—without being immediately dismissed on ideological grounds or pulled into a hyper-partisan vortex that prioritizes political gamesmanship over practical problem solving.

Community wealth building efforts are defined by four distinctive features:

- inclusive community participation, on the front end, in the process of change;
- establishment of bold equity goals and corresponding metrics for tracking progress;
- use of holistic strategies encompassing physical, financial, and human capital to build wealth for individuals and communities;
- use of inclusive economic tools and strategies that build on existing assets and bring more capital and resources into communities.

A comprehensive community wealth building approach necessarily involves and integrates to the degree possible the fundamental policy systems driving the development and distribution of wealth: not only economic development, but also education, workforce development, housing, transportation, and the systems of governance that ultimately allocate resources in communities.

To be sure, effort—in the form of political engagement, political leadership, and community organizing—is required to create these conversations and move them to the forefront of local political agendas. In the absence of such effort, local politics and governance will often continue to revolve around ribbon cuttings, pet projects, and political careerism, at best focusing on problem mitigation rather than root-cause problem solving. Community wealth building offers a new paradigm, not only for policy, but also for the practice of democratic citizenship. It requires individuals from diverse backgrounds living in close proximity to engage with one another, debate, disagree, build consensus, and ultimately, build community. It is rooted in a renewed appreciation that the legitimacy of any democratic government, including our own, is anchored in its ability to solve problems effectively and meet the concrete needs of the people.

II.

> Deep down, many Americans know our country is in a state of total failure. That's true for folks on the left and the right. We know that our futures have been sold and that our children's futures have been sold [...] Politicians pay lip service to the middle class but spend no time helping them. Black lives matter more and illegal immigrants who break the law get a free pass. Evangelical Christians in this country no longer feel that they have the right to religious freedom and have watched what they perceive as a sacred institution in marriage gutted. All the while, politicians they voted for to represent them just plain don't. Now enter Trump. (Friedersdorf, 2015)

> Stephanie Delgado-Garcia had volunteered for Clinton in Pennsylvania and went to vote with her formerly undocumented immigrant parents. She took a picture of her mother wearing a Hillary button in the voting booth. "I felt like I lost my country that night," she said. "Here was a man who essentially told the American public that the America I thought was great was in fact broken for making my story possible." (Khazan, 2017)

At first glance, it is hard to believe the individuals referenced in the passages above live in the same America. While both are sincere in their convictions and concern for our country, it appears they inhabit two very different worlds. Yet, what they have in common is hiding in plain sight: both are appealing to an America that never existed. That is a strong—and painful—claim, so let us pause to explain.

Consider four prominent frames for understanding our current political moment. These frames are not mutually exclusive; each of them taps into deep currents of American political thought and practice to try to comprehend the challenges we face.

American nostalgia

One traditional lens celebrates America as a beacon of liberty for the world: the freest, most powerful, and most just nation in human history. In the words of Ronald Reagan (in turn channeling John Winthrop), this view interprets America as a "shining city on a hill [...] still a beacon, still a magnet for all who must have freedom, for all the Pilgrims from all the lost places who are hurtling through the darkness, toward home." This narrative points to the durability of American political institutions, the triumphs in the hot and cold wars of the twentieth century, and the nation's material prosperity. Yet, versions of this narrative warn that America's favored place is fragile and indeed under threat: by the weakening of traditional moral values; the decline in religious institutions; the rise of identity politics and affirmative action empowering racial minorities, sexual minorities, and women; and the presence of immigrants.

American insecurity

A related but distinct frame declares that the American Dream is over. Many Americans fear they are not doing as well as their parents and their children will do worse. The next rung of the economic ladder appears permanently out of reach, and the 1 percent have a firm hold on wealth. Income inequality in the United States has been steadily increasing since 1980, with notable increases during the last 15 years. In 2016, the U.S. Gini coefficient, a formula that has been used for a century to measure inequality in national economies on a scale from 0 to 1 (with 1 being the most unequal), was 0.48—worse than Iran, and the worst among advanced industrialized nations (Guzman, 2017, Table 1). In addition, as a result of poorer physical and mental health, declining job opportunities, and other challenges, mortality rates across race, ethnicity, and gender lines are rising. "Deaths of despair" among middle-age white men and women with a high school degree or less have doubled since 1990 (Case and Deaton, 2017). To make matters worse, Washington and Wall Street are synonymous. Well-heeled lobbyists have the ear of our elected officials, and when democratic institutions work—which is rare—they work for those writing big checks, not for those working a job or two to make ends meet. If democratic institutions did work, things would be different, so we need to try something new. This perspective, commonly labeled *populism*, argues that achieving real change will require sweeping aside an entrenched status quo in Washington.

As we have learned all too well, the political upshot of the populist critique is indeterminate. Consider the case of Bernie Sanders and Donald Trump, two very different men with very different goals. In 2016, both in effect ran against each of the major political parties, and both argued that they would stand up for folks who work hard and play by the rules. Sanders created a campaign and a movement promising a significant redistribution of wealth and dedication of sizable new government resources to address the concerns of those feeling economically adrift. The substance of Sanders's populism focused on the nexus between corporate power, the political influence of the affluent, and the ways an entrenched elite perpetuates and extends economic inequality and insecurity.

At the other end of the spectrum, Donald Trump positioned himself (however improbably) as someone who could "tell it like it is" by giving voice to the angst and frustration of those who "don't recognize [their] country." Trump at times also criticized specific companies, but his version of populism primarily targeted immigrants and government, which he portrayed as a "swamp" needing to be drained. Trump's stunningly effective slogan "Make

America Great Again" astutely taps into a combination of each of the views described above: uncritical reverence of the past and severe anxiety about the present and future.[5] Trump's version of populism produced an Electoral College victory in 2016 and has allowed him to retain enthusiastic support from his base, which regards all challenges to Trump as evidence of an unaccountable, anti-democratic "deep state" that is nefariously thwarting the president, and hence, the popular will.

Durable America

A third lens, associated with much academic political science and some mainstream politics, stresses the durability of American democracy and its economy. Rhetoric about the United States as the shining beacon on the hill, a light to all nations, is understood as more mythology than fact. The power and global ascent of the United States is attributed to economic factors and natural geographic advantages rather than the inherent morality of American institutions and the American people. This view holds that while America was never as great as some imagine, its future is not as bleak as current anxieties on the left and right might suggest. American political institutions and associated norms are generally stable and domestically and globally battle tested, and the economic stress of much of the working class and the poor must be considered in the context of overall rising wealth and improved technology. (The working class may not have secure jobs anymore, but they certainly have cellphones and often Netflix.) The United States has shown a capacity for self-correction and moral progress in the past and will again in the future. In this view, anxieties about present and future are either exaggerated or addressable by discrete policy initiatives to counter specific problems. While the Trumpian moment is not without serious dangers, the probability is that once he leaves office—or is removed—this too will pass. The American project will muddle through in the end.[6]

American sham

A fourth lens, associated with some activist movements and an increasing number of Americans, holds that rhetoric about democracy and American community is inherently a sham. The personal flaws of the Founders only magnify the deeper flaw of a nation built on white supremacy and oppression. This view does not deny the impact of democratic social movements to build a measure of social justice in America, but considers these movements as fundamentally an uphill struggle. Democracy is "fugitive," consisting of episodic moments in which hard-won progress is secured, moving us only one step closer on a 1000-mile journey.[7] Most of the time, the real work is resisting inherently oppressive institutions and carving out small spaces of collective and personal freedom. Bolder aspirations for what America might become are largely pointless, because the powerful, rich, white elites who have held power from the beginning and hold most of the power now will never let such aspirations come to fruition.

***

Each of these views has considerable plausibility, and versions of each are widespread in our political discourse. Certainly, some elements of these views would resonate with both the Trump voter and the Clinton voter quoted, above. But none offers either a fully accurate diagnosis of our unique historical moment or a promising response. Instead, they leave us in a box of our own design. Trumpist politics purports to speak to nostalgia for lost American community, but in practice offers a disturbing politics of white nationalism and nativism that fails to serve the vast majority of Americans. Saber-rattling about trade is a cover for tax giveaways to the wealthy and deregulation that will accelerate our march to plutocracy rather than renew or expand the American Dream. On the left, while there is an important place for the demythologizing (often protest) politics recommended by the American sham view in driving change forward, this is not a substitute for a governing vision. Finally, the centrist notion that the historical durability of American institutions and society assures that we will inevitably muddle through offers no practical assistance at all: it is merely wishful thinking based on the erroneous assumption that the future will be just another version of the past.

III.

Our view is rather different. The way out of the unpromising box drawn above is to act upon a compelling vision of community wealth building, even as our country is being riven by cultural and economic angst in a seemingly zero-sum national environment. To have vision is to see possibilities for a future that transcends the limitations of the past and to map out a practical pathway to move from here to there. That vision must pay equal attention to *identity*—who we are and aspire to be as a people and as a nation—and to the *economic structure and policy* that assure that these aspirations are translated into the experiences of Americans.

Unquestionably, those Americans who find comfort in a nativist path for the country and those who have a winner-take-all/zero-sum point of view will reject what we propose. But we believe most Americans are looking for both a common vision of who we are and a new economic paradigm to secure opportunity for all.

That means we must claim our agency and responsibility as democratic actors in this moment of American history. The dangers of Trumpian frames to democracy and equality are obvious, as are the dangers of centrist complacency or leftist fatalism. Responsibility in this moment entails having the courage and imagination to plough a new path for American democracy in the twenty-first century, judiciously combining political imagination with hard-eyed realism. As Abraham Lincoln (1862) put it in another moment of crisis, "As our case is new, so we must think anew, and act anew."

Part of thinking and acting anew must involve affirming the value of democracy itself and the positive possibilities of political engagement. Community wealth building is not just about policies and structural changes; it is also about ordinary citizens getting deeply engaged in the work of democracy.

To fulfill our promise, however, we must reckon with the past. America's framers believed that a nation of citizens, secure in their inalienable rights, could give their consent to be governed by representatives of their choosing, creating a constitutional republic. But a republic for whom and for what purpose?

PART TWO: THE PAST

Nowhere have the conflicting answers to that question been more violently and poignantly expressed than in Richmond, Virginia. Richmond is our home, and we are deeply aware of the city's painful history and legacy. In Richmond, violent racial oppression collided with efforts not only to resist that oppression, but also to build and sustain an inclusive community, even when the odds seemed long. The city is a unique place, but its connection to our nation's earliest mistakes and its contemporary effort to build a more equitable society reflect a more universal narrative. In so many ways, the following section tells the story not only of Richmond, but also of America.

The English settlement that eventually became the city of Richmond survived years of war and conflict between the British and the indigenous Powhatan. The British hoped to settle land northwest of Jamestown and ultimately brokered a limited 1646 treaty. The Virginia Assembly later voided the treaty, leading to an influx of settlers and marginalization of the Powhatan. Decades later, the neighborhoods of Shockoe Bottom, Shockoe Slip, and Church Hill were cobbled together into one entity, chartered as a town, and governed by the British Crown's representatives in Jamestown. By the time Richmond became a city in 1782, it had also become a force in the political and economic life of the colonies and the new nation. Revolutionary activism was part of its lifeblood. During the Revolutionary War, the state capital was moved from Williamsburg to Richmond—a year before the city was decimated by fire by the British troops.

Simultaneously, Richmond was becoming a major center for the American slave trade and ultimately became the second largest slave port in the United

States after New Orleans. Between 1800 and 1861, it is estimated that 300 000 to 500 000 enslaved men, women, and children were bought and sold at the Shockoe Bottom slave auction, then transported to the American South and the Caribbean. By 1857, the Richmond-based slave trade, fueled by the production of cotton, was worth about $100 million in today's currency (Campbell, 2012, pp. 108–9). Cotton replaced tobacco as the crop of choice, and the result was a national economy engaged in cotton production and international trade, predicated upon increasingly valuable and profitable slave labor.

By the time the Civil War ended, the legacy of slavery in Richmond was at least twofold. First, there was an entrenched belief in white supremacy and a system for maintaining that fiction. Second, there was a significant African American population, including descendants of enslaved men and women, some of whom—given Richmond's urban industrial slave system—may have lived independently of their owners. Some slaves could earn and keep wages, and they built institutions, including several of the African American churches still in existence today. Some became active participants in political life in the city and the Commonwealth of Virginia after the Civil War.

For a brief period after the war, most registered voters in Richmond were African American, and from 1865 until 1895, 25 African Americans served on the city council. Yet, every effort by African Americans to build community was met by white establishment efforts to undermine black progress. A strict vagrancy law accompanied compulsory labor with depressed wages for newly freed slaves. Segregation laws separated African Americans and whites at voting sites, on street cars, and in schools and cemeteries. Annexation— increasing the size of the city by absorbing contiguous county land—became a tool to dilute African American voting power. In 1871, a single majority– minority district was drawn to contain that voting strength within the Jackson Ward neighborhood (Campbell, 2012, pp. 134, 137). By the end of the nine-teenth century, resistance to African Americans in economic and political life was feverish and accompanied the rising "Lost Cause" sentiment that led to the establishment of statues depicting Confederate generals across the city.

The new state constitution adopted in 1902 cemented segregation in Virginia and set the stage for generations to come. Customs and Jim Crow laws hardened segregation across almost every aspect of public and private life in Virginia: public transportation, public assembly, public facilities, party primaries, employment, marriage, housing, and secondary and post-secondary education.

Even in this oppressive atmosphere, Richmond generated extraordinary leaders like Maggie L. Walker, who utilized fraternal organizations, the black-owned bank over which she presided, and other collective self-help tools to build community and wealth in Jackson Ward, one of the most prosperous

African American urban neighborhoods in the South in the early twentieth century.

But Jackson Ward itself could not survive post-World War II urban renewal, a policy aimed at concentrating African Americans in particular Richmond neighborhoods, while prioritizing highway construction and commuter mobility in the rapidly suburbanizing region. City leaders armed themselves with robust tools to achieve their goal, namely, a master plan and a new city charter that created a city manager and a nine-member city council elected at-large. From 1941, when the Richmond Housing Authority was created, until the 1970s, one African American community after another was destroyed in the name of "renewal." The men, women, and children who lived in those communities were displaced, with many pushed into public housing.

In the 1950s alone, the city destroyed 4700 units of housing and replaced them with 1736 units of public housing (Campbell, 2012, p. 153). It used significant portions of the land so acquired to facilitate the building of new federal highways (the Richmond–Petersburg Turnpike, I-95, and I-64) that almost encircled the new public housing projects, denied walkable access to other parts of the city, and aided easy ingress and egress for white residents who were moving to Federal Housing Administration-supported suburbs. The city also built public facilities and industrial sites on some of the land.

Richmond's "renewal" eliminated and destabilized African American communities. It clustered many of Richmond's lowest-income residents—predominantly African Americans who were two or three generations from slavery—in eight public housing projects and encouraged white residents to flee to suburbs in Henrico and Chesterfield counties. In short, it initiated economic free-fall in the city of Richmond.

The story of deliberate racial segregation in Richmond's housing is intertwined with Richmond's equally tragic experiences with racial segregation in public education and the establishment of a political structure that prevented African Americans from having a political voice for many years.

By the time Richmond's first African American mayor, Henry L. Marsh, claimed the helm in 1977, Richmond was plagued with significant challenges that were the progeny of white supremacy and had been created to thwart city growth and prosperity: the concentration of public housing and poverty in the East End, largely segregated schools, middle-class exit and a declining tax base, lack of a regional transportation system, and the inability to annex. By the 2010s, the city of Richmond had a poverty rate of 25 percent, including a child poverty rate of 40 percent; was consistently appraised as having one of the three most challenged public school systems in Virginia; and was ranked by national scholars as being one of the worst 2 percent of localities in the United States in fostering upward social mobility.[8]

PART THREE: COMMUNITY WEALTH BUILDING AND LOCAL LEADERSHIP

I.

Here then is the question for 21st-century Richmond: is it possible for local political and civic leadership, combined with ordinary citizens, to work together to forge a future path that confronts our deep legacy of racial inequality? Must Richmond forever be simply the capital of the Confederacy or could it instead be known as a capital of community wealth building? Our answer to that question is yes: and we further add, if it can happen in a place as challenged as Richmond, it can happen almost anywhere.

A standard view of the politics of the American South is that whereas local and state political institutions tend to be fundamentally conservative and resistant to social equality, the federal government has generally been a progressive actor in enforcing federal civil rights laws and other basic standards. The federal government has indeed often been a critical, positive actor in Richmond's journey to redress its history of institutional racism. Congress and the courts were indispensable allies when Richmond's residents sought to lower or eliminate legal barriers to discrimination in housing, employment, education, and other areas. New Deal policies created a new relationship between the people and the federal government, and in so doing, ushered in decades of progressive change. It is clear to us—even during a time of conservative retrenchment—that the federal government plays a critical role protecting core civil liberties and rights and establishing a floor of protections for all who live and work in the United States. The authority needed to exercise that role must be protected where it continues to exist and reinvigorated where it has diminished.

However, as noted above, the federal government's track record of building rather than destroying community in Richmond—even in the mid- and late twentieth century—is mixed. The New Deal was replete with limitations and contradictions, sometimes leaving a legacy of discriminatory policies. In addition, the core idea of the New Deal—an ever-stronger federal government as the principal instrument of progressive social change—is under attack and, at least in the near term, will continue to struggle to provide solutions to our nation's most pressing challenges. While significant efforts must be devoted to enlivening the federal government as a partner in creation of a fair and just America, it is clear that journey is fraught with difficulty and engenders a loyal opposition.

From a Richmond perspective, our city's residents simply cannot wait for national politics to become more favorable, for more external resources from the federal government to suddenly appear, or for change to slowly trickle down I-95 from Washington. For the first time in our city's history, there is a broad, cross-cutting consensus and shared understanding among the city's political and civic leadership of the ways our current circumstances are shaped by the painful, racist historical legacy described above. Many Richmond residents, or all races and ethnicities, understand that our patterns of housing and educational segregation and concentrations of poverty result from decisions made in the nineteenth and twentieth centuries by both local and state policy-makers who were seeking to perpetuate patterns of white supremacy.

Our city's current young, African American mayor and young, white school superintendent speak regularly and comfortably about structural racism and legacies of exclusion. Richmonders are no longer interested in a theory of change once summarized as "waiting for the Yankees to come save us."[9] They are interested in taking action now, beginning with resources already on hand, and seeking support from other levels of government and policy wherever it can be found.

Central to Richmond's embrace of community wealth building is the idea that local political and civic leadership can drive a process aimed at fundamental change in the city's social and economic conditions. Richmond's recent municipal leaders have embraced the proposition that setting out on a bold course of change is both possible and necessary, even if we do not have all the answers at hand or all the needed resources in place. And even if we recognize that in seeking to reverse trends decades and centuries in the making, we will encounter roadblocks, challenges, failures, and reversals alongside moments of progress and promise.

II.

So, how does one go about overturning 400 years of history in the absence of significant new state and federal resources and in the context of a fiscally strained city? That is the practical challenge that confronted the members of the Anti-Poverty Commission formed by Mayor Dwight C. Jones in 2011 and the many community members who engaged in the deliberation and planning that ultimately led to the creation of the Office of Community Wealth Building and its constituent programmatic initiatives.[10]

We took fellow Richmonder and professional tennis player Arthur Ashe's advice to heart: "Start where you are, use what you have, do what you can." In our case, this meant simultaneously undertaking four strategic exercises:

• envisioning what it means to move a household sustainably out of poverty into economic thriving, and then identifying a broad strategy to achieve this goal (living wage, full-time employment combined with comprehensive support services);

- setting a broad community goal for transformation (in Richmond's case, cutting child poverty 50 percent in 15 years by lifting 1000 adults a year into stability), shifting the conversation from being satisfied with marginal improvements to the status quo to addressing and meeting needs at the scale they exist;
- taking an inventory of *existing* community wealth and resources to identify gaps and needs that must be filled if hundreds of residents are to be engaged in this strategy;
- developing a plan to generate the resources required to activate the plan, starting first with resources within our "zone of control."

Mayor Jones announced the creation of the Office of Community Wealth Building (OCWB) in April 2014 in conjunction with his budget proposal for the 2015 fiscal year. The office was charged with coordinating implementation of a series of initiatives recommended by the Mayor's Anti-Poverty Commission, spanning workforce development, economic development, transportation, education, and housing. In December 2015, Richmond City Council ratified the OCWB as a permanent agency of city government and formalized its dual function: developing and leading implementation of a citywide poverty reduction strategy and directly managing the city's workforce development programming. Legislation establishing the office also required the mayor to make an annual report on the city's poverty-fighting progress according to an established, consistent set of metrics. The office set a bold goal to achieve a 40 percent reduction in the city's overall poverty, including a 50 percent reduction in child poverty, by 2030. In practical terms, this meant building the capacity to move 1000 adults a year sustainably above the poverty line.

In 2017, Richmond's new mayor, Levar Stoney—who had made supporting the OCWB's work a key part of his platform in the 2016 municipal election—endorsed this goal and made expansion of the office a key highlight of his first budget. This support, combined with a new state grant from the Virginia Department of Social Services, allowed the OCWB's budget to nearly *triple* in one year. Consequently, the city now has four workforce centers (up from one in 2016) that serve city residents without restriction, and the OCWB as a whole now directly serves approximately 900 households annually with workforce services and related supports. These services, which include holistic support and the development of long-term career plans to move households to employment and on a trajectory toward long-term economic stability, are available without restriction to all city residents. Six hundred persons in OCWB case management obtained employment in the 2018–19 fiscal year. Allied educational and housing initiatives developed or supported by the OCWB have reached many additional families.[11]

Despite these promising steps and increased investment, the OCWB's work remains under development. The city of Richmond is currently working on extending the community wealth building paradigm throughout the whole of city government and expanding the capacity of the OCWB itself. But we are encouraged by the support this initiative has generated among not only elected municipal leaders but also business leaders, community organizations, city residents, and the Commonwealth of Virginia. Recent Census data also suggest the strategy is bearing fruit: the city's official poverty rate in 2018 fell to 21.9 percent, its lowest level in a decade (United States Census, 2018).

Equally important, the work in Richmond parallels work going on in dozens of communities nationwide that are informed by, or clearly consonant with, a community wealth building paradigm—that is, an effort to develop community-wide strategies for addressing long-standing inequities in effective ways. In the following section, we spell out the substance of this strategy.

III.

Community wealth building's aim is both to strengthen the asset and wealth base of low-income neighborhoods and cities and to expand the number of people who benefit from such assets, with the long-term aim of changing the entire structure of opportunity in American localities. As noted above, community wealth building efforts are defined by four distinctive features designed to achieve these ambitious goals: inclusive participation, bold equity goals, a holistic approach to wealth, and inclusive economic strategies. The following subsection details each component part of community wealth building.

Inclusive participation

Whatever their social class, race, or income level, Americans resent being treated as "problems" to be managed or acted upon, rather than being respected as equal civic agents. We know just how difficult—and rewarding—it can be to build strong relationships of mutual respect across lines of difference as a critical component of inclusive community-building processes. We also know that conflict and disagreement are inevitable in a pluralistic society. But without this relational foundation, even the best policy ideas and initiatives will eventually founder and fade away.

Setting bold equity goals

Achieving lasting systemic change is by definition a long-term process. It requires taking a long view, while simultaneously working day-by-day with a sense of urgency and a determination to take advantage of immediate opportunities.

Setting clear goals is essential to both galvanizing and sustaining this work. Such targets, in our view, must be bold: bold enough to motivate sustained, committed work and bold enough to motivate changes in practices, resource distributions, and the institutional status quo. Communities like Richmond cannot become markedly better places by continuing to do more and more of the same.

Concrete goals help in three ways: in motivating the work, organizing the work, and communicating the work. But for goals to have teeth, they must be widely promulgated and shared across the community and rigorously tracked through a system of metrics and regular reporting.

Defining wealth holistically

Community wealth building is about building wealth in an inclusive manner. But what do we mean by *wealth*? Our use of the term intends a holistic meaning: wealth is the total sum of the resources an individual may access or use in support of both their daily activities and in pursuit of their long-term, lifetime goals. We are concerned with eight major categories of wealth: public assets (like parks and libraries), shared community assets (nonprofit spaces, congregation-owned properties), business ownership, residential ownership, other assets held by households, and individuals' financial capital, human capital, and social capital. A strong community has an abundance—and equitable distribution—of *each* of these forms of wealth; yet, even neighborhoods and cities classified as poor have at least some significant assets and strengths to build upon.

Economic tools and integrating policy systems

We have contended that public policy must aim to tackle deep-seated economic, racial and gender inequalities, starting from a ground-up, community-driven perspective. Community wealth building identifies five broad economic tools, which in turn allow for countless variations, combinations, and innovations.

First, community wealth building seeks to utilize or unlock existing community assets that are not fully used. Second, over time, it aims at the holistic development of assets: in particular, the skills and experience of people, but also more tangible assets such as buildings and infrastructure. Third, community wealth building focuses on being more intentional about the flow of income streams within communities in two ways: by seeking to keep local dollars more frequently circulating in the community (enhancing local economic multipliers) and by redirecting income streams flowing through anchor institutions and other institutions of concentrated wealth to support the needs of low-wealth neighborhoods through contracts and employment opportunities. These strategies can strengthen the tax bases of cities, benefiting all residents. Fourth, community wealth building seeks to broaden ownership of assets within communities by encouraging local ownership, and where feasible, employee and community ownership. Successful employee-owned firms can help individuals build wealth above and beyond wage earning, while community land trusts help secure long-term affordable housing within communities to offset the impacts of gentrification in urban neighborhoods. Finally, community wealth building welcomes—and in some cases seeks to catalyze—the attraction of new public and private investment to communities, according to rules and policies aimed at assuring maximum local benefit from the new investment, whether in the form of employment, ownership, or contracting opportunities.

Economic strategies like these have a vital role to play in directly building wealth. Even more important from a policy point of view is the work of integrating different policy functions into a common strategy. In a city like Richmond, the economic development agencies, public transit company, public housing authority, public school system, and social service agencies all may be pursuing independent strategies rather than working off a single, integrated community plan. The result, too often, is economic development projects that do not actually lead to sustained employment for people in poverty or school progress plans that do not deliver tangible results because underlying neighborhood challenges are not being addressed simultaneously. In general, our localities tend to be program rich but system poor.

That is why, in our rendering, it is critically important for community wealth building to be viewed as a *policy paradigm*: a lens for organizing and integrating a community's major agencies and systems around shared, transformative goals.

There are many possible ways to structure larger-scaled community collaboration incorporating both collective impact principles and a community-organizing mindset. Adopting this approach does not in itself guarantee success: additional resources are needed, as well as competent execution of strategies supporting the stated goals. But the process of a *community organizing itself for change* is a prerequisite for having a reasonable chance of achieving sustained change in larger-scale community outcomes; a prerequisite for taking maximum advantage of additional external resources, if and when they become available; and a prerequisite for generating the sustained political pressure needed to obtain additional resources and support.

PART FOUR: COMMUNITY WEALTH BUILDING AS NATIONAL POLICY PARADIGM

Community wealth building is thus an emerging policy paradigm for locally driven, systemic change. Community wealth building strategies are fully consonant with *collective impact* and *community-organizing* approaches to achieving measurable change through harnessing local resources in pursuit of shared goals. And community wealth building is aimed not just at any particular set of discrete outcomes (important as these may be), but also at systemic change in the distribution of wealth and power in our communities and, hence, in our larger democracy.

Understanding the potential of community wealth building as a local strategy is important in itself. But we make the further contention that community wealth building can and should also be understood as a promising *national* policy paradigm. By *policy paradigm* we mean an approach to governance that articulates both the ends of policy and an account of how public authority (in law and governance) ought to advance those ends.

A compelling policy paradigm for the 21st century must do two things: explicitly state a theory of American national identity and purpose and develop the social and economic policies capable of realizing that purpose. All Americans want to live in communities that provide employment opportunities, education, healthy public amenities, vibrant civic and social networks, and safety and security. A successful governing paradigm must demonstrate how democratic engagement and the political process can help communities achieve those goals, as directly and as tangibly as possible.

In recent decades, neither political party has offered a persuasive account of, or sustained commitment to, policies which might address the core, common concerns of citizens: jobs, housing, education, and safety and security. As suggested above, this failure helped open the door for Donald J. Trump, who as a presidential candidate claimed to offer something different. Setting Trump aside, the predominant policy approaches championed by political leadership have consisted of what we might term Goldwater-Reagan conservatism, Democratic Leadership Council (DLC) centrism, and New Deal liberalism.

Goldwater-Reagan conservatism is clear about the ends it seeks to promote: interfering as little as possible with the established socio-economic order and providing businesses with a minimum of constraints on operations. These goals are represented as "liberty," and the characteristic policy strategies are threefold: reducing taxes, limiting government spending, and limiting or repealing government regulation of business. This bundle of ideas is clear, internally consistent, and aligned with the collective self-interest of many powerful groups and individuals.[12] Further, Goldwater and Reagan each articulated a soaring vision of human liberty and portrayed government as the primary threat to such liberty.[13] It is little wonder that this set of ideas—despite being subject to scores of critiques from academic observers—remains politically potent. Our disagreement with this viewpoint rests at both the level of goals and means. First, most politicians and policy writers in this paradigm do not regard rectifying our current inequalities of race, class, and gender as a top priority. Second, those who do seek to address these concerns in some form believe we must do so through the market or by relying primarily on nongovernmental entities.

DLC centrism aims to carve a so-called third way between Goldwater-Reagan conservatism and New Deal liberalism. This approach, strongly associated with President Bill Clinton and the allied Democratic Leadership Council (DLC), generally acknowledges the desirability of expanding educational and economic opportunity, is broadly supportive of gains made by women and racial minorities, and believes that government has an important role to play in fostering a good society. The DLC in the 1990s stated that it sought "to define and galvanize popular support for a new public philosophy built on progressive ideals, mainstream values, and innovative, non-bureaucratic, market-based solutions" (DLC Mission Statement, quoted in Goethals, Sorenson and Burns, 2004, p. A24). Similarly, William Galston and Elaine Kamarck's influential white paper that helped shape the early agenda of the DLC stressed the importance of Democratic leadership showing an understanding of the "social values and moral sentiments of average Americans" and recommended "the consistent use of middle-class values—individual responsibility, hard work, equal opportunity—rather than the language of compensation" (Galston and Kamarck, 1989, pp. 18–19). Market-based policy interventions are seen as the best avenue for promoting equity. The DLC thus supported President Clinton's welfare reform and free trade policies of the 1990s and also supported expansion of the Earned Income Tax Credit and market-based healthcare reform. Discussion of inequities associated with race, gender, and income inequality were to be framed not in terms of structural injustices, but within a language of individual responsibility. This approach also favored get-tough-on-crime messaging in response to the 1988 presidential election; as Galston and Kamarck (1989, p. 16) remarked, "By concentrating on race alone, Democrats avoid confronting the fact that for years they have been perceived as the party that is weaker on crime and more concerned about criminals than about victims."

Our disagreement with this framework reflects disagreement about both ends (we believe a bold articulation of our commitment to inclusive community is essential for any governing framework) and means (we do not think that the market or market mechanisms are always or automatically the best policy tool). It is also based on the sober observation that, to date, DLC-recommended policies have shown little to no capacity to arrest, let alone reverse, long-standing trends toward increased economic disparity; in fact, these policies have exacerbated inequity in our criminal justice system. At the same time, we do not think that simply sweeping aside all policy tools or ideals that reflect DLC centrist thinking is wise or necessary; instead, such tools should be re-evaluated and assessed from a community wealth building framework.

New Deal liberalism, associated with the presidency of Franklin D. Roosevelt (FDR) and his political heirs Harry Truman, John Kennedy, and Lyndon Johnson, as well as many other politicians, offered a breakthrough in American political history: the New Deal, while internally contradictory in many ways, stood consistently and compellingly for the idea of using public power proactively both to mold the market and to reshape market outcomes. Taken together, the various reforms of the 1930s represented a fundamental shift in the relationship between government and capitalism as well as in the scope of the federal government. To simplify greatly, the four fundamental planks of the New Deal included provision of social insurance; regulation of business activities, especially with respect to finance; support for organized labor; and establishment of the government's ability to manage economic conditions through both fiscal and monetary tools.[14] Well into the 1960s and even 1970s, liberal politicians and academics expressed confidence that this approach could bring about sustained prosperity, and even, with proper focusing, an end to poverty and the worst consequences of economic disparity.[15]

Since the 1970s, however, two of the core planks of the New Deal—support for organized labor and support for assertive government regulation of business activities in the public interest have weakened substantially (cataclysmically in the case of labor). While aspects of the social insurance systems established in the New Deal remain intact (e.g., Social Security), the safety net itself has largely weakened since the 1970s, with the significant exception of the 2010 Affordable Care Act. Further, history shows that the capacity of New Deal-type policies to expand depends on rare alignments of political forces: the huge Democratic supermajorities FDR enjoyed between 1932 and 1938 in response to the Depression and the huge majorities President Johnson enjoyed in the 1965–66 term in which most Great Society legislation passed. In the far more common periods of mixed government, the accomplishments of the New Deal have been either in a holding pattern or on the defensive.

Although the New Deal continues to be revered by many progressives, it is unclear whether a paradigm based on a rapid growth in federal power can win the lasting support of most Americans, at least in the near term.[16] Further, it is important not to lose sight of the very real limitations of the New Deal, even from a progressive point of view. Founded as a compromise with conservative Democratic Southerners fully committed to the region's racial caste system, the New Deal never named racial equity as a key goal. African Americans did benefit from specific New Deal policies, and as a group, shifted political loyalties from the party of Lincoln to the party of Roosevelt in the 1930s, but impactful federal civil rights legislation was delayed until the 1960s. In the meantime, as we have seen in Richmond, many federal policies associated with the New Deal in fact helped underwrite the patterns of housing (and educational segregation) associated with postwar suburbanization.

Hence, there is much justifiable skepticism about whether the federal government can be the sole driver of an agenda focused on racial, economic, and gender equity. More importantly, we believe a compelling policy paradigm must put political agency in the hands of ordinary citizens and not rest alone on hopes for what elected officials in Washington may or may not be willing or able to do. Traditional policy thinking encourages us to think of local experimentation as a laboratory for what national policy might someday undertake. Community wealth building flips this frame by stating clearly that the end goal of local *and* national policy is *the transformation of local communities so as to promote economic security, inclusivity, and equity, while promoting meaningful opportunity for all*. Importantly, achieving these goals both implies and requires a *broadening and rebalancing of power within local communities*. Building wealth and promoting equity in the communities where people live is the ultimate measure of success; the pathway to that success will require forging a new partnership between local, state, and federal government. The role of state and federal policy—and it is a crucial, indispensable role—is to support, facilitate, and enable this partnership through law, policies, and direction of resources. Bold local leadership and action can catalyze change that has national impact; at the same time, activity at the federal level should establish a nationwide baseline of civic rights and economic opportunity that allows localities to pursue and implement change.

For instance, Richmond and many other communities are undertaking work involving elements of a community wealth building agenda: bold equity goals, a holistic approach to wealth building, establishment of shared metrics, and community participation on the front end. But there is as yet no federal effort to extend this work to other communities, to establish and promulgate best practice standards, or to systematically steer federal resources to communities that are taking this approach. Indeed, the experience of many local communities with federal agencies is one of frustration at both the sheer lack of resources available and the difficulty of less politically connected communities in accessing larger grants.

We see community wealth building as a paradigm based on all levels of government working together on a shared understanding that the goal is systemic, community-level change in fundamental patterns. The key question in assessing any policy should be: does this help *build* wealth and equitable community at the local level? Sometimes these goals are best advanced by state-wide or nation-wide initiatives and programs mirroring the most success-ful elements of the New Deal, such as the Rural Electrification Administration, or by reforming or reversing policies that undermine these goals. But the *sine qua non* of this approach is communities organizing themselves—perhaps with assistance and encouragement from higher levels of government—to set bold goals and marshal available resources in support of those goals.

Without well-organized efforts to establish transformative community goals, achieving and sustaining measurable change will be nearly impossible. Equally important, this process does what the New Deal paradigm and the other dominant paradigms do not: it brings individual citizens to the table. Few people will ever be in a position to alter federal policy, and few people are bold enough to claim to know what is best not only for one community, but also for every other community. But everyone has a view—and tangible knowledge—about their own community's needs and possibilities. Community wealth building invites these views and this knowledge to the table—on the front end—and deliberately seeks out not only the most informed, expert, and involved local voices, but also the voices of the whole community in an equitable fashion. In this way, community wealth building gives substance to the idea of democratic participation, involving everyone, in shaping the goals and agenda of one's community. Only a process such as this, we contend, can reinvigorate faith in democracy among the many citizens who now feel both ignored by policy and powerless in the political arena.

The path we have sketched out here is hard work, no doubt. Community wealth building is not a snappy slogan or a one-size-fits-all policy gimmick. Rather, it is a process for rebuilding both the fabric of our communities on an equitable basis and citizen engagement in our frayed democracy. It requires thinking about processes of change from a decades-long perspective, even while acting with immediacy and urgency on shared community problems and citizens' most tangible needs. This is the long road to rebuilding community from the roots up. There is, we contend, no viable shortcut that is consistent with our aspirations to create a truly inclusive democracy.

EPILOGUE

Richmond's initial efforts in community wealth building are a work in pro-gress. Whether the city achieves its ambitious goals remains to be seen, and depends in part on factors beyond the city's control. Certainly, the overall national economic climate has an important effect both on municipal budgets and the ability of underemployed persons to find jobs. As noted above, state and federal policy significantly impact the policy flexibility available to cities to pursue innovative strategies—against a backdrop of protected rights—as well as the scale of resources available to drive transformative change.

Indeed, in Richmond as elsewhere, policies and structural arrangements that reinforce economic and racial segregation and exclude communities from wealth have to be challenged and changed, whether through incremental means or more radical steps. Communities do not exist in a vacuum but within a larger state and national structure. Hence, a community wealth building approach must encompass local, state, and national governance systems to be effective. Bold community goals should inspire reassessment of policies at all levels of government.

The significance of the work done in Richmond, Rochester, Philadelphia, and numerous other cities is that it represents the first steps on a path towards more direct civic participation in the policy process, more equitable outcomes, and identification of practical solutions to problems at the local level. Participation and the hope that one's efforts can make a difference are critical to sustaining the legitimacy of democratic institutions.

Equally important, the hard work of building community together creates engagements and relationships that cannot happen when citizens stay in their own comfort zones and narrow spheres of influence. Democracy cannot work if people who disagree do not engage with one another—and if people do not learn how to work (and argue) with people who have different interests or points of view. As theorists since Alexis de Tocqueville (1835 [2000]) have recognized, this democratic competency is best learned at the local level, where the problems are practical and there is opportunity for real civic dialogue, rather than partisan shouting.

We believe that community wealth building—led at the local level but with ample support from the state and federal level, and with a supportive architecture of federal rights and policy— should be at the core of a progressive, inclusive, and effective governance paradigm. It offers a framework for challenging America's deep legacies of inequality, racism, and sexism in fundamental ways; expanding democratic participation, one community at a time; and building the American community that never has been but should and must be.

NOTES

1. As historian Jill Lepore (2018, p. xv) writes concerning the founding propositions of the United States, "The real dispute is between 'these truths' and the course of events: Does American history prove these truths, or does it belie them?"
2. Gallup polling from late December 2018 shows that just 51 percent of all Americans characterize relations between whites and blacks as "good" or "very good," compared to 70 percent in the late 2000s. Notably, the same poll shows that 59 percent of blacks rated black–white relations as "somewhat" or "very" bad, compared to 28 percent in 2001 and 33 percent as late as 2013 (Younis, 2019).

3. A recent Pew survey found wide support for democratic values, but that 61 percent of Americans believe "significant changes" are needed in the "fundamental design and structure of American government" (Pew Research Center, 2018).

4. The term *community wealth building* was coined in a report written by the non-profit research organization The Democracy Collaborative (2005) and published by The Aspen Institute. As used in that report and in subsequent publications from The Democracy Collaborative, community wealth building refers to innovative local economic-development strategies aimed at broadening ownership of wealth while meeting local needs. Richmond, Virginia, adopted the term in 2014 to describe its comprehensive poverty-reduction efforts by establishing the Office of Community Wealth Building, directed by Thad M. Williamson (who previously worked with The Democracy Collaborative as an affiliated researcher). Our usage of the term in this chapter builds on and extends earlier work by proposing community wealth building not only as a set of local economic development tools but as an entire paradigm for governance.

5. The nativist strain in Trump's politics stands in sharp contrast to Reagan's view, however: in his 1989 farewell address, Reagan remarked that, in his vision of the shining city on the hill, "if there had to be city walls, the walls had doors, and the doors were open to anyone with the will and the heart to get here" (Reagan, 1989).

6. David Runciman (2018, p. 19) thus writes:

   It is possible to argue that since Trump was elected, American democracy has been working as it is meant to. There has been an ongoing contest between Trump's disruptive menace and a system designed to withstand a lot of disruption, especially when it emanates from demagoguery. The demagogue is discovering the world of difference between words and deeds [...] Beyond his narrow circle, which is shrinking all the time, the institutions of American democracy are proving relatively resistant to capture.

   In a similar vein, The Bright Line Watch (2018) project assessing democratic performance in the United States finds that academic experts tend to have a significantly more positive assessment of the condition of American democracy than the wider public. The project's ongoing survey of academic political scientists shows a mild but not catastrophic erosion of democratic norms under the Trump administration across 27 discrete metrics of democratic practice.

7. The definitive academic statement of this viewpoint is political theorist Sheldon Wolin's (1994 [2016]) essay "Fugitive democracy."

8. This account of Richmond history draws on several key sources, including Campbell (2012); the Office of Community Wealth Building's first report (City of Richmond, 2016), accessed February 20, 2020 at http://www.richmondgov.com/CommunityWealthBuilding/index.aspx; Drake and Holsworth (1996); Hayter (2017); Mayor's Anti-Poverty Commission (2013) report; Moeser and Dennis (1982); Silver (1984); and Williamson (2014).

9. Private communication of Rev. Benjamin Campbell to Thad Williamson, 2013.

10. Disclosure: Thad Williamson served on the Mayor's Anti-Poverty Commission and was primary author of its final report. He was co-chair (with Councilwoman Ellen Robertson) of the subsequent Maggie L. Walker Initiative for Expanding Opportunity and Fighting Poverty, which developed specific action plans to implement Anti-Poverty Commission recommendations. He served as the first director of the Office of Community Wealth Building under Mayor Dwight C. Jones from June 2014 to May 2016 and then as transition director and a senior policy advisor for Mayor Levar M. Stoney from November 2016 to June 2018.

11. For further detail, see Office of Community Wealth Building Annual Reports, 2016–20, accessed February 20, 2020 at http://www.richmondgov.com/ CommunityWealthBuilding/index.aspx.
12. The contemporaneous description of President Reagan's program by policy analysts John Palmer and Isabel Sawhill (1984, p. 2) is helpful here:
    What is distinctive about Ronald Reagan is his conviction that prosperity requires a much more limited role for government, while the preservation of peace and of traditional values, requires, in many cases, an expanded role. He combines the libertarian's distrust of government in the economic sphere with a more traditionally conservative belief in moral absolutes and the need for a strong defense against external threats. It is a consistent philosophy given its premises that economic growth will flow from the inherent entrepreneurial spirit and enterprise of the American people; that social problems can be largely solved by church, family, and neighborhood; that freedom is our greatest national asset; and that its protection requires, above all, military strength.
13. Thus, Barry Goldwater (1960, p. 70):
    We can shatter the collectivists' designs on human freedom if we will impress upon the men who conduct our affairs this one truth: that the material and spiritual sides of man are intertwined; that it is impossible for the State to assume responsibility for one without intruding on the essential nature of the other; that if we take from a man the personal responsibility for caring for his material needs, we take from him also the will and the opportunity to be free.
14. See Leuchtenburg (1963) for a detailed programmatic overview.
15. Peter Edelman (2012, p. 4), former policy adviser to Robert F. Kennedy, thus writes with respect to the 1964 Economic Opportunity Act, "To those involved, the new law was truly a war on poverty, and confidence abounded that it would be a war that could be won." Reflecting on the persistence of poverty in an affluent society, influential economist John Kenneth Galbraith (1958 [1998], Chapter 22) attributed the "disgraceful" persistence of poverty in an affluent society to lack of political will to commit the necessary resources to provide an income base for all and employment opportunities for all those able to take advantage of them.
16. This observation does not mean we are opposed to bold national efforts in support of critical policy goals such as redressing climate change. Policy advocates continue to cite the New Deal as a kind of synonym for the idea of a bold national effort, as in the now-current term "Green New Deal." We have no criticism of invocations of the New Deal for this purpose; rather, we raise questions about whether future bold national efforts can or ought to follow the paradigm Roosevelt developed of necessity, featuring rapidly expanding, federally designed initiatives as the primary or sole driver of change.

REFERENCES

Belsches, Elvatrice (2015), "When freedom came, part 2," *Richmond Free Press*, April 4, accessed January 3, 2020 at http://richmondfreepress.com/news/2015/apr/02/ when-freedom-came-part-2/?page=1.
Bright Line Watch (2018), "Wave 7 report," October/November, accessed January 7, 2020 at http://brightlinewatch.org/wave7/.
Campbell, Benjamin (2012), *Richmond's Unhealed History*, Richmond, VA: Brandylane Publishers.
Case, Anne and Sir Angus Deaton (2017), "Mortality and morbidity in the 21st century," *Brookings Papers on Economic Activity*, March 23, accessed January 7, 2020 at https://www.brookings.edu/bpea-articles/mortality-and-morbidity-in-the -21st-century/.

City of Richmond (2016), *Office of Community Wealth Building Year One Annual Report* (2016), Richmond, VA: City of Richmond.

Democracy Collaborative at the University of Maryland (2005), "Building wealth: the new asset-based approach to solving social and economic problems," working paper published by the Aspen Institute, May 22.

Drake, W. Avon and Robert Holsworth (1996), *Affirmative Action and the Stalled Quest for Black Progress*, Champaign, IL: University of Illinois Press.

Edelman, Peter (2012), *So Rich, So Poor: Why It's So Hard to End Poverty in America*, New York: The New Press.

Friedersdorf, Conor (2015), "What do Donald Trump voters actually want?" *The Atlantic*, August 17, accessed January 7, 2020 at https://www.theatlantic.com/politics/archive/2015/08/donald-trump-voters/401408/#Top.

Galbraith, John Kenneth (1958 [1998]), *The Affluent Society, 40th Anniversary Edition*, New York: Houghton Mifflin Harcourt Publishing Company.

Galston, William and Elaine Kamarck (1989), "The politics of evasion: democrats and the presidency," Progressive Policy Institute, September, accessed January 11, 2020 at https://www.progressivepolicy.org/wp-content/uploads/2013/03/Politics_of_Evasion.pdf.

Goethals, George, Georgia Sorensen and James McGregor Burns (2004), *The Encyclopedia of Leadership, Vol 1*, Thousand Oaks, CA: SAGE Publications.

Goldwater, Barry (1960), *The Conscience of a Conservative*, Shepherdsville, KY: Victor Publishing.

Gordon, Robert (2017), *The Rise and Fall of American Growth: The U.S. Standard of Living Since the Civil War*, Princeton, NJ: Princeton University Press.

Guzman, Gloria G. (2017), "Household income: 2016: American Community Survey briefs," United States Census Bureau, September, accessed January 7, 2020 at https://www.census.gov/content/dam/Census/library/publications/2017/acs/acsbr16-02.pdf.

Hayter, Julian Maxwell (2017), *The Dream Is Lost: Voting Rights and the Politics of Race in Richmond, Virginia*, Lexington, KY: University Press of Kentucky.

Khazan, Olga (2017), "Strangers in their own land," *The Atlantic*, March 7, accessed January 7, 2020 at https://www.theatlantic.com/science/archive/2017/03/strangers-in-their-own-land/518733/.

Lepore, Jill (2018), *These Truths: A History of the United States*, New York: W.W. Norton & Company, Inc.

Leuchtenburg, William E. (1963), *Franklin D. Roosevelt and the New Deal, 1932–1940*, New York: Harper & Row.

Lincoln, Abraham (1862), "Annual message to Congress—concluding remarks," December 1, accessed January 7, 2020 at http://www.abrahamlincolnonline.org/lincoln/speeches/congress.htm.

Mansbridge, Jane (2012), "On the importance of getting things done," *PS: Political Science and Politics*, 45(1), 1–8, accessed January 3, 2020 at https://www.cambridge.org/core/journals/ps-political-science-and-politics/article/on-the-importance-of-getting-things-done/23A7AF6FC633DB2CEF05CBE3E1901F3A.

Mayor's Anti-Poverty Commission (2013), *Mayor's Anti-Poverty Commission Report*, Richmond, VA: City of Richmond.

Moeser, John and Rutledge Dennis (1982), *The Politics of Annexation: Oligarchic Power in a Southern City*, Cambridge, MA: Schenkman Publishing Company.

Palmer, John and Isabel Sawhill (eds) (1984), *The Reagan Record: An Assessment of America's Changing Domestic Priorities (An Urban Institute Study)*, Cambridge, MA: Ballinger Publishing Company.

Pew Research Center (2018), "The public, the political system and American democracy," April 26, accessed January 3, 2020 at https://www.people-press.org/2018/04/26/the-public-the-political-system-and-american-democracy/.

Reagan, Ronald (1989), "Transcript of Reagan's farewell address to American people," *The New York Times*, January 12, accessed January 7, 2020 at https://www.nytimes.com/1989/01/12/news/transcript-of-reagan-s-farewell-address-to-american-people.html.

Ruane, Michael E. (2015), "War's end," *The Washington Post*, March 27, accessed January 3, 2020 at https://www.washingtonpost.com/sf/style/2015/03/27/wars-end/?utm_term=.72fcebf9dec9.

Runciman, David (2018), *How Democracy Ends*, New York: Basic Books.

Shapiro, Thomas M. (2004), *The Hidden Cost of Being African American: How Wealth Perpetuates Inequality*, New York: Oxford University Press.

Silver, Christopher (1984), *Twentieth-Century Richmond: Politics, Planning, and Race*, Knoxville, KY: University of Tennessee Press.

Snow, David, Sarah Soule and Hanspeter Kriesi (eds) (2007), *The Blackwell Companion to Social Movements*, Malden, MA: Blackwell Publishing Ltd.

Stokes, Keith W. (2014), "The symbol of one America," *Richmond Times-Dispatch*, April 3, accessed January 7, 2020 at https://www.richmond.com/opinion/columnists/stokes-the-symbol-of-one-america/article_5badf73b-5904-5327-8be1-d88edbeba7c3.html.

Stone, Chad, Danilo Trisi, Arloc Sherman and Roderick Taylor (2019), "A guide to statistics on historical trends in income inequality," *Center on Budget and Policy Priorities*, August 21, accessed January 3, 2020 at https://www.cbpp.org/research/poverty-and-inequality/a-guide-to-statistics-on-historical-trends-in-income-inequality.

Tocqueville, Alexis de (1835 [2000]), *Democracy in America, Volume 1*, translated and edited by Harvey Mansfield and Delba Winthrop, Chicago, IL: Chicago University Press.

Tufekci, Zeynep (2018), "Russian meddling is a symptom, not the disease," *The New York Times*, October 3, accessed January 3, 2020 at https://www.nytimes.com/2018/10/03/opinion/midterms-facebook-foreign-meddling.html.

United States Census (2018), American Community Survey, Table S1701, "Poverty status in the past 12 months, 2018," accessed January 21, 2020 at https://data.census.gov/cedsci/.

Williamson, Thad (2014), "The tangled relationship of democracy, leadership, and justice in urban America: a view from Richmond," in John Kane and Haig Patapan (eds), *Good Democratic Leadership: On Prudence and Judgment in Modern Democracies*, Oxford: Oxford University Press.

Wolin, Sheldon (1994 [2016]), "Fugitive democracy," in Sheldon Wolin with Nicholas Xenos (ed.), *Fugitive Democracy and Other Essays*, Princeton, NJ: Princeton University Press.

Younis, Mohamed (2019), "Most blacks rate race relations with whites as bad," *Gallup*, February 21, accessed January 3, 2020 at https://news.gallup.com/poll/246899/blacks-rate-race-relations-whites-bad.aspx.

PART II

Racial justice and American democracy

3. Repairing American democracy?[1]

Lawrie Balfour

Past injustices and crimes against African Americans need to be addressed with reparatory justice.
(United Nations, General Assembly, 2016)

REPARATIONS NOW

Demands for reparations for slavery and its legacies are not new. They have long played a vital role in the agendas of antiracist activists; they have been parsed and debated by academics and lawyers; and they are periodically held up by conservative commentators as emblematic of the dangers of race-conscious policies. While public signals of support by Democratic candidates for the presidency *are* new, it is unclear that this moment of political respectability will last or whether it will have concrete, positive effects. Indeed, the career of black reparations in the United States is one of persistent disconnection— between the enduring work of black-led social movements over the past two centuries on the one hand, and the relatively short-lived character of public attention to the political implications of white supremacy on the other. Rather than assessing the candidates' mostly undeveloped proposals, this chapter seizes on the renewed interest in reparations as an opening for inquiring into their history and assessing their promise and limitations as a response to deeply entrenched political and economic inequality. What distinguishes the language of reparations is that it names debts that can never be repaid in full, and yet must be paid down for the sake of present and future generations. Approaching reparations as a framework for democratic thought and action resonates with Melody C. Barnes and Thad M. Williamson's community wealth building paradigm described in Chapter 2 of this book. Like their chapter, this chapter asks how to connect an understanding of US history to the realization of a more equal society. Where they lay out a compelling policy paradigm that joins local empowerment initiatives to state and federal resources, I call attention to reparations as a political language or framework that, I contend, ought to shape a wide range of policies aimed at democratic reconstruction.

   The history of black reparations claims is a transnational story of demands made by the relatively powerless against states and corporate entities that have profited from roughly 500 years of Euro-American policies of conquest, extraction, enslavement, and disenfranchisement. It is a history of resistance to the closure that calls for reconciliation too frequently enjoined and a vision of substantially different arrangements of power. In the United States, this resistance dates back to the early days of the Republic. For example, when African American abolitionist David Walker ([1829] 1965, p. 70) issued his blistering "Appeal to the Coloured Citizens of the World" in 1829, he argued: "The Americans may do as they please, but they have to raise us from the condition of brutes to that of respectable men, and to make a national acknowledgment to us for the wrongs they have inflicted on us."

Subsequent generations have joined the call for acknowledgment and immediate liberation to a far-reaching set of programs designed to make real the promise of equality and freedom for all. The Black Panthers' Ten-Point Program links the broken promise of "forty acres and two mules" to demands for "Land, Bread, Housing, Education, Clothing, Justice and Peace" (Black Panther Party, 1966). And the National Black Economic Development Conference's 1969 "Black Manifesto" sought reparations in the form of individual payments as well as a land bank for African Americans, investment in communications and education, welfare rights, and assistance for striking workers. The turn of the 21st century witnessed a resurgence of visible reparations-related activity. In every Congress between 1989 and his retirement in 2017, Rep. John Conyers (D-Michigan) introduced H.R. 40, a bill to acknowledge the horrors of slavery and establish a commission to study the idea of reparations;[2] Randall Robinson published *The Debt: What America Owes to Blacks* (2000); grassroots organizations, such as the Black Radical Congress and the National Coalition of Blacks for Reparations in America (N'COBRA), pressed the case; law professors and legal activists filed a series of reparations lawsuits against governmental and corporate entities; and expressions of regret for slavery, race riots, lynching, and related crimes proliferated at federal, state, and local levels. That momentum was largely stopped in its tracks in 2008 by the election of Barack Obama, which appeared to support the ideas that the United States had entered a post-racial epoch and that legal and legislative efforts to produce concrete remedies had failed. Still, the plausibility of black reparations as a political project emerged—once again—with the rise of the Black Lives Matter movement and the publication, in June 2014, of Ta-Nehisi Coates's *Atlantic* article, "The case for reparations."[3] Together, these varied moments and movements indicate the importance of reparations activism as "one arc of the centuries long struggle for Black racial equality" (Aiyetoro and Davis, 210, p. 692).[4] They also constitute a deep reservoir for political thinking.

Although often dismissed as backward looking, reparations demands have historically advanced positive steps that can/must be taken to realign radical asymmetries of wealth and power rooted in past and present injustice.[5]

Advocates have been castigated for sowing division, even though their words often emphasize collective benefits and social healing. And although reparations claims are trivialized as purely symbolic and dangerously anti-political (Reed, 2000), they are often the outcome of egalitarian forms of collective organizing. When Martin Luther King Jr. declared (1967 [2010], p. 95; original emphasis) that "a society that has done something special *against* the Negro for hundreds of years must now do something special *for* him," for example, he followed that claim with a call for the abolition of poverty and for a range of programs to transform education, employment, rights, and housing in the United States. Noting that his proposal would primarily aid white Americans, King nevertheless linked the history of anti-black racism to broad plans for material reconstruction, remarking that Americans' treatment of all poor people (at home and abroad) is as "cruel and blind as the practice of cannibalism at the dawn of civilization" (King, 1967 [2010], p. 175). More recently, the organizations that comprise The Movement for Black Lives have laid out a demand for reparations that cites harms stretching "from colonialism to slavery through food and housing redlining, mass incarceration, and surveillance" (The Movement for Black Lives, n.d.). And their platform articulates a list of specific actions that can be taken at local, state, and national levels to address issues that include inequities in access to high-quality education; the need for a living wage; monetary compensation that can be used to invest in decent food, housing, and land; curricular reform and support for cultural programming; and legislative initiatives that acknowledge and redress the effects of slavery (ibid.). Beyond the United States, the Reparations Commission established by the Caribbean Community (CARICOM) in 2013 articulates a Ten-Point Plan comprising an imaginative range of policy proposals (Beckles, 2013).

Perhaps the most distinctive feature of all these demands is their insistence on challenging the invisibility and presumed inevitability of current injustices, while also asking how those injustices have emerged over time and envisioning their undoing. In the United States, where so many of the race-conscious policies put in place during the civil rights era have been stripped of their efficacy, speaking of reparations involves naming both the contemporary significance of race and its pivotal role in American political development. The movement for reparations, writes Dorothy Roberts (2002, p. 271), undermines "the obfuscation of race" through which "universal" policies disguise the degree to which present-day inequalities flow from prior policies that were designed to exclude or suppress African Americans. This view complements Deborah Thomas's insight that reparations ought to serve as "a framework for thinking," rather than any single policy or narrowly conceived compensatory program (Thomas, 2011, p. 4), and Michael Dawson's view that reparations constitute "a demand for a conversation" (Dawson, 2013, p. 197). In a nation with a history of engaging in conversation as a substitute for action, however, it is crucial that any discussion is construed as a beginning, not the end. And not all perspectives can carry equal weight. Talk of redress for slavery and its legacies should be rooted in African American history and political thought, offering an accounting of the continuing costs of historic injustice and envisioning concrete proposals for redress.[6] Crucially, reparations arguments resist cultural explanations for poverty and violence in racialized communities; instead, they focus on the ways that a purportedly democratic polity has been structured along racially inegalitarian and often deadly lines. Thus, reparations arguments can help us to see what democracy requires in a sense that is both general and specific.

This chapter focuses on one dimension of that aspiration by exploring how demands for reparations offer an avenue for dramatizing and redressing costs that accumulate when a democratic society directs much of its energy toward the violent control and confinement of citizens and immigrants, particularly poor, nonwhite men, women, and children. If we accept Ian Haney-López's contention that "race helped make security and punishment seemingly obvious goals of government across a stunning array of disparate contexts" (Haney-López, 2010, pp. 1037–8), then undoing the deep penetration of punitive practices into public policy and everyday experience entails acknowledging the enduring effects of official and unofficial forms of racial subordination and dehumanization. And the language of reparations, which keeps these harms in view, indicates why transforming those communities hardest hit by mass incarceration and over-policing is both the least that is owed to them and essential to the health of democracy in the United States. The next section inquires how the temporal framework of reparations, which emphasizes the residual and cumulative effects of historical forms of racial power and violence, reveals connections between present and past in policing and punishment. The third section draws on the language of reparations to disclose how the carceral polity undermines the promise of equal citizenship and to suggest how that language enables us to develop a more robust account of shared responsibility for racial injustice. In spite of this democratic promise, however, there are good reasons to worry that successful reparations claims would forestall any ongoing commitment to social change. In the fourth section, I review some of these dangers and suggest why approaching reparations as a framework, rather than a single policy, offers a constructive rebuttal to Americans' recurrent efforts to declare that "the past is passed."[7]

RESETTING DEMOCRATIC TIME

One of the basic features of reparations language is the challenge it poses to conventional ways of measuring time. Thinking through reparations unsettles historical narratives that overemphasize the uniqueness of different historical periods and figure the movement from one era to another as progress. It also disturbs the apparent timelessness of the principles animating debates in political theory—debates that too regularly transpire in what Charles Mills (2014) calls "white time"—and presses us to begin our analysis from the fact of existing injustices. Such an orientation emphasizes both the unfinished business bequeathed by the re-foundations that followed the Civil War, the modern civil rights movement, and the invention of new anti-democratic practices from the ruins of the old. Because temporal inequalities have played a crucial role in structuring and reproducing racialized relationships of dominance and exploitation, the language of reparations illuminates contemporary discrepancies in the ways that time is experienced, distributed, and measured by situating the present within an expanded temporal frame (Hanchard, 1999). One of the most pernicious of these inequalities, clearly, is the gap between those who must "do time" (and their loved ones and communities) and those of us who largely live beyond the reach of the carceral apparatus.[8]

Approaching the democratic damage of American investments in policing and punishment through the lens of reparations could, for example, extend conversations inaugurated by Michelle Alexander's *The New Jim Crow* and other recent critiques of mass incarceration. Alexander's landmark study inspired many readers to join her in "com[ing] to see that mass incarceration in the United States had, in fact, emerged as a stunningly comprehensive and well-disguised system of racialized social control that functions in a manner strikingly similar to Jim Crow" (Alexander, 2012, p. 4). Like Douglas Blackmon's argument that the widespread practice of convict leasing that emerged after the Civil War was "slavery by another name" (Blackmon, 2008), Alexander's book presses readers to grapple with the afterlives of institutions and practices often presumed to be dead and buried. Despite important disanalogies between slavery and Jim Crow, Alexander's scholarship spurs us to question any claim that it is time to move on or that slavery and legal segregation were fully abolished in 1865 and the mid-1960s, respectively.[9]

Indeed, because mass incarceration developed *after* the major legislative and judicial achievements of the civil rights movement, focusing on its democratic costs can also fruitfully complicate the temporal perspective of many reparations arguments. These arguments begin by demanding a reckoning with the legacies of slavery, lynching, debt peonage, and the multitude of other crimes associated with earlier racial regimes. For example, H.R. 40 proposes a commission "to acknowledge the fundamental injustice, cruelty, brutality, and inhumanity of slavery in the United States and the 13 American colonies between 1619 and 1865" and the injustices that have followed from it. While this approach could "bring to light the broken promises of freedom" (Hartman, 2002, p. 760), viewing reparations in the context of mass incarceration also highlights the degree to which the United States continues to innovate, producing new forms of racial subjugation and violence against communities of color. Such inventiveness is on display, argue Mary Katzenstein and Maurcen Waller (2015), in new forms of "cash extraction" through which the state and its corporate partners demand money from the incarcerated poor, who rely on loved ones to cover fees, fines, and charges for everything from access to prison libraries to medical care. Katzenstein and Waller's research uncovers the degree to which the state now relies on the poor (primarily women) to finance their own governance. In other words, a focus on the carceral dimensions of US democracy reorients reparations claims so that they not only emphasize the crimes that were left unredressed in previous periods of reconstruction, but also reckon with forms of subjugation that creatively combine new practices with vestiges of slavery and Jim Crow.[10] In this light, it is telling that prison abolitionists, who advocate the elimination of a wide range of punitive practices with roots in racial slavery, have invoked the language of reparations.[11]

A reparative framework could thus engender more creative responses to a present that does and does not look like the past. For instance, critics have rightly noted the relationship between mass incarceration and the withdrawal of public investment in poor communities on the one hand, and the replacement of norms of collective responsibility with a discourse of "personal responsibility" on the other. While these developments are hallmarks of neo-liberal governance, a longer historical perspective reminds us that new structures of power may build on deeply rooted features of the American political tradition. In this light, we might re-view the contradictory status of poor citizens of color, who are held accountable for any failure to adhere to the demands of a state that demonstrates no accountability for their protection or well-being. When we consider their susceptibility to what Lisa Miller (2014) calls "racialized state failure" through the temporal frame of reparations, we find echoes of a system that once regarded the slave "as a member of the society, [...] as a moral person" for the purposes of punishment or that held, without apparent irony, that the slave was protected "in his life and in his limbs, against the violence of all others, even the master of his labor and his liberty" and that he was "punishable himself for all violence committed against others" (Madison, 1788 [2009], p. 278). Without collapsing crucial differences between racial regimes, we can nevertheless ask whether a similar logic underwrites today's criminalization of blackness or surmise how the massive expansion of a carceral system that disproportionately punishes poor citizens of color could evolve from a promise of protection from "lawless racial violence."[12]

Regarding policing and punishment through the long arc of racial history also sheds light on the antidemocratic implications of the prison as a "gendering apparatus" (Davis, 2012, p. 147). On the one hand, the prison is one of the most rigidly sex-segregated institutions in the United States today, and the use of genitalia to determine housing assignments can compound the injuries of punishment by requiring that transsexual and intersex prisoners conform to binary sex categories and subjecting them to additional violence (Pemberton, 2013). Reparations discourse enlarges our understanding of the sexual abuse that is endemic to police stations, jails, and prisons by connecting contemporary institutions to prior formations of racial power and their role in the constitution of masculinity and femininity. For example, Adrienne Davis's study of sexual harassment in the context of slavery enhances our understanding of carceral violence: "[S]lavery's sexual economy calls attention to the ways women working in certain geographic configurations are particularly vulnerable to sexual abuse, especially when combined with other axes of social power(lessness), such as race, age, immigrant/document status, or imprisonment" (Davis, 2002 [2004], p. 471). Such an approach also alerts us to the ways in which historically specific, but overlapping, figurations of black masculinity have been allied to popular conceptions of criminality.

If the temporal frame of reparations can illuminate the gendering effects of the carceral polity, it can also assist in our thinking about racialized practices of *un*-gendering that transpire on streets, in courtrooms, and behind prison walls. As Hortense Spillers (1987) argues, the Middle Passage and New World slavery amounted to a "theft of the body," in which what was left to be exploited and discarded, as needed, was purely "flesh." In such a schema, differentiations between men and women were not relevant. Looking to the roles of women under slavery, Angela Davis (1998, p. 117) uncovers a "deformed equality of equal oppression" in a system that expected enslaved women to work as hard as men. Today, a logic of formal equality engenders what she calls "this presumptive equality [...] grounded in violence," whereby "women's prisons are rendered equal to men's by making them equally punitive, equally dehumanizing" (Davis, 2012, p. 78).[13] Ensnared by the association of blackness and criminality that captures women as well as men, African American women and other women and girls of color are particularly susceptible to being treated as criminals when they seek protection from gender violence in what Beth Richie (2012) calls the "prison nation." Despite "the dramatic growth in punishment in women's lives," furthermore, they are too easily overlooked as subjects of concern in public discourse about imprisonment and policing, particularly arguments that focus on the "endangerment" of black men (Crenshaw, 2012, p. 1471).[14] Insofar as reparations claims are informed by feminist analysis—crucially, by black feminist thought—they can provide a way of reckoning with the complex interactions of time, gender, race, and class at work in carceral practices from the Middle Passage to the present.

Further, thinking through and speaking of reparations bring explicit attention to the politics of time itself. Challenging a temporal orientation in which past practices are eclipsed, the language of reparations highlights those elements of the past that linger on or that are reborn in new forms. Crucially, it provokes acknowledgment of the limits of what can be redressed, admitting the fact that it is "too late" to make many victims whole. Nonetheless, reparations claims can operate as a source of both counter-narratives about what has been and an expression of hope for alternative futures. Reparations demands differentiate between "the past as bygone," which characterizes the approach of most official mnemonic projects, and "the past as prologue" (Westley, 2005, p. 85). These differences are registered in the experiences of citizens and in the body politic itself. George Jackson's account of the connectedness between his own imprisonment and the time of slavery captures this relation:

> My recall is nearly perfect, time has faded nothing. I recall the first kidnap, I lived through the passage, died on the passage, lain in the unmarked shallow graves of the millions who fertilized the American soil with their corpses; cotton and corn growing out of my chest "until the third and fourth generation," the tenth, the hundredth. (Jackson quoted in Best and Hartman, 2005, p. 4)

Where Jackson reflects how the heritage of slavery is lived as a deeply personal experience, the language of reparations also addresses ways in which slavery and its aftermath haunt the polity as a whole. Hence Haney-López's approach to race through the concept of "cumulation": "Race's full force cannot be grasped by examining the consequences of particular discriminatory episodes, but must be measured in the folds and knots of a whole social fabric woven and rewoven with reinforcing racial bands" (Haney-López, 2010, p. 1056).

Addressing the time of mass incarceration and racialized policing through the lens of reparations entails keeping the myriad ways in which past habits and institutions are both discredited and reconstituted in a present that is new and not new. Although crimes associated with slavery and Jim Crow have been the subject of a growing number of official apologies and public history projects since the turn of the twenty-first century, these efforts too frequently dissociate bygone injustices from contemporary conditions. In such cases, Salamishah Tillet (2012, p. 165) warns, "[T]he living suddenly risk becoming more invisible than the dead." The aim of reparations advocates, by contrast, is to vivify how abuses ranging from police harassment and violence, to unequal arrest and prosecution rates, to the exclusion of former prisoners from a host of essential services and rights of citizenship, to the continued practice of capital punishment must be understood in conjunction with a reckoning with history.

THE (CIVIL) DEATH OF CITIZENSHIP

What does it mean to approach reparations claims as "discursive instruments" through which the norms of democratic citizenship are critically examined and affirmed (Rubio-Marín, 2008, p. 212)? One way to address this question is to consider how the development of mass incarceration since the end of the civil rights era threatens the very possibility of democratic citizenship. Indeed, activists and scholars note that the United States stands apart from the rest of the world in its punitiveness and in the degree to which the effects of punishment ripple outward. First, the United States defines offenders by their convictions and, for many, permanently obliterates their political person-hood.[15] Second, it traps many children, women, and men who may be guilty of nothing, but who are detained, imprisoned, and even killed because they are presumed to pose a threat. Finally, the geographic and demographic concentration of police surveillance and imprisonment effectively denies whole communities of offenders and nonoffenders the full enjoyment of their rights as citizens.

Imprisonment, as incarceration scholars have observed, is a form of "banishment." James Forman Jr. (2012, p. 28) notes that "even those most familiar with our criminal justice system may fail to recognize how completely we banish those who are convicted of crimes."[16] Dylan Rodríguez (2006, p. 227; original emphasis) describes prison as "a point of *massive human departure*" that cuts the incarcerated off from affective or institutional connection to the world beyond. Long after completing their sentences, offenders are stigmatized in myriad ways, unable to gain access to employment or basic public services; and the age of mass incarceration marks an astonishing rise in the number of convicted felons who exist beyond the scope of democratic citizenship, as many scholars and activists have noted. Efforts to grapple with the implications of this form of civil death remain limited without an inquiry into how the present is conjoined to the history of slavery and forms of racialized power that developed to control and suppress black citizens in the aftermath of emancipation. Such an approach might begin with Colin Dayan's genealogy of the cruelties of racialized imprisonment, which tracks the ways in which the "shifting body of the slave was reborn in the body of the prisoner" (Dayan, 2011, p. 60). What forms of violation and exclusion might emerge from such a remaking of the imprisoned body? Viewing the polity through the lens of reparations spurs a reckoning with the links between practices that we condemn and those we take for granted; it opens up new questions about the degree to which citizenship in the United States has been circumscribed by convict leasing, solitary confinement, the chain gang, felon disenfranchisement, and the legally sanctioned deprivation of a wide range of rights.

As the history of such practices intimates, the scope and weight of racialized punishment are also felt by those who have committed *no* crime. Bryan Stevenson's best-selling memoir of his work among men and women who have been convicted, and often sentenced to death, for offenses in which they were not involved or in which their culpability was terribly distorted, challenges any insouciance about the protections provided by the legal order (Stevenson, 2014). Among the crucial findings of Amy Lerman and Vesla Weaver's study of what they call "custodial citizenship" is the degree to which encounters with the state through its policing apparatus serve as the primary avenue through which many poor black men experience citizenship. Indeed, the proliferation of practices of supervision and punishment constitute a distinctive "custodial lifeworld." Even for citizens who have not lost the right to vote through felon disenfranchisement, "punishment and surveillance themselves activate a process of political withdrawal, alienation, and fear of government" (Lerman and Weaver, 2014, p. 200). Effectively, Traci Burch contends, the geographic concentration of criminal justice enforcement disenfranchises whole neighborhoods; proximity is sufficient for citizens to be caught up in the carceral web, regardless of their actual involvement in criminal activity (Burch, 2013). Cathy Cohen (2010) likewise remarks that a significant number of young black Americans practice what she calls a "politics of invisibility," and she suggests that their decision to disengage from political life reflects their experiences of government surveillance and control. If we consider the violent, and often deadly, character of encounters between residents of impoverished, hyper-segregated neighborhoods and the police, the conclusion that the safest course is to stay under the radar, escaping the state's attention, appears strikingly reasonable.

While American punitive practices since the Civil War have often targeted the status of African Americans *as* citizens, their effects are also felt beyond the boundaries of US citizenship. The spread of anti-immigrant statutes and the subjection of would-be Americans to degrading and often violent detention demonstrates how policies that criminalize black citizens can ease the way for cruelty and disregard toward other racialized groups. Like the policies that established mass incarceration, Marie Gottschalk (2014, p. 220) observes, "the strikingly punitive turn in immigration policy has been fiercely bipartisan." If there is no clear causal line from slavery to mass incarceration to the detention of immigrants, it remains crucial to ask how a history of unredressed anti-black violence shapes a society that also abuses prisoners at Abu Ghraib, Guantanamo Bay, and other sites outside the continental United States, while profiling individuals marked as members of "terrorist" communities. Thinking through reparations helps us to see connections between different moments in the history of racial violence (both legal and extra-legal) and understand how the devaluation of black life has made it easier for the polity to target and devalue members of other vulnerable or dispossessed communities (Gilmore, 2007; Gottschalk, 2014). It both dramatizes the extent to which punishment and surveillance function as the primary mode of political communication from the state to many citizens of color and offers an alternative language through which to articulate democratic aspirations.

The vantage offered by reparations not only enables us to reconceive the relationship between a history of racial slavery, terror, exploitation, and exclusion on the one hand, and the operations of apparently race-neutral criminal justice practices and policies on the other, but it also forces a reckoning with the implications of the carceral polity for those of us who are *not* under state control. Although the spread of punitive policies is destructive of democratic life and thus a threat to all citizens, individuals who have never experienced custodial supervision or feared arbitrary police stops may reap both affective and material rewards from the pretense that locking up criminals will safeguard the innocent from harm. We are not required to see the products of our democratic failures—unsafe neighborhoods, unfit schools, lack of access to basic services, and so forth—as long as they can be explained by the deviant behavior of the people who are confined to them. Consideration of the kinds of investments that are owed to these citizens, in other words, is not *our* problem. Glenn Loury (2008, p. 27) makes this point with particular sharpness: "We law-abiding, middle-class Americans have made decisions about social policy and incarceration, and we benefit from those decisions, and that means from a system of suffering rooted in state violence, meted out at our request." Katzenstein and Waller (2015, p. 648) press the matter farther, asking whether "law-abiding middle-class Americans" enjoy "a system of welfare socialism for the better-off that is dependent on the predation by the state of the poor."

Such propositions reinforce Angela Davis's observation that mass incarceration not only relieves some citizens from thinking about the conditions within prison walls but also preserves a wider innocence about the desperate condition of communities that have withstood generations of disinvestment and disregard (Davis, 2012, p. 51). Here, the work of innocence is twofold: it signifies a bright line between those of us who are not branded as criminals, whether or not we have actually broken the law, and those who carry the mark; and it also provides a ready explanation for these divisions that inoculates the privileged from cultivating a sense of shared responsibility for targeted individuals and communities.

The language of reparations, by contrast, emphasizes shared, plural forms of responsibility as a cornerstone of democratic politics. Loosening the grip of a discourse of "personal responsibility" that has targeted disadvantaged groups with particular ferocity, reparations calls upon the concern of the citizenry as a whole and insists that individual action can take place only within a fabric of relations.[17] In this sense, it resonates with Iris Marion Young's "social connection model" of political responsibility and discredits any efforts on the part of the beneficiaries of the carceral polity to shield ourselves from owning up to the costs of punitive practices and structures of oppression (Young, 2011). Otherwise, the concept of responsibility devolves into what Toni Morrison (1993 [2008], p. 200) decries as "official language smitheryed to sanction ignorance and preserve privilege." Such language, she declares, "is a suit of armor polished to shocking glitter, a husk from which the knight departed long ago." Responsibility, in other words, is both a marker of contemporary inequality—where some members of the polity are presumed responsible in the criminal sense, while others are presumed responsible in the sense of independent, upstanding, dutiful citizens—and a vehicle for entrenching inequality. Popular uses of the term, furthermore, often conjure degrading images of black existence and efface white supremacist structures and practices that have been sedimented over generations.[18] Among the signal contributions of reparations is the refusal to accept such a degradation of our political vocabulary and its attentiveness to forms of inequality that can be redressed only through collective investments in the polity we are supposed to hold in common.

REPARATIONS: A FRAMEWORK, NOT A POLICY

Calling for reparations as a framework (or a language), and not a policy, may sound hopelessly abstract. My aim, however, is to suggest that the reverse is true. The idea of reparations is not any one thing; but it is, concretely, relevant to any area of political organizing or policy that has been affected by white supremacy. To invoke reparations as a response to the legacies of slavery, in general, as some presidential candidates have done, may simply invite new disillusionment among nonwhite citizens and violent reactions by their white neighbors. To consider reparations as a one-time program is to lose the opportunity to reshape the way we approach a broad range of specific policies. Still, rather than abandon the language of reparations, I argue that citizens and policy-makers should draw upon its distinctive capacity to join history to future-oriented objectives when we debate issues in which slavery's legacies live on. In addition to policing and punishment, discussions of housing, education, the regulation of financial institutions, taxes, and the environment are among the many areas of politics and policy in which unacknowledged effects of white supremacy shape present conditions and ought not be allowed to determine future decisions.

To be sure, such an approach has its risks. There is no guarantee that appeals to the collective responsibility of US citizens will spark a fundamental remaking of the society that has enforced racial hierarchies across its history. Indeed, such appeals could reinforce the legitimacy of the norms and institutions that reparations advocates aim to discredit or transform. Robert Westley's classic brief for black reparations suggests how a public admission of responsibility could be interpreted as the end of the complaint: "[T]he closure afforded by reparations means that no more will be owed to Blacks than is owed to any citizen under the law" (Westley, 1998, p. 476). Admirable though this objective may be, it obscures the role of law as an ongoing source of the devaluation of black life and citizenship. And this worry acquires particular force when we consider that any official move toward reparations could, like calls for reconciliation, shut down/out criticism of continuing and unredressed harm. There is always a danger that a successful reparations campaign could preclude other democratizing policies once enough citizens believe enough (or too much) has been done or that the language of reparations will mean different things to different Americans. As King (1967 [2010], p. 8) observed after the passage of the Voting Rights Act: "There is not even a common language when the term 'equality' is used. Negro and white have a fundamentally different definition." If *reparations* offers "a compelling language of political criticism and mobilization" (Scott, 2014) when uttered by women and men who oppose the status quo, what different valences might the same word have as an instrument of public policy? What are the dangers of success?[19]

Acknowledging that such risks are unavoidably part of the discussion that reparations claims instigate, I would like to conclude with an example. Consider the City of Chicago's 2015 decision to provide reparations to the survivors of police torture under Jon Burge's 20-year command. In light of the persistence of police brutality, gun violence, and deep economic inequality in Chicago, the limitations of the ordinance are only too obvious. Furthermore, the language of the resolution passed by the city council uses the past tense and the passive voice in ways that could be construed to insulate the present leadership from its predecessors; and the focus on Burge's crimes individualizes harms that were representative of broad system failures (City of Chicago, 2015). As *The Guardian* recently reported, the ordinance earned little media attention and constituted a very small part of the city's budget (Baker, 2019). Nevertheless, another lesson of Chicago is that reparations can serve as a language through which democratic aspirations are articulated and partially realized, when official gestures of repair constitute a first, rather than the final, word. The $5.5 million reparations package not only provides some relief to survivors and descendants of deceased victims, it also incorporates a number of forward-facing initiatives in job placement, psychological services, educational access, and a mandatory high school curriculum (Chicago Public Schools, 2017). These efforts indicate how reparations might be understood as a preliminary step toward community rebuilding. Equally importantly, the pivotal role of grassroots activism in advancing the case for reparations and assessing Chicago's continuing efforts to address police violence precludes city leaders from either figuring reparations as an act of beneficence or considering the case closed. Speaking of reparations thus honors the democratic participation of everyday citizens who fight for meaningful redress. In the words of historian and activist Barbara Ransby (2018, p. 133), "This creative and far-reaching settlement was an important landmark in the struggle to hold police and city officials accountable and to reimagine what reparations might look like."

Can reparations demands play a meaningful role in making our democracy work? If they are detached from grand vision statements and linked to the kinds of concrete political and economic changes that have long been articulated by black activists and their allies, there is reason for hope. Can they help to "state a theory of American national identity and purpose," as Barnes and Williamson (in Chapter 2 of this book) propose for community wealth building? Perhaps not. The language of reparations calls us all backward to a deep and careful examination of US history and forward to an appreciation for our mounting debts to future generations. Whether the long entanglement of American democracy with these practices suggests that we should relinquish our loyalty to an idea of Americanness or seek instead to become the *democratic* community that "we have never been" is a question worth asking. It is a question, I believe, King put to his audience in his final year's effort to alchemize tragedy into a more democratic future. "No society," he writes, "can fully repress an ugly past when the ravages persist into the present. America owes a debt of justice which it has only begun to pay" (King 1967 [2010], p. 116).

NOTES

1. I am grateful to Melody C. Barnes, Corey D.B. Walker, and Thad M. Williamson for their astute comments. I have presented elements of this chapter at the University of Richmond, University of Virginia, Ohio State University, Brown University, the University of Minnesota, and at sessions in San Francisco, Bad Homburg, and Prato; and I have benefited from the generous feedback of the participants in each of these cases.
2. See Commission to Study and Develop Reparation Proposals for African-Americans Act, H.R. 40, 16th Congress (2019). Rep. Sheila Jackson Lee (D-Texas) has assumed primary sponsorship of the bill. In April 2019, presidential candidate Cory Booker (D-New Jersey) introduced a companion bill in the U.S. Senate, and Elizabeth Warren (D-Massachusetts) has also expressed support for Jackson Lee's bill.
3. This chapter is part of a project that explores reparations as a *democratic* idea. Where much of the scholarly literature on reparations has focused on the case for reparations as a matter of justice, my aim is not to supplant that work but to enlarge it by considering reparations as a question of political reconstruction. In addition to making legal and moral demands, I contend, reparations claims also call into question the terms by which the polity is organized; and democratic theorists have both an opportunity and a responsibility to think through the implications of these

claims. I elaborate this argument in Balfour (2014, 2015). One question I have not addressed is that of the desirability of democracy itself. The recent success of racist populisms may challenge all of us to reconsider an unthinking fidelity to democratic norms and institutions that have allowed these movements to emerge and flourish.

4. Adjoa Aiyetoro and Adrienne Davis approach reparations as a social movement, highlighting both the degree to which the concept has animated black political activism since the 19th century and the ways it reveals the ideological complexity of black politics.
5. For a recent study of reparations as a response to the racial wealth gap, see William Darity Jr. et al. (2018).
6. Nothing in this argument is meant to exclude other groups' claims for reparations or to forestall consideration of the ways in which different forms of racial violence, exploitation, and dispossession have intersected in U.S. history.
7. This line is famously associated with Herman Melville's Captain Delano in *Benito Cereno*, although Melville captures a sentiment that reverberates more than 150 years after the publication of his novella (Melville, 1856 [1987]).
8. P.J. Brendese (2014) helpfully clarifies how "those who are compelled to 'do time' are literally and figuratively 'out of time'."
9. Rhetorically powerful though it may be, any neat equation of mass incarceration and Jim Crow, or convict labor and chattel slavery, risks obscuring the specific forms of brutality that defined earlier periods and eliding changes, such as the geographic concentration of today's targeted populations, new class dynamics within racial groups, and the degree to which Latinx and other communities have been ensnared in the custodial web. For a sympathetic critique of the New Jim Crow literature, see Forman (2012).
10. This claim is informed by Lisa Lowe's (2015) distinction between *residual* elements of the past and *emergent* practices, subjectivities, and relationships.
11. See, for example, Patrisse Cullors (2019). Angela Davis (2005, p. 35) argues that anti-prison arguments can also reshape the reparations movement.
12. On the last point, see Naomi Murakawa (2014). On the association of blackness with criminality after Reconstruction, see Khalil Gibran Muhammad (2010).
13. Davis (2012, p. 57) extends this critique of perverted forms of equality, remarking that "we are in very difficult straits if the measure of equality has become the right to execute white people for killing people of color."
14. For an example of a serious treatment of mass incarceration in which women are invisible as targets of policing and punishment, see VICE (2015).
15. On the threat posed to democracy by felon disenfranchisement, see Andrew Dilts (2014).
16. See also Marie Gottschalk (2014, pp. 249–50).
17. For a helpful account of the interactive character of agency and the plural conception of responsibility, see Sharon Krause (2015).
18. See, for example, the United States Department of Justice's "Investigation of the Ferguson Police Department" (2015), which found that city officials relied on a "personal-responsibility refrain" to account for the disparate treatment of white and black citizens.
19. For a thought-provoking investigation of the "underside" of reparations, the ways in which compensation and apology can thwart, rather than advance, transformative political and social change, see Eric K. Yamamoto (1998).

REFERENCES

Aiyetoro, Adjoa A. and Adrienne D. Davis (2010), "Historic and modern social movements for reparations: the National Coalition of Blacks for Reparation in America (N'COBRA) and its antecedents," *Texas Wesleyan Law Review*, 16, 687–766.

Alexander, Michelle (2012), *The New Jim Crow: Mass Incarceration in the Age of Colorblindness*, New York: New Press.

Baker, Peter (2019), "In Chicago, reparations aren't just an idea. They're the law," *The Guardian*, March 8, accessed February 3, 2020 at https://www.theguardian.com/news/2019/mar/08/chicago-reparations-won-police-torture-school-curriculum.

Balfour, Lawrie (2014), "Un-thinking racial realism: a future for reparations?" *Du Bois Review*, 11(1), 43–56.

Balfour, Lawrie (2015), "Ida B. Wells and 'color line justice': rethinking reparations in feminist terms," *Perspectives on Politics*, 13(3), 680–96.

Beckles, Hilary McDonald (2013), *Britain's Black Debt: Reparations for Caribbean Slavery and Native Genocide*, Kingston, Jamaica: University of the West Indies Press.

Best, Stephen and Saidiya Hartman (2005), "Fugitive justice," *Representations*, 92(1), 1–15.

Black Panther Party (1966), "Ten-Point Program," October 15, accessed January 28, 2020 at https://www.marxists.org/history/usa/workers/black-panthers/1966/10/15.htm.

Blackmon, Douglas A. (2008), *Slavery by Another Name: The Re-Enslavement of Black Americans from the Civil War to World War II*, New York: Doubleday.

Brendese, P.J. (2014), "Black noise in white time: segregated temporality and mass incarceration," in Romand Coles, Mark Reinhardt and George Shulman (eds), *Radical Future Pasts: Untimely Political Theory*, Lexington, KY: University Press of Kentucky, pp. 81–111.

Burch, Traci (2013), *Trading Democracy for Justice: Criminal Convictions and the Decline of Neighborhood Political Participation*, Chicago, IL: University of Chicago Press.

Chicago Public Schools (2017), *Reparations Won: A Case Study in Police Torture, Racism, and the Movement for Justice in Chicago*, accessed February 3, 2020 at https://blog.cps.edu/wp-content/uploads/2017/08/ReparationsWon_HighSchool.pdf.

City of Chicago (2015), "Establishment of reparations fund for victims of torture by Police Commander Jon Burge," accessed February 3, 2020 at https://chicago.legistar.com/LegislationDetail.aspx?ID=2262499&GUID=6DCDD51B-2234-4713-93FC-26D647905536&Options=&Search=&FullText=1.

Coates, Ta-Nehisi (2014), "The case for reparations," *The Atlantic*, June, accessed January 28, 2020 at https://www.theatlantic.com/magazine/archive/2014/06/the-case-for-reparations/361631/.

Cohen, Cathy J. (2010), *Democracy Remixed: Black Youth and the Future of American Politics*, Oxford: Oxford University Press.

Crenshaw, Kimberlé W. (2012), "From private violence to mass incarceration: thinking intersectionally about women, race, and social control," *UCLA Law Review*, 59, 1418–72.

Cullors, Patrisse (2019), "Abolition and reparations: histories of resistance, transformative justice, and accountability," *Harvard Law Review*, 132(6), 1684–94.

Darity, William Jr., Darrick Hamilton and Mark Paul et al. (2018), *What We Get Wrong about Closing the Racial Wealth Gap*, Durham, NC: Samuel DuBois Cook Center on Social Equity, Duke University, and Insight Center for Community Economic Development.

Davis, Adrienne D. (2002 [2004]), "Slavery and the roots of sexual harassment," in Catharine A. MacKinnon and Reva B. Siegel (eds), *Directions in Sexual Harassment Law*, New Haven, CT: Yale University Press.

Davis, Angela Y. (1998), "Reflections on the black woman's role in the community of slaves," in Joy James (ed.), *The Angela Y. Davis Reader*, Malden, MA: Blackwell.

Davis, Angela Y. (2005), *Abolition Democracy: Beyond Empire, Prisons, and Torture*, New York: Seven Stories Press.

Davis, Angela (2012), *The Meaning of Freedom and Other Difficult Dialogues*, San Francisco, CA: City Lights Books.

Dawson, Michael (2013), *Blacks In and Out of the Left*, Cambridge, MA: Harvard University Press.

Dayan, Colin (2011), *The Law Is a White Dog: How Legal Rituals Make and Unmake Persons*, Princeton, NJ: Princeton University Press.

Dilts, Andrew (2014), *Punishment and Inclusion: Race, Membership, and the Limits of American Liberalism*, Bronx, NY: Fordham University Press.

Forman, James, Jr. (2012), "Racial critiques of mass incarceration: beyond the new Jim Crow," *New York University Law Review*, 87(1), 21–69.

Gilmore, Ruth Wilson (2007), *Golden Gulag: Prisons, Surplus, Crisis, and Opposition in Globalizing California*, Berkeley, CA: University of California Press.

Gottschalk, Marie (2014), *Caught: The Prison State and the Lockdown of American Politics*, Princeton, NJ: Princeton University Press.

Hanchard, Michael (1999), "Afro-modernity: temporality, politics, and the African diaspora," *Public Culture*, 11(1), 245–68.

Haney-López, Ian F. (2010), "Post-racial racism: racial stratification and mass incarceration in the age of Obama," *California Law Review*, 98, 1023–72.

Hartman, Saidiya (2002), "The time of slavery," *South Atlantic Quarterly*, 101(4), 757–77.

Katzenstein, Mary Fainsod and Maureen R. Waller (2015), "Taxing the poor: incarceration, poverty governance, and the seizure of family resources," *Perspectives on Politics*, 13(3), 638–56.

King, Martin Luther, Jr. (1967 [2010]), *Where Do We Go from Here: Chaos or Community?*, reprinted with a foreword by Coretta Scott King and introduction by Vincent Harding, Boston, MA: Beacon Press.

Krause, Sharon (2015), *Freedom Beyond Sovereignty: Reconstructing Liberal Individualism*, Chicago, IL: University of Chicago Press.

Lerman, Amy E. and Vesla M. Weaver (2014), *Arresting Citizenship: The Democratic Consequences of American Crime Control*, Chicago, IL: University of Chicago Press.

Loury, Glenn (2008), *Race, Incarceration, and American Values*, Cambridge, MA: MIT Press.

Lowe, Lisa (2015), *The Intimacies of Four Continents*, Durham, NC: Duke University Press.

Madison, James (1788 [2009]), "No. 54," in Alexander Hamilton, James Madison and John Jay, *The Federalist Papers*, edited by Ian Shapiro, New Haven, CT: Yale University Press.

Melville, Herman (1856 [1987]), "Benito Cereno," in Harrison Hayford, Alma A. MacDougall and G. Thomas Tanselle et al. (eds), *The Writings of Herman Melville. The Piazza Tales and Other Prose Pieces 1839–1860*, Evanston and Chicago, IL: Northwestern University Press and The Newberry Library.

Miller, Lisa (2014), "Racialized state failure and the violent death of Michael Brown," *Theory & Event*, 17(3), supplement.

Mills, Charles W. (2014), "White time: the chronic injustice of ideal theory," *Du Bois Review*, 11(1), 27–42.

Morrison, Toni (1993 [2008]), "The Nobel lecture in literature," in Carolyn C. Denard (ed.), *What Moves at the Margin: Selected Nonfiction*, Jackson, MS: University Press of Mississippi, pp. 198–208.

Muhammad, Khalil Gibran (2010), *The Condemnation of Blackness: Race, Crime, and the Making of Modern Urban America*, Cambridge, MA: Harvard University Press.

Murakawa, Naomi (2014), *The First Civil Right: How Liberals Built Prison America*, New York: Oxford University Press.

National Black Economic Development Conference (1969), "Black manifesto," April 26, accessed January 28, 2020 at https://episcopalarchives.org/church-awakens/exhibits/show/specialgc/item/202.

Pemberton, Sarah (2013), "Enforcing gender: the constitution of sex and gender in prison regimes," *Signs*, 39(11), 151–75.

Ransby, Barbara (2018), *Making All Black Lives Matter: Reimagining Freedom in the 21st Century*, Oakland, CA: University of California Press.

Reed, Adolph L., Jr. (2000), "The case against reparations," *The Progressive*, December, 15–17.

Richie, Beth (2012), *Arrested Justice: Black Women, Violence, and America's Prison Nation*, New York: New York University Press.

Roberts, Dorothy (2002), *Shattered Bonds: The Color of Child Welfare*, New York: Basic Civitas Books.

Robinson, Randall (2000), *The Debt: What America Owes to Blacks*, New York: Penguin Publishing Group.

Rodríguez, Dylan (2006), *Forced Passages: Imprisoned Radical Intellectuals and the U.S. Prison Regime*, Minneapolis, MN: University of Minnesota Press.

Rubio-Marín, Ruth (2008), "Gender and collective reparations in the aftermath of conflict and political repression," in Will Kymlicka and Bashir Bashir (eds), *The Politics of Reconciliation in Multicultural Societies*, Oxford: Oxford University Press.

Scott, David (2014), "Preface: debt, redress," *Small Axe*, 18(1), vii–x.

Spillers, Hortense J. (1987), "Mama's baby, papa's maybe: an American grammar book," *Diacritics*, 17(2), 64–81.

Stevenson, Bryan (2014), *Just Mercy: A Story of Justice and Redemption*, New York: Spiegel & Grau.

The Movement for Black Lives (n.d.), "Reparations," accessed June 19, 2020 at https://m4bl.org/policy-platforms/reparations/.

Thomas, Deborah A. (2011), *Exceptional Violence: Embodied Citizenship in Transnational Jamaica*, Durham, NC: Duke University Press.

Tillet, Salamishah (2012), *Sites of Slavery: Citizenship and Racial Democracy in the Post-Civil Rights Imagination*, Durham, NC: Duke University Press.

United Nations, General Assembly (2016), *Report of the Working Group of Experts on People of African Descent on its Mission to the United States of America*, August 18, accessed January 28, 2020 at https://www.refworld.org/docid/584073d34.html.

United States Department of Justice, Civil Rights Division (2015), "Investigation of the Ferguson Police Department," March, accessed February 3, 2020 at https://www.justice.gov/sites/default/files/opa/press-releases/attachments/2015/03/04/ferguson_police_department_report.pdf.

VICE (2015), "VICE special report: fixing the system" [documentary], accessed June 19, 2020 at https://video.vice.com/en_us/video/fixing-the-system/584ae51c0226b0e6061f54e0.

Walker, David (1829 [1965]), "David Walker's appeal to the coloured citizens of the world," in Charles M. Wiltse (ed.), *David Walker's Appeal in Four Articles; Together with a Preamble, to the Coloured Citizens of the World, but in particular, and very expressly, to Those of the United States of America*, New York: Hill and Wang.

Westley, Robert (1998), "Many billions gone: is it time to reconsider the case for black reparations?" *Boston College Third World Law Review*, 19(1), 429–76.

Westley, Robert (2005), "The accursed share: genealogy, temporality, and the problem of value in black reparations discourse," *Representations*, 92(1), 81–116.

Yamamoto, Eric K. (1998), "Racial reparations: Japanese American redress and African American claims," *Boston College Third World Law Journal*, 19(1), 477–523.

Young, Iris Marion (2011), *Responsibility for Justice*, Oxford: Oxford University Press.

4. *Paideia*, politics, and the people: deep democracy and the new urban commons

Corey D.B. Walker

INTRODUCTION

Nancy Fraser begins her 2018 American Philosophical Association presidential address by stating:

> Capitalism has always been deeply entangled with racial oppression. That proposition clearly holds for the slave-based plantation capitalism of the eighteenth and early nineteenth centuries. But it is equally true of the Jim Crow industrialized capitalism of the twentieth century. Nor can anyone reasonably doubt that racial oppression persists in the deindustrializing, sub-prime, mass-incarceration capitalism of the present era. Despite the clear differences between them, none of these forms of "really existing" capitalism was nonracial. In all of its forms to date, capitalist society has been entangled with racial oppression. (Fraser, 2019)

Fraser's address is a recent entry in the critical and contentious discourse on the relationship between modes of racial oppression and capitalist political economy. Joining a long list of scholars such as W.E.B. Du Bois, Oliver C. Cox, Angela Davis, C.L.R. James, Cedric Robinson and others, Fraser's argument rests on an inquiry into the nature of racial oppression as a necessary and sufficient condition for the elaboration of capitalist economic relations in the modern era. Recognizing the distinctive relationship between capitalism and racial oppression, Fraser underscores the ways in which capitalism reinforces racist oppression across space and time. Evading the circular issue of origins, Fraser's argument directs our attention to the ways in which historic and contemporary material conditions of existence form and inform social and political relations. By denaturalizing capitalist political economy *and* forms of racial oppression—a move inspired by the pioneering work of Cedric Robinson—Fraser opens up new opportunities to consider new forms of social relations that do not pivot on exploitative and competitive economic and social arrangements (see Cedric Robinson, 2000, pp. 1–28). According to Fraser:

> What is needed to overcome capitalism's stubborn nexus of expropriation and exploitation is to transform the overall matrix, to eradicate both of capitalism's exes by abolishing the larger system that generates their symbiosis. Overcoming racism today requires cross-racial alliances aimed at achieving that transformation. Although such alliances do not emerge automatically as a result of structural change, they may be constructed through sustained political effort. (Fraser, 2019)

In the wake of Fraser's intervention, we may ask ourselves, "What does a non-exploitative and non-competitive democracy look like in a nation with a history of racialized chattel slavery, state-sanctioned anti-black discrimination, and systemic and enduring racial inequality?" Of course, any such response must critically confront the twin issues of capitalist political economy and America's enduring problem with race. However, the question forces an analysis of the economy that is not restricted to the economy in a narrow sense. Nor is it one that is narrowly tailored to combatting invidious forms of racism. Rather, this question implicates us in a broader vision of democracy. In other words, the critical issue is how and in what ways might we organize our social life to shape, support, and give meaning and expression to new and authentic relations of human being and belonging. The deep imbrications of historic and contemporary arrangements in the economic sphere with regimes of racial oppression must be untangled in order to enable all citizens to flourish. This entails a broad rethinking of the prospects and possibilities of democracy and democratic politics.

There are no easy answers to what must be done in order to facilitate a transition to such a state of affairs. Indeed, additional questions readily come to mind and haunt our theoretical imagination when we begin to seriously consider this matter. Melody C. Barnes and Thad M. Williamson, in Chapter 2 of this book, appropriately frame this nexus of issues with their question, "Can we create and sustain the America that never was?" In other words, what are the conditions of possibility for *creating* a robust American democracy? Barnes and Williamson's response to this question is community wealth building. Community wealth building is conceived as "both a strategy for directly confronting entrenched inequalities of wealth, power and opportunity and a method of community-driven problem-solving that aims at inclusivity and empowerment" (Barnes and Williamson, Chapter 2). As strategy and as method, community wealth building seeks to leverage local, grassroots democracy in shifting public discourse, public policy, and public resources to be responsive to the needs and aspirations of empowered citizens. A key pillar in the proposal is an active and organized citizenry. Ordinary citizens engage in robust dialogue with one another, elected representatives, and public officials in determining the critical priorities and resources needed to enable the community to thrive. Through dialogue, deliberation, and shared decision-making in a context defined by recognition, reciprocity, and trust, democracy is renewed and validated. Democracy thus becomes the practice of citizenship that is active, participatory, collaborative, inclusive, and creative.

Barnes and Williamson's proposal of community wealth building is animated by a vision of a revitalized democracy from a low-intensity spectator sport to a deliberative *demos* guided by ethical norms of inclusivity and collaboration. The proposal is not a mere restatement of the "opportunity zones" framework and logic that continues to dominate much of urban development and revitalization schemes (Baradaran, 2017). Instead, they seek to leverage novel forms of capital of local communities in transforming Richmond from just the "capital of the Confederacy" to the "capital of community wealth building." The arc of this narrative of Richmond is vital to this project. As the former capital of the Confederacy, Richmond occupies a unique space in the narrative of America and American democracy. Richmond materializes the inability of the nation to recognize the humanity of enslaved Africans, the perpetual arrested development of American democracy, and an ever-vigilant politics of nostalgia that patrols the legitimate boundaries of historical memory. Richmond as aspirant "capital of community wealth building" seeks to shift this narrative to the fulfillment of an inclusive and broad realization of "We the People." Such a narrative shift is particularly resonant in a political moment animated by the national Black Lives Matter movement and the Commonwealth of Virginia still wrestling with the August 2017 events in Charlottesville (Howard-Woods, Laidley and Omidi, 2019; Lebron, 2017; Nelson and Harold, 2018; Spencer, 2018). The resonance of this shift is amplified in economically precarious urban contexts characterized by historic wealth inequality, deepening poverty, ongoing wage stagnation, and increasing labor market stratification.

Suturing the prospects of democratic renewal, or rather democratic rebirth, to the project of community wealth building is intriguing. This aspect of the project is elegantly captured in Barnes and Williamson's statement, "Community wealth building's aim is both to strengthen the asset and wealth base of low-income neighborhoods and cities, and to expand the number of people who benefit from such assets, with the long-term aim of changing the entire structure of opportunity in American localities" (see also Guinan and O'Neill, 2019). Deploying what is ostensibly a policy framework that registers with the dominant keywords and frames of democratic politics to achieve structural transformation within the limits of actually existing politics in a fractured democratic polity may not seem novel. Indeed, it may be that the proposal concedes too much to the current constellation of forces that have structured the political terrain around a politics of austerity, thus limiting the structural impact of the effort by design (see Blyth, 2013). To be sure, community wealth building is not the project of the freedom budget (Le Blanc and Yates, 2013). But, by saturating the proposal with normative aspirations of revaluing the economic and political lives and life chances of the least of these in American society, Barnes and Williamson's proposal affords us an opportunity to draft new knowledges into our political discourse, thereby opening new avenues for conceptualizing deep democracy. This chapter reoccupies the democratic imagination by articulating the critical import of local knowledge in facilitating the emergence of new practices of being and belonging. In so doing, I hope to extend the boundaries of politics and political thinking to consider alternatives to ground and authorize new modes of democratic community.

LOCAL KNOWLEDGE AND DEEP DEMOCRACY

The prospects of deep democracy in the United States must, among other things, fully confront and mitigate the lingering effects of America's history of racialized chattel slavery while managing the competing (and conflicting) interests of a pluralistic polity whose prospects and privileges hinge on the continuing legitimacy of white racial normativity. Minimally, this entails critically negotiating a political context that has a demonstrated ability to absorb and marginalize change efforts while continually developing and deploying new strategies and tactics to reconfigure societal arrangements and empower political subjects. The shift in municipal governments from regimes of management to governing coalitions exhibiting forms of (limited) shared governance opens up the potential terrain to new actors to engage in democratic deliberation and resource allocation. However, with financialization and the resultant ramifications for municipal governments along with the ascendancy of a dominant conservative political regime, the prospects for systemic change powered by local initiatives seem bleak.[1] Indeed, the local is always already bisected by broader forces that dramatically curtail the effectiveness of community-based coalitions seeking to express alternative preferences for economic and political organization (e.g., Turbeville, 2015).

Yet, the return to local, community-inspired and community-driven initiatives have been and continue to be staples in development thinking (Immerwahr, 2015). But the effectiveness of these projects centers on the ability to scale these initiatives to achieve critical mass for system change. This entails understanding the limits of the "lure of the local" as well as how best to conceive the "local" in leveraging a multi-scale effort to instantiate system change (Spicer, 2018). The local must then operate and be understood as more than just the mobilization of a prefigured community. It must also function without nostalgia and fetishization of the grassroots. It must operate critically in denoting a method of conceptualizing and mobilizing power/knowledge of disempowered citizens.

In the midst of the European–American crisis of the 1960s, the German social theorist Jürgen Habermas offered his inaugural lecture at Frankfurt on the theme "Knowledge and Human Interests." Habermas's lecture marks the beginning of his project to provide a "historically oriented attempt to reconstruct the prehistory of modern positivism with the systematic intention of analyzing the connections between knowledge and human interests" (Habermas, 1971, p. vii).[2] Revisiting the continual attempts within the German intellectual tradition from Schelling to Husserl of renewing the emancipatory potential of knowledge, Habermas challenges the very foundation that connects and supports these different efforts in articulating "an idea of knowledge that preserves the Platonic connection of pure theory with the conduct of life" (ibid., p. 302). For Habermas, this is the critical aporia of these efforts and subverts their potential from within. Indeed, through a rigorous interrogation of these efforts along with the positing of five theses on knowledge and human interests, Habermas concludes:

> These practical consequences of a restricted, scientistic consciousness of the sciences can be countered by a critique that destroys the illusion of objectivism. Contrary to Husserl's expectations, objectivism is eliminated not through the power of renewed *theoria* but through demonstrating what it conceals: the connection of knowledge and interest. Philosophy remains true to its classic tradition by renouncing it. The insight that the truth of statements is linked in the last analysis to the intention of the good and true life can be preserved today only on the ruins of ontology. However even this philosophy remains a specialty alongside the sciences and outside public consciousness as long as the heritage that is has critically abandoned lives on in the positivistic self-understanding of the sciences. (Ibid., pp. 316–17)

Habermas develops a preliminary outline of a critical intellectual practice that challenges the reinforcing tendency of purported "emancipatory projects" in their uncritical acceptance of the theoretical conditions of positivist objectivity. That is, the illusion that only through "true" objectivity—an Archimedean perspective—is it possible to yield substantive knowledge that will support the advancement of human existence. It is only through the reconstruction, in the sense of "taking a theory apart and putting it back together again in a new form in order to attain more fully the goal it has set for itself," of philosophy proper that we can develop an emancipatory knowledge with a proper theoretical temper (Habermas, 1979, p. 95).

Habermas's turn to Max Horkheimer's distinction between theory and critical theory and his explication and re-examination of this theme in his lecture is suggestive for a turn to a conceptualization of an epistemological position that can (in)form political projects seeking to inaugurate deep democracy. That is, forms of deep democratic practice not only welcome a plural polity without differential standing, they also host multiple knowledge formations beyond the dominance of current prevailing knowledge regimes. Instead of holding out the possibility of radicalizing democracy from within one dominant epistemic frame—thus, reinscribing us within the prison house of what already exists—Habermas directs us to reconsider how particular epistemological privileges and positions are linked with and underwrite certain interests. Dominant and dominating configurations delegitimize alternative ways of knowing along with certain knowledge epistemes that underwrite emerging democratic projects. The task that Habermas's project gestures toward but is unable to face is a thoroughgoing critique of the epistemic model that underwrites this logic. The political import of this recognition is that the opportunity, indeed the necessity, to begin to think anew about a plurality of epistemic positions that have been/are overlooked, to state it politely, in a politics structured on a systematic forgetting. It is here were we may turn to the idea of local knowledge to begin to create deep democracy.

With Jack Goody, I readily recognize that "local knowledge is essential, but for many purposes it is a beginning rather than an end" (Goody, 1991, p. 21). There are limits to local knowledge—its applicability, its utility in politics, and its import in policy (see e.g., Pecora, 1994). But these limits are not fatal. Rather, they are generative of political possibility. That is, the limits of local knowledge reflexively entail a recognition of its own limitation, thus exposing the space of noncoercive dialogue. In this manner, a turn to local knowledge inheres within it an ethic of the opacity. Inspired by the work of Charles H. Long (1995), this ethical posture recognizes the knowledges of marginal groups that have yet to be fully engaged in dominant projects of world making. It also recognizes that the knowledges of the opaque hold open the opportunity for generating new worlds in which all humans thrive. Such an ethical imperative interrupts an economy of knowledge that conquers through a commitment to legitimacy and authority. The forms, codes, rules, and frameworks that govern delegitimize those knowledges of "other" citizens who do not conform to the exercise of democracy proper. Chantal Mouffe highlights this situation in rehearsing Stanley Cavell's critique of John Rawls:

> As Cavell points out in his Carus Lectures, Rawls' account of justice omits a very important dimension of what takes place when we assess the claims made upon us in the name of justice in situations in which it is the degree of society's compliance with its ideal that is in question. He takes issue with Rawls' assertion that "Those who express resentment must be prepared to show why certain institutions are unjust or how others have injured them" […] In Rawls' view, if they are unable to do so, we can consider that our conduct is above reproach and bring the conversation on justice to an end. But, asks Cavell, "What if there is a cry of justice that expresses

a sense not of having lost out in an unequal yet fair struggle, but of having from the start being left out?" (Mouffe, 1999, p. 750)

Deep democracy welcomes those local knowledges that have been left out from the start and tempers those imperial knowledges that seek to dominate through exercises of legitimacy. In other words, the space of deep democracy is animated by an agonistic politics marked by a rich tapestry of collaborative and conflicting knowledge forms.[3] To undertake such a project is to embark on a political process that does not seek to conquer. Instead, an ethic of opacity develops a critical posture that welcomes knowledge pluralism as a generative condition in developing new frameworks for dialogue, deliberation, and collaboration. It is a reflexive injunction that reminds us that we are always already thinking with ourselves and the epistemic traditions and cultures that (in)form us. The question thus becomes, how do we develop a democratic politics with the capacity to recognize, welcome, and adjudicate multiple forms of local knowledge in creating sustainable social lives and democratic cultures?

By moving to a generative conception of local knowledge, I would like to open up for exploration the democratic possibilities between knowledge and politics, theory and experience. My particular production of local knowledge refers to the historically informed linguistic and material structures, devices, and discourses in and through which situated communities theorize, comprehend, and articulate meanings and understandings of their world while simultaneously producing requisite critical apparatuses that interrogate these mental and material constructions and webs of meaning. The term "local" does not seek to absolutize or (re)inscribe the binary of local–global. Nor does it serve as a place holder or metaphor for the concept of particular in the universal–particular binary. Instead, local gestures to, among other things, a critical understanding and awareness of the contingent and qualified foundations of these (and all) knowledge systems without collapsing into a vacuous relativism that rejects any and all possible foundations. This serves as a "reaffirmation of the possibility of (a postpositivist) objectivity." In other words, such contingent foundations "replace a simple correspondence theory of truth" with a dialogical "theory of reference" (Moya and Hames-Garcia, 2000, p. 12).[4]

This conception of local knowledge entails a renewed emphasis on mapping the micro-logics of ordinary, everyday practices. Such a move necessitates critical attention to how and in what manner societies and sectors of societies produce and reproduce knowledge systems. The distinction between knowledge and culture underscores the epistemic status of these knowledge systems and advances a perspective of these societies and communities as epistemic communities. Multiple and varied epistemic communities thus engage in democratic politics and these communities and their knowledges should find expression in public life. In other words, it is not only black lives that matter, but also black minds and black ways of knowing matter. Deep democracy hosts these epistemic communities in creating and recreating the conditions of possibility for human flourishing. In this configuration, culture and knowledge are not absolutes isolated within themselves. Nor are they jettisoned for a thin politics of representation. Rather, they are held in dialogical tension whereby the permeable boundaries between them are not simply collapsed. Thus, the critical task that remains is the close examination and analysis of how knowledge and culture operate together. The conception of local knowledge that I advance seeks to facilitate a deep, nuanced, and thoroughgoing exploration of the "personal experiences, social meanings, and cultural identities," that make up worlds of meaning and informs how and in what ways actors engage the political terrain of action. This move echoes the prescient observation by Moya and Hames-Garcia regarding the epistemological significance and salience of identity:

> Who [and how] we understand ourselves to be will have consequences for how we experience and understand the world. Our conceptions of who we are as social beings influence—and in turn are influenced by—our understandings of how our society is structured and what our particular experiences in that society are likely to be. (Ibid.)

Pointing out the epistemological significance of local knowledge has potentially significant implications for understanding the possibilities of deep democracy. "Every established order tends to produce (to very different degrees and with very different means) the naturalization of its own arbitrariness" (Bourdieu, 1977, p. 164). The naturalization of the arbitrariness of American democracy has had the effect of limiting the prospects of systemic change to support the lives and aspirations of those who have lived on the underside of the American democratic experience. Moreover, the knowledges, habits, and customs of those actors have been deemed illegitimate if not in compliance with dominant democratic habits and practice. This has placed minoritized communities in perpetual and permanent democratic deficits whereby the marginal inclusion of some affirms and legitimates the permanent exclusion of the knowledges of the many who are deemed other.[5] Democracy as such justifies its account of how different and differentially situated communities view the prospects, perils, and possibilities of democratic politics through this self-reinforcing register. By recourse to an epistemological investigation and interrogation of local knowledge, we can begin to read more critically and carefully how situated communities construct, mobilize, and deploy knowledge systems that navigate and negotiate this contested terrain. The (re)turn to local knowledge focuses our attention on a strategic trajectory announced by Leora Auslander and echoed by Thomas Holt:

> The challenge […] is to simultaneously grasp the manifestations of the very large and abstract structures and transformations of the world in the small details of life; to re-capture people's expressions—in all media—of their experiences of those abstractions, while also attempting to understand the forces shaping the multiple grids mediating those expressions; and finally, to analyze how concrete and mundane actions in the everyday may themselves transform the abstract structures of polity and economy. (Holt, 1995, p. 8)

In this regard, the problem of democracy is not enough democracy that recognizes production and reproduction of multiple knowledge systems as well as the interrelatedness between other knowledge systems and the exercise of democratic politics. Deep democracy seeks to engage the micro-logics and technologies upon which situated communities elaborate contextualized worlds of meanings and possibilities. The flow and exchange of meanings and possibilities constitute the fabric of deep democratic discourse and the substance of democratic citizenship.

The conceptual import of this particular production of local knowledge is the recognition and understanding of the manner in which situated communities shape and form knowledge systems that express particular political preferences and aspirations. These knowledges shape democratic politics and offer dialogic sites of engagement for making democracy real in the lives of everyday citizens. In turn, we can trace how these epistemic positions serve as an orientating framework for what Lefebvre describes the everyday as the "empirical organization of human life" as well as "a repertory of 'representations which mask that organization'" (ibid., p. 11). Knowledges produced by situated communities may reveal logics of the multi-positionality of ideas and instantiations democracy thus revealing new spaces for democratic possibility. Deep democracy facilitates a conception of the space of democratic politics as something akin to what Michel Foucault has termed "heterotopia":

> The space in which we live, which draws us out of ourselves, in which the erosion of our lives, our time and our history occurs, the space that claws and gnaws at us, is also, in itself, a heterogeneous space. In other words, we do not live in a kind of void, inside of which we could place individuals and things. We do not live inside a void that could be colored with diverse shades of light, we live inside a set of relations that delineates sites which are irreducible to one another and absolutely not superimposable on one another. (Foucault and Miskowiec, 1986, p. 23)

Thus, democratic politics engages the messiness of everyday life. Evading neat and clean divides, democratic politics creates the space for adjudicating forms of local knowledge and plays a crucial role in radically pluralizing ideas and conceptions of ways of life that may hold open the chance for realizing authentic community.

PAIDEIA AND DEEP DEMOCRACY

The ethos that hosts the idea of engaging local knowledge in cultivating and forming deep democracy is animated by a reading of Augustine's *Confessions* (Martin, 2008). Deep democracy requires critical attention to the habits that form political subjects. Those habits are formed in cultures, traditions, and heritages that do not necessarily find expression and support in public life. They are bound up with the ways in which individuals and communities build interpretative grids of meaning to make sense and give expression to their lives. The pedagogy of *Confessions* enables us to be attentive to how individuals and communities learn how to live in the world. Reading, or rather learning to read again, is the process of learning to live as an enduring exercise in (self-)transformation. This type of reading draws Augustine and others into "the opacity that surrounds the relation between words and the fugitive sources they draw on" (Connolly, 2000, p. 45). It is an exercise in reading intimately linked with a broader reading and understanding of the world. The text extends an invitation and cultivates the imagination to respond. Charles Mathewes instructively writes:

> In brief, Augustine suggests that questioning, and "seeking" more generally, is not simply a prolegomenon to faith or praise but, in fact, a vital expression of it. Hence it is no accident, nor any little thing, that Augustine ends his book with a beginning—both stylistically with *aperietur* and materially through the concluding discussion of the Sabbath with no evening—or that that inconclusive conclusion comes at the end of a book riddled with questions. (Mathewes, 2002, p. 542; see also Mathewes, 2010)

Augustinian questioning presupposes that the knowledge requisite for a response is not always already given. It is a knowledge that seeks to truly host the question and respond authentically. Analogously, deep democracy invites political subjects to engage in a reflective and reflexive exchange of knowledges cognizant of the formations of each subject.

In *Politics and the Order of Love: An Augustinian Ethic of Democratic Citizenship*, Eric Gregory "does not offer another politics of meaning or a science of techniques that delivers us from the disappointing realities of human relations" (Gregory, 2008, p. 31). Rather, he seeks a more constructive approach that will enable scholars and citizens to acknowledge the limits of the human social endeavor while striving to create a more hospitable community. For Gregory, "Augustine's moral psychology of love—often taken to be his most antiliberal feature—can help Augustinians develop a more positive account of the social virtues proper to good citizenship in a liberal polity" (ibid., p. 32). Gregory draws our attention to the necessity of cultivating an ethos supportive of citizens embodying and enacting a culture of responsible and responsive ethical citizenship. To do so, society must recognize and understand the dialogical relationship between the *ethos* of good citizenship and the *cultus* of good citizenship. That is, the spirit that is signature of good citizenship—marked by recognition and reciprocity, for instance—and the system of practices that make it possible. Such a democratic *cultus* grounds an ethic of deep democracy in welcoming a knowledge pluralism that welcomes and enables cultures of social and political flourishing.

Gregory's Augustinian account of love underscores the political and intellectual resources available by a return to a critical account of love. Indeed, in our hyper-partisan and divided nation and world, love's moment is seemingly over. But Gregory is right to return to Tillich in reminding us that:

> love has been "rejected in the name of a formal concept of justice, and under the assumption that community is an emotional principle adding nothing essential to the rational concept of justice—on the contrary endangering its strictness." At best, love must wait until liberty and equality have their say. (Ibid., p. 37)

Love is more than sentiment and affect. It has the ability to bind political actors together for noble political ends. In so doing, political acts are imbued with substantive ethical and moral significance. In a deep democratic space, love facilitates a transformation of democratic politics from mere process and procedure in a competition between adversaries to substantive principles that bind and commit communities to engage in deep dialogue to facilitate collaboration designed to enhance the lives and life chances of all.

Perhaps no other public figure in modern American history has articulated a comprehensive love ethic in public life than Martin Luther King, Jr. King is inextricably linked with the concept of "beloved community" and is part of a long and extensive tradition of African American social, political, and religious thought on the concept of community. African American historian Lawrence N. Jones writes:

> [E]ver since blacks have been in America, they have been in search of the "beloved community," that is, that community which to paraphrase Martin Luther King, accepts a person on the basis of the "content of his or her character rather than upon the color of his or her skin [...] Black Christians grounded their confidence in a theology of history. Their efforts were to actualize on earth the vision of the 'beloved community' embodied in the Declaration of Independence and explicit in the Bible." (Jones, 1981, pp. 12, 19)

While Jones advances a unique genealogy of the concept of "beloved community" in African American thought, he makes explicit the political claim on "beloved community" as a particular set of relations of people and ways of life that are actualized in the everyday and properly reflects the worth, value, and dignity of African Americans as legitimate political subjects in American democracy. In many ways, Jones's project establishes a normative claim that guides and forms his political vision. We should also keep in mind that the idea of "beloved community" also operates as a regulative ideal in African American and American social and political thought on community. Given the varieties of black ways of being, the notion of "beloved community" is not so much a given as an argument that must be posited, supported, and advocated. To be sure, "Understanding African American political attitudes requires an analysis of seemingly mundane interactions and ordinary circumstances of daily black life, because it is in these circumstances that African Americans often do the surprising and critical work of constructing meaningful political worldviews" (Harris-Perry, 2010, p. 2).

In King, the concept of "beloved community" is inspired by the local knowledge of African American religious ideas, cultures, and practices that provides the framework for formulating an ethico-political conception of human community that resonates with the principles of deep democracy. It does not act imperially in King's thinking, as it is framed in a minimalist manner cognizant of Kant's second and third formulation of the categorical imperative: "'all human beings must be treated as ends and never as mere means' [...] [and] [...] 'act in accordance with the maxims of a member giving universal laws for a merely possible kingdom of ends'" (Jensen and King, 2017, p. 18). But the concept of beloved community offers more than a mere regulatory ideal for human interaction or a rhetorical norm of human community. It is a holistic vision of human existence and practice that requires systemic and institutional transformation. King's ideal recognizes the import of Ronald Walter's understanding of political change, "The political history of Blacks suggests that political strategies designed to produce large changes should be system challenging" (Smith, Johnson and Newby, 2014, p. 140). Beloved community seeks to fundamentally transform American society and global humanity. It offers (and suffers) a vision of human existence beyond the current configurations of our world. At its heart, it is a conceptual revolution that offers a new social and political horizon for human community.

In offering this understanding of beloved community, it may prove beneficial to revisit the thinking of an exemplary scholar who provides a frame for this conceptual revolution beloved community. Nathan A. Scott, Jr. expresses the lasting power Ralph Ellison's mid-twentieth century classic, *Invisible Man*, continues to exert over us. As one of "the great masters of this century," Ellison joins James Joyce, Thomas Mann, William Faulkner, and T.S. Eliot in attempting "to give a 'shape and [...] significance to the immense panorama of [...] anarchy which is contemporary history" (Scott, 1995, p. 310). Through his unnamed narrator in *Invisible Man*, Ellison offers up a liminar, a marginal figure who exists on the fringes of society but whose existence is not a "merely negative state of privation: on the contrary [...] it can be and often is an enormously fruitful seedbed of spiritual creativity, for it is precisely amidst the troubling ambiguities of the liminar's *déclassement* that there is born in him a profound hunger for *communitas*" (ibid., p. 313). Scott continues:

> Ellison's essays are often being controlled by the same vision of *communitas* that guided *Invisible Man*. "The way home we seek," [Ellison] says, "is that condition of man's being at home in the world which is called love [...]." In short, he took it for granted that the regulative norm to which our social and cultural life are accountable is what the *koiné* Greek of the New Testament denominates as *agape*. But he had a clear sense of how infinitely difficult any full realization of this ultimate norm is. (Ibid.)

To be sure, the unnamed narrator in *Invisible Man* raises that most probing of questions, "Can politics ever be an expression of love?" Nathan A. Scott, Jr. reminds us of the capacity of the *liminar* to be a prophetic harbinger of *communitas*: "the vision of an open society in which all the impulses and affections that are normally bound by social structures are liberated, so that every barrier between *I* and *Thou* is broken down and the wind of *communitas* may blow where it listeth" (ibid.). Ellison's thinking of community and Scott's reflection on community via Ralph Ellison remind us the singular place of this concept in the intellectual tradition of African American social, political, and religious thought and culture. In many ways, Scott enables a rethinking of community in King as the spirit of *communitas* that is bound up with his vision of beloved community. In other words, beloved community facilitates a critical *thinking* of community captured in King that moves along a logic that reimagines the human being and belonging not through dominant peoples, institutions, and ideas, rather through the liminar who:

> lift[s] *communitas* into the subjunctive mood: [...] dwelling on the edges of the established order [puncturing] "the clichés associated with status incumbency and role-playing" and [filling] [...] the open space of absolute futurity with a vision of what the theologians of Russian Orthodoxy call *sobornost*—which is nothing other than that "catholicity," that "harmony," that "unanimity," that free "unity-in-diversity," which graces the human order when a people gives its suffrage to the "open morality" (as Bergson would have called it) of *agape*. (Ibid., pp. 313–14)

Political philosophers have recognized the unique dimensions of King's conception of beloved community as well as his political philosophy (e.g., Moses,

1997; Shelby and Terry, 2018; Walton, 1971). Kipton Jensen and Preston King write:

> What King espoused then was not just any community, for community could be counterfeit. What he embraced in particular was beloved community, which was a society of friends, a colloquy of equals, a practice of concern, caring, giving—in which each person had standing, each stone in place, none rejected, in a rising tumult of aspiring mutuality. (Jensen and King, 2017, p. 16)

Jensen and King recognize the critical political import of King's concept fully appreciating the manner in which it contributes to the formation of political subjects and political community. Despite community being a "many *splendored* and *splintered* thing," to appropriate the words of ethicist Walter Fluker, the analytical and normative dimensions of this concept are not exhausted within the confines of a particular disciplinary lens (Fluker, 1989; original emphasis).

King's understanding of community unfolds within his deep and evolving conception of beloved community. The intellectual and experiential roots of this concept are broad and complex. To be sure, however, King's notion is deeply rooted in a genealogy of black Baptist thought and culture. More specifically, King draws on the local knowledge gleaned from the history, culture, and practices of the black Baptist Church in providing the architecture for his ideal of beloved community. The historical dimensions of this claim are not straight forward and requires a revision of our methods of interrogating black Baptist thought and culture. Indeed, Baptist history in America is grounded in negotiating the dialectic of spiritual freedom and political unfreedom. Baptist history and identity are indeed shaped by the compromises—politically and theologically—within this dialectical relationship. Recently, John Saillant (2016) has offered a revision of black Baptist history that authorizes and supports a critical genealogy of a distinctive black Baptist thinking of community. Saillant's historiographical excursion into black Baptist history facilitates a critical thinking of how and in what ways Martin Luther King, Jr. articulated a distinctive black Baptist conception of beloved community that challenges the dominant coordinates of democratic theory. King's formulation of beloved community often suffers from either simplistic reduction to the quest for the end of anti-black racism in America democracy while the practices and norms of democracy continue apace or it is rendered as an eschatological vision that is untenable in light of the condition of society and humanity. In either formulation, what is missing is a full engagement with this ideal as shaped by the practices and cultures of the African American ecclesial imagination, which in turn shapes a deep democratic ideal cast as beloved community.

In the formulation of King's unique conception of beloved community, Walter Fluker correctly reminds us that "From his early childhood until his death, there is a progression in [King's] personal and intellectual understanding of the nature and goal of human existence which he refers to as 'the beloved community'" (Fluker, 1989, p. 81). Fluker recognizes the evolution of King's thinking. The concept of the beloved community was not a static ideal for King. It was a living phenomenon that responded to his continual thinking, practices, and relationships. His experiences with local black Baptist churches in Alabama, Georgia, and Pennsylvania informed him about the history and possibility of these unique communities. King inaugurates a synthesis of ethics, epistemology, and experience into an evolving and protean ethico-political concept of beloved community.

While the idea of beloved community received its initial expression in the philosophy of Josiah Royce, King's formulation of beloved community shifts the grounds of Royce's project to take account of the knowledges and cultures of the African American religious imagination in formulating his unique mid-century ideal. To be sure, Royce and King looked to the church as a model for beloved community:

> Royce's notion of the invisible church is the closest he comes to being specific in his philosophy of religion. It is the notion of an ideal kingdom whose present reality (insofar as it has any present reality) is the closet possible human approximation to the perfect community which bears the label "beloved." As means for approaching this ideal, the Church is seen by Royce as the instrument through which he hopes ultimately to solve the "religious paradox." (Briody, 1969, p. 234)

While Royce's ideal is inspired by the church he is apprehensive to an all-encompassing intellectual commitment to doctrinal Christianity. Nevertheless, he recognizes the significance of religious ideas in his two-volume *The Problem of Christianity* and engages them in his philosophical work. Indeed, Royce's philosophy owes a great deal to its religious underpinning:

> Although Royce generally speaks of [...] love in terms of loyalty, it is love which makes interpretation possible in the Community of Interpretation; it is love which makes existent the communal reality of Church; it is love which forms the basis of Royce's hope for a Great Community. Finally, it is Love personified which founds the reality of the Beloved Community. As Peter Fuss suggests, love thus becomes a fourth condition for community, one which Royce does not list as such, but which he presupposes in his exposition of the other three. Without love, or its universal form of loyalty, there is no community—whether as end or means. (Ibid., p. 238)

Whereas Royce is reticent to engage the religious infrastructure of his conception of beloved community, King's formulation is established on an explicitly religious architecture but unfolds beyond the boundaries of religion proper. King seizes and deploys the radical framework of congregational polity and local democracy to offer up new modes of being, acting, and belonging in the world. It is this vision that lies at the heart of King's ideal of beloved community. King is shaped by the cultures and habits of African American religion and its cultivation of the promise of human community. King views the black Baptist Church as a continuation of a sacred promise and desire for right community despite the loss of African American experience as a result of the Middle Passage, chattel slavery, Jim Crow, and the arrested development of democracy (Lowe, 1993). The history of black Baptist Church formation and development not only affirms the worth, value, and dignity of black humanity, it also instantiates a politically redemptive vision of democracy for the marginal and the oppressed of society. The black Baptist Church's history of affirmation and creation of a community that welcomes and practices a deep hospitality for all, particularly the oppressed, is the animation logic and *telos* of beloved community. As Walter Fluker writes, "The black church symbolized the authentic mission of the church in society through its redemptive suffering for injustice in the Civil Rights Movement" (Fluker, 1989, p. 152). King's deep democratic commitment is evident at the beginning of his involvement in the modern black freedom struggle when he "state[s] that the purpose of the Montgomery bus boycott 'is reconciliation; the end is redemption; the end is the creation of the beloved community'" (Smith and Zepp, 1974, p. 130).

The witness of the black Baptist Church, past and present, authorizes and sustains King's vision of beloved community. These communities contain the ability to animate new practices of human society and offer a wider range of possibilities for human beings in the world. Nonviolence as a way of life cultivates the requisite habits to form new subjects and a new humanity for the world. For King, the church "demonstrate[s] in its fellowship the power of *agape* to create community" (Fluker, 1989, p. 152). The *ekklesia* is the beloved community—a space set apart to inculcate, cultivate, nurture, and shape behaviors and practices of *human* modes of being in the world:

> "Ekklesia" bears an etymology stemming from both ancient Athenian citizen assemblies and, later, early Christian churches; each was a local congregation gathered in the name of either the polis or the body of Christ, of the demos or of God [...] Jean-Luc Nancy notes that the word *ekklesia* was "drawn from" or gestured to institutions of the Greek city yet marked the birth of a new mode of assembly distinct from the social or political. (Johnson, Klassen and Sullivan, 2018, pp. 1–2)

The *ekklesia* signals a new entity that opens up a new social and political space that belongs to a community in formation. In this sense, King's beloved community is not synonymous with or affirmative of actually existing American democracy. It is an alternative political community created and sustained by the local knowledge of African American religious practices. King's notion of beloved community beyond a narrow and provincial theological reading opens new possibilities of deep democracy—a true beloved community.

***

In his 1871 classic, *Democratic Vistas*, Walt Whitman writes:

> We have frequently printed the word Democracy, yet I cannot too often repeat that it is a word the real gist of which still sleeps, quite unawakened, notwithstanding the resonance and the many angry tempests out of which its syllables have come, from pen or tongue. It is a great word, whose history, I suppose, remains unwritten, because that history has yet to be enacted. (Whitman, 1871, p. 37)

Whitman reminds us of the unfinished state of American democracy. In the space of absence, in the confrontation with this necessity—to speak of a "frequently printed word," a word whose history "remains unwritten"—there still remains the urgent task to not only speak the word but to enact practices to realize this ideal in the lives of all citizens. In this sense, this chapter sketches a mode of thinking about the prospects and possibilities of a political project "whose history […] remains unwritten."

NOTES

1. On financialization, see Davis and Kim (2015); on financialization and municipal governments, see Weber (2010).
2. This argument builds and extends on my essay in Walker (2012).
3. For a fuller treatment, see Chantal Mouffe (2013).
4. "Postpositivist realists assert both that (1) all observation and knowledge are theory mediated and that (2) a theory-mediated objective knowledge is both possible and desirable" (Moya and Hames-Garcia, 2000, p. 12).
5. See my discussion of "A/democracy" in Walker (2008).

REFERENCES

Baradaran, Mehrsa (2017), *The Color of Money: Black Banks and the Racial Wealth Gap*, Cambridge, MA: Belknap Press of Harvard University Press.

Blyth, Mark (2013), *Austerity: The History of a Dangerous Idea*, New York: Oxford University Press.

Bourdieu, Pierre (1977), *Outline of a Theory of Practice*, Cambridge, UK: Cambridge University Press.

Briody, M.L. (1969), "Community in Royce: an interpretation," *Transactions of the Charles S. Peirce Society*, 5(4), 224–42.

Connolly, William E. (2000), *The Augustinian Imperative: A Reflection on the Politics of Morality*, Lanham, MD: Rowman & Littlefield.

Davis, Gerald F. and Suntae Kim (2015), "Financialization of the economy," *Annual Review of Sociology*, 41, 203–331.

Fluker, Walter E. (1989), *They Looked for a City: A Comparative Analysis of the Ideal of Community in the Thought of Howard Thurman and Martin Luther King, Jr.*, Lanham, MD: University Press of America.

Foucault, Michel and Jay Miskowiec (1986), "Of other spaces," *Diacritics*, 16(1), 22–7.

Fraser, Nancy (2019), "Is capitalism necessarily racist?" *Politics/Letters*, 15, accessed May 30, 2019 at http://quarterly.politicsslashletters.org/is-capitalism-necessarily -racist/.

Goody, Jack (1991), "Toward a room with a view: a personal account of contributions to local knowledge, theory, and research in fieldwork and comparative studies," *Annual Review of Anthropology*, 20, 1–23.

Gregory, Eric (2008), *Politics and the Order of Love: An Augustinian Ethic of Democratic Citizenship*, Princeton, NJ: Princeton University Press.

Guinan, Joe and Martin O'Neill (2019), "From community wealth-building to system change: local roots for economic transformation," *IPPR Progressive Review*, 25(4), 383–92.

Habermas, Jürgen (1971), *Knowledge and Human Interests*, translated by Jeremy J. Shapiro, Boston, MA: Beacon Press.

Habermas, Jürgen (1979), *Communication and the Evolution of Society*, translated by Thomas McCarthy, Boston, MA: Beacon Press.

Harris-Perry, Melissa V. (2010), *Barbershops, Bibles, and BET: Everyday Talk and Black Political Thought*, Princeton, NJ: Princeton University Press.

Holt, Thomas C. (1995), "Marking: race, race-making, and the writing of history," *American Historical Review*, 100(1), 1–20.

Howard-Woods, Chris, Colin Laidley and Maryam Omidi (eds) (2019), *Charlottesville: White Supremacy, Populism, and Resistance*, New York: OR Books.

Immerwahr, Daniel (2015), *Thinking Small: The United States and the Lure of Community Development*, Cambridge, MA: Harvard University Press.

Jensen, Kipton and Preston King (2017), "Beloved community: Martin Luther King, Howard Thurman, and Josiah Royce," *AMITY: The Journal of Friendship Studies*, 4(1), 15–31.

Johnson, Paul Christopher, Pamela E. Klassen and Winnifred Fallers Sullivan (2018), *Ekklesia: Three Inquiries in Church and State*, Chicago, IL: University of Chicago Press.

Jones, Lawrence N. (1981), "Black Christians in antebellum America: in quest of the beloved community," *The Journal of Religious Thought*, 38(1), 12–19.

Le Blanc, Paul and Michael D. Yates (2013), *A Freedom Budget for All Americans: Recapturing the Promise of the Civil Rights Movement in the Struggle for Economic Justice Today*, New York: Monthly Review Press.

Lebron, Christopher J. (2017), *The Making of Black Lives Matter: A Brief History of an Idea*, New York: Oxford University Press.

Long, Charles H. (1995), *Significations: Signs, Symbols, and Images in the Interpretation of Religion*, Aurora, CO: The Davies Group.

Lowe, Walter (1993), *Theology and Difference: The Wound of Reason*, Bloomington, IN: Indiana University Press.

Martin, Thomas F. (2008), "Augustine's *Confessions* as pedagogy: exercises in trans- formation," in Kim Paffenroth and Kevin L. Hughes (eds), *Augustine and Liberal Education*, New York: Routledge.

Mathewes, Charles T. (2002), "The liberation of questioning in Augustine's *Confessions*," *Journal of the American Academy of Religion*, 70(3), 539–60.

Mathewes, Charles T. (2010), *The Republic of Grace: Augustinian Thoughts for Dark Times*, Grand Rapids, MI: Eerdmans.

Moses, Greg (1997), *Revolution of Conscience: Martin Luther King, Jr., and the Philosophy of Nonviolence*, New York: Guilford Press.

Mouffe, Chantal (1999), "Deliberative democracy or agonistic pluralism?" *Social Research*, 66(3), 745–58.

Mouffe, Chantal (2013), *Agonistics: Thinking the World Politically*, London: Verso.

Moya, Paula M.L. and Michael R. Hames-Garcia (eds) (2000), *Reclaiming Identity: Realist Theory and the Predicament of Postmodernism*, Berkeley, CA: University of California Press.

Nelson, Louis P. and Claudrena N. Harold (eds) (2018), *Charlottesville 2017: The Legacy of Race and Inequity*, Charlottesville, VA: University of Virginia Press.

Pecora, Victor (1994), "The limits of local knowledge," in H. Aram Veeser (ed.), *The New Historicism Reader*, New York: Routledge.

Robinson, Cedric (2000), *Black Marxism: The Making of the Black Radical Tradition*, Chapel Hill, NC: University of North Carolina Press.

Saillant, John (2016), "'This week black Paul preach'd': fragment and method in early African American studies," *Early American Studies: An Interdisciplinary Journal*, 14(1), 48–81.

Scott, Jr., Nathan A. (1995), "Ellison's vision of *communitas*," *Callaloo*, 18(2), 310–18.

Shelby, Tommie and Brandon M. Terry (eds) (2018), *To Shape a New World: Essays on the Political Philosophy of Martin Luther King, Jr.*, Cambridge, MA: Belknap Press of Harvard University Press.

Smith, Kenneth L. and Ira G. Zepp, Jr. (1974), *Search for the Beloved Community: The Thinking of Martin Luther King, Jr.*, King of Prussia, PA: Judson Press.

Smith, Robert C., Cedric Johnson and Robert G. Newby (eds) (2014), *What Has This Got to Do with Liberation of Black People? The Impact of Ronald W. Walters on African American Thought and Leaders*, Albany: SUNY Press.

Spencer, Hawes (2018), *Summer of Hate: Charlottesville, USA*, Charlottesville, VA: University of Virginia Press.

Spicer, Jason S. (2018), "Exceptionally un-American? Why co-operative enterprises struggle in the United States, but scale elsewhere," Ph.D. dissertation, Massachusetts Institute of Technology.

Turbeville, Wallace C. (2015), *Financialization and Equal Opportunity*, New York: Demos, accessed May 30, 2019 at https://www.demos.org/sites/default/files/ publications/Financialization%20and%20Equal%20Opportunity.pdf.

Walker, Corey D.B. (2008), *A Noble Fight: African American Freemasonry and the Struggle for Democracy in America*, Champaign, IL: University of Illinois Press.

Walker, Corey D.B. (2012), "'How does it feel to be a problem?': (local) knowledge, human interests, and the ethics of opacity," *Transmodernity: Journal of Peripheral Cultural Production of the Luso-Hispanic World*, 1(2), 104–19.

Walton, Jr., Hanes (1971), *The Political Philosophy of Martin Luther King, Jr.*, New York: Praeger.

Weber, Rachel (2010), "Selling city futures: the financialization of urban redevelopment policy," *Economic Geography*, 86(3), 251–74.

Whitman, Walt (1871), *Democratic Vistas*, New York: Smith & McDougal.

PART III

Political economy and community wealth building

5.   Capitalism and the future of democracy

Isabel Sawhill

America is a mess. So are many other Western nations. Populism is on the rise because our existing system of a market-based liberal democracy is falling short of producing what citizens need and want.[1] The argument made by Francis Fukayama in 1992 that liberal democracy has won in the competition for ideas now seems quaint. History has by no means ended. Its next phase is, to many people, extremely worrying. Some of the problems are economic: rising inequality, stagnant wages, lack of employment, lower intergenerational mobility, disappointing levels of health and education in the United States despite large costs, rising levels of public and private debt, and growing place-based disparities. Some are political: hyper-partisanship, influence-buying and corruption at the highest levels, paralysis, and declining trust in government. Some are cultural: resentment of migrants and growing tensions over race and gender in America.

These problems are interrelated. We can no longer address them in isolation from one another. A failure in one domain creates failures in the others. Economic and cultural anxieties elected Trump. Trump and his ilk in other countries are using these anxieties to gain and maintain power and further erode confidence in our institutions. Government paralysis is undermining efforts to deal with economic disparities and those left behind.

Underlying these discontents at a deeper level is a mindset that has treated markets as the ultimate arbiter of human worth—a mindset I will label *capitalism* or *market fundamentalism* for short. The basic idea is that markets work, governments don't. This ideology has been especially strong in the United States in recent decades. This chapter argues that this mindset has led to ever-rising inequality and a government that has been captured by business interests and the wealthy. It is creating a spiral that can only end in crisis unless the intellectual foundations of the current system are better understood and challenged.

THREE TYPES OF SOCIETIES

Most modern societies are made up of three sectors: the state, the market, and civil society. Most political philosophies contain an implicit bias toward one of these three sectors.

Socialists tilt toward the state. They believe that government bears primary responsibility for improving the lives of its citizens. To this end, state ownership of the means of production is favored. A softer version of this model, which I will call democratic socialism, sees some role for markets, given the past failure of planned economies, but a bigger role for government than currently exists in many European countries and especially in the United States. The Nordic countries come closest to embodying this philosophy and left-leaning politicians in other countries point to their example as one that is worth copying.

Capitalists believe that free markets are the best way to organize a society. Markets, they argue, are not only the most efficient way to allocate resources, but also preserve individual freedom in the process. Markets produce good outcomes precisely because, when unfettered, they optimize growth, efficiency, and a distribution of income that is acceptable because it is assumed to reflect each person's contributions to the economy.[2]

A softer version of capitalism, which we might call liberal democracy or the mixed-economy model, accepts the importance of markets but recognizes the need for government to correct market failures and address distributional questions. This type of a mixed economy prevailed in the three decades following World War II in the United States and was championed in a weaker way by Third Way leaders, such as Tony Blair and Bill Clinton in the 1990s and Obama in the 2000s.

Social capitalists believe that the good society is built on a foundation of respect for tradition and authority and for the civic virtues or morals that enable us to fulfill various responsibilities to one another. That society is based on private property, but also on "the little platoons" of family, church, and voluntary associations. It celebrates virtuous social norms and habits that shape how people behave. I call this social capitalism, not because of its emphasis on private property (although that institution is celebrated), but because of its emphasis on the little platoons that in the aggregate create social capital.

These three models are archetypes. In most societies, all three sectors—the state, the market, and civil society—play a role. The question is not whether there is a role for each; the question is what's the right balance or mix. If we got the mix right, we might have a Goldilocks economy and a well-woven society—one in which all three sectors play a prominent role, but in which they complement each other and provide a kind of checks and balances against the weaknesses of each.

Right now, the predominant paradigm in the United States is market fundamentalism.[3] But it is being challenged on both the left and the right, by both left-leaning Democrats (e.g., Elizabeth Warren and Bernie Sanders) and some conservative intellectuals (e.g., David Brooks and Yuval Levin).

HOW MARKET FUNDAMENTALISM BECAME AN IDEOLOGY

Advocates of the mixed economy model argue that we don't need to disparage the market; we just need a more capacious understanding of its strengths and weaknesses, of where government needs to intervene to improve overall welfare. As taught in most upper-level university courses, we can rely on markets to allocate resources, but that won't resolve distributional questions or a variety of market failures. As Paul Collier (2019) puts it, "capitalism needs to be managed, not defeated."

In practice, most ordinary citizens are never exposed to this more sophisticated and nuanced version of capitalism. Instead, conservatives have transformed it into a caricature of its academic self.[4] They have created a narrative about markets that supports tax cuts, deregulation, and limited government. They argue that safety nets create hammocks when what we need is trampolines. They have celebrated free trade with little concern for its adverse effects on local workers and communities.

I will argue that the ideological mindset that the capitalist model has engendered, the attitudes it has fostered among well-intentioned leaders and citizens, and the kind of policy regimes it supports have damaged the social fabric, and with it, the strength of democracy—especially in the United States. The free market model has had an outsized influence on the policy debate and has produced progeny such as supply-side economics that has dominated policy-making at least since the Reagan-Thatcher years. Supply-side economics has spawned supply-side (donor-dominated) politics with very troubling consequences for the survival of democracy.

I am not the first or only person to voice these concerns. Larry Kramer (2018), the president of the Hewlett Foundation, has called for a longer-term effort to create a new paradigm to replace what he calls neoliberalism. The Niskanen Center has been thinking creatively about these issues (Lindsey et al., 2018), along with Eric Liu and Nick Hanauer (2011) on the left and Oren Cass (2018) and Abby McCloskey (2019) on the right. My colleagues, Homi Kharas, Geoff Gertz, and Kemal Dervis are rethinking the so-called Washington Consensus (Dervis, Conroy and Gertz, 2019; Gertz and Kharas, 2019). *The Economist* (2018) magazine celebrated its 175th anniversary by reviewing the history of liberalism (in the classical British sense) and called for newer and much bolder thinking. Economists, as members of the discipline most associated with capitalism and market primacy, are branching out to form groups such as the Center for Equitable Growth, the Institute for New Economic Thinking, and Economics for Inclusive Prosperity. They are becoming more empirical, less wedded to abstract models with no institutional detail, and more willing to join with those from other disciplines to study economic and social behavior.

Political scientists have also tackled the issue. In their comprehensive and impassioned book *American Amnesia*, Jacob Hacker and Paul Pierson (2016) tell the story of how a market-based ideology—what they call Randianism (after author Ayn Rand)—led to the undermining of the earlier mixed economy model in the United States. The mixed economy had married the nimble fingers of the market with the powerful, but much clumsier thumb of government to produce widespread prosperity from the early 1940s to the mid-1970s.[5] Capitalism played a major role, but democratic government added the key ingredients that enabled its success.

Starting earlier in the twentieth century, we saw the creation of the Federal Reserve, the income tax, antitrust laws, the regulation of food and drugs, social insurance, collective bargaining rights, the G.I. Bill, the interstate highway system, and the 1960s' War on Poverty. All these added the guiding hand of government to the dynamism of the market during this period. After about 1980, according to Hacker and Pierson (2016, p. 19), this "constructive balance shattered under the pressure of an increasingly conservative Republican party and an increasingly insular, parochial, and extreme business leadership"—the latter exemplified by the Business Roundtable, the Chamber of Congress, and the Koch brothers.

By starving the public sector of the resources and support it needed to be effective, the market purists have created a self-fulfilling prophecy. Government *has* become less effective in meeting a variety of challenges, new and old, and this, in turn, has sowed public distrust and loss of confidence in public institutions, creating a vicious circle. Business leaders went from recognizing the need to partner with government and to take constructive positions on a broad array of policy concerns, as exemplified by the Committee for Economic Development during the 1950s and 1960s, to later opposing almost all government intervention and focusing only on their own narrow interests.

The shift wasn't all about partisanship either. After all, it was President Eisenhower who created the interstate highway system and President Nixon who called for a guaranteed income, while President Clinton talked about "ending welfare as we know it" and went on to say, "the era of big government is over." Government went from being seen as good to being seen as bad. *Liberal* became a pejorative word. At the same time, markets grew in esteem and began to be celebrated as having almost magical powers. In the words of Hacker and Pierson (2016, p. 71), "the siren song of 'free markets' is simple and catchy. The anthem of market failure is not so hummable, made up of a series of rich but complicated themes." As I will argue below, the siren song was seductive, its intellectual pedigree strong, and its composers and popularizers all too powerful. Or as Hacker and Pierson (2016, pp. 171–2) put it, "Ideas *were* crucial [...] [and] they intersected with and guided powerful economic interests" (original emphasis). Warren Buffet put it even more succinctly: "There's a class war and my class is winning" (Hacker and Pierson, 2016, p. 196).

In the U.S. political context, we are hearing a lot of talk now about a revival of socialism. Some politicians, such as Bernie Sanders and Alexandria Ocasio-Cortez, are self-described socialists, and President Trump and many Republicans are having a field day trashing ideas such as the Green New Deal, Medicare for All, or a national jobs guarantee program. Whatever one thinks of these ideas, they do not fit the usual definition of socialism, which entails government ownership of the means of production. Still, they have moved the discourse way to the left and are challenging the more moderate mixed-economy version of capitalism that calls for markets and governments to work together to achieve a variety of goals.

The good news is that this wide-ranging discussion about alternatives to capitalism has paved the way for new understandings and possibly new politics, making it a good time to debate their intellectual foundations. Between market fundamentalism on one end of the spectrum, to a Nordic-style welfare state on the other, there are many choices.

CHALLENGES TO THE MARKET PARADIGM

Old paradigms give way to new ones when some combination of actual events and new ways of understanding those events appear on the scene. Then the ice begins to crack. More and more people question the status quo and come to embrace new ways of thinking and new directions for policy. Right now, cracks in the ice are appearing for three reasons: (1) the disruptive effects of trade and technology on individual lives and communities; (2) virtually unprecedented levels of inequality and the possibility that ever-rising inequality is baked into a market economy; and (3) the failure of supply-side economics to deliver on its promises along with some deeper questioning of its goals (Sawhill, 2018a, ch. 3).

Effects of Trade and Technology

Free trade and technology are believed by many to have led to a loss of jobs and stagnant wages among less-skilled Americans. In the academic version of capitalism, the overall benefits of trade and technology far exceed the costs, but many people and places are hurt in the process. It's assumed that the winners can and will compensate the losers. It's assumed that those living in declining communities can and will move to areas that are thriving (Austin, Glaeser and Summers, 2018; Hendrickson, Muro and Galston, 2018; Shambaugh and Nunn, 2018). But that's like "assuming a can opener" and it hasn't happened.

The winners are riding high and the losers have seen their jobs disappear, their communities decline, their neighbors die from opioids or suicide, and their trust in government and in elites plummet. They handed an electoral victory to President Trump in 2016 because he promised to fix both trade and immigration, not with the kind of adjustment assistance called for by most economists, but with tariffs and a wall. To be sure, there was a large element of cultural alienation or status anxiety mixed in with the economics. These grievances have produced a populist moment with all its attendant effects on political norms, respect for the truth, and other democratic values. But in crisis lies opportunity. The reaction to Trumpism is now leading to a counter-reaction, most decidedly on the left, but spreading to thoughtful people on the right as well.

Ever-rising Inequality

Inequality has been increasing now for many decades. It partly reflects technological advances that have raised the wages of skilled workers, but that can't explain most of the trend, especially at the top. And even if it does reflect the fact that the demand for skills has outpaced the supply, it doesn't explain why the supply has not adjusted to meet that demand over many decades. In the neoclassical economic model, such adjustments are expected to happen more rapidly than that.

Even more troubling is the prospect of a never-ending trend of rising inequality. Inequality, unless counteracted by government policy or other extra-market forces, tends to feed on itself. The rich save more than the poor, causing an accumulation of capital at the top, and that accumulation automatically produces more inequality, as the rich reap unearned gains from an ever-growing stock of financial assets.

That prospect was the essence of Thomas Piketty's book *Capital in the Twenty-First Century*. He argued that when the rate of return to capital, r, is higher than the growth rate of the economy, g, asset holders will amass ever more income to add to their existing assets and capital's share of national income will grow (Piketty, 2014). Since most of the people with significant amounts of capital are in the upper ranks, those ranks will grow as well.

Piketty explains that the period from about 1950 to 1980—when inequality declined in the United States—was an anomaly caused by the destruction of capital or lower rates of return on that capital, as the result of war and depression along with government policies that recognized the importance of unions, minimum wages, and social insurance. What we are seeing now, he argues, is a reassertion of the inherent contradiction in a capitalist society, which is its tendency to produce ever-rising inequality and to spawn political tensions and a threat to democracy in the process. Consistent with his thesis were declines in inequality in the early post-World War II decades, followed by huge increases since then, especially at the very top of the distribution. That, in turn, has arguably led to the torqueing of the rules of the game to favor capital—everything from less antitrust enforcement, more financial deregulation, excessive patent protection, and other anticompetitive measures.

Piketty ends up calling for a very high tax on top incomes (80 percent) and a global tax on capital. Elizabeth Warren is calling for something similar—a 2 percent tax on wealth over $50 million and 3 percent tax on wealth over $1 billion. While the political feasibility of such proposals is slim, the fact that they are even being discussed makes the point that we may be near a tipping point in the battle between market capitalism as philosophy and its alternatives.

If one buys the Piketty story, there is no alternative to government intervention to ensure that incomes at the top don't get even more out of line. Distributional outcomes of the sort we have been experiencing in recent decades are not self-correcting, nor can they be addressed by modest tweaks in current policies, as I document in my book *The Forgotten Americans* (Sawhill, 2018a).

The Failure of Supply-side Economics

Despite rising inequality, economic growth continues to motivate much policy-making on both right and left. On the left, the agenda has included a call for more investment in education, research, and infrastructure. On the right, it has included such supply-side policies as lower taxes, less regulation, and more fiscal responsibility (granted that adherence to the latter goal is now in tatters). While right and left may have disagreed about the means of achieving more growth and how it should be distributed, they have shared a belief in the ability of growth to improve people's lives.

Economic growth has many benefits. It makes it easier to tackle a host of social and environmental problems. If broadly distributed, it makes everyone better off, and it has been the single most important reason for the reduction in global poverty and improvements in health and longevity.

But here again, the ice is cracking. And it is cracking for two reasons: first, because supply-side policies have mostly failed to deliver more growth; and second, because the objective itself is under greater scrutiny. Given a choice, for example, between more growth and a healthier environment, many people would choose the latter.

With the purported aim of raising the growth rate, supply-side policies were implemented under Ronald Reagan, George W. Bush, and Donald Trump. There is little evidence that they have produced the promised increase in long-run growth. Tax cuts can lead to a sugar-high for the usual Keynesian reasons, but they have not necessarily put the economy on a higher long-term growth path. Indeed, because most of these tax cuts have been financed by adding to the national debt, many economists believe that in the long run, growth may be impaired. Rising debt eventually leads to higher borrowing costs for both the public and the private sectors, and since much of the money is being borrowed from foreigners, any increase in U.S. production and incomes will need to be earmarked in large part to repay foreign lenders with interest (Page and Gale, 2018). While the new 2017 tax law could have a small effect, no serious economist predicts it will raise long-term growth rates by the one percentage point predicted by President Trump. Credible estimates from both liberal and conservative economists suggest an increase one-tenth as large at best (Barro and Furman, 2018). This underscores Charles Schultze's statement that there is nothing wrong with supply-side economics that dividing by ten doesn't solve (Schultze, 2011).

But it is not just the failure of supply-side economics that is causing increased doubts about economic growth. The objective itself is being questioned—and not just on the left. The Manhattan Institute's Oren Cass argues in his book *The Once and Future Worker*, that the focus on economic growth has led us down the wrong path. He likens GDP to a pie and the ideology surrounding growth as "economic piety." That piety has not produced the kind of jobs and wages that support strong families and communities (Cass, 2018).

Another articulation of this theme from a center-right intellectual can be found in a *National Affairs* essay by Abby McCloskey entitled "Beyond growth." She argues that growth alone has left too many workers behind, frayed our social fabric, and caused people to lose a sense of purpose, dignity, and connection to one another (McCloskey, 2019).

Former Federal Reserve Chairman Ben Bernanke has also chimed in. In a speech called "When growth is not enough," he notes that "the credibility of economists has been damaged by our insufficient attention, over the years, to the problems of economic adjustment and by our proclivity toward top-down, rather than bottom-up, policies." Stagnant wages, declining mobility, social dysfunction, and political alienation have been the result (Bernanke, 2017).

In my own book *The Forgotten Americans* (Sawhill, 2018a), I make a similar argument. Everyone likes to promise more growth, but actual understanding of what fuels the growth process is quite limited. My metaphor for growth is that it is like a car. Its engine—or what moves it forward—remains something of a mystery. Its speedometer (the GDP) is a flawed measure of welfare. Finally, and most importantly, even when we get to our destination, we may not be much happier. More material prosperity in an advanced country like the United States has not led to greater life satisfaction (Graham, 2017; Sawhill, 2018a, ch. 4). In fact, when it is accompanied by rising inequality, deteriorating communities, a lack of decent jobs, and environmental degradation, it may lead to dysfunction and even so-called "deaths of despair." New efforts by the United Nations, the World Bank, and others to create broader measures of national welfare are showing little correlation between GDP and other metrics of well-being.

The problem with making economic growth a priority is that it makes it far harder to achieve other goals. For example, if one's goal is to provide a safety net for the poor, but that undermines their willingness to work and thus growth, we will end up being stingy. If we think raising the minimum wage reduces hiring of the most disadvantaged, even though it makes the vast majority of workers better off, we may opt not to raise it. Too much contemporary debate is about the costs in lower efficiency or less growth caused by policies aimed at achieving other goals. Of course, policies should be designed to mitigate such costs, but not necessarily to avoid them entirely. As former French prime minister Lionel Jospin put it, we can say "yes to the market economy, no to a market society" (Lawday, 2001).

Another way to think about economic growth is as a by-product of a healthy society, not the other way around. Political stability and responsiveness, a well-educated population, new scientific advances and access to knowledge, lack of corruption, and the rule of law establish a platform for growth, which then happens spontaneously once the conditions are right. Bill Gates and Mark Zuckerberg weren't thinking about marginal tax rates or regulatory barriers when they began activities that have transformed our society.

Declining marginal utility further reduces the value of growth. At an everyday level, we are all aware of the many things we buy that we don't really need. Some of my favorite examples are an egg tray that syncs with your phone to alert you to buy more eggs, a snow sauna that creates artificial snow for those pining for a winter wonderland in Florida, pre-peeled bananas in plastic wrap, and neuticles (artificial testicles) for dogs whose owners are worried about their self-esteem (really! I didn't make this up) (CTI Corporation, 2019; Monbiot, 2017, p. 119). Granted what seems like a luxury in one generation becomes a necessity in another; but most people don't miss what they don't have, especially if they can't even imagine having it, because it doesn't yet exist. I don't think the baby boom generation felt deprived growing up without cell phones, for example.

In sum, these three developments—stagnant wages and employment for a large portion of the population, rising income inequality, and new skepticism about the overriding importance of economic growth—may finally be creating a counter-reaction to the market fundamentalism that has dominated policy-making in recent decades. At the same time, new ideas have been bubbling up from below—ideas that strike at the intellectual foundations of a pure market economy and further widen the cracks in the ice. I turn now to those ideas.

INTELLECTUAL CHALLENGES TO THE NEOCLASSICAL MODEL

Economics students are taught that markets are, under certain assumptions, the most efficient way to allocate scarce resources. But the story is highly stylized and the assumptions too rarely hold. We must assume that there is perfect competition, economies of scale are rare, information is costless and equally available to all, individuals are rational and far-seeing and know how to maximize their own well-being, one person's well-being doesn't depend on the well-being of others, individual behavior doesn't impose costs or provide benefits to others (no "externalities"), and wages and prices are flexible—responding to any changes in demand or supply almost immediately, thereby assuring that markets clear and that full employment will be achieved.

There is nothing wrong with this stylized picture except that it doesn't exist in the real world. Its logic and its elegance, including its mathematical precision, are extraordinarily seductive. Despite its simplifying assumptions (or because of them), it has influenced countless generations of students, produced thousands of articles in peer-reviewed journals, and arguably had more influence on public policy than almost any other discipline. As Keynes (1936, p. 383) famously wrote, "Practical men who believe themselves to be quite exempt from any intellectual influence, are usually the slaves of some defunct economist. Madmen in authority, who hear voices in the air, are distilling their frenzy from some academic scribbler of a few years back."

Professional economists are well aware of the shortcomings of the basic model. The problem is not so much with the "academic scribblers" as it is with the way the "madmen in authority" have used these scribblings to create a market-based ethic that is not always consistent with human welfare. Here I briefly discuss three key weaknesses in the neoclassical paradigm: neglect of the business cycle, neglect of the institutional determinants of wages, and the challenge posed by behavioral economics.

The Business Cycle

Keynes himself challenged the neoliberal view that wages and prices adjust to inadequate demand. Many contemporary economists have not only accepted his view, but also are careful to distinguish between an economy that grows because it is recovering from a downturn and still has excess capacity and high unemployment and one that is growing because the labor force or worker productivity is increasing. Yet, many politicians, journalists, and ordinary citizens continue to conflate the two, failing to distinguish between policies affecting overall demand and those affecting supply.

The financial crisis of 2007 to 2008 and the long recession that followed were not predicted by economists and remain an embarrassment to this day. Even Alan Greenspan admitted after the fact that economists got this wrong. Leading observers of today's economy, such as Janet Yellen, are still worrying about the economy's financial stability and the potential for more crises. No one thinks the task of stabilizing the economy is easy or yet within our reach.

A related but more controversial view is that growth itself is no more than a series of short runs in which keeping the economy on an even keel with all its resources employed is the trick to ensuring long-run growth. Economists like to distinguish between cycles and growth, aggregate demand and aggregate supply, and actual and potential GDP. But, as Larry Summers and others have suggested, perhaps it's the case that demand creates its own supply. When businesses see their markets expanding, they make the investments and come up with the innovations critical to productivity growth. They entice sidelined workers back into the labor force and train them. If that's the case, it further undermines the priority attached to supply-side measures and suggests that policy should focus on aggregate demand instead.

Jared Bernstein notes that the economy's resources have been fully employed much less frequently over the last few decades than they were in the earlier postwar period. Perhaps that's why growth has been sluggish as well. This "demand-creates-its-own-supply" view of the world is at odds with neoclassical growth theory and with supply-side economics. That theory suggests instead that if labor, capital, and productivity are all growing and output is expanding, that will create the income needed to fuel demand. In the contrarian demand-side view, if the 2017 tax cut does have a positive effect, it will not be because it provided new tax incentives for investment, but because it revved up demand by expanding debt.

The Determinants of Wages

Although many economists would admit that neoclassical economics is hard to reconcile with major fluctuations in the economy, fewer quarrel with how it treats distribution. In theory, wages are set equal to an individual's productivity, which then determines what income that individual receives from the market. But to what extent does this assumption hold true in the real world?

No one would deny that there is, and should be, some relationship between productivity and market wages. However, producing goods and services is a team sport. Identifying the specific contribution of each member of the team is very difficult, especially in a knowledge-based and service-oriented, high-tech economy. Workers often know more about their productivity than their managers. Human resource departments establish wage or salary scales based on very rough proxies for productivity, such as education and years of experience, often constraining pay for some and overcompensating others. Unions can and have raised wages above productivity, helping workers share in revenues (VanHeuvelen, 2018). Earnings gaps by race or gender have been hard to explain away after adjusting for differences in productivity, and audit studies have found clear and convincing evidence of discrimination by race and gender (Bertrand and Mullainathan, 2004; Blau and Kahn, 2017). Monopolistic elements in both product and labor markets affect how much people are paid (Benmelech, Bergman and Kim, 2018; Furman and Orszag, 2018). Workers in superstar firms earn big premiums relative to comparable workers in other firms (Furman and Orszag, 2015). Workers who suffer a negative shock to their wages rarely recover, suggesting that path-dependence is as important as one's human capital in determining income (Kletzer and Fairlie, 2003). One lucky break may propel someone into a position from which they can't easily be dislodged and send misleading signals to future employers. In recent decades, compensation has not grown in parallel with productivity and labor's share of national income has fallen (Economic Policy Institute, 2018).

Not only can there be many departures from the basic wages-equal-productivity theorem, but productivity may itself depend on wages. Good management, trust, and peer pressure may work better than economic incentives in facilitating effort and creativity in the workplace. When Henry Ford doubled his wages, and simultaneously reduced hours of work, productivity in his plants rose about 30 percent. Fast food franchises that share profits with their workers actually earn higher profits than those that don't, according to data collected in a randomized trial (Sawhill, 2018a, p. 152). Higher minimum wages and better benefits, such as health care, child care, and paid leave, can reduce turnover and absenteeism and pay for themselves by raising productivity and reducing hiring costs (AEI-Brookings Working Group on Paid Family Leave, 2018). Of course, there are limits to adopting such measures and cases where overregulation of labor markets and overly generous benefits have gone too far. But, in general, the market paradigm has little or no room for the possibility that productivity is a function of wages paid as well as the other way around.

The problem is that once wage norms establish a certain standard of pay for a certain occupation or job, market forces may not correct it. Human resource departments and compensation committees establish benchmarks based on what other firms are doing. It becomes a circular process, not easily upset in the face of limited information, imperfect competition, and collective action problems. Take CEOs. Once very high compensation packages are established for whatever reason, no one firm can afford to ignore them for fear of losing their own top executive. Instead, they are likely to engage in leapfrogging the competition for fear of sending a signal that their executive is (horror of horrors) "below average." One interesting provision in the 2017 tax bill is a prohibition on deducting CEO pay above $1 million a year. Market-oriented conservatives will see this provision as inimical to efficiency. Progressives will see it as a bulwark against runaway rent-taking. My view is that it also deals with a collective action problem: no one firm can afford to pay less than the competition, even if doing so would have little or no effect on productivity and profits. Only an externally set limit can achieve this goal.

At a still deeper level, productivity itself depends on circumstances over which most individuals have little control. We don't have the kind of equal opportunity enshrined in our founding documents. We don't get to pick our parents, our genetic endowments, our race or gender, our neighborhoods, or our early schooling. That lack of choice provides an additional rationale for sharing income with those whose productivity is limited for one of these reasons.

Behavioral Economics

Behavioral economics has mounted a serious challenge to more orthodox thinking. Two of its practitioners, Daniel Kahnemann and Richard Thaler, have now been awarded Nobel prizes, and with good reason. Thaler calls the people who populate neoclassical models "Econs." Econs are always rational, all knowing, and far-sighted. They never lack willpower. They have stable and known preferences, independent of the effects of advertising or other social influences. They always optimize and are never content with second choices. They are self-interested and don't care about other people. The only problem is that Econs are not "Humans" (Thaler, 2016).

Humans care about other people. Research suggests that an ethic of fairness is virtually innate. It may be the product of an evolutionary history in which cooperation with others was essential to survival. A common test of the proposition that people care about fairness as much as about self-interest is the so-called Ultimatum Game. In the game, a player is given a fixed amount of money and told they must offer some of it to a second player. If that second player accepts the offer, the first one can keep whatever is left. We would expect the first player to provide a small sum to the second player, both of whom would then be better off. But in multiple trials and versions of this basic game, pure self-interest rarely prevails. Most players offer either an equal amount of money, or a slightly-less-than-equal amount to the other player. In cases where the second player is offered a very low amount, they often refuse to take the money. They are indignant and feel disrespected. They have been treated unfairly. But far more common are cases where the first player understands this and behaves like a Human, not like an Econ.

It follows that people may prefer to live in a society in which there are no beggars on the streets and limited wage premiums for those who happen to have been lucky enough to have been born with the talents of an opera star or a major league quarterback. They may want government to intervene to shore up incomes at the bottom and limit them at the top. They may support a higher minimum wage even if, in some cases, it causes employers to hire fewer low-skilled workers. Neoliberals focus on the inefficiencies of such policies and give short shrift to perceptions of fairness.[6] But trade-offs of this sort are ubiquitous. The purpose of a democracy is to find the right balance.

Put simply, markets are amoral. To be sure, they do a reasonable job of allocating resources, a far better job than any planned economy. But they can't deal with the larger issue of what kind of society we want to live in. They cannot be left to decide what benefits should be provided to the least well-off, what kind of environment our children will inherit, and what kind of guard rails are needed to maintain competition and prevent unchecked economic power from influencing the political system.[7]

In an earlier era, market failures were given more emphasis than now. Students were taught that, because of these flaws, a mixed economy would perform far better than one in which markets dominated. Hacker and Pierson (2016, pp. 167–8) provide an account of how the intellectual terrain has shifted over time. They compare the earliest version of Paul Samuelson's widely used economic textbook to later versions and show that the arguments for a mixed economy have waned. In his earliest version (1948, p. 412), Samuelson said, "The private economy is not unlike a machine without an effective steering wheel or governor." In later versions, he retreated, dropping this sentence entirely, and his publisher promoted the revised textbook as more market oriented (Hacker and Pierson, 2016, p. 168). The lesson that markets don't flourish unless government provides a variety of complementary inputs has been weakened, if not lost.

POLITICAL FAILURES

The argument that markets work best when complemented by government requires still another assumption—that government is capable of intervening in ways that are both smart and responsive to democratic values. The current reality, however, is that government is not addressing such issues as growing inequality and climate change. We should be asking why.

In part, it's because the market mindset and supply-side ideologies I've just described have blocked the way forward. It has now been almost 40 years since Ronald Reagan told us that government is the problem and not the solution. It has been almost as long since a "no new taxes" ideology has gripped the Republican Party and cowed many Democrats into submission as well. It's also true that the American public is more conservative than the citizens of many other rich countries and U.S. politics more dominated by racial discord (Alesina, Glaeser and Sacerdote, 2001). Add to that the fact that no one likes to pay the higher taxes that a more activist government requires.

While all these reasons for inaction can be invoked, polls also show that over the past 25 years, a majority of Americans have wanted higher taxes on the rich and on corporations. The tax law of 2017 took the country in just the opposite direction. That law has been unpopular with the public—more evidence perhaps that the ice is cracking. But the fact that it has been so hard to raise taxes on the rich, despite consistent support for doing so, suggests that the problem might be less with the reigning economic paradigm or with a conservative-minded public and more with the difficulty our political system has in translating public preferences into legislative form.

Political theory has long contended that democracies are generally responsive to the will of the people. Empirical evidence supporting the theory is mixed (Burstein, 2003). The most recent research by Martin Gilens and Benjamin Page suggests that economic elites at the 90th-income percentile and organized business interests have a large influence, while the average citizen has virtually no impact. The so-called *median voter* celebrated in political theory—the swing voters that all politicians should, in theory, want to cultivate—may, in effect, have very little say about what happens legislatively. In contrast, business interest groups have an outsized impact on policy. In the words of Gilens and Page (2014, p. 576), "In the United States, our findings indicate, the majority does not rule—at least not in the causal sense of actually determining policy outcomes. When a majority of citizens disagrees with economic elites or with organized interests, they generally lose. Moreover, because of status quo bias built into the U.S. political system, even when fairly large majorities of Americans favor policy change, they generally do not get it." This is a devastating critique of democracy itself. It suggests that government has been captured by business interests and wealthy individuals. If we combine this conclusion with the earlier argument made by Thomas Piketty and others that capitalism leads to ever- greater inequality then we are headed for ever-greater concentrations of income and wealth at the top. It's not a pretty picture.

We may now have an economic system that is not self-correcting and which has spawned a political system that is not self-correcting either. Supply-side economics has created supply-side politics—a political system dominated by those who supply the money.

The feedback loops between economic and political institutions makes the threat to democracy that much greater. More inequality leads to more capture, and more capture leads to more inequality ad infinitum, until a crisis of some sort ends the process. In the words of Bill Galston (2018, p. 135): "[I]t is unarguable that beyond a certain point economic inequality is a threat to liberal democracy."

It would help, of course, if we could restructure a variety of political institutions from an Electoral College now biased toward smaller states, gerrymandered congressional districts, primaries dominated by activists who don't represent the typical voter, and a finance system epitomized by Citizens United. But it's hard to see how to do this as long as those who benefit from the status quo remain in charge, while voters are poorly informed, disengaged, and vulnerable to populist appeals.

Strengthening political parties and substituting representative for popular democracy could help. As Jonathan Rauch argues, political parties need to exercise more influence on the choices provided to the voters. In a well-intentioned attempt to make the system more open and more democratic, parties have forfeited their ability to serve as restraining intermediaries and inadvertently created political chaos (Rauch, 2016). If the Republican Party were institutionally stronger, it would have checked Trump long before now. Instead, the party is now at a crossroads; it can cynically exploit the anxieties of its political base, while continuing to serve the interests of its donor base, or it can rebuild a principled vision of society that deals with today's economic and social divisions in a coherent fashion.

SHIFTING THE PARADIGM

Although political reform is badly needed, so is a shift in the market mindset. My critique of market fundamentalism is not a narrative about evil people or simple greed. It's a story about the alleged miracle of markets turned into an ideology that has permeated policy-making for almost half a century. Business leaders, as well as the ordinary citizens who might have otherwise put up greater resistance, have been socialized to think of markets as basically good and government as basically bad. Markets, they are told, grow the pie and eventually everyone will get a piece of it.

This view has now entered the country's DNA. To be sure, progressives have derisively labelled it "trickle-down economics," but they have no grand theory to explain the world that can begin to compete with the neoliberal paradigm. Instead, they sound like special pleaders or bleeding hearts, socialists or communists in the making.

Most people have simply bought into the idea that income is based on effort and talent, wages mirror individual productivity, and those at the top are superstars and thus deserving of their riches. Those in the top ranks are able to justify their good fortune via a similar logic: they earned it. Companies create jobs. They are the wealth creators, and as such, need to be freed from taxes and regulations. This worldview has animated a starve-the-beast agenda and deprived government of the resources it needs to work effectively, ensuring further public disappointment and distrust of the one sector that has the power to turn the tide.

My point here is that the market narrative is so pervasive that we don't even know when we are dancing to its tune. It has affected the entire zeitgeist and provided a powerful rationale for the rich and powerful to justify their good fortune. The successful tell themselves they achieved their wealth because of their extraordinary accomplishments, not because of luck or having been born in privileged circumstances. The unsuccessful blame themselves rather than their bad luck or modest beginnings for not having won the brass ring. They have been left in the lurch and turn to social assistance with regret, if not outright shame.

WHAT'S THE ALTERNATIVE?

Although the ice may be cracking, with the weaknesses in a pure market economy becoming more apparent, an alternative narrative that is widely accepted still eludes us. I see three possible directions for our politics. All of them reject the primacy of markets.

The first is what I will call *social democracy* (or *democratic socialism*). It is an ambitious agenda of government intervention in the economy epitomized by the Green New Deal, Medicare for All, a guaranteed-jobs program, an extension of social insurance to include such things as paid leave and lifelong learning, higher benefits for the less advantaged, a universal basic income, and the like. It is expensive, requires big tax increases, and a major disruption of existing institutions, including the labor market and the health care system. It places faith in the ability of government not to be "all thumbs." It is mainly favored by those on the political left. It promises bold, not incremental change. Whether it can be adopted or sustained in a country whose citizens are more moderate than their elected officials remains to be seen. But it represents a revolt against the status quo and is further evidence that the ice is cracking.

The second approach I will call *democratic liberalism*. It would embrace an updated version of the mixed economy of the earlier postwar period. It would restrain the worst aspects of capitalism without going as far as the social democratic model. It would emphasize opportunity and pre-distribution over large transfers of income after the fact, because of the kind of public conservatism and hostility to taxes and transfers noted above. It would rebuild confidence in government by making the existing tax system much simpler and public spending more transparent, perhaps by substituting a VAT for most income taxes and earmarking these or other revenues for specific purposes, so that the public could see where their money was going. It would rely on public–private partnerships to rebuild infrastructure, train workers, and create a more efficient health care system. It would recognize climate change as a national emergency but address it via a tax on carbon or other market mechanisms. It would, in short, redirect rather than supplant the market. It would reject the idea that markets perform miracles, but also the idea that government can always provide the solution. Government can be clumsy, inflexible, and too easily captured by narrow interests for whom the benefits of particular policies loom large.

The third is what I will call *social capitalism*. This social-capital approach is favored mainly by those on the political right, including such public intellectuals as David Brooks, Yuval Levin, and Ben Sasse. It's not clear what kind of government they envisage, only that—like their more progressive counterparts—they see markets as flawed and inadequate. They emphasize the need for a renewal of social capital and trust. A thriving middle class is not just people with a certain level of income. It's people with other resources, including the kind of social and human capital that make them self-sufficient, self-respecting, and part of a community. Social capitalism substitutes for markets; not big government, but rather such intermediaries as families, churches, nonprofits, grassroots organizations, and local communities. By relying more on civic virtue and nongovernmental institutions, government policies are less necessary. Its advocates typically support national service, new incentives for charitable giving, and more devolution of authority to the local level, as well as strengthening "the little platoons" of a robust civic- and faith-based society. Families are foundational and traditional marriage celebrated. Government can support or nudge the civic virtues in light-touch ways. For example, low rates of saving for retirement can be countered by automatic enrollment in a retirement plan with an opt-out provision to retain some freedom of choice. Teenage pregnancy has fallen in response to a television program depicting the difficulties of becoming a young, single parent. Many other examples could be cited (Thaler and Sunstein, 2009). These approaches owe much to the insights being provided by behavioral economics, and their success often flies in the face of the assumptions embedded in the neoclassical paradigm.

Of course, there are overlaps between these models and still other models now hard to imagine. In any of these models, there will be space and need for the kinds of place-based community wealth building strategies aimed at bolstering employment and meeting community needs that Barnes and Williamson describe in Chapter 2 of this book. My point is not to argue for a particular model (although I tilt toward the second, with increasing sympathy for the third), but for the need to have a more robust debate about the alternatives to market fundamentalism.

All three of the above models would lean against the current paradigm with its emphasis on markets and economic growth. They all recognize that more material goods in an already affluent society, if badly distributed, make people less happy, not more.[8] Those at the bottom suffer a loss of relative status, even if their incomes are still growing. They are more aware of what they can't buy than what they can. They may have a cell phone and a microwave, but not a Porsche, Rolex, or house in The Hamptons. Behavioral economists call this *loss aversion* and understand that it is about relative, not absolute, status in one's own society. Having citizens who feel fairly treated, respected, and engaged in productive activity is the primary goal of a liberal democracy and cannot be left to accidents of the market.

An affluent society can and should make different choices than a poor one. As a society becomes wealthier, the pursuit of growth—a little more GDP, but at the expense of less equity or a degrading environment—begins to pale in comparison to the benefits of living in a society that prioritizes other goals. More growth for growth's sake has diminishing returns. French GDP per capita is about two-thirds that of the United States. But once one adjusts for differences in leisure time, life expectancy, and inequality and translates them into what a reasonable model suggests would produce equivalent satisfactions, then the typical French citizen is 92 percent as well off as the typical American citizen (Jones and Klenow, 2016). In terms of such values as equity, good health, good food, good wine, more leisure, longer lives, and happy farmers, the French have chosen a different, and arguably superior, path.

What is fair or equitable or contributes to "the good life" will be debated by philosophers and contested in the political arena. That's as it should be. If economics is mostly about production, politics is mostly about distribution. Some, following John Rawls, will define the ideal distribution as one about which most people would feel comfortable, even if they didn't know in advance their own place in that distribution. They may favor the social democratic approach, including a universal basic income, as a way to achieve a Rawlsian world. Others will simply conclude that whatever the current amount of inequality, it is too great. They may simply prefer less inequality than we now have. We don't need to agree on the exact end point to know the direction in which to move. Many people's preferences will be based not just on how the current distribution affects them but also on how it affects others. Unlike Thaler's self-interested Econs, they are Humans; they care about the kind of society in which they live.

Herbert Stein, a much-respected conservative economist, once said that the problem with inequality is that "it is unlovely." So are climate change, crumbling roads, workers who have not seen a boost in real wages for decades, dilapidated buildings and ruined lives in small towns, and many other aspects of American life. The fact is that we know more about how to repurpose growth than we know about how to speed it up (Sawhill, 2018a, pp. 81–2).

Some might object that growth, even in a rich country, enables that country to help the global poor or to compete more effectively with rising hegemons, such as China. But altruism is bounded by ties of family, community, and nation, and a better way to deal with global inequalities is to be open to trade and immigration. As for preventing the rise of a new hegemon, that may depend more on modelling democratic values and maintaining strong alliances than on faster economic growth.

If one agrees with my assessment about the dangers of market fundamental-ism and the need to reprioritize fairness and human flourishing, what exactly should be done? A good first step would be to enact legislation calling for more explicit attention to this goal. There should be a Council of Social Advisers in the White House that would report every year on the well-being of American families, the overall distribution of income and other valued goods such as health and education, and the health of civic society and confidence in dem-ocratic institutions. The report would produce credible metrics against which to measure progress, lay out the administration's goals, and describe what the council was doing or proposing as a way to achieve those goals. There would be hearings on the report and a more robust discussion about how to achieve greater fairness, a stronger middle class, and a healthier society.

In the end, of course, the solutions will have to come from the political system and the serious engagement of the public in the electoral process along with political reforms that more effectively translate their preferences into constructive action. If we want a "weaver's" society, one in which markets and government work together, we will need to do better.

CONCLUSION

Supply-side economics has spawned supply-side politics—the capture of politics by those who benefit from the status quo. The ability of our existing political institutions to respond to ever-rising inequality and the threat it poses to democracy is by no means assured. In this context, it is encouraging that a market-based ideology appears to be on the wane. It is being challenged both by events and by new intellectual stirrings on the right and the left. What will replace it is unclear. But the cracking of the ice is a good sign. In the meantime, the state of the nation is not good. Market fundamentalism is only one of the reasons, but it has shaped minds and hearts in ways that have made it difficult to move forward. The ice may be cracking, but we have a long way to go before spring.

NOTES

1. For more details on these failings and their political consequences, see Sawhill (2018a, 2018b).
2. See Milton Friedman (1962, p. 4), who argues that economic freedom is a "necessary condition for political freedom."
3. In an earlier version of this chapter, I used the term *neoliberalism* as a synonym for market fundamentalism, but the term is used to mean different things to different people, so I abandoned it.
4. As Dani Rodrik (2017) says, "A proper understanding of the economics that lies behind neoliberalism would allow us to identify—and to reject—ideology when it masquerades as economic science."
5. This metaphor is originally credited to Charles Lindblom, but is used extensively in Hacker and Pierson (2016).
6. Empirical evidence suggests the efficiency costs of a modest increase in the federal minimum wage (from $7.25 to $10.10) are very small, causing about half a million people to lose jobs and about 17 million to see their wage rise by about 15 percent (Congressional Budget Office, 2014).
7. One of the most trenchant critiques of the flaws in market capitalism comes from Steven Pearlstein, the Pulitzer Prize-winning business columnist for *The Washington Post* (Pearlstein, 2018). For a summary and review, see Sawhill (2019).
8. This same point as been made by Cornell University professor Robert Frank and a number of others.

REFERENCES

AEI-Brookings Working Group on Paid Family Leave (2018), *The AEI-Brookings Working Group Report on Paid Family and Medical Leave*, September, accessed January 23, 2020 at http://www.aei.org/wp-content/uploads/2018/09/The-AEI-Brookings-Working-Group-Report-on-Paid-Family-and-Medical-Leave.pdf.

Alesina, Alberto, Edward Glaeser and Bruce Sacerdote (2001), "Why doesn't the United States have a European-style welfare state?" *Brookings Papers on Economic Activity, 2:2001*, accessed January 23, 2020 at https://www.brookings.edu/wp-content/uploads/2001/06/2001b_bpea_alesina.pdf.

Austin, Benjamin, Edward Glaeser and Lawrence Summers (2018). "Saving the heartland: place-based policies in 21st century America," *Brookings Papers on Economic Activity, 3:2018*, accessed January 23, 2020 at https://www.brookings.edu/bpea-articles/saving-the-heartland-place-based-policies-in-21st-century-america/.

Barro, Robert and Jason Furman (2018), "Macroeconomic effects of the 2017 tax reform," *Brookings Papers on Economic Activity, 3:2018*, accessed January 23, 2020 at https://www.brookings.edu/wp-content/uploads/2018/03/4_barrofurman.pdf.

Benmelech, Efraim, Nittai Bergman and Hyunseob Kim (2018), "Strong employers and weak employees: how does employer concentration affect wages?" *National Bureau of Economic Research Working Paper No. 24307*, February, accessed January 23, 2020 at https://www.nber.org/papers/w24307.

Bernanke, Ben S. (2017), "When growth is not enough," speech presented June 26 at the European Central Bank Forum on Central Banking, accessed January 22, 2020 at https://www.brookings.edu/blog/ben-bernanke/2017/06/26/when-growth-is-not-enough/.

Bertrand, Marianne and Sendhil Mullainathan (2004), "Are Emily and Greg more employable than Lakisha and Jamal?" *American Economic Review*, 94(4), 991–1013.

Blau, Francine and Lawrence Kahn (2017), "The gender wage gap: extent, trends, and explanation," *Journal of Economic Literature*, 55(3), 789–865.

Burstein, Paul (2003), "The impact of public opinion on public policy: a review and an agenda," *Political Research Quarterly*, 56(1), 29–40.

Cass, Oren (2018), *The Once and Future Worker: A Vision for Renewal of Work in America*, New York: Encounter Books.

Collier, Paul (2019), *The Future of Capitalism: Facing the New Anxieties*, New York: HarperCollins.

Congressional Budget Office (2014), "The effects of a minimum-wage increase on employment and family income," February 18, accessed January 23, 2020 at https://www.cbo.gov/publication/44995.

CTI Corporation (2019), accessed January 22, 2020 at https://neuticles.com/.

Dervis, Kemal, Caroline Conroy and Geoffrey Gertz (2019), "Politics beyond neoliberalism: history does not end," in Geoffrey Gertz and Homi Kharas (eds), *Beyond Neoliberalism: Insights from Emerging Markets*, Washington, DC: Brookings Institution, pp. 74–81, accessed January 22, 2020 at https://www.brookings.edu/wp-content/uploads/2019/05/beyond-neoliberalism-final-05.01.pdf.

Economic Policy Institute (2018), "The productivity–pay gap," August, accessed January 20, 2020 at https://www.epi.org/productivity-pay-gap/.

Friedman, Milton (1962), *Capitalism and Freedom*, Chicago, IL: University of Chicago Press.

Fukayama, Francis (1992), *The End of History and the Last Man*, New York: Free Press.

Furman, Jason and Peter Orszag (2015), "A firm-level perspective on the role of rents in the rise in inequality," presented at "A Just Society," Centennial Event in Honor of Joseph Stiglitz, Columbia University, October 16.

Furman, Jason and Peter Orszag (2018), "Slower productivity and higher inequality: are they related?" *Working Paper 18-4*, Peterson Institute for International Economics, June, accessed January 23, 2020 at https://piie.com/system/files/documents/wp18-4.pdf.

Galston, William (2018), *Anti-pluralism: The Populist Threat to Liberal Democracy*, New Haven, CT: Yale University Press.

Gertz, Geoffrey and Homi Kharas (eds) (2019), "Introduction: beyond neoliberalism in emerging markets," in *Beyond Neoliberalism: Insights from Emerging Markets*, Washington, DC: Brookings Institution, pp. 7–16, accessed January 22, 2020 at https://www.brookings.edu/wp-content/uploads/2019/05/beyond-neoliberalism-final-05.01.pdf.

Gilens, Martin and Benjamin Page (2014), "Testing theories of American politics: elites, interest groups, and average citizens," *Perspectives on Politics*, 12(3), 564–81.

Graham, Carol (2017), *Happiness for All? Unequal Hopes and Lives in Pursuit of the American Dream*, Princeton, NJ: Princeton University Press.

Hacker, Jacob S. and Paul Pierson (2016), *American Amnesia*, New York: Simon & Schuster.

Hendrickson, Clara, Mark Muro and William Galston (2018), "Strategies for left-behind places," Brookings Institution, November, accessed January 23, 2020 at https://www.brookings.edu/wp-content/uploads/2018/11/2018.11_Report_Countering-geography-of-discontent_Hendrickson-Muro-Galston.pdf.

Jones, Charles I. and Peter J. Klenow (2016), "Beyond GDP? Welfare across countries and time," *American Economic Review*, 106(9), 2426–57.

Keynes, John Maynard (1936), *The General Theory of Employment, Interest, and Money*, Basingstoke, UK: Palgrave Macmillan.

Kletzer, Lori and Robert Fairlie (2003), "The long-term costs of job displacement for young adult workers," *Industrial and Labor Relations Review*, 56(4), 682–98.

Kramer, Larry (2018), "Beyond neoliberalism: rethinking political economy," William and Flora Hewlett Foundation, April 26, accessed January 23, 2020 at https://hewlett.org/library/beyond-neoliberalism-rethinking-political-economy/.

Lawday, David (2001), "The New Statesman profile—Lionel Jospin," *New Statesman America*, February 26, accessed January 22, 2020 at https://www.newstatesman.com/node/152948.

Lindsey, Brink, Steven Teles, Will Wilkinson and Samuel Hammond (2018), "The center can hold: public policy for an age of extremes," Niskanen Center, December 18, accessed January 23, 2020 at https://www.niskanencenter.org/the-center-can-hold-public-policy-for-an-age-of-extremes/.

Liu, Eric and Nick Hanauer (2011), *The Gardens of Democracy: A New American Story of Citizenship, the Economy, and the Role of Government*, New York: Penguin Random House.

McCloskey, Abby M. (2019), "Beyond growth," *National Affairs*, No. 42, accessed January 22, 2020 at https://www.nationalaffairs.com/publications/detail/beyond-growth.

Monbiot, George (2017), *Out of the Wreckage: A New Politics for an Age of Crisis*, New York: Verso.

Page, Benjamin and William Gale (2018), "CBO estimates imply that TCJA will boost incomes for foreign investors but not for Americans," Brookings Institution, May 10, accessed January 23, 2020 at https://www.brookings.edu/blog/up-front/2018/05/10/cbo-estimates-imply-that-tcja-will-boost-incomes-for-foreign-investors-but-not-for-americans/.

Pearlstein, Steven (2018), *Can American Capitalism Survive? Why Greed Is Not Good, Opportunity Is Not Equal, and Fairness Won't Make Us Poor*, New York: St. Martin's Press.

Piketty, Thomas (2014), *Capital in the Twenty-First Century*, translated by Arthur Goldhammer, Cambridge, MA: Belknap Press of Harvard University Press.

Rauch, Jonathan (2016), "How American politics went insane," *The Atlantic*, July/August, accessed January 23, 2020 at https://www.theatlantic.com/magazine/archive/2016/07/how-american-politics-went-insane/485570/.

Rodrik, Dani (2017), "Rescuing economics from neoliberalism," *Boston Review*, November 6, accessed January 23, 2020 at http://bostonreview.net/class-inequality/dani-rodrik-rescuing-economics-neoliberalism.

Samuelson, P. (1948), *Economics*, New York: McGraw-Hill.

Sawhill, Isabel (2018a), *The Forgotten Americans: An Economic Agenda for a Divided Nation*, New Haven, CT: Yale University Press.

Sawhill, Isabel (2018b), "What the forgotten Americans really want and how to give it to them," Brookings Institution, October, accessed January 23, 2020 at https://www.brookings.edu/longform/what-the-forgotten-americans-really-want-and-how-to-give-it-to-them/.

Sawhill, Isabel (2019), "Book review: Steven Pearlstein's 'Can American Capitalism Survive?'" Brookings Institution, January 16, accessed January 23, 2020 at https://www.brookings.edu/opinions/book-review-steven-pearlsteins-can-american-capitalism-survive/.

Schultze, Charles (2011). "Slaying the dragon of debt: fiscal politics and policy from the 1970s to the present," University of California-Berkeley: Regional Oral History Project. Interviews conducted by Martin Meeker, accessed January 23, 2020 at https://digitalassets.lib.berkeley.edu/roho/ucb/text/schultze_charles.pdf.

Shambaugh, Jay and Ryan Nunn (2018), "Place-based policies for shared economic growth," Brookings Institution, September 28, accessed January 23, 2020 at https://www.brookings.edu/multi-chapter-report/place-based-policies-for-shared-economic-growth/.

Thaler, Richard (2016), *Misbehaving: The Making of Behavioral Economics*, New York: W.W. Norton & Company.

Thaler, Richard and Cass Sunstein (2009), *Nudge: Improving Decisions about Health, Wealth, and Happiness*, New York: Penguin Random House.

The Economist (2018), "*The Economist* at 175: reinventing liberalism for the 21st century," September 13, accessed January 22, 2020 at https://www.economist.com/essay/2018/09/13/the-economist-at-175.

VanHeuvelen, Tom (2018), "Moral economies or hidden talents? A longitudinal analysis of union decline and wage inequality, 1973–2015," *Social Forces*, 97(2), 495–530.

6.   Community wealth building: lessons from Italy

Margaret Kohn

Community wealth building (CWB) is an established global paradigm with a long history. In Italy, 10 percent of private employment is in the cooperative sector, which makes it a particularly successful example of CWB. In this chapter, I provide an overview of the organizational and regulatory structure of the cooperative movement in Italy and explain the features that have played a role in its growth. The Italian cooperative movement provides an illustration of the benefits of state support for the solidarity economy. In the past 40 years, the movement has expanded to include new types of cooperatives that directly aim to advance the common good rather than just the mutual benefit of members. Social cooperatives work with local governments to provide social services to vulnerable populations and/or employment to disadvantaged people. Community cooperatives are hybrids that promote economic activity in regions that have experienced disinvestment. They do so by involving multiple stakeholders who are interested in broader, non-commodifiable benefits that are rooted in a specific place. A key feature of the Italian cooperative movement is its integrated and pluralistic character that links together a range of different forms of solidaristic economic activity. The regulatory framework developed in Italy can serve as a model for emerging solidarity economies in the United States.

CWB approaches the economy as a kind of delicate ecosystem that, when healthy, enables people to flourish. CWB reanimates ideas embraced by movements around world, including radical republicans in late 19th-century France and social democrats in inter-war Sweden (Gide, 1905; Stjernø, 2009). These movements mobilized disadvantaged citizens and promoted a range of tools to combat inequality, including worker management, public goods, municipal ownership, mutual aid societies, limited equity housing, and tax-funded redistribution. The progressive movement in the United States also aspired to combat poverty through participatory democracy, the development of human, social, and economic capital, and the expansion of property ownership (Caspary, 2018; Knight, 2008). Globally, the left has embraced the idea of social and solidarity economies as a way of transforming capitalism (Utting,

2015). CWB is an established global paradigm, and there is much to be learned from the long history of successes and failures in other countries, particularly in Italy, the country with the largest cooperative sector.

There is a scholarly literature that contrasts the benefits of a society modeled on a decentralized, popular "commons" with the harmful effects of bureaucratic control by the state (Dardot and Laval, 2015; Hardt and Negri, 2011). CWB rejects this juxtaposition and recognizes the relationship between the state, political participation, and property. An economic order oriented toward the common good requires a regulatory framework. The state is an important mechanism for exercising democratic control over the terms of social cooperation, but it only plays this role when citizens are mobilized and hold the state accountable. The Italian cooperative movement provides an illustration of the benefits of state support for the solidarity economy. In using the term solidarity economy, I intend to highlight forms of economic organization that enable the fair sharing of the benefits and burdens of cooperation in order to counteract the inequalities produced by unregulated markets. The record of the cooperative movement in Italy shows that CWB is a realistic strategy. The regulatory framework developed in Italy can serve a model for emerging solidarity economies in the United States.

THE COOPERATIVE MOVEMENT IN ITALY

Cooperatives seem like a good idea in theory, because economic activity benefits members rather than external investors. Furthermore, the governance structure enables democratization of the management of firms. Despite these normatively desirable features, cooperatives are not very common in the United States and are widely viewed as marginal or utopian (Singer, 2018). The success of the cooperative sector in Italy, however, demonstrates the viability of the model. Based on the most recent data (2013), the cooperative sector in Italy employs over 1 800 000 workers, which is 9.5 percent of total private sector employment (Carini, Borzaga and Fontanari, n.d.). During the global financial crisis, the cooperative sector also increased its share of total employment. This suggests that CWB is not inevitably a marginal, precarious strategy of last resort.

The growth of the cooperative sector in Italy was supported by two distinctive political ideologies. The first is the "red" ideology associated with the socialist and communist movements of the early 20th century. In the pre-fascist period, socialists encouraged the formation of cooperatives made up of workers and landless agricultural laborers. The associated political parties helped create umbrella organizations to provide training, support, and investment to fledgling cooperatives. Excluded from national political power in the post-war period, the Partito Comunista Italiano (PCI) focused on building a strong, local red subculture. In the regions where the PCI participated in the government, it actively fostered the growth of worker and consumer cooperatives. The Catholic or "white" subculture also endorsed the cooperative movement, based on the principle of solidarity and self-help. The Catholic leadership saw cooperatives as part of the church's mission of helping the poor. Mutualism was considered a form of economic organization that was an alternative to both state socialism and usurious forms of capitalism.

The cooperative movement dated back to the late 19th century, but it was reorganized and consolidated in the post-war period. The Italian Constitution contains a provision explicitly recognizing the value of cooperation. Article 45 states that the Republic should promote and encourage cooperatives because the state "recognizes the social function of co-operation of a mutually supportive, non-speculative nature" (Senato della Repubblica, 1947, Art. 45). The social function could be construed in different ways, and the framers of the constitution debated the meaning and purpose of cooperation. The left saw cooperatives as the partial realization of socialism within the capitalist system (Bagnoli, 2010, p. 66). The centrists viewed them as a form of private enterprise that could be placed along the continuum between the sole proprietorship and the limited liability cooperation.

Due to the tensions between these different ideological approaches, the constitution did not include criteria defining the meaning of "cooperative" (Bagnoli, 2010, p. 68). Article 2511 of the Civil Code, however, defined a cooperative as a company with "variable capital and mutual purpose" (Fici, 2010, 2013). The provision requiring variable capital is a way to implement the principle of "open and variable membership." This principle is one of the seven defining values endorsed by the International Co-operative Alliance (ICA), which was founded in 1895 (ICA, 2018). In this document, cooperatives were defined as voluntary associations open to all without discrimination.

The second component of the definition from the Civil Code, mutual purpose, has been interpreted in different ways. The doctrine of mutualism holds that interdependence is necessary to human flourishing, but this can describe bonds between members of an association or a broader form of social solidarity. The narrow interpretation emphasizes that an association should advance the common interests of the members. In a broader sense, however, mutualism could also suggest solidaristic ties to non-members and responsibilities to the broader community. This is explicit in two of the seven principles of the ICA: concern for the community and cooperation with other cooperatives. The original Italian statute governing cooperatives did not incorporate these principles but, as I will explain in more detail below, a new type of cooperative called the "social cooperative" was introduced in 1991. These cooperatives have a different structure and an explicitly solidaristic objective.

Traditional cooperatives, however, are based on the principle of mutualism among members. What exactly constitutes their shared interests and how does mutualism create social benefits that distinguish cooperatives from corporations? In the case of capitalist firms, the unifying interest is the highest return on invested capital. In Italy cooperatives are forbidden from distributing reserves to members, and they cannot provide a return on invested capital above a rate set to the interest rate on postal bonds (Fici, 2010, p. 10). Departing members can only withdraw invested capital and a portion of the value of the firm itself. These rules ensure that Italian cooperatives meet the constitutional requirement that the goal cannot be speculation. The law also stipulates that 30 percent of total annual profit be allocated to the reserve fund and 3 percent must be contributed to an umbrella organization for the promotion and support of new cooperatives. The rest of the profit can be allocated to members.

Since cooperatives are designed to further the interests of their members, the objectives vary across different types of cooperatives. Consumer cooperatives try to lower the price of consumer goods, and worker cooperatives aim to ensure the stability of employment and to increase the compensation of the members. Unlike the original by-laws governing the well-known Mondragon cooperatives in Spain, the Italian legislation does not provide any restrictions on the ratio of compensation between the highest- and lowest-paid workers. Managers can be paid at market rates, but the overall budget must be approved by the assembly of all members. In accordance with the ICA principles, the basic governance structure is one member one vote.[1] According to amended legislation, however, this can be modified under certain circumstances—for example, in agricultural cooperatives where some members participate more extensively and have a proportionately larger vote.

There is debate in the cooperative movement about the tension between mutualism (the shared economic interests of members) and the common good. Before addressing this question, it is important to note that there are normative reasons for supporting cooperatives that are independent of the economic or social benefits. In *After Occupy*, Tom Malleson argued that the same principles that justify political democracy also apply to workplace democracy (Malleson, 2014). Workplace democracy is an important mechanism for preventing domination. A strong cooperative sector also increases freedom by providing workers with the possibility of joining worker-managed firms.

During the original debate about cooperation in the constituent assembly, participants outlined a number of benefits that justified the special treatment of cooperatives. Cooperatives were described as a mechanism for local economic development. They could also enhance equal opportunity by removing the social and economic obstacles that prevent some people from flourishing (Bagnoli, 2010, pp. 105–6). Finally, by reorienting economic activity away from speculation, and ensuring that economic benefit was retained in the community, they could improve the living standards of workers. The constituent assembly granted constitutional recognition to cooperatives due to their potential as mechanisms of CWB and equity. In recognition of these contributions to social equality, cooperatives were granted considerable preferential treatment under the tax code. In many types of cooperatives, the profits are not taxed as long as they are reinvested in the co-op (Corcoran and Wilson, 2010). Some regions also provide additional benefits such as funding for research and development, training, and marketing support (Bagnoli, 2010; Fici, 2009).

There is an extensive literature assessing the relationship between the practice of cooperation and the solidaristic objectives that justified it. The more business-focused research suggests that Italian cooperatives have been successful at maintaining and even increasing employment, even under the adverse conditions of the post-2008 economic crisis (Ammirato, 2018). Another recent study explored the degree to which managers and directors embraced values associated with the cooperative movement. A survey of co-ops in Trento found that 60 percent of respondents thought that the well-being of the community was a primary value and another 30 percent agreed that it was an important value. There was considerable difference across different types of cooperatives. Among worker/producer cooperatives, only 42 percent identified the well-being of the community as a primary objective, but among credit cooperatives 80 percent chose this response. The survey also asked respondents to rate the importance of seven values. The two most important were "the economic stability of the co-op" and "respect for the will of the majority." Of lower priority but still significant were the development of participation, equity, and shared ideals (Bagnoli, 2010).

The legal structure also ensures that cooperatives differ from business partnerships. In workers' cooperatives, 50 percent of all labor costs must be compensation for work by members and there is a similar 50 percent threshold in other kinds of cooperatives (Fici, 2010, p. 10). This ensures that the organization remains primarily mutualistic and doesn't exploit the labor of non-members. Together with democratic control of management and limits on return to capital, this creates a distinctive kind of firm.

This research suggests that the cooperative movement still has distinguishing characteristics and values. There have been legitimate critiques of co-ops that are almost indistinguishable from private businesses, or ones that use the cooperative structure fraudulently to get tax benefits, but, overall, the movement has maintained a commitment to cooperative values while also advancing the interests of members. Much of the growth in the cooperative sector has been due to the introduction of a new kind of cooperative: the social cooperative.

Starting in the 1970s, new organizations emerged that focused on the needs of marginalized individuals rather than the mutual interests of members (Borzaga and Ianes, 2006; Ianes, 2016). These groups formed through Catholic religious networks, activist circles or professional associations. They responded to the deficiencies of the welfare state by providing services to individuals whose needs were not met by state institutions (Borzaga and Santuari, 2001). This "third sector" composed of non-profit and non-governmental organizations came to play an important role in providing social services across Europe and North America. In Italy, however, many of these organizations eventually took the distinctive juridical form of the social cooperative, and, more recently, this model been adopted in other European countries such as France and Portugal. This new kind of cooperative, however, is not strictly mutualist because it focuses on the interests of non-members. In the next section, I will describe the structural and normative characteristics of social cooperatives. In the final section of the chapter, I will explain an emerging type called community cooperatives, and discuss how these different types form an integrated "solidarity economy."

SOCIAL COOPERATIVES

According to Carlo Borzaga and Alceste Santuari, the expansion of the post-war welfare state replaced pre-existing charitable and mutual aid societies. In the 1970s, however, the welfare state had increasing difficulty in meeting growing social needs. Most government spending was allocated to pensions, education, and health care, leaving few resources for new needs produced by the transformation of family structures. These included child care, support for people with disabilities, and home-based elder care. At the same time, the period of post-war economic growth was slowing, producing increasing levels of unemployment (Borzaga and Santuari, 2000). According to Alberto Ianes, the public sector also suffered from significant organizational problems. Excessive bureaucratization undermined its ability to meet the needs of citizens and limited its ability to innovate new solutions (Ianes, 2016). This was true in spite of the fact that in 1990, public spending accounted for 53 percent of GDP (Borzaga and Santuari, 2000).

Voluntary organizations formed to try to address some of these government failures, but as the organizations grew, they needed a legal structure that enabled them to raise money and pay salaries. In the Italian legal code, associations were not allowed to hire permanent paid employees. Cooperatives, on the other hand, are able to engage in all the normal functions of businesses and were introduced in order to produce social benefit rather than profit. This combination seemed promising, and early social cooperatives were started as worker cooperatives that provided social services. Professionals who could not gain state employment took advantage of the demand for services by organizing co-ops that satisfied these unmet needs. The members were the workers who staffed day cares or provided elder care.

Nevertheless, the cooperative was not a totally appropriate structure for these complex organizations. Many of the organizations were started by volunteers and still relied heavily on volunteer labor, but volunteers couldn't be members (Borzaga and Santuari, 2000). Some of the new cooperatives provide training and work experience for disabled individuals, but they were not intended to be businesses that would compete with other private enterprises on the free market. What was needed was a multi-stakeholder governance model that included volunteer members, paid staff, and "consumers" who received services. Over time, a fourth stakeholder was included: the local government or state agency that contracted out services to these providers.

Initially, the courts did not recognize these hybrid organizations as legal cooperatives because they did not adhere to the principle of mutualism. Mutualism was interpreted narrowly to describe the shared interest of members. The definition, however, was contested. Proponents of social cooperatives emphasized that the language of the Italian Constitution highlighted the "social function" of cooperative enterprise. Mutuality need not refer exclusively to the internal relations among members. It could also describe the reciprocal obligations among members of a broader community.

In 1991, after ten years of debate, Law 381/91 was passed defining the structure of social cooperatives. One area of disagreement had been the degree to which social cooperatives should rely on voluntary labor. The Catholic wing of the movement strongly emphasized volunteerism, but the red wing rejected a charity-based model. The final legislation included no minimum number of volunteers and specified that no more than half of the members could be volunteers. Social cooperatives could take two forms. Type A co-ops are involved in the provision of social, health, and educational services, and Type B co-ops integrate disadvantaged people in work activities (Borzaga and Ianes, 2006). Both types aim at providing benefits to society as a whole rather than just to the individual members (Thomas, 2004).

Once the legal framework was secured, social cooperatives expanded quickly because they were able to secure social service contracts from local government. They were able to keep costs low and, due to their embeddedness in local communities, they could flexibly design and implement new, more effective ways of meeting local needs. When the new law was approved in 1991, there were around 1000 social cooperatives; by 2011 this had grown to 11 264, with 43 368 volunteers and 320 513 paid personnel (Ianes, 2016).

In recognition of their public benefits, social cooperatives also receive preferential treatment from the state. Type A cooperatives pay a lower value-added tax and indivisible reserves are not taxed. Donations to social cooperatives receive the same tax-exempt treatment that non-profit charities receive. Local government also provides direct financial support to these organizations. A 2011 study estimated that 69 percent of the revenue of Type A cooperatives and 46 percent of Type B cooperatives come from government contracts (cited in Ammirato, 2018, p. 125). Initially, cooperatives had to compete against private firms in a competitive bidding process, but since 2006, local governments can take social goals into account when tendering certain types of contracts. This has led to the creation of an accreditation process that identifies preferred partners based on social criteria (ibid.). Total employment in social cooperatives has grown from 27 510 in 1991 to 390 079 in 2013, which represents just under half the national social services workforce (ibid., p. 126).

THE SOLIDARITY ECONOMY

Why have cooperatives been so successful in Italy? In addition to the legislative framework, a key factor is the role played by the national federations and consortia, which provide support and financing. The cooperative sector in Italy does include some very large firms, but the majority of social cooperatives are small. Half have fewer than 19 employees (Ammirato, 2018). In order to support these small cooperatives, the Consorzio Nazionale Gino Mattarelli has promoted the rhizomatic "strawberry field" model, which creates a network of horizontal ties. Especially in the social sector, cooperatives thrive when they are small enough to sustain worker participation in governance and connections with local communities and clients. At the same time, however, they must be large enough to compete for contracts and to benefit from economies of scale in administrative, legal, and financial services. The consortium has contracts with its affiliated cooperatives, and the uniformity of the protocols helps streamline management and facilitates relationships between the 766 affiliated cooperatives (ibid., p. 127). This has helped them compete with private firms.

The concept of mutualism is a key feature of the cooperative movement. At its most basic level, mutualism means that people must work together to solve collective problems and to achieve objectives they could not accomplish in isolation. The cooperative movement is also animated by a deeper principle of solidarity, which means that members consider others not just as an instrumental means to obtain individual ends; they also value one another's well-being and are inclined to engage in conduct to benefit others and to consider their views. The legal structure of a cooperative by itself does not necessarily advance equity or decrease poverty or other forms of disadvantage. There are private membership clubs and real estate cooperatives that enable wealthy people to jointly own assets, but they are exclusive rather than egalitarian. The cooperative movement in Italy, however, developed as a way of responding to the needs of the disadvantaged. How well does the movement realize the normative and political objectives of CWB?

CWB aims to ensure that economic activity benefits workers and the local community. Worker cooperatives attain this objective through the rules governing the distribution of surplus. There are limits to the return on capital, and the rules require that profit be allocated to strengthen the firm, and to build the cooperative movement. After discharging the legal requirements, the remainder of the profit can be distributed to members according to criteria selected by the general assembly of members. Cooperatives can pay dividends to worker-members or subsidize welfare benefits and collective activities. According to Ammirato, the value-added produced by cooperatives is distributed quite differently from capitalist firms. Publicly traded companies typically distribute between 70–85 percent of profit to shareholders. A study of the way that Italian cooperatives operate found that 68.3 percent of value added went to labor, 6.9 percent went to private capital and 20.8 percent went to community or enterprise capital (the undivided reserve) (ibid., p. 195).

There is strong evidence that demonstrates that cooperatives behave differently from private firms when faced with an economic downturn or crisis. Instead of shedding labor, they usually decide to reallocate labor among members, decreasing the hours worked while maintaining employment. The cooperative law does not regulate the wage differentials between the highest- and lowest-paid workers, but the egalitarian culture of the movement and the democratic decision-making still produce a more solidaristic wage structure. The average salary differential is 6–1, which is higher than the 2–1 in the early days of the movement but still considerably lower than the differential in the private sector (ibid., p. 193).

While cooperatives are primarily focused on the interests of members, the movement as a whole also emphasizes benefit to the broader community. The charters of the cooperative Coop Italia (a large consumer cooperative) purchases 90 percent of its products from local suppliers. Cooperative banks devote 96 percent of their portfolios to families and businesses in their catchment area and donate 7 percent of their profit to community activities (Ammirato, 2018).

A key component of CWB is participation. As Barnes and Williamson explain in Chapter 2 of this book, it is not enough to combat poverty by treating people as passive beneficiaries of the well-intentioned but paternalistic initiatives of others. Instead, the disadvantaged should be seen for what they are—people with capacities, resources, and ideas that have often not been recognized and mobilized due to structural injustice. Participatory institutions are a way to ensure that the people have a say over how wealth is produced and shared. How well have cooperatives performed at sustaining meaningful participation?

Italian law requires democratic oversight of cooperative governance. There must be an annual general meeting where members approve the budget and financial statements. The board is elected by the members, and members must hold the majority of board positions. Elections are largely based on one member one vote. In practice, however, professional managers and boards play an important role, especially in larger cooperatives. Participation is higher in smaller cooperatives and in times of internal crisis moments. Research suggests that the level of participation varies across different types of cooperatives, and often functions as a check on management rather than a genuinely participatory form of governance.

An important goal of CWB is to involve different local stakeholders into an integrated system. The growth of the Italian cooperative movement is a product of its collaboration with local government. The movement has also introduced innovative programs for diffusing understanding of the values and benefits of cooperatives. In high schools in Bologna, a city at the heart of the cooperative movement, there is an "Invent a Cooperative" competition in which students develop a business plan. At the university level, Legacoop (one of the three federations) organizes seminars about cooperative ideals, law, and logistics. The Trentino federation has seminars that allow students to study the practice of democratic decision-making in an enterprise environment. In 2016, 600 students took part (Ammirato, 2018, p. 114). Italians who perform civil service in lieu of military service can work to complete this service in a social cooperative, which provides an opportunity to learn about the cooperative movement and ideals. Together these programs ensure that broad sectors of society understand the theory and practice of cooperation.

The cooperative movement has also focused on equity goals, particularly by trying to address the problem of youth unemployment, which, at 29.3 percent, is the third highest in Europe (Eurostat, 2020). One of the cooperative federations introduced a program to encourage unemployed youths to form cooperatives. Program participants must complete an online training course and develop a business plan. Those who are selected receive additional in-person training about cooperative governance and coaching to further develop the business strategy. Winners receive start-up capital of 15 000 euros that is provided by the co-op federation and partners. After the new co-ops are launched, they receive an additional 36 months of management, marketing, and accounting support at a subsidized rate and are eligible for micro-credit loans. Coopstartup has funded 30 new cooperatives and the related CoopUP program supported the formation of 40 more (Ammirato, pp. 117–18).

The legal structure of the cooperative enterprise has also proved to be a flexible tool for advancing local development projects. These "community" cooperatives are organized to revitalize small communities that are experiencing disinvestment and out-migration. One of the first community cooperatives was founded by local residents in Valle dei Cavalieri. The initiative began after the last bar and shop closed in 1991. Without a place to serve as the focal point of social life, local residents thought the community seemed "destined to die" (Cooperativa di Communità Valle dei Cavalieri, 2020). The residents organized an "agricultural tourism" enterprise with a restaurant and a small farm that produced pecorino cheese. The community cooperative eventually hired seven employees (including two disabled workers), several seasonal workers, and 33 volunteer members (Grella, 2016). The cooperative expanded to provide services for the community, including transportation for elderly people and school children.

Community cooperatives are consistent with the core objective of the movement: promoting the well-being of economically vulnerable people through mutualism. In another sense, however, they are also innovative, because they focus more on the sustainability of the local community rather than the economic interests of individual members. They provide goods and services that are in the collective interest, but the real objective is to strengthen social relations. Often, the goal is the revitalization of communal property or cultural infrastructure that been abandoned or decayed. This happens both in rural areas experiencing depopulation and also in blighted urban centers. The local dimension is decisive (Bodini et al., 2016, p. 7). The goal is to unleash dormant social capacities, strengthen social ties, and sustain collective infrastructure.

Community cooperatives are often a response to market failures. In villages that are losing population, the market is not large enough to sustain for-profit business, yet there is still demand for some type of social space. The solution is to share the responsibility to provide a desired good or service, such as a café or public transportation (ibid., p. 14). According to Riccardo Bodini and his collaborators, solidarity emerges out of the search for solutions to collective problems. When this problem-solving takes place on a sufficiently circumscribed scale, it can overcome the feeling of individual powerlessness in the face of complex problems (ibid., p. 1).

The community cooperative is a structure that enables members of the community to address local needs, but it is also part of a broader movement that is structured by the principles of mutualism. According to a White Paper published by the European Research Institute on Cooperative and Social Enterprises (EURICSE), a community cooperative must have the following distinctive features (ibid., pp. 32–3):

1. It is an enterprise that is capable of producing goods or services (including public or communal goods) in a stable, sustainable manner.
2. It is a cooperative, which means that it is governed completely, or to a large degree, by its members through democratic procedures.
3. It is tied to the community. Its objective is the flourishing of a particular place, understood broadly to include diverse forms of interests, values, and connections.

4. It is open. It tries to provide access to collective goods to the community (members and non-members) in a non-discriminatory fashion. In distributing benefits to members, it also maintains a commitment to sustainability and future generations.

This definition is helpful in distinguishing a community cooperative from elitist, exclusive organizations that provide collective consumption goods to members. The objective of the community cooperative is the good of the local community as a whole. Of course, the meaning of both "the common good" and "the community" are contestable, but the values of the cooperative movement provide some guidance about how to approach these concepts. Priority is placed on basic needs and economic development is understood as a means to an end, which is the flourishing of the members of the community (ibid., p. 34). The cooperative movement also recognizes that there can be conflicting interests and judgments, and therefore it emphasizes that active, democratic participation is necessary.

Community cooperatives differ from traditional cooperatives insofar as they place more emphasis on the production of non-economic value. According to EURICSE, these cooperatives produce "collective benefits that are not divisible into individual shares." Community cooperatives are hybrids that promote economic activity as well as broader, non-commodifiable benefits that are rooted in a specific place. For example, the Cooperative Sociale L'Innesto in La Val Cavallina is made up of 20 members. The cooperative was founded in response to the decline of traditional agricultural and artisanal activity in the area. The objectives of the cooperative are two-fold: to provide employment for disadvantaged people and also to reverse the decline of the built environment by restoring historic buildings. To finance this project, the cooperative also introduced educational and cultural activities to attract tourists. Social cooperatives have also been formed in urban areas. For example, Isola Pepe Verde is a community garden in Milan. It organizes educational activities for all ages and fosters practices of collective management of shared space (ibid., p. 42). While the cooperative movement originally prioritized the economic benefit of members, it has come to support the emergence of new, hybrid organizations focused on community benefits.

CONCLUSION

The cooperative movement helps us imagine a different kind economy, one in which self-interest and social interest are intertwined rather than opposed. Community cooperatives are an innovative sector of the Italian cooperative movement. It is tempting to conclude that it is this type of cooperative that fits best with the aspirations of CWB, but I think this would be incorrect. CWB is best understood as an integrative policy paradigm made up of local initiatives connected in a way that facilitates systematic change. The complex structure of the Italian cooperative movement, which has evolved over 100 years, shows that the solidarity economy can be an integrative policy paradigm. The key features of the paradigm are the following: state support, a federated structure, institutional pluralism, and public education to diffuse understanding of norms and institutional structures. The cooperative movement has both a rhizomatic and a pyramidal structure. We see the rhizomatic structure in the way that community cooperatives emerged from the grassroots and integrated features of consumer cooperatives and social cooperatives to generate a new type of structure. Social cooperatives emerged in a similar way. At the same time, the mandatory contributions to federated associations ensure that there is an institutional framework that promotes and nurtures new cooperatives, by providing training and legal advice. The federations also lobby the government to secure a favorable regulatory framework. The various types of cooperatives have different objectives: advancing the economic interests of members, providing social services, securing employment for the disadvantaged, and strengthening the community. This pluralism has enabled the growth of an integrated solidarity economy that engages in an ongoing process of deliberation on how to balance the dual imperatives of building wealth and building community.

NOTE

1. This is consistent with the definition of a workers' cooperative provided by Bowles and Gintis (1996, Chapter 5). They define a workers' cooperative as a firm in which workers choose the management and determine the administrative structure using democratic procedures.

REFERENCES

Ammirato, Piero (2018), *The Growth of Italian Cooperatives: Innovation, Resilience and Social Responsibility*, Abingdon, UK: Routledge.

Bagnoli, Luca (2010), *La funzione sociale della cooperazione: teorie, esperienze e prospettive*, Rome: Corocci.

Bodini, Riccardo, Carlo Borzaga and Pierangelo Mori et al. (2016), *Libro Bianco: La Cooperazione Di Comunità*, EURISCE, April.

Borzaga, Carlo and Alberto Ianes (2006), *L'economia della solidarietà: storia e prospettive della cooperazione sociale*, Rome: Donzelli.

Borzaga, Carlo and Alceste Santuari (2000), "Social enterprises in Italy: the experience of social co-operatives," *Institute for Development Studies of Non Profit Enterprises Working Papers*, No. 15.

Borzaga, Carlo and Alceste Santuari (2001), "Italia: dalle cooperative tradizionali alle cooperative sociali," in Carlo Borzaga and Jacques Defourny (eds), *L'impresa sociale in una prospettiva europea*, Trento: Edizioni 31, pp. 161–82.

Bowles, Samuel and Herbert Gintis (1996), "The distribution of wealth and the viability of the democratic firm," in Ugo Pagano and Robert Rowthorn (eds), *Democracy and Efficiency in the Economic Enterprise*, New York: Routledge, pp. 64–81.

Carini, Chiara, Carlo Borzaga and Eddi Fontanari (n.d.), "Il valore economico e occupazionale della cooperazione nel 2013 e la sua evoluzione negli anni 2011–2013," EURICSE.

Caspary, William R. (2018), *Dewey on Democracy*, Ithaca, NY: Cornell University Press.

Cooperativa di Communità Valle dei Cavalieri (2020), "La nostra storia," accessed January 5, 2020 at https://valledeicavalieri.it/wp/.

Corcoran, Hazel and David Wilson (2010), *The Worker Cooperative Movements in Italy, Mondragon and France: Context, Success Factors and Lessons*, Calgary, AB: Canadian Worker Cooperative Federation.

Dardot, Pierre and Christian Laval (2015), *Commun: essai sur la revolution au XXIe siècle*, Paris: La Découverte.

Eurostat (2020), "Youth unemployment rate in EU member states as of August 2019," accessed January 5, 2020 at https://www.statista.com/statistics/266228/youth-unemployment-rate-in-eu-countries/.

Fici, Antonio (2009), "Cooperatives and social enterprises: comparative and legal profile," in Bruno Roelants (ed.), *Cooperatives and Social Enterprises: Governance and Normative Frameworks*, Brussels: CECOP Publications, pp. 77–101.

Fici, Antonio (2010), "Italian co-operative law reform and co-operative principles," *EURICSE Working Papers*, No. 02.

Fici, Antonio (2013), "Cooperative identity and the law," *European Business Law Review*, 24(1), 37–64.

Gide, Charles (1905), *Économie sociale*, Paris: Larose.

Grella, di Diletta (2016), "Succiso, il paese-cooperativa dove ogni giorno si cambia lavoro," *Vita*, accessed January 5, 2020 at http://www.vita.it/it/article/2016/05/23/succiso-il-paese-cooperativa-dove-ogni-giorno-si-cambia-lavoro/139495/.

Hardt, Michael and Antonio Negri (2011), *Commonwealth*, Cambridge, MA: Belknap Press of Harvard University Press.

Ianes, Alberto (2016), "Exploring the origins of social enterprise: social co-operation in the Italian welfare system and its reproduction in Europe (from the 1970s to the present)," *EURICSE Working Papers*, No. 88.

International Co-operative Alliance (ICA) (2018), "Cooperative identity, values and principles," accessed January 5, 2020 at https://www.ica.coop/en/cooperatives/cooperative-identity.

Knight, Louise W. (2008), *Citizen: Jane Addams and the Struggle for Democracy*, Chicago, IL: University of Chicago Press.

Malleson, Tom (2014), *After Occupy: Economic Democracy for the 21st Century*, Oxford: Oxford University Press.

Senato della Repubblica (1947), *Constitution of the Italian Republic*, accessed January 5, 2020 at https://www.senato.it/documenti/repository/istituzione/costituzione_inglese.pdf.

Singer, Abraham A. (2018), *The Form of the Firm: A Normative Political Theory of the Corporation*, Oxford: Oxford University Press.

Stjernø, Steinar (2009), *Solidarity in Europe: The History of an Idea*, Cambridge, UK: Cambridge University Press.

Thomas, Antonio (2004), "The rise of social cooperatives in Italy," *Voluntas: International Journal of Voluntary and Nonprofit Organizations*, 15(3), 243–63.

Utting, Peter (ed.) (2015), *Social and Solidarity Economy: Beyond the Fringe*, London: Zed Books.

7. A place to call home? Property, freedom, and the commonwealth[1]

Richard Dagger

Within the republican tradition of political thought, ownership of property is typically considered an important means of securing the citizens' independence and promoting their capacity for self-government. Accompanying this regard for private property is the corresponding concern, as Jean-Jacques Rousseau (1762 [1978], p. 58) put it, that everyone should have something and no one too much. That is, everyone should have enough property to provide a foundation for an independent life, and no one should have so much as to be in a position to render others dependent on his or her favor. Finding this balance is a persistent challenge, and dramatically so in those times and places in which many people are homeless; for how are we to ensure that everyone has sufficient property when some own nothing more than the clothes on their backs and the contents of a backpack or shopping cart? What has republican theory to say about that problem, other than to deplore its existence?

My aim in this chapter is to answer this question by showing that republicanism provides a helpful diagnosis of the political implications of homelessness and a frame of reference for overcoming homelessness itself. To prepare the groundwork for this answer, it is first necessary to explain how republicanism relates to the topic of community wealth building and to clarify the connection between property and self-government.

COMMUNITY, WEALTH, AND THE COMMONWEALTH

To understand the project of community wealth building requires a grasp of the meaning of *community*, which is a term both widely used and variously defined. For present purposes, though, it should be sufficient to say that the community in community wealth building falls into the middle ground between strict and loose conceptions of community. On the strict side are those who want to distinguish community from terms such as *aggregation*, *group*, *society*, and *association*. John Rawls (1993, pp. 40–43, n. 43), for instance, defines "a community as a special kind of association, one united by a comprehensive doctrine," such as a church, whereas an association is a group of people pursuing a particular end, as the members of a parent–teacher association or professional group may do. For Rawls, moreover, neither a community nor an association is equivalent to a society, which is both more encompassing and more diffuse than either of the others, for a society "is complete in that it is self-sufficient and has a place for all the main purposes of human life" (ibid., p. 40). Michael Taylor (1982, p. 32) provides a different, but similarly strict definition when he identifies the following three characteristics of community: "shared values and beliefs, direct and many-sided relations, and the practice of reciprocity." The last two characteristics especially make this a narrow definition of community, for in "a large and changing mass of people, few relations between individuals can be direct or many-sided, and reciprocity cannot flourish on a wide scale, since its continuation for any length of time requires *some* actual reciprocation, which in turn requires stable relations with known individuals" (ibid.; original emphasis).

For Rawls, Taylor, and others who define community in strict or narrow terms, the United States and other nation-states, or even multinational states, may well be societies or polities, but they cannot be communities. Such a restrictive view is at odds, of course, with those who apply the term community not only to states but also to larger and even international entities, such as the academic community and the global community. References to such communities are widespread today, as is reference to communities of color. Such usages are far too loose to satisfy either Rawls's or Taylor's restrictive conceptions of community, both of which require substantial agreement among those who compose the community, whether it be agreement on a comprehensive conception of the good for Rawls or shared values and beliefs for Taylor. The fact that there is a remarkable diversity of beliefs and values among the people who populate the globe, however, or a similar diversity among people who share a skin color, is not as important to those who use community loosely, as in the sense of a common fate or standing. In their view, it is reasonable to say that we are global citizens who share a global community because we all have reasons to fear the effects of climate change and the loss of biodiversity; or that people of color form communities of color, notwithstanding their differences, because their social and political standing are largely constrained by their color. To conceive of community expansively is, in their view, both fitting and proper.

Between these two conceptions of community is a broad middle ground, and it is on this ground that the project of *community* wealth building is likely to prove most fruitful.[2] Taylor's narrow or strict conception of community may apply to small towns or regions, such as Lexington and Buena Vista in Rockbridge County, Virginia, but a city the size of Richmond is too large to generate the direct, many-sided, and reciprocal relations that he takes to be the hallmarks of a genuine community. The same is even more obviously true of metropolitan areas such as Greater Richmond and larger entities, such as the Commonwealth of Virginia and the United States as a whole. However, all four of these entities—city, metropolis, state, and nation-state—display two features, shared with intermediate bodies such as townships and counties, which justify the appellation of community. One is that they are limited territorially, so that the residents of Richmond share a common set of boundaries and common geographical features, as do, more expansively, the residents of Greater Richmond, Virginia, and the United States. The second is that these residents find their lives defined by a common set of laws, even though their legal standing is sometimes complicated by the fragmented jurisdictions within Greater Richmond and by the multiple jurisdictions within the United States and its subordinate parts. Despite these complications, there is enough commonality in the legal standing of towns, cities, counties, states, and the United States as a whole to make it reasonable to apply the term *community* to each of these entities.

What, though, of wealth building? Again, there seem to be three distinct ways to conceive of this aspect of the project of building community wealth: the aggregative, the distributive, and the communal. According to the first conception, the measure of a community's wealth is simply the sum of its members' wealth. In keeping with classical utilitarianism, the aim of a program of community wealth building so conceived would be to increase the aggregate wealth of the community without regard to how that wealth is distributed. If providing tax breaks and other incentives to the rich will increase the aggregate wealth of the community, even though they diminish the wealth of some portion of its residents, then these breaks and incentives will count, on this view, as proper methods of building community wealth.

This is a conclusion that neither of the other two conceptions will allow. According to the second conception, what matters is the distribution of wealth within the community, not its aggregate amount. Any scheme that enhances or reinforces the wealth of the wealthy at the expense of the poor or middling elements may count as wealth building of a sort, in other words, but not as community wealth building. To achieve the latter, on this view, it is necessary to distribute wealth throughout the community in ways that work to the advantage of as many of its people as possible. There are various ways of specifying the terms of this distribution—for example, the Pareto criterion, which would block any program that makes anyone worse off, and Rawls's difference principle, which allows unequal distributions of wealth only when such distributions benefit the worst-off members of society—but in every case, the emphasis is on the distribution of the community's wealth. The number that counts, then, will be the number of people who benefit from a program of wealth building, rather than the total gain in wealth.

This refusal to settle for straightforward aggregation is also characteristic of the third conception, but here the emphasis is on the distribution of wealth only to the extent that it strengthens the community as such. There is a sense, that is, in which the aggregative and distributive conceptions of wealth building are both individualistic, with one focusing on the sum of the wealth achieved by individuals within the community and the other on the distribution of that wealth among its individual members. Missing from both, however, is any concern for the communal aspects of community wealth that are central to this third conception. According to this view, many elements of community wealth, and many of the most important elements, are not readily divisible into individual assets. Parks, libraries, roads, schools, police and fire protection, and other public goods may benefit some community members more directly than others, but they benefit everyone, and thus the community as a whole, by contributing to various forms of well-being that cannot be assessed in the ways that income and property values are. Among these forms are the sense of community itself—of being a part of a shared enterprise with a history and a future—together with the social capital and civic virtue that accompany it.[3]

By shifting the center of attention from the aggregation and distribution of individual wealth within the community to the wealth of the community as such, this communal conception is in two ways superior to either of the other conceptions. First, it is more capacious. The communal conception does indeed shift the center of attention away from aggregative and distributive concerns, but it neither displaces nor neglects them. To the contrary, those who aspire to build the wealth of a community in this communal sense will find that they often will need to devote their efforts to increasing its aggregate wealth and seeing to its proper distribution. Those, however, are narrower aims to be brought together and reconciled with one another in the interests of the community as a whole. In doing so, moreover, those who follow the communal model will act with a broader and richer sense of wealth in mind. This is the second way in which the communal conception is superior to the aggregative and distributive. By aiming to secure and enhance the institutions and practices that generate social capital, civic virtue, and other elements of the public good, the communal conception concentrates less on wealth understood in monetary terms than on the older sense of weal, or well-being.

Here, moreover, is where the connection between community wealth building and the republican tradition in political thought becomes evident. The simplest and most direct way to mark this connection is with a word often used in English as a translation of *res publica* and a synonym of the word *republic*. That word is *commonwealth*. *Commonwealth* is an appropriate translation because the *res publica* is the people's business, or the property of the public, and the weal or wealth or well-being of the public is a matter of common concern. It is not only the business of one ruler or a few rulers, nor merely the concern of a faction or sect, but of the people in their common capacity as citizens. In the words of Cicero (1999, p. 18), whose *De Re Publica* is often translated as *On the Commonwealth*, the republic is "not any group of men assembled in any way, but an assemblage of some size associated with one another through agreement on law and community of interest." Indeed, for Cicero and subsequent republican thinkers, sustaining the rule of law is one of the foremost interests the members of the commonwealth will have in common—as central to their common weal as their economic productivity is. For that reason, it will be as vital to community wealth building as anything that promotes wealth or prosperity in the narrower sense those terms typically convey in our time.

For republicans, the rule of law is a matter of common concern not only because all members of the commonwealth must be subject to it, but also because all citizens are entitled to play a part in making the laws that govern them. To reduce republicanism to a formula, it is a theory of publicity and self-government (Dagger, 2004, esp. pp. 168–70). To be a republican, as Margaret Jane Radin (1993, p. 159) says, is thus to dedicate oneself "to the flourishing of citizens in a community by means of their self-government." This same description applies to those who dedicate themselves to community wealth building, at least when they conceive of wealth building in accordance with the communal model. Radin's views also underscore this point by connecting "the flourishing of citizens" to the possession of property. As she argues in "Property and Personhood" (1982), there is an important distinction between two kinds of property, personal and fungible, with the former playing a crucial role in self-government. To be precise, personal property, such as a place to call home or a family heirloom, is of great importance to one's sense of self or identity—of personhood—in contrast to fungible possessions one would happily exchange for money or some item of fleeting interest. Personal property is thus vital to self-government as *self*-government. In particular, the home is more than a place of sanctuary in which one is free from interference; it is, as Radin (1982, p. 992) says, "[T]he scene of one's history and future, one's life and growth […] [O]ne embodies or constitutes oneself there. The home is affirmatively part of oneself—property for personhood—and not just the agreed upon locale for protection from outside interference."

But what, one may ask, has any of this to do with the homeless? What can talk of "the flourishing of citizens" mean to those who are simply trying to "get by"? Why should those who are preoccupied with self-preservation care about self-government? How can distinguishing personal from fungible property help those who have almost none of either? To these questions I now turn.

PROPERTY, LAW, AND THE PLIGHT OF THE HOMELESS

Anyone who is concerned with the plight of the homeless must recognize that they have pressing needs. Of these there are many. The homeless need food and shelter, of course, but they also need warm clothing in cold weather, health care of various kinds, and counseling that will help them move from mere survival to a significant degree of security. Their needs are so overwhelming, in fact, that talk of self-government or freedom or anything but sheer need may seem to be pointless. Nevertheless, addressing the plight of the homeless is more than a matter of meeting their basic needs.

To appreciate this point, it may help to consider two examples. The first is of a man who appears to be homeless; the second is of a woman who does not. The man appears to be homeless because he has no fixed abode; he is one of those whose wanderlust takes him from place to place as the fancy strikes him. Unlike the "rambling man" of folk songs, however, he has an SUV in which he occasionally sleeps and credit cards backed by well-funded bank accounts that enable him to buy food, lodging, and anything else he needs in the course of his wandering. He is even wealthy enough to buy a house and call it is his home, although he chooses not to do so. Is such a man really homeless? In contrast, consider the woman Mary Wollstonecraft described in 1792, who "was left by [her] parents without any provision" and had to rely on the benevolence of her brother for the roof over her head and the food on her plate. She has a home, it seems, but only by the grace of her brother—and perhaps of her brother's wife, who is likely to be scheming, Wollstonecraft suggests, to force her out of the house and into the cruel world. Meanwhile, the unfortunate sister has a home only because she is "eating the bitter bread of dependence" (Wollstonecraft, 1792 [1997], pp. 182–3).[4] Does such a woman really have a home?

In both examples, pressing needs are met. In other respects, though, the situations are quite different. The man who appears to be homeless clearly does not have to be. The woman who appears to have a home, however, lives on the brink of homelessness, at best. I say "at best" because there is a sense in which she is already homeless, despite the shelter her brother affords her. What she lacks, and what the well-to-do wanderer has in abundance, is property. She shares the plight of the homeless, and he does not, because her lack of property leaves her dependent on the grace and favor of others in a way that the man of independent means will not experience. It is true, of course, that a home is more than a house. The latter is fungible, in Radin's terms, while the former is perhaps the paradigmatic form of personal property. Even so, owning a house—or even the kind of property that one can use to buy a house—gives one a measure of independence and provides the prospect of the sanctuary to which Radin refers, because it gives the owner a substantial degree of control over what happens to and within that house. This control is something that the homeless lack, including those homeless people who are fortunate to have shelter but owe that good fortune to the benevolence of others.

Property and ownership are concepts that almost everyone uses, implicitly if not explicitly, almost all the time. But they are also notoriously complicated concepts. According to A.M. Honoré's (1961) oft-cited analysis, there are at least 11 "incidents" of ownership, such as the right to use and the right to possess, but not one of them is a necessary condition of "owning" something.[5] Still, three of these "incidents" appear to be central to the legal analysis of property. As Christopher Essert (2016, p. 281) observes, "Since at least ancient Rome, lawyers have explained property rights in terms of the three 'incidents' of possession, use, and alienation," with possession understood to include the right to exclude others from one's property. Furthermore, Essert takes these three "incidents" to be "elaborations of property's *core idea* of *normative control* over others' presence and actions" (ibid., pp. 281–2; emphasis added). To own property is to have a measure of independence, that is, in the sense of a measure of normative control, or rights, over what others may do within one's property. To lack this control is, both in effect and by definition, to be homeless. As Essert (ibid., pp. 274–5) says, "The homeless are homeless because they lack any right to decide how things will be as between them and others in the space where they live. In other words, they are homeless because they lack property."

This is why the plight of the homeless is much more than a matter of responding to their most urgent needs. Even if we somehow arranged to provide every homeless person, every day, with sufficient food and temporary shelter, we would not have addressed, either fully or directly, the problem of homelessness itself. To do that, we must find a way for the homeless to overcome their lack of property. To put the point another way, we must help them find a way out of their paradoxical relationship with the law.

The relationship is paradoxical because property ownership is largely a matter of legal standing, and the homeless are in an uncomfortable position with regard to the rule of law. On the one hand, they rely on law for both protection and guidance, much as those who own houses, cars, and bank accounts do, if not to the same extent. The homeless need protection from violence and the theft of what little property they have, and they depend on traffic laws for the safe use of streets and sidewalks. On the other hand, property laws exclude them from every privately owned place unless the property owners grant them permission to enter. In this respect, the homeless person is close to being an outlaw. As Jeremy Waldron remarks:

> there is no place governed by a private property rule where [a homeless person] is allowed to be whenever *he* chooses, no place governed by a private property rule from which he may not at any time be excluded as a result of someone else's say-so. As far as being on private property is concerned—in people's houses or gardens, on farms or in hotels, in offices or restaurants—the homeless person is utterly and at all times at the mercy of others. (Waldron, 1991, p. 299; original emphasis)

To be sure, the homeless may avail themselves of parks, libraries, and other forms of public property. Waldron and others have pointed out, however, that the law is not always on their side even when public property is concerned, largely because of "the increasing regulation of the streets, the subways, parks, and other public places to restrict the activities that can be performed there" (ibid., p. 301).[6] The homeless are thus within the law—they are certainly subject to it—while being excluded outright, in many important instances, from its protection.

Compounding this paradox is a challenge that homelessness poses to the idea of legality. Together with limited and impersonal government, this idea forms the core of the rule-of-law ideal. In brief, *legality* refers to the defining features of law itself, such as generality and publicity; that is, laws must be general in their application, rather than aimed at specific persons or events, and they must be published so that those who are subject to them can conduct themselves in accordance with the law. Another characteristic of legality—the possibility of compliance—proves especially troublesome with regard to the homeless. The idea here is that the law cannot reasonably command people to do what they cannot possibly do.[7] "Laws" requiring us to leap tall buildings in a single bound or to stay awake for days on end fail this test of legality, which means that they are not proper laws at all. The homeless, however, find themselves in a position where the laws protecting private property and prohibiting trespass make it difficult, if not quite impossible, to meet their basic needs—eating, sleeping, bathing, eliminating bodily wastes—without either trespassing or securing the permission of property owners. The latter may be easy enough to do if they have the money to pay for a meal in a restaurant or a place to sleep, but the lack of money is one of the main reasons for homelessness in the first place. Moreover, their opportunity to acquire money by begging is often subject to laws that prohibit panhandling. The alternative is to rely on public facilities, but these opportunities also are limited by laws against loitering, sleeping in public, camping in public parks, and other "quality-of-life" offenses (Skolnik, 2016, 2018). In such circumstances, Waldron (1991, p. 302) declares, the homeless are "comprehensively unfree," for "a person who is not free to be in any place is not free to do anything." To be banned from doing what one cannot help but do, furthermore, raises questions not only about the justice of their treatment but also about the legitimacy of the legal system that renders them "comprehensively unfree."

With regard to freedom, those who have called attention to homelessness as a problem of freedom have taken different paths. Waldron's claim is that the homeless are deprived of negative freedom, which is typically construed as the absence of interference or restraint. On the face of it, this seems to be an odd claim, for the homeless are not the victims of obvious interference. In Waldron's judgment, however, "[h]omelessness is partly about property and law, and freedom provides the connecting term that makes those categories relevant. By considering not only what a person is allowed to do, but where he is allowed to do it, we can see a system of property for what it is: rules that provide freedom and prosperity for some by imposing restrictions on others" (ibid., p. 324). The homeless may be free to go where they want, one might say, but they are not free to go where they are not wanted; and if there is nowhere they are wanted, or at least permitted, they are "comprehensively unfree."

The rival view is the republican conception of liberty, which is usually defined, in accordance with Philip Pettit's influential analysis, as freedom from domination.[8] According to this view, what limits one's freedom is not necessarily interference or restraint, which may in some cases serve to preserve one's freedom, but domination by and dependence on others, including those who may neither interfere with nor even notice what one is doing. What matters, though, is that one must be wary of attracting the attention or losing the favor of those who are in a position of dominance, for they may interfere in one's life when and as they see fit. Wollstonecraft's example of the sister who must depend on the benevolence of her brother is an example of someone who lacks freedom from domination, according to this analysis, as do the "homeless who depend on charity to get a bed for the night," as Pettit says (2014, p. 2). Freedom in this republican sense is thus linked to independence—that is, freedom from dependence—and to self-government. It is also linked to property, which provides some degree of "normative control" and thus some security against domination and dependence. Those who lack property, however, lack this control, this security, and freedom itself. "To be homeless," Essert insists, "is to be always and everywhere subject to others' rights and therefore to the possibility of their enforcing those rights. It is to be under the power of others, dependent on them, dominated by them, unfree" (Essert, 2016, p. 276; see also Skolnik, 2018, esp. §§IV and V).

Whether we should conceive of freedom in the negative or the republican sense is a matter of much debate, but Essert is not alone in thinking that the republican view captures Waldron's concern about the comprehensive unfreedom of the homeless better than the negative conception Waldron advocates. One reason to take this position is that the republican view points toward a more helpful program for alleviating the plight of the homeless than Waldron offers.

BUILDING COMMUNITY WEALTH BY HOUSING THE HOMELESS

In one of his more provocative comments, Waldron (1991, p. 302) asserts that "the homeless have freedom in our society only to the extent that our society is communist." As the lower-case *c* indicates, Waldron is not proposing the adoption of a Marxist or Soviet-style regime. What he intends, instead, is a society in which more property is held in common and more of that common property is available to the homeless—more places, in short, in which the homeless are free to meet their basic needs without violating the laws of property. There is, of course, something to be said for such a society, which would make life better in important ways for the homeless. But the policy of extending common property fails to address the core problem of homelessness, which is the lack of homes.

This is the point that Essert makes in response to Waldron. If people are homeless because they lack property, then we should strive to ensure that they have it. Essert agrees with Waldron in holding that "*everything* that is to be done needs to be done somewhere," but he goes further than Waldron in drawing the connection between individual freedom and private property. As he observes, "it might seem that we could do these things without property [i.e., as long as we had access to communal property, but] we would always be able only to do them subject to others' forbearing from interfering, which is just to say we would be under their power regarding whether or not we could do them, so we could not do them freely" (Essert, 2016, p. 279; original emphasis). To overcome homelessness, then, we must find ways to extend not only access to common or communal property but also ownership of private or personal property, so that almost everyone has a legally secure place to call home.

From the standpoint of community wealth building, this suggests a two-pronged approach to homelessness. In keeping with the communal conception of community wealth I set out earlier, the first prong aims at strengthening the public institutions that bear the brunt of homelessness and at enhancing their ability to provide the basic services the homeless need. The second prong aims at providing housing for the homeless that they may come to regard not as temporary shelter but as a long-term home. Exactly how this is to be done is too complicated a topic to pursue here, but a clear implication is that the housing-first approach is the proper policy. That is, debates about how best to deal with homelessness tend to pit housing-first advocates against those who maintain that the homeless have a prior need for other kinds of assistance, such as drug counseling and mental health treatment, if they are to be capable of living in homes of their own. There is now sufficient evidence to believe, though, that providing housing should come first, largely because housing enables homeless persons "to stabilize their existence before moving into service delivery in other areas (such as drug or mental health treatment)" (Tars and Egleson, 2009, p. 212).[9]

Whether it comes first or second, however, the aim must be to find homes for the homeless so that they have the sanctuary that Radin extols and the normative control that Essert links to property rights. A corollary is that preventing homelessness is as important as finding a remedy for it. For that reason, any attempt to deal with homelessness must be part of a larger project to advance home ownership and, more broadly, housing security—a project that recognizes that leaseholders also have an interest in normative control. Attacking homelessness, in other words, is in the end a part of a larger program of building a property-owning democracy.[10]

CONCLUSION

One should expect, of course, that some will object to any policy that aims to find or provide homes for the homeless, because they believe that such a policy will take property from some in order to give it to others. It is fine, the objectors may say, for a person to contribute to Habitat for Humanity, which builds houses for those who can meet minimum financial requirements and are willing to invest sweat equity in the construction, but that is charity, not a government program at the expense of taxpayers. We should note, however, that the homeless are members of the community, even if they are more transient than the propertied typically are. In their homeless condition, they contribute little to the community's wealth, while consuming its resources and putting a strain on its parks, libraries, and other institutions. If we can find ways to provide them with a place to call home—perhaps by transforming abandoned buildings and converting decommissioned government property—we also will be helping them to become independent citizens who will contribute to building the wealth of their communities (e.g., Siegel, 1991, esp. pp. 1063–4; and National Law Center on Homelessness and Poverty, 2018).

Another objection may be that any attempt to transform the homeless into property owners is far too ambitious for any community—any local community, that is—to undertake on its own. After all, no local community has the resources to control the economic conditions that drive housing costs or the social and psychological forces that contribute to homelessness through racial discrimination, drug addiction, and mental illness, among other factors. Even so, there are two effective responses to this objection.

The first is that local communities have a critical role to play in the attempt to eradicate homelessness, even though they must rely on assistance from other sources. In keeping with the old idea that the best judge of the quality of a shoe is the person who must wear it, those who must deal with the effects of homelessness most directly, in their own lives and communities, will have an especially valuable perspective on the problem and the possibilities of solving it. Moreover, the fact that local communities cannot fully control economic, social, and psychological forces does not mean that they cannot have an important effect in these areas. As zoning regulations and schooling policies indicate, local communities have significant powers, and these they may employ in a conscious effort to eliminate homelessness. Finally, those who share this local perspective need not shun outside advice or assistance. On the contrary, they will find it wise to look for such advice and call upon such assistance from other sources, private as well as public. In fact, one of the central features of the Canadian city of Abbotsford's plan to address homelessness is to form an agency that coordinates the city's efforts with agencies of the Province of British Columbia, the federal government of Canada, and various nongovernmental organizations.[11] Such an agency may also play a part in promoting housing-friendly policies at higher levels of government that will help to promote home ownership and stable-housing arrangements.

The second response to the objection concerning the weakness of local communities is that confronting homelessness on the local level is itself a way of building community wealth. Among the anticipated impacts of Abbotsford's action plan, for example, are these: "Social capital is increased and invested throughout the community" and "[t]he community wellbeing of Abbotsford is increased" (Abbotsford, 2014). That is to say, the community that makes a concerted effort to address this problem is likely to foster the independence and civic contributions of those who were formerly homeless, and especially so if these people are given a voice in the shaping of the policies that will most directly affect them. More broadly, it is also likely to strengthen the bonds of trust and reciprocity that enhance the social capital of the community as a whole. To build that kind of capital is to build community wealth in a form that is capable of providing a significant response not only to homelessness but also to other problems that are likely to beset any community. In Richmond, for example, the newly created Office of Community Wealth Building began its efforts by focusing on three concerns—education, employment, and housing for the homeless—that bear on one another and together have broad implications for the well-being of the community as a whole. For both practical policy-makers and republican champions of freedom from domination and dependence, in sum, there is ample reason to believe that the local community should be at the heart of the attempt to build community wealth by overcoming homelessness.

NOTES

1. I am grateful to my Jepson School colleagues, and particularly Thad M. Williamson, for comments on earlier drafts of this chapter.
2. For other dimensions of the concept of community, see Dagger (2009), esp. pp. 311–17.
3. The central reference for social capital is Putnam (2000). See esp. p. 19, where Putnam notes:

    The term *social capital* itself turns out to have been independently invented at least six times over the twentieth century, each time to call attention to the ways in which our lives are made more productive by social ties" (original emphasis). He also says, on the same page, that "social capital is closely related to what some have called 'civic virtue.' The difference is that 'social capital' calls attention to the fact that civic virtue is most powerful when embedded in a dense network of reciprocal social relations. A society of many virtuous but isolated individuals is not necessarily rich in social capital." It is likely, though, that the virtue of these isolated individuals would be something other than *civic* virtue.
4. Christopher Essert employs similar examples in Essert (2016), esp. pp. 273–4.
5. For helpful discussion of the problems of defining property and ownership, see Alexander and Peñalver (2012), esp. pp. 1–6.
6. See also Siegel (1991); Skolnik (2018); and Waldron (2000).
7. For discussion of this and the other elements of legality, see Fuller (1969), esp. pp. 70–79.
8. Pettit has elaborated and defended this conception of freedom in numerous works, the most accessible of which is Pettit (2014).
9. Tars and Egleson draw on evidence from Scotland's attempt to end homelessness, but recent evidence from Helsinki's housing-first program is also apposite (see, e.g., Henley, 2019).
10. For elaboration of this conception of democracy, see the essays in O'Neill and Williamson (2014) and Thomas (2016).
11. For details, see https://www.abbotsford.ca/community/housing_and_homel essness/Homelessness_Action_Plan.htm, accessed December 27, 2019. Thanks to Peggy Kohn for calling my attention to Abbotsford's efforts.

REFERENCES

Abbotsford, British Columbia, Canada (2014), *Homelessness Action Plan*, accessed December 27, 2019 at https://www.abbotsford.ca/community/housing_and _homelessness/Homelessness_Action_Plan.htm.

Alexander, Gregory and Eduardo Peñalver (2012), *An Introduction to Property Theory*, Cambridge, UK: Cambridge University Press.

Cicero (1999), *On the Commonwealth; and, On the Laws*, edited and translated by James E.G. Zetzel, Cambridge, UK: Cambridge University Press.

Dagger, Richard (2004), "Communitarianism and republicanism," in Gerald F. Gaus and Chandran Kukathas (eds), *Handbook of Political Theory*, London: SAGE Publications, pp. 167–79.

Dagger, Richard (2009), "Individualism and the claims of community," in Thomas Christiano and John Christman (eds), *Contemporary Debates in Political Philosophy*, Malden, MA: Wiley-Blackwell, pp. 303–21.

Essert, Christopher (2016), "Property and homelessness," *Philosophy and Public Affairs*, 44(4), 266–95.

Fuller, Lon (1969), *The Morality of Law*, New Haven, CT: Yale University Press.

Henley, Jon (2019), "'It's a miracle': Helsinki's radical solution to homelessness," *The Guardian*, 3 June, accessed 21 January 2020 at https://www.theguardian.com/cities/2019/jun/03/its-a-miracle-helsinkis-radical-solution-to-homelessness.

Honoré, Anthony Maurice (1961), "Ownership," in Anthony Gordon Guest (ed.), *Oxford Essays in Jurisprudence*, Oxford: Oxford University Press, pp. 107–47.

National Law Center on Homelessness and Poverty (2018), *Public Property/Public Need: A Toolkit for Using Vacant Federal Property to End Homelessness*, accessed July 1, 2020 at https://nlchp.org/wp-content/uploads/2018/10/Public-Property-Public-Need.pdf.

O'Neill, Martin and Thad Williamson (2014), *Property-Owning Democracy: Rawls and Beyond*, Malden, MA: Wiley-Blackwell.

Pettit, Philip (2014), *Just Freedom: A Moral Compass for a Complex World*, New York. W.W. Norton & Co.

Putnam, Robert (2000), *Bowling Alone: The Collapse and Revival of American Community*, New York: Simon & Schuster.

Radin, Margaret Jane (1982), "Property and personhood," *Stanford Law Review*, 34(5), 957–1015.

Radin, Margaret Jane (1993), *Reinterpreting Property*, Chicago, IL: University of Chicago Press.

Rawls, John (1993), *Political Liberalism*, New York: Columbia University Press.

Rousseau, Jean-Jacques (1762 [1978]), *On the Social Contract*, edited by R.D. Masters, translated by J.R. Masters, New York: St. Martin's Press.

Siegel, Norman (1991), "Homelessness: its origins, civil liberties problems and possible solutions," *Villanova Law Review*, 36(5), 1063–84.

Skolnick, Terry (2016), "Homelessness and the impossibility to obey the law," *Fordham Urban Law Journal*, 43(3), 741–87.

Skolnick, Terry (2018), "How and why homeless people are regulated differently," *Queen's Law Journal*, 43(2), 297–324.

Tars, Eric and Caitlin Egleson (2009), "Great Scot! The Scottish plan to end homelessness and lessons for the housing rights movement in the United States," *Georgetown Journal on Poverty Law and Policy*, 16(1), 187–216.

Taylor, Michael (1982), *Community, Anarchy and Liberty*, Cambridge, UK: Cambridge University Press.

Thomas, Alan (2016), *Republic of Equals: Predistribution and Property-Owning Democracy*, Oxford: Oxford University Press.

Waldron, Jeremy (1991), "Homelessness and the issue of freedom," *UCLA Law Review*, 39(2), 295–324.

Waldron, Jeremy (2000), "Homelessness and community," *University of Toronto Law Journal*, 50(4), 371–406.

Wollstonecraft, Mary (1792 [1997]), *The Vindications: The Rights of Men, The Rights of Woman*, edited by D.L. Macdonald and K. Scherf (eds), Peterborough, ON: Broadview Press.

PART IV

The politics of democratic reform

8. Achieving accountability—or not—in contemporary times

Kenneth P. Ruscio

It was only 30 years ago, roughly a generation, that the fall of the Berlin Wall and the collapse of communist rule signaled—or seemed to signal—the ascendancy of liberal democracy. The rule of law, protection of fundamental rights, freedom of expression and religion, and the belief that authority legitimately resides with the governed rather than the governors—were all principles that had achieved unrivalled status as the cornerstones of political life. Those countries not yet democracies soon would be. How could they possibly resist the tide? Not only was the moral argument won, but also democracies promised economic prosperity, at least compared to the decrepit conditions in late-century authoritarian states. Winston Churchill's faint praise of democracy as the "worst form of government except for all the others that have been tried" seemed uncharitable. Democracy was, many felt, the best form of government, not just the least worst. The evidence was obvious and compelling.

But the script changed. The "end of history" story gave way to "the end of the democratic century" (Fukuyama, 1992; Mounk and Foa, 2018). Watching the fall of the Berlin Wall, the dissolution of the USSR, the end of the Cold War, and the rising influence of the United States as the sole superpower in the 1990s, few would have predicted that in 2020 there would be so many concerns whether democracy can work. The Great Recession dented democracy's armor. Adam Tooze, the economic historian, believes the economic shock over a decade ago ushered in a governance crisis today. "Since 2007," he writes, "the scale of the financial crisis has placed the relationship between democratic politics and the demands of capitalist governance under strain." He looked in vain for the political leadership capable of addressing "unpopular but necessary actions" within as well as across countries (Tooze, 2018, p. 614). Moreover, as Mounk and Foa (2018, p. 4) point out, in 1990 countries rated "not free" accounted for only 12 percent of global income. By 2018, their share had increased to 33 percent. Maybe other forms of governance could be as effective as those complex, cumbersome, plodding, polarized, and highly regulated democracies.

But the moral argument suffered as much as, if not more than, the economic one. Populists, authoritarians, and nationalists prevailed over liberal democrats. Skepticism about the rule of law, impatience with institutional structures of policy-making, and questions about the definition of citizenship and whose rights should be protected—all led to a rejection, sometimes direct and sometimes indirect, of those long-standing touchstones. A columnist noting the recent electoral successes of Donald Trump in America, Viktor Orbán in Hungary, Jair Bolsonaro in Brazil, and others with equally wavering devotion to democratic ideals worried that democracy "does not have to die in darkness. It can also be starved of oxygen in well-lit polling booths" (Luce, 2019).

Democracies haven't vanished. At least so far. But their weakening means a weaker commitment to the principles that gave rise to them in the first place. Asking whether democracy works leads to asking whether the rationale for democracy still resonates. One of those principles is that government and its leaders must be held accountable.

THE BASIS FOR ACCOUNTABILITY

At the heart of liberal constitutional democracy are several beliefs. Individuals consent to being governed. They do so in order to be protected from harm and to be secure in the exercise of their rights. They possess those rights by virtue of their humanity, not because a political authority has seen fit to bestow them. If government fails to secure the people's rights or violates them in the exercise of its own powers, citizens may justifiably withdraw their consent.

And so (to paraphrase Thomas Jefferson): there are self-evident truths; all persons are created equal and endowed with certain inalienable rights; among these are life, liberty, property, and the pursuit of happiness; to secure those rights, governments are instituted and derive their just powers from the governed; and whenever a government becomes destructive of those ends, it is the right of the people to alter or abolish it.

Jefferson did his own deriving, of course, in this case from the work of John Locke. Locke's early writings, especially the *Second Treatise on Government*, are the pillars upon which liberal democratic thought rests to this day. Any grant of power to a political authority is conditional, the result of an agreement—a contract of sorts—and it depends upon abiding by the terms of the contract. Governments are constrained:

> And so whoever has the legislative or supreme power of any common-wealth, is bound to govern by established standing laws, promulgated and known to the people, and not by extemporary decrees; by indifferent and upright judges, who are to decide controversies by those laws; and to employ the force of the community at home, only in the execution of such laws, or abroad to prevent or redress foreign injuries, and secure the community from inroads and invasion. And all this to

be directed to no other end, but the peace, safety, and public good of the people. (Locke, 1689 [1764], Book II, Chapter 9, §131)

Locke was a realist, however. He understood there would be occasions, especially in times of crisis, when the formal constraints imposed on leaders and governments would be ambiguous or irrelevant. Stuff happens. Unforeseen problems arise inevitably and often require quick action, not the deliberative, intentional, careful balancing of interests on the ponderous path to compromise. Leaders must be accountable but must also have the ability to act in the absence of specific guidance from the people or the legislature. The balancing of power and constraint, not the exclusion of one for the other, was always part of liberal democratic theory. A constitution cannot be a suicide pact.

Locke (ibid., §160) called it the prerogative power of the executive:

> This power to act according to discretion, for the public good, without the prescription of the law, and sometimes even against it, is that which is called prerogative: for since in some governments the lawmaking power is not always in being, and is usually too numerous, and so too slow, for the dispatch requisite to execution; and because also it is impossible to foresee, and so by laws to provide for, all accidents and necessities that may concern the public, or to make such laws as will do no harm, if they are executed with an inflexible rigour, on all occasions, and upon all persons that may come in their way; therefore there is a latitude left to the executive power, to do many things of choice which the laws do not prescribe.

When Abraham Lincoln, for example, enlarged the army and navy beyond their authorized strength, spent public money without appropriation, suspended *habeas corpus*, and otherwise proceeded without clear authority at the outbreak of the Civil War, he justified his actions in precisely these terms. The occasion for his remarks to Congress was an extraordinary one, and while he conceded he might have overstepped his formal constraints, his higher duty to preserve the Union justified the breach; the greater breach would have been to watch passively as many laws were broken because of the overly prudent desire to abide by just one. "Must a government, of necessity, be too *strong* for the liberties of its own people, or too *weak* to maintain its own existence?" he asked (Lincoln, 1861 [1953], p. 426; original emphasis).

But it was indeed the extraordinary set of circumstances, not the everyday pressures of tough dilemmas that led Lincoln to color outside the lines of normal decision-making. And as the historian Arthur Schlesinger later explained in his classic work, *The Imperial Presidency*, the object of a liberal constitutional democracy is to have leaders who are neither puppets nor czars, who act strongly but responsibly and wisely, always guided, as Locke first noted, by the public interest. When emergencies arise, presidents—for those are the executives Schlesinger had in mind—who venture into the land of prerogative must, therefore, check off certain boxes: "the threat must be unquestionably dire; time must be unquestionably of the essence; Congress must be unable or unwilling to prescribe a national course; the problem must be one that can be met in no other way; and the President must do everything he can to explain himself to Congress and the American people" (Schlesinger, 1973 [2004], p. 323).

And, Schlesinger argued, a president "must not be encouraged to treat every trouble as if it were a crisis or be led to suppose that everything he does in response to a crisis thereby becomes constitutional" (ibid.). In short, whatever the simplicity and clarity offered by the theory of accountability, in practice it becomes complicated by the messiness of circumstances, by the leader's surplus or deficit of trust. The use of prerogative is rare and extraordinary, the exception that proves the rule that in times of normal democratic decision making, the sometimes convoluted and cumbersome mechanisms required by accountability must prevail.

WHY WE SEEK ACCOUNTABILITY

The democratic justification for holding leaders accountable rests on two presumptions. One is that governments make mistakes. They are fallible. Leaders will try hard and will occasionally enjoy modest success and progress, but they usually fall short of their highest aspirations and must revise and adjust their approaches. The theory of democracy does not rest on the perfectibility of people or those who govern them; rather, it accepts their limitations. The other presumption is that leaders always have the opportunity and often the propensity to abuse the powers granted them. Without constraints on power—and the safeguards to react if those constraints are violated—tyranny and corruption are likely, if not inevitable.

The Fallibilist Presumption

George Washington was hardly a reticent leader. A reluctant one perhaps. Called out of retirement time and again, whether to head the Constitutional Convention or the new Republic, he always demurred before being finally convinced to accept yet another position of responsibility. Mount Vernon was his refuge; the call to civic duty and the sacrifice of a private life for a public one were burdens sacrificially borne—perceived obligations rather than a lust for power or recognition. But reluctance should not be confused with timidity. He was confident in his abilities, assured in his leadership, and embracing of the responsibilities once assumed.

So, it is of some significance that he ended his public life with an apology for his mistakes. At the conclusion of his famous Farewell Address, in a passage overshadowed by the advice to avoid entangling alliances and the evils of partisanship, the general who had won the War for Independence and whose presidency stabilized the emerging democracy, asked for forgiveness:

> Though I am unconscious of intentional error, I am nevertheless too sensible of my defects not to think it probable that I have committed many errors. Whatever they may be I fervently beseech the Almighty to avert or mitigate the evils to which they may tend. I shall also carry with me the hope that my Country will never cease to view them with indulgence, and that after forty-five years of my life dedicated to its Service, with an upright zeal, the faults of my incompetent abilities will be consigned to oblivion, as myself must be to the Mansions of rest. (Washington, 1796 [1997], p. 977)

Thomas Jefferson was so certain of making mistakes he didn't wait until the end of his presidency to seek forgiveness. He began it that way in his First Inaugural Address. Humbled by the responsibilities of the office he was to assume, he admitted he needed the help—the wisdom—of those surrounding him, his cabinet, and the legislators. He knew "that it will rarely fall to the lot of imperfect man to retire from this station with the reputation and the favor which bring him into it." He predicted he would often "go wrong through defect of judgment." And therefore, "I ask your indulgence for my own errors, which will never be intentional, and your support against the errors of others" (Jefferson, 1801 [1990], pp. 169–70).

Washington's and Jefferson's self-awareness of their personal fallibility was a reflection of the type of government they were fashioning. Democracy assumes leaders, citizens, or the institutions will never achieve perfection. No law would ever be perfect; no leader would ever have a mythic combination of abilities and judgment; no philosopher-king was waiting in the wings. On the contrary, democracy will repeatedly fall short. That may be a simple recognition of the modest capacities of individuals, their flawed nature, and therefore the modest capacities and flawed nature of any government they establish. As Madison (1788a [1987], pp. 319–20) famously wrote, "But what is government itself but the greatest of all reflections on human nature? If men were angels, no government would be necessary. If angels were to govern men, neither external nor internal controls on government would be necessary." Government of the people, by the people, and for the people does not flow from the presumption of the infinite wisdom of the governed or the governors but rather their imperfections.

When Alexis de Tocqueville left France in the 1830s to observe the new democracy called the United States, he couldn't help but notice more than a few complexities. For one thing, the freedom of the press was remarkable, certainly different from what he knew back in the old-world aristocracies. But that freedom brought dangers, among them a press that could excite the passions and emotions rather than appeal to the reason of the people. On the other hand, censorship in a land of universal sovereignty and freedom of opinion and expression was dangerous, if not impossible. Caught between the rock and the hard place of "servitude and license," Tocqueville could find no middle ground, no way to rein in the press a little without infringing on its freedom a lot. And so, he concluded, the benefit of an inevitably unchained press, the reason to accept the risks it created, "was for the evils it prevents much more than the good it does" (Tocqueville, 1835 [2002], p. 172).

So, too, with democracy in general. The leaders chosen by the people were not the most distinguished or capable. Aristocracies like the one Tocqueville knew in France were ruled by leaders with both talents and virtues who were "more skillful in the science of the legislator than democracy can be." But democratic leaders were in touch with the interests of the people, and while talents and virtues were important, if leaders did not understand and work on behalf of the people, the "virtues could become almost useless and the talents fatal" (Tocqueville, 1835 [2002], p. 222). Seeking protection from the worst mistakes of inevitably fallible leaders was a far more prudent approach than searching in vain for the one who gets it just right. The processes of democracy are imperfect and, therefore, so its outcomes will be imperfect.

But, Tocqueville (1835 [2002], p. 216) concluded, the "great privilege of the Americans is to be able to have repairable mistakes." As one contemporary theorist, David Runciman (2018, p. 186), explained, drawing directly from the work of the French observer:

> Even if democracy is often bad at coming up with the right answers, it is good at unpicking the wrong ones. Moreover, it is good at exposing people who think they always know best. Democratic politics assumes there is no settled answer to any question and it ensures that is the case by allowing everyone a vote, including the ignorant. The randomness of democracy—which remains its essential quality— protects us against getting stuck with truly bad ideas. It means that nothing will last for long, because something else will come along to disrupt it.

In his work, *The Passions and Constraints*, Stephen Holmes elevates this core proposition to a central place in contemporary liberal theory. It is, he believes, a defining quality of constitutional democracy, the essence of its legitimacy and durability, a recognition that what some may view as a less than glorious defense of democracy is actually its most compelling rationale. We "embrace constitutionalism not only because it increases the probability of intelligent decision making, but also because it maximizes the opportunity for correction later on," he writes. He continues:

> The present electoral majority will submit to irritating criticism of its decision by the opposition because it knows it may want to change its mind in the future and that

it needs to hear and consider, on an ongoing basis, possible reasons for doing so. Constitutional democracy, in short, is a fallibilist democracy [...] Constitutionalism is a technique. It assumes that the passions of men will not conform to the dictates of reason and justice without constraint. It is the way a democratic nation strives to make itself into a community that can continue to learn and adapt itself intelligently to unfamiliar circumstances as they arise. (Holmes, 1996, p. 274)

The inevitability of mistakes and the need to correct them call for one form of accountability. Public officials will err, sometimes in minor and easily corrected ways and sometimes in severe ways that call into question their competence and our continued consent to their governing. When additional information or new conditions require nothing more than a simple recalibration, leaders should adjust and join in the collective effort to achieve accountability. Such leaders possess a kind of public humility, neither arrogance nor timidity, but enough of a sense of self to modify policy or strategy. It helps when they share the temperament of a Jefferson or Washington, well aware their own leadership should be measured not by their infinite wisdom but by their ability to learn from and respond to setbacks.

When leaders' mistakes are more severe, significant, or harmful, there could well be a need for a more forceful reaction: a change in the laws, a change in administrators, or a change in leadership through an election. But never in these cases are the accountability steps punitive, which is how we often think of "holding leaders accountable." Accountability in response to the fallibilist presumption is an ordinary correction achieved through ordinary politics. Under the second presumption, however, things get more complicated.

The Tyrannical Presumption

Politics is like dice: the better the player the worse the man. (Sansom, 2010, p. 55)

James Madison was trying to thread the needle. In *The Federalist Papers*, he had to make the case that the people were capable of governing themselves and choosing able leaders. Indeed, it would have been odd to argue the contrary in the name of democracy. "As there is a degree of depravity in mankind which requires a certain degree of circumspection and mistrust," Madison (1788b [1987], p. 339) wrote, "so there are other qualities in human nature which justify a certain portion of esteem and confidence. Republican government presupposes the existence of these qualities in a higher degree than any other form." In his view, there was "sufficient virtue" for self-government.

And yet, Madison knew all about the self-interest that led to factions, about the dynamics of power that made it necessary to divide governmental functions so that the ambition of one branch would check the ambition of another. He worried about the tendency of people to act on their passions and emotions rather than their reason. It was in the nature of individuals as well as the nature of how they act collectively. "Had every Athenian citizen been a Socrates," Madison (1788b [1987], p. 336) remarked, "every Athenian assembly would still have been a mob." A self-governing democracy was a precarious proposition that, at one and the same time, granted power to leaders and protected citizens from the inevitable tendencies for leaders to abuse that power.

Alexander Hamilton faced the same dilemma. Yes, there would be energy in the executive under the proposed Constitution, but the office would seldom "fall to the lot of any man who is not in an eminent degree endowed with the requisite qualifications [...] there will be a constant probability of seeing the station filled by characters pre-eminent for ability and virtue" (Hamilton, 1788a [1987], p. 395). And yet, "The history of human conduct does not warrant that exalted opinion of human virtue which would make it wise in a nation to commit interests of so delicate and momentous a kind, as those which concern its intercourse with the rest of the world, to the sole disposal of a magistrate created and circumscribed as would be a President of the United States" (Hamilton, 1788b [1987], pp. 425–6). He worried, too, about the tendencies of leaders who appeal duplicitously to the people, vowing to protect their rights in their glorious promises but in reality "paying an obsequious court to the people, commencing demagogues and ending tyrants" (Hamilton, 1787 [1987], p. 89).

In the often-overlooked *Federalist Paper #64*, written by the often-overlooked John Jay, the high-wire act of the Founders found one of its most vivid expressions. Jay, the seasoned diplomat, was explaining why the Constitution's provisions for negotiating and approving treaties were sound, even as the critics thought too much discretion and power had been granted to the executive branch. There were practical reasons. Delicate discussions with foreign entities required secrecy and flexibility. Treaties were essentially bargains struck, and if a legislature demanded either fully transparent discussions or the authority to constantly revise or walk away entirely from the bargain, the position of the new democracy would be untenable on the international stage. Wise and experienced administrators would have to be granted a degree of trust.

They would deserve that trust because corruption "is not supposable." Perish the thought, Jay seemed to say. For someone to imagine that administrators would not act in the best interests of their country, "he must either have been very unfortunate in his intercourse with the world, or possess a heart very susceptible of such impressions." Those entrusted with these important responsibilities deserve and require proper authority. "Every consideration that can influence the human mind, such as honor, oaths, reputations, conscience, the love of country, and family affections and attachments, afford security for their fidelity," Jay asserted. They will be "men of talents and integrity," and therefore the treaties they produce will be as good as they possibly could be

(Jay, 1788 [1987], pp. 379–80). But then in a remarkable pirouette, after a few pages of explaining why officials deserve trust, Jay turned to the skeptics and advised them in a blunt sentence or two not to worry: "So far as the fear of punishment and disgrace can operate, that motive to good behaviour is amply afforded by the article on the subject of impeachments" (ibid., p. 380). If leaders violate the trust, the Constitution provides the remedy.

When it came to predicting the character, virtues, and talents of leaders in the newly formed democracy, Madison, Hamilton, and Jay hoped for the best but prepared for the worst. How could the new government cultivate the highest virtues of public officials while guarding against the likelihood that even the best could abuse the power granted to them? At some cost to government's efficiency, at some cost to its ability to act with dispatch, at some cost even to its capacity to achieve great things, it was important to prevent leaders from doing bad things contrary to the public interest.

Many years later, in *Ex parte Milligan* (1866), Justice Davis put it best: the nation had "no right to expect that it will always have wise and humane rulers, sincerely attached to the principles of the Constitution. Wicked men, ambitious of power, with hatred of liberty and law, may fill the place once occupied by Washington and Lincoln" (US Supreme Court Reports, 1866). Which brings us to the present day.

THE CONTEMPORARY CHALLENGE

I think it's great. Maybe we'll want to give that a shot someday. (President Trump on China's president, Xi Jinping, when Xi was designated "president for life," cited in Perlex, 2018)

I can tell you, knowing the president for a good 25 or 30 years, that he would love to have the situation that Viktor Orbán has, but he doesn't. (David B. Cornstein, US ambassador to Hungary, cited in Baker, 2019)

Our constitutional system never contemplated a President like Donald Trump. (Toobin, 2019)

It is difficult these days to step back from the deluge of headlines, tweetstorms, investigations, careening shifts in domestic and international policies and strategies, revelations, scandals, personalities, cable news competition, battles between the parties, and even the pending presidential election. Overreacting to the current political chaos is a constant risk. The democratic system in the United States has endured crises before. Those who lived through a Civil War, prior impeachments, the Depression, the Great Recession, or bitter disputes over foreign interventions might wonder if this is any worse. Then, as now, there were credible cries of alarm and foreboding, charges that the executives had overstepped their authority or that the courts and legislatures had acted ineffectively or inappropriately.

The current angst is also undoubtedly colored by the deliberately polarizing personality of the elected president. He generates intense opposition or support because of his temperament, attitudes, and impulses as much as for his policies and philosophies. He divides rather than unites. He craves the coverage and is most comfortable with an adversary to oppose or blame. He measures success by the attention he receives and welcomes any reaction, especially an overreaction.

But there is also the risk of discounting the severity of the present challenge. If Jeffrey Toobin is correct that the constitutional system never anticipated a president like Trump, then we are facing a constitutional crisis, but not one defined simply as a subpoena showdown between the executive and Congress. It may be much larger. Antagonism to a free press, resisting the authority of Congress, questioning the integrity of the electoral process, politicizing the courts and law enforcement, and using the powers of the office to investigate and impugn opponents should be seen not as separate daily outrages in isolation from each other, but as a pattern.[1] They reflect not necessarily a methodical Machiavellian plot to seize power, for that may grant the president more credit for purposeful thinking than he deserves (Frank Bruni, 2019 describes his reasoning process as "more narcissistic than syllogistic"). It may be instead a governing style completely at odds with one suited for a liberal democracy.

When a president—and, it must be said, his defenders—reject the very premises of accountability in a democracy; and when, because of their positions, they have the capacity to throw sand in the gears of the processes, the challenges are formidable. Can the mechanisms drawn for a liberal democracy check a president who rejects the underlying values of the system he was elected to lead? Can a president so reflexively inclined toward authoritarianism and illiberal democracy be held accountable within the normal processes and established structures of a liberal democracy?

As an example, consider the recently declared national emergency at the southern border of the United States, an extraordinary step by the president in response to a congressional refusal to appropriate funds to build a wall the president felt was necessary to stop the flow of immigrants. Both houses of Congress—the Democratic-controlled House and the Republican-controlled Senate—denied the president's request, mainly on grounds that it was a misdirected and simplistic solution to a complex problem. In response, the president forced a governmental shutdown and threatened to declare a national emergency if Congress did not acquiesce. That step presumably would give him the authority to build the wall over the objections of Congress.

Consistent with at least the basic logic of Locke's view of prerogative, presidents have had the authority to declare national emergencies in recent history and have done so typically in response to either foreign threats or natural disasters. Once the immediate threat was addressed, the declarations often remained on the books with little practical long-term effect. Many were essentially forgotten or left by the wayside. By the mid-1970s there were 580 emergencies in force, including Roosevelt's during the Depression, Truman's during the Korean War, and Johnson's and Nixon's during Vietnam. Taken together, one senator argued in 1973 that they "confer the power to rule this country without reference to normal constitutional processes" (US Senate, 1973, p. 1). The extraordinary was becoming ordinary.

In 1976, as part of the legislative correction to the overreach of executive power during the Nixon presidency, and perhaps in a classic expression of what Madison might have seen as ambition counteracting ambition, Congress passed the National Emergency Act. A president could still declare a national emergency. But congressional participation in the decision was enlarged, not at the point where immediate action was called for, but during a subsequent period when the legislature had the opportunity to weigh in. A concurrent resolution by Congress requiring a simple majority in both houses would bring an end to the emergency.

In testimony during the committee hearings that took up the proposed bill, the constitutional scholar Robert S. Rankin told of the time when as a boy he drove a car for a country doctor. He once noticed a bottle of morphine in the doctor's bag. The doctor described it as one of the most powerful medicines he had. Used correctly, the doctor explained, it relieves pain. Abused, it brings great suffering. Rankin likened it to emergency powers: "Used properly and within bounds set up by the Constitution it becomes restorative in nature and has a proper place within a democracy. Used improperly it is the very essence of tyranny" (ibid., p. 8). In those same hearings, Senator Mathias noted, "When you look at the Constitution itself, it is cast primarily as a series of prohibitions. It recognizes the weakness of men who hold power. These prohibitions are an attempt to limit those weaknesses of men who hold this power" (ibid., p. 13). Senator Church pointed to the Vietnam War and the "very big mistakes" presidents can make. "There is no degree of infallibility vested in the Chief Executive of this country, or his advisers. The Founding Fathers were right when they undertook to divide the powers of government between the three branches, guarding against excessive mistakes in any one place" (ibid., p. 16).

The National Emergency Act of 1976 was a statute that hoped for the best among chief executives but prepared for the worst. It was a legislative check on executive power. In 1983, the Supreme Court complicated the process. In *INS* v. *Chadha*, a case not directly related to the National Emergency Act, it declared legislative vetoes unconstitutional. That is, a concurrent resolution such as the one called for in the 1976 Act was not, in the court's view, consistent with the original intention of the system of checks and balances.

If Congress wanted to nullify a national emergency, it must pass a law; but that would require a president's signature. The president could instead veto the legislation—a more likely step if the president had claimed an emergency existed in the first place. Then, of course, Congress could execute its will only with a two-thirds vote. A simple majority for a concurrent resolution would not be enough. The executive regained some leverage and Congress's check was weakened (Pildes, 2019).

President Trump's declaration of the emergency and his subsequent successful veto of Congress's bill declaring the emergency void is noteworthy, not necessarily because he possibly exceeded his formal authority. That remains to be seen. When Congress has expressed its intentions, as it did when it refused to provide funds for the construction of a wall, and when it acts in accordance with one of its expressed powers, which in this instance is the power of the purse, it is generally understood that the burden on a president to find ways around the legislative branch gets considerably heavier, or so courts have ruled in the past. They will undoubtedly have the chance to consider that question in this matter.

But whether or not the president exceeded his formal authority, the declaration of a national emergency over border-wall funding is of a piece with his propensity to stretch to the breaking point well-established norms of democratic leadership. Well before the Trump presidency, Arthur Schlesinger (1973 [2004], p. 458) put it well: "The perennial question is how to distinguish real crises threatening the life of the republic from nightmares troubling the minds of paranoid presidents."[2] Bypassing Congress, stoking the perception of a crisis, expressing offense because of the resistance to a pet project, and worrying about his loss of face, the president's steps were both an escalation of previous actions to push against the boundaries of reasonable executive behavior and a foreshadowing of even greater ones to come, such as the Ukraine affair and the subsequent attempted impeachment of the president.

The Trump presidency raises fundamental problems for accountability in modern American democracy. For all its ingenuity, the American constitutional system of checks and balances is not self-executing. Madison (1788c [1987], p. 312) himself warned that "a mere demarcation on parchment of the constitutional limits of the several departments is not a sufficient guard against those encroachments which lead to a tyrannical concentration of all the powers of government in the same hands." Institutions matter, but so do the people who reside within them. The hope expressed by the Founders that leaders of the newly formed democracy would possess a set of virtues suitable for leadership was not simply a rhetorical strategy of advocacy to convince the public to support a proposed constitution. They knew a limited, constrained government resting on the consent of the governed required leaders with a kind of public humility who could acknowledge and learn from mistakes and act with an awareness of their own fallibility and the imperfections of the political system.

Steven Levitsky and Daniel Ziblatt have argued persuasively that democracy in general, and American democracy in particular, requires leaders to embrace the norm of forbearance. They should refrain from always using every lever of formal power in their arsenal and be mindful of the need to cultivate a broad respect for the principles of a democracy (Levitsky and Ziblatt, 2018, pp. 106–9). Those principles include using power for the greater public good and not the self-aggrandizement of the person who holds the power. Violating the norm of forbearance may yield short-term advantages for the ruler but at the expense of overall respect for the democratic institutions exploited by the ruler. Exercising forbearance requires, however, a democratic disposition, the kind of public humility shown by a Washington, Jefferson, or Lincoln, and more recently expressed by Michael Ignatieff (2013, pp. 180–81), whose own experience in Canadian politics led him to this realization:

> You are the custodian of a democracy, of a relationship of trust with the people, but also of the institutions of your country. If you get to serve in a legislature, try not to forget the wonder you felt on your first day, when you took your seat and you understood it was the votes of ordinary people that put you there. Try to remember, too, that you are not smarter than your institutions. They are there to make you better than you are. Respect for traditions, for the rules, even some of the silly ones, is part of respect for the sovereignty of the people and for the democracy that keeps us free. Respect for the institution means you shoulder an obligation to treat your adversaries as opponents, never as enemies.

In seeking accountability we typically look for bright legalistic/constitutional lines. If a leader has violated the law or exceeded the formal bounds of power in a technical sense or even just made simple errors, the corrective steps are easier to execute and explain. They flow from the presumption of fallibility.

But when a leader's repeated actions erode the legitimacy of the political system and when it begins to appear that the individual's intentions behind the use of power are for self-aggrandizement, it calls upon a hazier but even more fundamental standard for pursuing accountability, a political or even a moral standard that flows from the presumption of authoritarian or even tyrannical tendencies. That is to say, a nation's public officials have a broad responsibility to democracy and its values, and threats to the system's values require public officials to go beyond the usual calculus of political self-interest and expediency and recognize the overriding danger to the system. A bright legalistic line is often an inadequate guide in such cases. The pattern becomes more significant than any individual act.

When the United States set up internment camps for Japanese in America during World War II, and the action was challenged in the Supreme Court case of *Toyosaburo Korematsu* v. *US*, Justice Robert Jackson (1944) wrote—sadly, in a dissenting opinion—"The chief restraint upon those who command the physical forces of their country, in the future as in the past, must be their responsibility to the political judgments of their contemporaries and to the moral judgments of history." One must wonder whether we have reached that point today where holding a president accountable is appropriately based on political, even moral judgments, beyond any legalistic or constitutional bright line.

NOTES

1. On using the powers of the office to investigate political opponents, Harvard law professor and constitutional scholar Jack Goldsmith commented, "It's a terrible breach of norms for the president to publicly advocate prosecutions of his opponents" (Haberman et al., 2019).
2. Revisiting Schlesinger's classic work, *The Imperial Presidency*, during the present is informative in many ways. In the first edition in 1973, he wrote: "We have noted that corruption appears to visit the White House in fifty year cycles [...] Around the year 2023 the American people would be advised to go on the alert and start nailing down everything in sight." His prediction was well within a reasonable margin of error (Schlesinger, 1973, p. 458).

REFERENCES

Baker, Peter (2019), "Trump praises Hungary's Viktor Orbán, brushing aside criticism," *The New York Times*, May 13.

Bruni, Frank (2019), "Donald Trump is not America," *The New York Times*, May 15.

Fukuyama, Francis (1992), *The End of History and The Last Man*, New York: The Free Press.

Haberman, Maggie, Annie Karni, Kenneth P. Vogel and Katie Brenner (2019), "Trump's demands for investigations of opponents draw intensifying criticism," *The New York Times*, May 20.

Hamilton, Alexander (1787 [1987]), "Number I," in Isaac Kramnick (ed.), *The Federalist Papers*, London: Penguin Books, pp. 87–90.

Hamilton, Alexander (1788a [1987]), "Number LXVIII," in Isaac Kramnick (ed.), *The Federalist Papers*, London: Penguin Books, pp. 392–6.

Hamilton, Alexander (1788b [1987]), "Number LXXV," in Isaac Kramnick (ed.), *The Federalist Papers*, London: Penguin Books, pp. 424–8.

Holmes, Stephen (1996), *Passions and Constraints: On the Theory of Liberal Democracy*, Chicago, IL: University of Chicago Press.

Ignatieff, Michael (2013), *Fire and Ashes: Success and Failure in Politics*, Cambridge, MA: Harvard University Press.

Jackson, Robert (1944), "Dissenting opinion," in *Korematsu* v. *US*, 323 US 214, accessed December 19, 2019 at https://www.law.cornell.edu/supremecourt/text/323/214#writing-USSC_CR_0323_0214_ZD2.

Jay, John (1788 [1987]), "Number LXIV," in Isaac Kramnick (ed.), *The Federalist Papers*, London: Penguin Books, pp. 375–80.

Jefferson, Thomas (1801 [1990]), "First inaugural address," in *Jefferson: Public and Private Papers*, New York: Vintage Books, pp. 166–70.

Levitsky, Steven and Daniel Ziblatt (2018), *How Democracies Die*, New York: Crown.

Lincoln, Abraham (1861 [1953]), "Message to Congress in Special Session, July 4, 1861," in Roy B. Basler (ed.) and Marion Dolores Pratt and Lloyd A. Dunlap (assistant eds), *The Collected Works of Abraham Lincoln, Volume 4*, New Brunswick, NJ: Rutgers University Press, pp. 422–41, accessed December 19, 2019 at https://quod .lib.umich.edu/l/lincoln/lincoln4/1:741?rgn=div1;view=fulltext.

Locke, John (1689 [1764]), *Two Treatises of Government*, reprint, London: A. Millar et al., accessed December 19, 2019 at https://history.hanover.edu/texts/locke/j-l2 -001.html.

Luce, Edward (2019), "Donald Trump is building a populist global club," *The Financial Times*, April 11, accessed December 19, 2019 at https://www.ft.com/ content/19196876-5bee-11e9-9dde-7aedca0a081a.

Madison, James (1788a [1987]), "Number LI," in Isaac Kramnick (ed.), *The Federalist Papers*, London: Penguin Books, pp. 318–22.

Madison, James (1788b [1987]), "Number LV," in Isaac Kramnick (ed.), *The Federalist Papers*, London: Penguin Books, pp. 335–9.

Madison, James (1788c [1987]), "Number XLVIII," in Isaac Kramnick (ed.), *The Federalist Papers*, London: Penguin Books, pp. 308–12.

Mounk, Yascha and Roberto Stefan Foa (2018), "The end of the democratic century," *Foreign Affairs*, May/June, accessed October 11, 2018 at https://www.foreignaffairs .com/articles/2018-04-16/end-democratic-century.

Perlex, Jane (2018), "President for life? Trump's remarks about Xi find fans in China," *The New York Times*, March 4.

Pildes, Richard H. (2019), "The Supreme Court's contribution to the confrontation over emergency powers," *Lawfare* [blog], February 19, accessed February 21, 2019 at https://www.lawfareblog.com/supreme-courts-contribution-confrontation-over -emergency-powers.

Runciman, David (2018), *How Democracy Ends*, New York: Basic Books.

Sansom, C.J. (2010), *Heartstone*, New York: Viking.

Schlesinger, Arthur Jr. (1973 [2004]), *The Imperial Presidency*, reprint, Boston, MA: Mariner Reprint.

Tocqueville, Alexis de (1835 [2002]), *Democracy in America*, edited by Harvey C. Mansfield and Delba Winthrop, Chicago, IL: University of Chicago Press.

Toobin, Jeffrey (2019), "The constitutional system is not built to resist Trump's defiance of Congress," *The New Yorker*, May 10.

Tooze, Adam (2018), *Crashed: How a Decade of Financial Crisis Changed the World*, New York: Viking.

US Senate (1973), *National Emergency: Hearings Before the Special Committee on the Termination of the National Emergency of the United States Senate, Ninety-third Congress, First Session*, Washington, DC: US Government Printing Office.

US Supreme Court Reports (1866), *Ex parte Milligan*, 71 US 2, accessed December 19, 2019 at https://www.law.cornell.edu/supremecourt/text/71/2.

US Supreme Court Reports (1983), *INS* v. *Chadha*, 462 US 919, accessed December 19, 2019 at https://www.law.cornell.edu/supremecourt/text/462/919.

Washington, George (1796 [1997]), "Farewell address," in John Rhodehamel (ed.), *George Washington: Writings*, New York: Library of America, pp. 962–77.

9. Ranking ballots and policy juries: institutional reforms for further democratization in America

J.S. Maloy

The community wealth building (hereafter CWB) agenda is an important addition to the menu of reform for communities that wish to democratize—or re-democratize. Perhaps the most striking conceptual component of CWB, at least to the eyes of a scholar specializing in democratic theory and comparative politics, is *inclusive participation*. This principle, or something similar, has been central to many theories of democracy. In other words, it is a staple of imaginative efforts to democratize representative government. The reason is that representative government, both in intent and in effect, has always had a strong tendency (ironic to some observers, but difficult to ignore in any case) toward elite, oligarchic, or aristocratic forms of power—as far back as its seventeenth- and eighteenth-century appearances in Europe and North America (Maloy, 2008; Manin, 1997). The democratic deficits of our times occupy the latest chapter in a very long story.

But inclusive participation may be easier to conceptualize than to operationalize. Below I offer suggestions about how to conceptualize what would be required to close some of our democratic deficits, before turning to concrete proposals about how inclusive participation could be made operational in functioning political institutions. There are two specific sorts of institutional reform that might facilitate or complement the CWB agenda of democratic renovation in the United States, especially at the local level: ranking ballots and policy juries. Those who have followed political reform movements in the last 20 years have heard of ranked-choice voting, a specifically electoral type of reform, and citizens' assemblies or deliberative forums, which can be employed either outside of, or as adjuncts to, electoral processes. My contribution will be to make the connection between understanding how these reforms might affect the quality of democracy, through a comparative and global lens, and how they might actually function at the level of local government in American states, counties, and cities.

INSTITUTIONALIZED POPULAR INCLUSION

Political reform often requires institutional design, or rather redesign. The conceptual task of articulating what our goals are, and why we should expect them to be affected by particular institutional designs, comes before the operational task of designing and implementing reforms. I therefore begin with a proposed addendum to Barnes and Williamson's discussion of the concept of inclusive participation in Chapter 2 of this book.

In the last decade, I have been engaged with Devin Joshi and Timothy Peterson on a global and comparative analysis of "popular" vs "elite" democracies. This analysis examines national, constitutional, regime-level institutions, such as electoral systems and legislative structures. The key concept we use is *institutionalized popular inclusion*—a kindred concept to inclusive participation, with specific emphasis on the design of formal institutional structures. This research agenda is still a work in progress, but reviewing its conceptual premises and preliminary results may be useful for understanding the principle of inclusive participation in CWB.

The essence of our explanatory theory is that, under regimes with high levels of institutionalized popular inclusion (hereafter IPI), the political phenomenon of *elite dumping* should generally be found at low levels. Elite dumping occurs when a relatively small number of privileged citizens are able to unload heavy social costs onto a much larger number of ordinary citizens. Such costs may be personal and physical, as in human rights abuses, criminal justice sanctions, or public health outcomes. They may also be financial, as in fiscal policies concerning taxation and expenditure or levels of pecuniary corruption. Ecological degradation is another arena of elite dumping (often but not always) suffered by the many and imposed by the few. According to a long tradition of thought, most memorably associated with Machiavelli but also with numerous modern theorists, members of relatively small and cohesive factions within a community tend to use their superior wealth, education, and family reputation to create and entrench positions of privilege for themselves, even setting themselves against the interests of their more numerous but less distinguished and less talented neighbors when necessary. According to a shorter tradition of rational choice theory, it is natural (or at least rational) for any individual or group to reap benefits while free-riding on others' efforts to provide those benefits. Elite dumping may originate, therefore, in a variety of motives or impulses.

In the basic policy-making apparatus of a democratic regime, various ways of structuring legislative, executive, and electoral processes offer different degrees of room for maneuver to the political defenders of elite dumping. A low level of IPI characterizes an elite democracy; a high level of IPI characterizes a popular democracy. What makes a popular democracy special is an institutional environment in which elite agency and initiative are highly circumscribed by political pressures emanating from mass opinion.

In the global empirical analyses conducted so far, we have found that national-level democratic regimes with high levels of IPI tend to resist and restrict outcomes such as foreign military intervention (Joshi, Maloy and Peterson, 2015) and domestic human rights abuse (Joshi, Maloy and Peterson, 2019). The causal origin of these different outcomes appears to lie in three specific components of democratic regimes that show considerable variation around the world: voting access, electoral representation, and legislative structure (Joshi, Maloy and Peterson, 2019, pp. 115–16; see also Joshi, Maloy and Peterson, 2015, pp. 468–9):

1. *Voting access.* Democracies in general have converged on the formal model of universal adult suffrage, but further institutional variations make a significant difference for IPI. More popular democracies have instituted automatic voter registration and compulsory voting, rules that tend to reduce elites' room for maneuver in determining which segments of the population are more likely to cast ballots. More elite democracies have not adopted these rules, and constructing the electorate through selective strategies of voter mobilization and demobilization (by fair means or foul) is thereby enabled—becoming the focus of enormous time, energy, and money on the part of political professionals.
2. *Electoral representation.* More popular democracies elect legislators from multi-seat constituencies through proportional allocation rules, thereby opening up the halls of power to influence by a broad range of mass opinion. More elite democracies with single-seat constituencies, by contrast, allocate legislative representation through winner-take-all contests that manufacture silenced minorities (when 50 percent plus one obtains 100 percent of seated authority) as well as silent majorities (when a plurality, or less than 50 percent, obtains 100 percent of seated authority).
3. *Legislative structure.* More popular democracies make major legislative decisions through a unicameral structure, in which the primary assembly of elected representatives is relatively unimpeded by veto players. More elite democracies use multicameral legislative arrangements in which the popular assembly is "checked and balanced" by smaller, more elite bodies (such as senates, executives, and constitutional or quasi-legislative courts). To the extent that the real status quo of social and economic life tends to be inegalitarian, multicameralism offers protection for the privileges associated with elite dumping against the onslaughts of popular reform.

At this point we run into a limitation of the IPI framework for thinking about the kinds of democratic aspirations that the CWB agenda embodies. IPI, as laid out above, operates at the national-sovereign level of analysis, yet a great deal of democratic reform effort prioritizes subnational levels of political action. What we need to consider next is how to channel the conceptual spirit of IPI into the arena of subnational political institutions and processes.

DIRECT ELECTORAL REFORM: RANKED-CHOICE VOTING

Elite dumping is a broad social, economic, and political process at all levels of human endeavor, from the local to the global. Institutional room for elite maneuvering is the specifically political-structural aspect of communities large and small that, according to the theory behind IPI, enables elite dumping. IPI therefore implies a strategy of reducing elites' room for maneuver through institutional redesign. Since holding repeated competitive elections is the institutional core of all modern democratic systems, whether national or sub-national, what kinds of electoral reform would be compatible with CWB's principle of inclusive participation?

The theory behind IPI makes a clear distinction between proportional representation (PR) and single-seat plurality (SSP) types of electoral systems: the Netherlands represents an extreme form of the former, while the United States represents an extreme form of the latter. According to the explanatory theory of IPI described above, plurality systems tend to provide more favorable environments for the political defenders of elite dumping. But there are several problems with simply proposing PR as a reform in the American context. First, proportional electoral formulas work only with multi-member districts (with four or more seats filled per district, in most cases), but many citizens like having a single, easily identifiable representative for their locality. Second, important political offices such as mayor and governor are inherently single-seat choices, in which PR has no meaning or applicability. Third, proportional electoral systems usually share the same kind of ballot structure as plurality systems: an exclusive, all-or-nothing choice of one option on the ballot (i.e., the voter must pick one party under PR, one person under SSP).

This third point is usually overlooked, but crucial. To grasp its full import for the question of how inclusive participation is affected by the design of electoral institutions, consider the examples of Ireland and Australia: two countries that conduct both multi-seat and single-seat elections with a ranking type of ballot structure.

The Irish and Australian voting systems, with the single transferable vote (STV) in multi-seat districts and the alternative vote (AV) in single-seat races, use a multi-mark ballot structure with distributive input rules. With such an input rule, a voter's support for any given electoral contest may be distributed across more than one party or candidate, with each of the options supported potentially receiving varying fractions of the voter's total support (Maloy, 2019, ch. 4). By contrast, most American elections currently offer voters a single-mark, or exclusive, ballot structure, requiring the voter to give all or nothing, either 100 percent support or none at all. A ranking ballot uses one type of distributive input rule; grading and cumulative inputs are the other distributive types. My book *Smarter Ballots* presents a theoretical argument with empirical illustrations (Maloy, 2019, chs 3–5) for why, in general, the formal institution of distributive (or multi-mark) voting offers a higher level of structural accountability and voter empowerment than exclusive (or single-mark) voting.

Ireland and Australia (as well as the Mediterranean island of Malta) use ranking ballots for their national legislative elections (Bowler and Grofman, 2000). The British provinces of Scotland and Northern Ireland use STV in multi-seat districts for municipal and provincial elections, while some of the larger English cities use a version of AV for their mayoral elections (Lundberg, 2018). Several American cities also use the single-seat AV system, rebranded as ranked-choice voting (RCV) or instant runoff voting (IRV), to elect their mayors. And the voters of Maine's two U.S. House districts used RCV to elect their two representatives in 2018.

From the voter's vantage, the process is virtually identical under (multi-seat) STV or (single-seat) RCV. The voter is presented with a list of individual candidates for an office, be it mayor, councilor, or what have you. The voter's job is to rank candidates in the order of his or her preference: first choice, second choice, third choice, and so on. The voter can mark every single candidate, as long as each one gets a different ranking, or only one candidate. The number of marks on the ballot is entirely up to the voter; the general rule is that any and all candidates considered worthy should get some ranking, while any and all candidates considered unworthy should be left blank. Every candidate's first-choice rankings will be counted first, and those candidates with the weakest levels of support across the electorate as a whole will be eliminated, so that their supporters' votes can be transferred to their later preferences. As soon as one candidate collects a majority of all votes, whether they are first- or second- or third-choice votes, and so on, the election is over. If no one obtains an absolute majority, the eliminations and transfers proceed until only two candidates are left.

By comparison with the plurality vote or "first-past-the-post" system of American, British, and Canadian elections for national legislatures, the implications of ranking for the voter are rather dramatic. The possibility that a first-choice vote for your favorite candidate will be "wasted" if that candidate is not viable across the electorate as a whole is removed, since your vote would

Table 9.1   *Irish presidential election, 1990*

	1st Count	2nd Count	Total
Mary Robinson	612 265 (38.9%)	205 565 (13.0%)	817 830 (51.9%)
Brian Lenihan	694 484 (44.1%)	36 789 (2.3%)	731 273 (46.4%)
Austin Currie	267 902 (17.0%)	−242 354 (15.3%)	25 548 (1.7%)

Note: The number of second-choice votes transferred from Currie supporters was less than the total number of Currie's first-choice votes because 25 548 of those ballots (1.7% of all votes cast) did not indicate a second preference but left both remaining candidates blank.
Source: Took and Donnelly (2018).

then be transferred to another, more viable candidate. You the voter determine the order in which your vote gets transferred. As a result, there is no reason for anyone to discourage multiple qualified candidates from getting on the ballot: it is impossible to have a spoiler throw a close election to an unpopular candidate when vote splitting is ruled out by the formal structure of the input rules. In turn, that means voters should encounter fewer "lesser evil" choices where ranking ballots are used, since multiple candidacies per contest are not discouraged for fear of splitting the vote. The ranking inputs enable the transfers of votes, and the transfers of votes ensure that vote splitting and vote wasting are not a problem for voters to fret about when judging the candidates.

Consider the example of Mary Robinson's election as president of Ireland in 1990 (Table 9.1), or of Jean Quan's election as mayor of Oakland, California, in 2010. Robinson came second after the first count, but finished first after the second count, thanks to transfers from the third-place candidate, Austin Currie. Brian Lenihan voters complained that they would have won with a more restrictive, exclusive ballot. Because ranking ballots were in place, however, Currie voters never had to face the alternative of "wasting" their votes on their favored candidate or giving their first-choice votes to Robinson as a "lesser evil" option. Under a US-style election for mayor, governor, or presidential electors, Lenihan would have been the winner, Robinson the loser, and Currie the spoiler. A similar dynamic played out in Quan's leapfrog victory in Oakland, from a second-place position, when the third-place candidate's supporters overwhelmingly favored her compared to the initial leader. In Maine's second House district in 2018, Jared Golden earned a leapfrog win over an incumbent who failed to get a majority of first-choice votes, thanks to transfers from two independent candidates who finished third and fourth. Those independents were freed from the charge of being spoilers and wasters; instead, they became kingmakers.

As an additional example of the potential impact of ballot structure on electoral outcomes, consider the notorious presidential election of 2000 in the United States. The counterfactual of using ranking ballots rather than exclusive ballots to select statewide winners raises the intriguing possibility that up to 12 percent of all American states could have declared a different winner. In six states, the official winner's margin of victory was smaller than the number of votes cast for an ideologically opposed minor-party candidate. With second and third preferences counted after the elimination of their first choice, Ralph Nader's voters could have given victory to Al Gore in Florida and New Hampshire, while Pat Buchanan's voters could have made George W. Bush the winner of Iowa, New Mexico, Oregon, and Wisconsin. (For official state counts, see Berg-Andersson, 2020.)

What are the effects of distributive (multi-mark) ballots in general, and the ranking ballots of STV/RCV in particular, on elites' institutional room for maneuver? This is the key operational criterion for evaluating institutional structures in terms of democratic values like representation and accountability.

Though elections in general are often praised as powerful weapons of control for voters over politicians, the exclusive input rules of single-mark ballots have been a godsend to the cause of elite manipulation. With voters forced into all-or-nothing judgments, the list of options that actually appear on the ballot for a given contest becomes a powerful agenda-setting tool. Though having three or more candidates in a contest is good for voter choice, exclusive ballots make it possible for the spoiler logic to be deployed by larger parties against supporters of smaller parties: don't throw away your vote and hand a plurality victory to the greater of two evils. In this way, the range of issues up for electoral debate can be restricted, as smaller parties with new ideas get squeezed out of the arena of public discourse even as they fill ballot lines year after year. Occasionally, of course, the spoilers are stooges deliberately planted to split the vote on one side or the other—which explains why the Greens are Republican operatives' second-favorite party (Hill, 2002, p. 267), as the Libertarians are for many Democrats.

This situation changes fundamentally when voters have more than one mark to make on their ballots for each contest. In my conversations with academics in Ireland, the conventional wisdom among partisan elites is that stooge candidates and vote splitting are not tools that they can rely on. The formal structure of the ballot, by allowing voters to transfer support in case their first choice has a poor showing after the first count, reduces elites' room for maneuver.

American cities and counties have been noticing that the Irish model of elections offers a deepening of democracy. With about five million inhabitants, Ireland is a little smaller in population than the average American state. Though only Cambridge, Massachusetts, uses multi-seat STV for local councilors, almost a dozen other cities now use RCV for the mayor's seat. STV uses a more complicated counting process to accommodate multi-seat districts, but the voter's process is the same for all ranking-ballot systems, regardless of how many seats are up for election. In my conversations with election administrators in Scotland, where cities like Edinburgh and Glasgow have been using STV for over a decade, the perception is that most voters are content to trust professional staff to handle the counting process: there is no public clamor for a return to exclusive, single-mark ballots. In Maine, Secretary of State Matthew Dunlap was skeptical of RCV when I spoke to him in 2017, after the system was first passed by voters in a referendum. By the time of the U.S. House elections of 2018, after new administrative procedures had been designed and tested, he was vocally defending the integrity and administrability of RCV in the press.

The STV/RCV family of ranking ballots should be considered good for democracy on both of two registers: majority rule and minority rights. It is good for majority rule because unpopular incumbents cannot survive with relatively small bases of support by playing divide-and-conquer on the other side. It is good for minority rights because the process of eliminations and transfers sets up a structure within which even small blocs of voters can be seen, step-by-step and with data available on how many rankings went to which candidates, to swing any given election. Once political elites learn these two facts of life under ranking ballots, they adjust their approach to the electorate accordingly. They learn to maneuver in smaller spaces, more hemmed in by the public—which is what democratic theory led us to expect, after all.

ADJUNCTS TO ELECTORAL REFORM: POLICY JURIES

Ireland also offers the most compelling real-world model for the second path to inclusive participation which I wish to discuss here: policy juries. Different from a trial jury, this model is also called a *deliberative forum*; the proper name for Ireland's version is the Citizens' Assembly. Policy juries have also seen notable real-world applications in Canada, the Netherlands, and Belgium (Fournier et al., 2011).

The basic idea behind a policy jury is to institutionalize political power in an unelected body that is broadly representative of ordinary citizens, giving it some measure of genuine authority over policy change. Members of citizen assemblies in the broadest sense are randomly selected from pools of eligible citizens, much as trial juries are (in theory) selected in the United States, but the eligible pools may be non-randomly generated to some extent. In a process known as stratified sampling, random selections are made from different strata that are set aside to ensure representation on characteristics of interest, such as race or gender. For example, if the citizens who volunteer to serve on a policy jury happen to be 60 percent female and 40 percent male, randomly selecting the entire jury from the eligible pool is likely to approximate that disproportionality. If the pool were divided into female and male strata, however, equal numbers of selections could then be randomly made from each stratum.

It is important to note that the policy jury is one of many kinds of randomly selected popular assemblies that have been the focus of deliberative democratic theory, as well as practical experimentation and empirical testing, in the last two decades or so (Gastil and Levine, 2005). Deliberative polls (Fishkin, 2009) and the Deliberation Day proposal (Ackerman and Fishkin, 2004) are two of the best-known examples. More than capturing a snapshot of public opinion, to which policy-making elites may choose to refer prior to major decisions, policy juries may be considered distinctive (and more radical) in so far as they are supposed to constitute a necessary, and not purely advisory, step in the overall decision-making process. The case of the British Columbia jury on electoral-system reform in 2004 (Warren and Pearse, 2008) has long been the most famous and the most highly regarded example of a real-world policy jury: the government of the day was committed beforehand to placing the jury's proposals on a binding referendum ballot. But the 2016 Irish jury on abortion laws—having played a similar kind of role, but with greater practical success—is likely to take top billing in future debates over the democratic possibilities of policy juries.

The Irish Citizens' Assembly has gone through several iterations (Farrell, O'Malley and Suiter, 2013; Farrell, Suiter and Harris, 2019). The original template, in the Convention on the Constitution of 2013, was a jury of 99, composed of 33 members of parliament and 66 ordinary citizens, and presided over by a senior judge. For the second and third versions of the Citizens' Assembly, however, the 99 randomly selected jurors have not included any members of parliament, but have had a 100 percent lay membership. The jury hears witnesses and testimony on several proposed policy changes, especially constitutional amendments. The jury gets exposed to various sides of a particular issue, can request new information or research, and discusses matters among its members before voting on concrete proposals. Those proposals that receive majority support within the jury then, at the discretion of the sitting government, may be put to a national referendum. If a referendum is held and a proposition receives majority support at the national level, the constitutional amendment is passed.

Nations, regions, and municipalities hold referendums all the time. The Irish model of the policy jury is to have the ballot measures formulated, not by elected politicians or judicial experts, but by randomly selected citizens. This type of institution could be applied not only to a sovereign state's constitution, but also to an American city's charter.

In 2016, the difficult issue of abortion rights came before the Irish Citizens' Assembly. Up for debate was a constitutional clause that had the effect of placing strict limitations on abortion access. Politicians felt shifts in public opinion on this issue but were afraid to act against the Catholic Church by passing new, liberalized regulations. The members of a policy jury, however, did not have to run for re-election or worry about the church's campaign clout. Their task was to gather information about the effects of the constitutional clauses in question on the lives of their fellow citizens and to discuss the likely consequences of alternative arrangements (Caldwell, 2019). The result of the 2016–17 process was that the Citizens' Assembly formally proposed the liberalization of Ireland's abortion laws, and 66.4 percent of the electorate ratified that proposal in the ensuing referendum held in 2018 (McDonald, Graham-Harrison and Baker, 2018).

For democratic theory, the most important feature of the policy jury is not deliberation but randomness: its lay, nonpartisan, nonprofessional character. This characteristic is especially important when used as an adjunct to referendum processes, which often appear to be about manufacturing popular acquiescence to an elite agenda rather than constructing an autonomous or unmanipulated public judgment on an important issue. Importantly, the random selection of policy juries' members entails no significant disability in these bodies to represent the public; quite the contrary, in fact. Even the most ethnically, religiously, and sexually representative (in the descriptive sense) legislature in the world would still be composed of decision-makers who are set apart from 99 percent of their fellow citizens as a small class of professional legislators—and are generally dependent, to win elections, on a similarly tiny class of donors and professional consultants. A jury of ordinary citizens is a totally different kind of agency, and its representative character can be ensured through stratified sampling. In short, allowing policy juries, rather than state legislatures or city councils, to write referendum propositions for the voters does not threaten to open up new democratic deficits.

U.S. politician Boss Tweed allegedly said, "It's not who votes that counts; it's who counts the votes." We might add that, even where the integrity of the count is assured, "It's not only who votes that counts; it's also who sets the options to vote for." Elites have long realized that the power of agenda setting in elections depends on what goes on the ballot and what does not, and scholars have long realized that most referendums in the real world are therefore better described as instruments of oligarchy than democracy (Tierney, 2012). Citizen initiatives can place referendums in a different light, theoretically, but these are the exceptions rather than the rule, globally. The policy jury, when used as an adjunct to the electoral process, offers a way to reduce elites' room for maneuver in referendums: it is a more genuine type of citizen initiative than Astroturf campaigns funded by special interests.

Yet the Irish example is ambiguous on this point. Though it is encouraging that political elites in Ireland have relinquished their initial buy-in of a third of seats in the Citizens' Assembly, they still retain the veto power of keeping any proposal from reaching the voters. Would the residents of an American city or county bother to give their time and energy to an intensive deliberative process if they knew that the sitting mayor or council could simply ignore the findings? Advocates of deliberative polls believe that experience with those bodies shows that citizens' motivation is not difficult to come by. Yet the consequences of official neglect or defiance of citizens' deliberative efforts could be more distrust of democratic politics, not less. Advisory referendums on electoral reform in recent years have already suffered this fate at the hands of established factions in Memphis, Tennessee, and Prince Edward Island, Canada (on the latter, see Milner, 2017, p. 352).

Maybe the Irish example of constitutional juries is not a perfect model, but the general idea of taking difficult political issues and settling them through the participation of a randomly selected jury has considerable appeal in the early twenty-first century. As the zealotry, predictability, and intransigence of American partisans go up, the number of Americans identifying as partisans goes down. For better or worse, professional partisans are not trusted to come up with good-faith solutions to widely acknowledged problems. Too often they act in ways that vindicate the distrust rather than overturn it.

INCENTIVES AND IMPLICATIONS FOR CHANGE

There are multiple reasons for real-world reformers to give serious considera-tion to changes in the democratic process that, admittedly, might at first seem unfamiliar or farfetched. Particularly in the case of RCV, where basic changes to the electoral process might seem to threaten the very lifeblood of established elites and political professionals, it is important to state the case for why those players' own interests stand to gain from the change.

The elimination of vote splitting and spoiler/stooge candidacies under RCV seems to be an obvious benefit to voter empowerment, but it should appeal to elite incentives as well. In the context of partisan elections, both major parties can avoid the well-known perils of nominating unelectable extremists in low-turnout primaries if they embrace RCV. The reason is that RCV makes it possible to hold a single-round, blanket-primary type of election instead of a two-stage election with partisan primaries as a first step. With multiple candidates representing different strands of each major party on the same general election ballot, RCV's eliminations and transfers can reach a result in a single, high-turnout election: extremists will prosper only by building coalitions, appealing for voters' second and third preferences, and (in short) checking their extremism. All in all, the factions who have most to lose under RCV are those who aspire to sustained plurality rule with no compromises, simply by instigating vote splitting within the disunited majority that opposes them. The identity of such groups will vary from one locality to another, but in theory, they should have difficulty recruiting others to preserve a system that benefits such a small number—even of the already small number of political professionals.

Beyond considerations of elite interests and incentives, reformers should be prepared to articulate the positive values toward which RCV could move the democratic process, values such as CWB's inclusive participation. The RCV system is more *inclusive* than traditional plurality voting because small-party and other minority groups can demonstrate their numbers in the official public poll without fear of vote splitting, potentially gaining leverage in post-election bargaining and lobbying. Communities and groups whose interests are traditionally marginalized can gain more visibility by running their own candidates and giving them their first-preference votes. Even when such candidates do not prevail with the electorate as a whole, marginal voting blocs can still demonstrate their cohesion and impact, since the destination of their second- and third-preference votes is formally and publicly verified by the official count. In short, we are entitled to assert that RCV can benefit majorities and minorities alike in any given electoral context.

A related point is that the CWB project involves bold and innovative social and economic policies whose initial constituencies may be small in any given locality, and both RCV and policy juries are well suited to opening up space for new ideas. RCV allows single-issue candidacies to gain prominence, as with the Anti-Austerity Alliance in Ireland after the financial crisis of 2008, without fear of becoming spoilers for unintended beneficiaries. Policy juries allow lay citizens to discuss difficult issues face-to-face, and these discussions routinely reveal common ground in defiance of conventional wisdom about what is politically feasible, as with the abortion issue in Ireland. They can also offer needed cover for change to political elites who are reluctant to take bold steps, as elected officials otherwise demonstrate when deferring to judicial decisions. Transformative economic policies at the local or state level could therefore gain traction, in different ways, from both RCV and policy juries.

The model of the policy jury is also more *participatory* than traditional electoral politics because it gives substantial initiative and proposal power to ordinary citizens who are not elected officials or are not otherwise continuously engaged in the processes of local government. Since CWB entails difficult conversations about issues of fundamental fairness, the jury-like setting offers an institutionalized space for having those conversations that is less burdened with partisan baggage than other forums. To the extent that CWB requires tackling entrenched economic interests, standard selection procedures for making policy juries broadly representative of the community render it all but impossible that the perspectives of the One Percent (locally or nationally) dominate debate to the extent that they often do through established media channels.

Inclusive participation could mean many things, and formal institutional rules cannot in the end guarantee who participates or how much. But institutional structures construct opportunities and mobilize nudges. *Institutionalized space* is perhaps an apt metaphor. Further democratization in America may depend on decreasing the room for maneuver that the political defenders of elite dumping have carved out for themselves, correspondingly increasing the political room for maneuver of ordinary citizens. Ranking ballots and policy juries are two options, among others, for making American democracy roomier in this sense.

REFERENCES

Ackerman, Bruce and James S. Fishkin (2004), *Deliberation Day*, New Haven, CT: Yale University Press.

Berg-Andersson, Richard E. (2020), "General election Tuesday, November 7, 2000," accessed July 1, 2020 at http://www.thegreenpapers.com/G00/G00.html.

Bowler, Shaun and Bernard Grofman (eds) (2000), *Elections in Australia, Ireland, and Malta under the Single Transferable Vote: Reflections on an Embedded Institution*, Ann Arbor, MI: University of Michigan Press.

Caldwell, Louise (2019), "I took part in a Citizens' Assembly—it could help break the Brexit deadlock," *The Guardian*, January 16, accessed January 4, 2020 at www .theguardian.com/commentisfree/2019/jan/16/citizens-assembly-ireland-abortion -referendum.

Farrell, David M., Eoin O'Malley and Jane Suiter (2013), "Deliberative democracy in action, Irish-style: the 2011 *We the Citizens* pilot Citizens' Assembly," *Irish Political Studies*, 28(1), 99–113.

Farrell, David M., Jane Suiter and Clodagh Harris (2019), "'Systematizing' constitutional deliberation: the 2016–18 Citizens' Assembly in Ireland," *Irish Political Studies*, 34(1), 113–23.

Fishkin, James S. (2009), *When the People Speak: Deliberative Democracy and Public Consultation*, Oxford: Oxford University Press.

Fournier, Patrick, Henk van der Kolk, R. Kenneth Carty, André Blais and Jonathan Rose (2011), *When Citizens Decide: Lessons from Citizen Assemblies on Electoral Reform*, Oxford: Oxford University Press.

Gastil, John and Peter Levine (eds) (2005), *The Deliberative Democracy Handbook: Strategies for Effective Civic Engagement in the Twenty-First Century*, San Francisco, CA: Jossey-Bass.

Hill, Steven (2002), *Fixing Elections: The Failure of America's Winner-Take-All Politics*, New York: Routledge.

Joshi, Devin K., J.S. Maloy and Timothy M. Peterson (2015), "Popular vs. elite democratic structures and international peace," *Journal of Peace Research*, 52(4), 463–77.

Joshi, Devin K., J.S. Maloy and Timothy M. Peterson (2019), "Popular vs. elite democracies and human rights: inclusion makes a difference," *International Studies Quarterly*, 63(1), 111–26.

Lundberg, Thomas Carl (2018), "Electoral systems in context: United Kingdom," in Erik S. Herron, Robert J. Pekkanen and Matthew S. Shugart (eds), *The Oxford Handbook of Electoral Systems*, Oxford: Oxford University Press.

Maloy, J.S. (2008), *The Colonial American Origins of Modern Democratic Thought*, New York: Cambridge University Press.

Maloy, J.S. (2019), *Smarter Ballots: Electoral Realism and Reform*, New York: Palgrave Macmillan.

Manin, Bernard (1997), *The Principles of Representative Government*, New York: Cambridge University Press.

McDonald, Henry, Emma Graham-Harrison and Sinead Baker (2018), "Ireland votes by landslide to legalise abortion," *The Guardian*, May 26, accessed January 4, 2020 at https://www.theguardian.com/world/2018/may/26/ireland-votes-by-landslide-to -legalise-abortion.

Milner, Henry (2017), "Electoral system reform, the Canadian experience," *Election Law Journal*, 16(3), 349–56.

Tierney, Stephen (2012), *Constitutional Referendums: The Theory and Practice of Republican Deliberation*, Oxford: Oxford University Press.

Took, Christopher and Seán Donnelly (2018), "Presidential election, November 1990," *ElectionsIreland.org*, accessed December 31, 2018 at https://www.electionsireland .org/result.cfm?election=1990P&cons=194.

Warren, Mark E. and Hilary Pearse (eds) (2008), *Designing Deliberative Democracy: The British Columbia Citizens' Assembly*, Cambridge, UK: Cambridge University Press.

10. Gendered (and racialized) partisan polarization[1]

Nicholas J.G. Winter

INTRODUCTION

Barnes and Williamson, in Chapter 2 of this book, cite polarization and the resulting policy gridlock at the federal level as important reasons to pursue local community-building policies. In this chapter, I explore partisan polarization among the mass public over the past several decades, focusing on citizens' views on gender, race, and class. Specifically, drawing on data from the American National Election Studies, I trace the relationship from 1970 through 2016 between Americans' views on gender, race, and class on the one hand, and feelings about the political parties on the other. Although 2016 marks a high point for the impact of gender and race on views of the parties, it represents the culmination of trends that date back decades. Americans' evaluations of the political parties have been strongly and increasingly connected with their racial views, especially since 2000. Views on gender roles and feminism also powerfully shape evaluations of the parties, and have done so consistently since the mid-1980s. And feelings about social class steadily increased in importance through 2012 before fading a little in 2016.

These trends will trouble many. They mark a decline in cross-cutting cleavages within the population, and with them, partisan cooperation or at least tolerance. Such cross-cutting cleavages were central to constitutional design; Madison famously favored a large republic, arguing in *The Federalist* that size would:

> make it less probable that a majority of the whole will have a common motive to invade the rights of other citizens; or if such a common motive exists, it will be more difficult for all who feel it to discover their own strength, and to act in unison with each other. (Madison, 1787 [2005], p. 53)

Dahl and other pluralists similarly credited cross-cutting cleavages with moderating political parties and ensuring stability (Dahl, 1956, pp. 104–5). And empirical studies confirm that cross-pressured citizens—those whose policy views do not all align with one political party—are more likely to cross party lines, changing their vote from election to election and splitting their ticket between parties within an election (Hillygus and Shields, 2008).

Moreover, our ideas about gender and race are not mere policy preferences. They are central elements of identities that construct and symbolize who we are, individually and as a nation. As identities become closely tethered to the party system, political disagreements feel personal and political opponents represent existential threats. Aligning the party system with race- and gender-based fault lines in society is, therefore, an excellent recipe for partisan enmity and gridlock.

That said, and despite pluralists' valorization of cross-cutting cleavages, we might see some normative appeal in the alignment of the party system with views on gender and race. Even if cross-cutting identity cleavages limit polarization and allow bipartisan compromise, they do so at a cost: such cleavages motivate the parties to avoid discussing race and gender issues, which deflects political attention from these structural systems of hierarchy and power.

APPROACH

I do not aim to make causal claims about the direction of the changes I examine—that is, whether increasing alignment among views on race, gender, and class push the political parties to polarize at the elite level, or polarized elite parties push citizens to change their attitudes or partisan attachments. Rather, I document an underappreciated face of increasing polarization among the mass public: the increasing alignment, over the past several decades, of Americans' views on race, gender, and the political parties. In so doing, this analysis reveals that the powerful impact of sexism and racism on the 2016 election is but an extreme example of a much longer-term trend in the images of the political parties that transcends any one candidate or election.

My focus on views toward the groups associated with the parties departs from most studies of polarization. There is a robust literature on the role of policy attitudes in polarization. Some ask whether ordinary Americans are sharply divided in their views and whether they have become more so in recent decades (e.g., Abramowitz and Saunders, 2005; Fiorina, Abrams and Pope, 2006); others focus on the reciprocal relationships between polarization among political elites and division among the mass public (e.g., Hetherington, 2001; Levendusky, 2013). Taking a different path, I explore the connections between citizens' views of the parties on the one hand, and their feelings of the groups that make up the party coalitions and that are central actors in many policy disagreements on the other.

There are several reasons to focus on feelings about social groups. First, few citizens think about politics in ideological or even issue-based terms. Rather, most understand the parties—and politics more generally—in terms of groups (Campbell et al., 1960; Converse, 1964; Kinder and Kalmoe, 2017). Moreover, people are highly attuned to the social groups that make up the major political party coalitions, and party affiliation itself is a social identity that citizens understand in relation to other identities (Green, Palmquist and Schickler, 2002; Miller, Wlezien and Hildreth, 1991).

In addition, partisan conflict is structured by social group cleavages. For example, in his examination of partisan realignment in the 1980s, Petrocik argues that "One is hard pressed to find instances where issue conflict is independent of social cleavages. Issues and ideology may be the language of party conflict, but group needs and conflicts are its source in modern party systems" (1987, p. 353). Petrocik traces changes in the groups that make up the parties—that is, changes in the party identification of social groups like white Northern Protestants, white Southerners, African Americans, and others. Thus, he—like many others who study partisan realignment—focuses on the social make-up of party membership.

Considering racial groups, many analyses trace the movement of African Americans into the Democratic Party and white Americans—especially in the South—toward the Republicans as the parties polarized on civil rights in the mid-twentieth century (e.g., Carmines and Stimson, 1989; Schickler, 2016). The relative homogeneity of African Americans' views on civil rights and social and economic policy (Dawson, 1994) facilitates the conflation in these accounts of symbolic party image—Democrats stand for the interests of African Americans—and demographic party membership—African Americans are overwhelmingly Democratic. But of course, that symbolic image also led some white Americans—those with liberal views on civil rights—to favor Democrats and oppose Republicans.

The changing demographics of party membership is one important way that social groups intersect with the political parties. But groups play an important role in shaping each party's symbolic image among voters who may not be members of those groups (Green et al., 2002). For example, consider economic policy. The Democratic Party generally advocates for liberal economic policies and is allied with labor unions; the Republican Party pushes conservative economics and is allied with business groups. These positions and alliances shape each party's membership: union members are apt to identify as Democrats, business leaders as Republicans. But these policies and coalitions also affect citizens who are neither union members nor business leaders, because most citizens hold positive or negative views of those groups (labor unions and business), and use this information to make sense of the parties (Green et al., 2002; Nelson and Kinder, 1996). To call Democrats the party of labor and Republicans the party of business is not just to describe literal membership—at the mass and elite coalitional levels. It also communicates each party's image and what it stands for.

This conflation of image and membership particularly obfuscates the role of gender in the party system. Many scholars analyze group membership defined by gender: the gender gap in partisanship, opinions, and voting (Gilens, 1988; Kaufmann, 2002; Kaufmann and Petrocik, 1999; Manza and Brooks, 1998; Shapiro and Mahajan, 1986). Gender gaps have ebbed and flowed and have certainly been politically important at times (Ladd, 1997; Mansbridge, 1985). However, focus on gender gaps misses important ways that gender structures party competition because the politics of gender does not, generally speaking, divide men from women. Rather, it often engages questions of women's *and* men's roles, rights, and relative power; it pits those defending traditional gender arrangements against those advocating for egalitarian gender arrangements. In other words, the politics of gender divides supporters of gender egalitarianism and feminism—male and female—from gender traditionalists and anti-feminists of both sexes.

Though there are modest gender gaps in partisanship, voting, and policy views, these pale compared with the differences *among* men and *among* women in views on gender roles and feminism. And gender roles and feminism have increasingly structured elite partisan debate. Marjorie Spruill traces the role of anti-feminism in the construction of modern American conservatism beginning in the 1970s (2008, 2017). A key moment for the political parties came in 1980, when the Republican platform first included opposition to the Equal Rights Amendment (ERA); Greg Adams (1997) shows that abortion opinion also became more linked to partisanship following this shift. But men and women have differed little in their support for ERA and abortion rights, so these shifts on gender-based policy did little to create a gender gap in partisanship or voting (Cook and Wilcox, 1991; Mansbridge, 1985). And this is nothing new: for example, despite widespread expectations that one would form following suffrage in 1920, the United States has not seen a major women's political party (Andersen, 1996). In general, the social structure of gender, in which men and women are socially and functionally integrated—"dispersed among men" (Beauvoir, 1949 [2010], p. 8)—works against the formation of a sense of gender-group-based interest (e.g., Jackman, 1994).[2]

These intra-group differences on matters of gender—as opposed to inter-group difference *between* men and women—present a sharp contrast with the politics of race, where there are divides between white Americans and black Americans (Kinder and Winter, 2001); and to some extent with the politics of class, where rich and poor are relatively divided as well (McCall and Manza, 2011). To elucidate the gender- and race-based elements of citizens' images of the parties, I explore how the mass public views the social groups that make up each party's coalition at the elite level. Specifically, I explore citizens' views of three social cleavages that are fundamental to the post-1970s U.S. party system: race, class, and gender. Race has, of course, been central to American political competition and party systems since the founding. Since the 1960s, the Democratic Party has become increasingly the party of racial liberalism; the Republican Party the party of racial conservatism, and citizens have become aware of this and adjusted their party identification accordingly (Carmines and Stimson 1989).[3] Class, too, has been a central line of political disagreement that has structured partisan competition in many eras; since the New Deal, the association of Democrats with economic liberalism and the Republicans with economic conservatism has been a central feature of the party system (Sundquist, 1983).

DATA

To assess the contribution of feelings about social groups to Americans' views of the parties, partisanship, and voting, I need consistent measures of those feelings, and of reactions to the parties, over relatively long periods of recent American history. For this I turn to the American National Election Studies (ANES), which has conducted national surveys around the biennial federal elections since 1948 (ANES, 2018). These surveys represent the gold standard in sampling and other survey administration; as important, they have emphasized continuity in question inclusion and wording, which facilitates comparisons over time.

I draw on measures of respondents' views of the two major political parties, and of the social groups representing the politicized cleavages along lines of race, gender, and social class. I focus on these group-based evaluations—rather than views on policy issues having to do with race, gender, and class—for two reasons. First, I want to abstract from particular policy disputes that evoke myriad policy-specific considerations for respondents (Zaller, 1992) in order to focus on feelings about the broad social groups implicated in those issue debates. Second, the specific issues that appear in the ANES vary over time as the political agenda shifted; in contrast, instrumentation measuring group feelings has been more stable. My analysis begins in 1970, when the ANES first introduced a question asking respondents for their views of the women's movement.

I present three analyses. First, I document the increase in partisan affective polarization; that is, the increase in negative views that Democrats express toward Republicans, and that Republicans express toward Democrats. This is a relatively direct measure of the mass face of an increasingly polarized political system. Second, I analyze the feelings that partisans of each party hold toward race-, gender-, and class-based groups. Here I find increasingly polarized views of gender- and race-based groups, suggesting that these social cleavages may underlie the strengthening partisan antipathy. Finally, I run a series of regression models to explore directly—and simultaneously—the impact of views about gender, race, and class on partisan affective polarization. In all these analyses, I draw primarily on a long-standing series of ANES questions: the so-called "feeling thermometer," which asks respondents to rate on a zero-to-100 degree temperature scale how warmly or coldly (i.e., how favorably or unfavorably) they feel toward each of a series of groups.[4] This measure serves my purposes well: it solicits *affective* evaluations of each group in a general way that abstracts from any particular political issues, in a format that is comparable across different groups. And it has an extensive track record as a reliable and valid measure of group (and candidate) evaluations (Weisberg and Miller, 1980; Wilcox, Sigelman and Cook, 1989; Winter and Berinsky, 1999). Most importantly for my purposes, in most years since 1970 the ANES included among the thermometers both political parties, as well as groups relevant to race ("blacks" and "whites"), gender ("feminists" and/or "the women's movement"), and class ("labor unions" and "big business").

RESULTS

Partisan Affective Polarization

I begin with an analysis of the views of members of each political party: how they feel about their own party, and how they feel about the opposing party. Here I draw on two different pairs of feeling thermometer ratings: from 1972 through 1982, the ANES asked respondents to rate "Democrats" and "Republicans." From 1978 through 2016, respondents rated "The Democratic Party" and "The Republican Party." These items are somewhat different; the first pair refers to *members* of each party, while the second asks about the parties themselves. Happily, both pairs of items were included in 1980 and 1982, so I can calibrate the trends across this change of question wording.

Figure 10.1 shows the relevant averages. The left-hand panel shows the average ratings of each party by Democratic respondents,[5] along with the difference between these two average ratings. The right-hand panel shows the same set of evaluations, this time among Republican respondents.[6]

Looking first at Democratic respondents, Figure 10.1 shows that evaluations of the Democratic (in-)Party (and partisans) are quite high and relatively stable, averaging about 75 points on the 0-to-100 thermometer rating scale.[7] Evaluations of the Republican Party are lower—as we would expect. Over the past four-plus decades, Democrats' ratings of Republicans have fallen precipitously: from about 50 degrees in the 1970s and early 1980s to just above 25 degrees in the 2010s. The difference between ratings of the in-party and the out-party represents affective polarization. This has increased dramatically

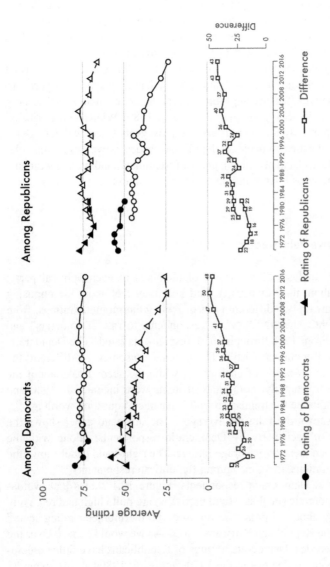

Source: ANES (2018).

Figure 10.1   Views of the parties by party members

among Democrats, from about 25–30 degrees in the late 1970s to about 50 degrees—fully half of the overall scale—by 2008 through 2016.

Turning to the right-hand panel, we see the mirror image among Republicans. Ratings of Republicans and the Republican Party are relatively high—in the mid-lower 70s, and are fairly stable over time. Ratings of Democrats are lower, and decline steadily from a difference of 25–30 points in the late 1970s to 43 points in 2012 and 2016. Thus, affective polarization has increased dramatically among members of both parties. The increase in polarization has been somewhat faster among Democrats, increasing by an average of 2.4 degrees per four-year presidential term, compared with 1.8 degrees every four years among Republicans.

Views of Groups at the Center of American Political Conflict

These findings mirror those of others who have documented increased affective partisan polarization over this period (Iyengar and Westwood, 2015). In this context of increasing antipathy between the parties, I will now trace parallel polarization in views of the race, gender, and class-based groups associated with each.

To measure feelings about gender and class groups, I continue to draw on the ANES feeling thermometers. For gender, I use ratings of two groups that have appeared on and off from 1970 through 2016 in the ANES: "feminists" and "the women's movement."[8] These items fit my needs well, because both "feminists" and "the women's movement" connote not simply women, but rather women who are politically active on behalf of a progressive gender agenda. That is, they capture quite well the *politicization* of gender rights, roles, and power. For class and economics, I make use of ratings of "big business" and of "labor unions." While big business, and to a lesser extent labor unions, are not as deeply politicized, these groups do both engage in political activity, each is a central member of a party coalition, and each is understood to have opposing economic interests.

Turning to racial groups, no ideal measure is available, so I pursue two strategies. First, I draw on thermometer ratings of "blacks" and of "whites," both of which have appeared consistently in the ANES. However, these do not directly engage *politicized* racial groups, and so they may under-state the role of views about politicized racial groups in the party system. And each may not measure white respondents' views very well: norms against open expression of racism may affect the ratings whites report of blacks (Mendelberg, 2001) and the invisibility of white racial identity may distort their ratings of whites as a group (Frankenberg, 1993). Therefore, I also draw on a two-pronged strategy. Through 1988, the ANES asked for thermometer ratings of "civil rights leaders." From 1986 forward, I also draw on a robust measure of racial sympathy, based on the canonical racial resentment battery of questions.[9] Though not parallel in form to the thermometer ratings, this measure precisely captures Americans' views on the contemporary *politics* of race, as opposed simply to their affective feelings about racial groups (Kinder and Sanders, 1996). In what follows, I focus primarily on the thermometer ratings of blacks and of whites, as they are available for the entire time period and are most comparable with the gender and class measures. I then supplement this with the combination of the thermometer rating of civil rights (CR) leaders (through 1988) and racial sympathy (from 1986).

Figure 10.2 shows the difference between Democrats and Republicans in ratings of each type of group.[10] The top-left panel plots the difference, in each year from 1970 through 2016, in the average ratings by Democrats and by Republicans of feminists and/or the women's movement. For example, the plot shows that in 1984 Democrats rated the women's liberation movement 12 degrees warmer, on average, than did Republicans.[11] From 1970 through 2016, Democrats rated feminists and the women's movement higher than did Republicans. This difference was modest—between 5 and 10 degrees—through the 1970s, then increased steadily from 10 degrees in 1980 to almost 20 degrees in the mid-1990s. After closing slightly, partisan polarization in ratings of feminists reached their most polarized level yet in 2016. That year, Democrats rated feminists at 67 degrees, compared with 43 degrees among Republicans, a difference of about a quarter of the 101-degree rating scale. This peak polarization in 2016 is consistent with the finding of others on the importance of sexism and views on gender to the 2016 election (e.g., Bock, Byrd-Craven and Burkley, 2017; Bracic, Israel-Trummel and Shortle, 2019; Frasure-Yokley, 2018; Ratliff et al., 2019; Schaffner, MacWilliams and Nteta, 2018; Setzler and Yanus, 2018; Valentino, Wayne and Miller, 2018; Winter, 2018). However, looking at the whole trend, it is clear that 2016 represents an extension and acceleration of a trend that has been in place for decades.

Turning to racial group perceptions, the right-hand panels of Figure 10.2 show the partisan polarization in racial group views, relying on my two different measurement strategies. Panel B shows the partisan difference in ratings of blacks and of whites; panel D presents the parallel differences in ratings of civil rights leaders and in racial sympathy.

Panel B shows moderate and relatively stable polarization in views of blacks and whites. Before 2008, the difference hovers between five and eight points. In 2008, the partisan difference climbs to about ten degrees, then to 12 degrees in 2012 and 15 degrees in 2016. This is consistent with the findings of many other scholars that the election of Barack Obama, and his administration, heralded an increase in the partisan political salience of race that continued into the Trump era (Kinder and Dale-Riddle, 2012; Tesler and Sears, 2010). The suspicion that this measure underestimates the *level* of polarization is con-

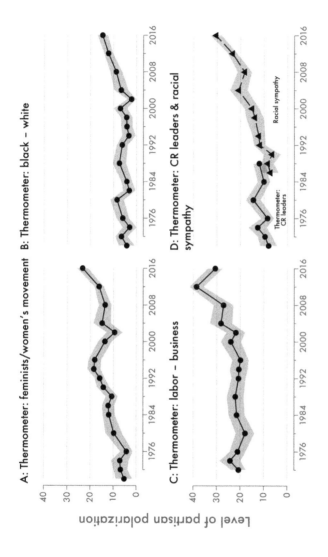

Source: ANES (2018).

Figure 10.2 Polarization in views of groups among party members

firmed in panel D of Figure 10.2, which presents partisan polarization using my alternate racial measures. Through 1988, polarization in feelings toward civil rights leaders is of relatively stable, albeit at a notably higher *level* than in panel B, with differences of about 10 degrees. From 1986, racial sympathy shows moderately increasing polarization through the 1980s and 1990s, followed by sharp increases in 2012 and 2016. It is worth noting that although partisan polarization on this measure dropped somewhat in 2008 relative to 2004, this did not reflect even a momentary flowering of racial sympathy in the electorate. Rather, it reflected an *drop* in racial sympathy among Democratic identifiers.[12] More broadly, while partisan differences in thermometer ratings of blacks and of whites were relatively steady, the metric of racial sympathy shows sharply increasing polarization between the parties on matters of race. By this measure the political salience of race started increasing in the 1980s, and the Obama years simply continue the trend.

I turn now to partisan polarization on matters of gender. Although *levels* of racial resentment are not directly comparable with the thermometer scores of feminists and the women's movement, the story each tells about partisan polarization is the same. Over several decades, Americans who identify with the two parties have grown steadily apart in their views on gender, just as they have on race. Polarization on both gender and race reached a peak in 2016, but in both cases those sharp differences are the culmination of longstanding trends in American politics.

Finally, turning to social class and the realm of economics, panel C of Figure 10.2 presents the partisan differences in ratings of class-based groups. The underlying measure is the difference in a respondent's rating of labor unions and big business. The figure shows the partisan differences in this rating; it indicates that Democrats are consistently more positive toward labor (and more negative toward business) than are Republicans. The partisan polarization here is very large and relatively stable: from 1970 through 2002 the parties differ by 20 to 25 degrees. This increases to the upper 20s in 2004 and 2008, then to almost 40 degrees in 2012. In 2016, it drops to a still-extreme 30 degrees, perhaps reflecting Trump's appeal among some white working-class voters.[13]

In sum, in all three areas—gender, race, and class—partisan polarization has increased sharply over the past 16 years. For gender and race, it is at its highest levels in 2016; for class, the peak was in 2012. Class-based polarization has been at a high level since the 1970s, with notable recent increases. Polarization in views on race looks less sharp in the 1970s and 1980s, but then increases dramatically beginning in the 1990s. Finally, partisan polarization in gender views has been generally increasing since the 1970s, although it dips somewhat in the 2000s before rebounding sharply since 2008.

Impact of Group Attitudes on Partisan Views, Partisanship, and Voting

In the last section, I demonstrated that Americans who identify with the two parties have grown increasingly polarized in their views about group that symbolize and represent gender-, race-, and class-based competition in American politics. In this final empirical section, I take up directly the question of the impact of these group views on Americans' evaluations of the parties. In order to do so, I estimate a series of regression models—one per year—that estimate the impact of attitudes toward each group, controlling for the simultaneous effects of the others. This analysis contributes two things beyond those that have come before. First, by estimating the impact of group-based views on partisan evaluation simultaneously, the regression model quantifies the impact of each group view, above and beyond the impact of the others. And second, this model includes all respondents, not simply those that identify with one party or the other.

For this analysis, my dependent variable is the individual-level evaluation of the parties, operationalized as the difference between a respondent's thermometer rating of Democrats and of Republicans.[14] Separately for each year, I estimate the following model:

$$\text{Affective polarization} = b0 + b1[\text{Gender-group affect}] + b2[\text{Racial-group affect}] + b3[\text{Class-group affect}] + b4[\text{Respondent female}] + b5[\text{Respondent African American}] + b6[\text{Respondent Latinx}] + b7[\text{Respondent other non-white race}]$$

The gender-group affect variable is the thermometer rating of the women's movement or of feminists, as available,[15] and class-group affect is the thermometer rating of labor unions minus the thermometer rating of big business. For racial-group affect, I use each of my two measures in turn: first the thermometer rating of blacks minus the thermometer rating of whites; and then the combination of thermometer rating of civil rights leaders and racial sympathy. The four respondent variables are indicators (0/1) for respondents who are female, African American, Latinx, or other/mixed race, respectively.[16]

The dependent variable—the partisan evaluation difference—is rescaled to run from −1 to +1, with higher values corresponding to more positive Democratic evaluations and more negative Republican evaluations. For the independent variables, higher values correspond to warmer evaluations of the women's movement or feminists; warmer evaluations of blacks (and colder of whites); warmer evaluations of civil rights leaders; higher levels of racial sympathy; and warmer evaluations of labor unions (and colder of big business). The thermometer difference variables are constructed from these 0−1 coded variables, and so run from −1 to +1. The estimated coefficients indicate the impact on the dependent variable of a one-point change in each independent variable.

Figure 10.3 shows the results for the model that uses as its measure of racial affect the thermometer ratings of blacks and whites. The top-left panel of the figure shows the estimated impact on relative party evaluations of respondents' views of the women's movement and/or feminists. For example, in 1980, the impact of the women's movement thermometer rating on relative party evaluations is 0.138 ($p < 0.01$). This means that if we compare a respondent who rates the women's movement at 100 degrees with one who rates it at 0 degrees, they will be 13.8 degrees higher on the party difference evaluation, holding constant racial and class evaluations. Surveying the trend, we see that evaluations of the women's movement and/or feminists has very little effect on evaluations of the parties in the 1970s. This changes, with the impact growing quickly through the 1980s and holding steady through the 1990s. It then drops slightly in 2008 and 2012, before peaking in 2016 with a regression coefficient of 0.552. The trajectory of these effects makes sense given the gender politics across this era: evaluations of the women's movement had little impact on partisan ratings in the 1970s ($b = 0.07$ to 0.10), before the second-wave feminist movement (and the Christian right backlash) became incorporated into the party coalitions. This changed in 1980 ($b = 0.138$, $p < 0.01$), when the Republican platform first opposed the ERA. The association between views of feminism and partisan evaluations grew through the 1980s and early 1990s, as the Republican Party adopted the gender agenda of the Christian right through the Reagan and Bush administrations. It is notable that views on feminism were particularly tightly connected with partisan evaluations in 1984, the year that the Democratic Party nominated Geraldine Ferraro for Vice-President, which sent a clear signal about the growing differences between the parties on gender issues and feminism. This association between views on feminism and the parties declined substantially in 2008, perhaps a result of Hillary Clinton's loss in the highly-contested Democratic primary race (e.g., McThomas and Tesler, 2016). In any case, this association then increased again in 2016, to 0.552 ($p < 0.01$).

The second panel, on the upper-right, shows that affective racial evaluations (the difference between ratings of blacks and of whites) had a rather modest impact on partisan evaluations through 2004, after which it increased in magnitude, ending with a coefficient of 0.285 in 2016 ($p < 0.01$). This means that in 2016, a respondent who evaluates blacks at 100 and whites at zero will have a party rating difference of about 28.5 degrees warmer toward the Democrats (and/or colder toward Republicans) compared with a respondent who rates the two racial groups equally.

Feelings about labor and big business have been strongly, and increasingly, associated with evaluations of the parties. This association has grown slowly

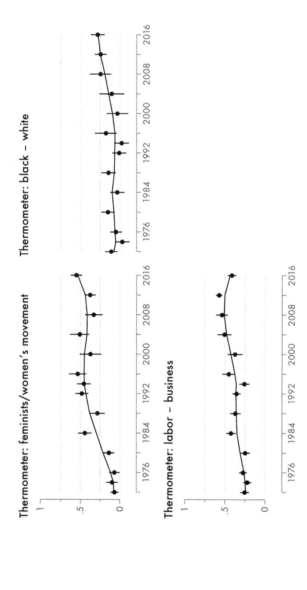

Note: OLS regression coefficients, with 95% confidence intervals; model includes controls for respondent gender and race.
Source: ANES (2018).

Figure 10.3   Impact of group views on party thermometer rating difference (model 1)

but steadily from about 0.25 in the 1970s to about 0.50 in recent presidential election years. While the impact of class-based views on partisan evaluations are quite strong in 2016—the regression coefficient is 0.415—it is notable that this association is weaker than that between party evaluations and gender groups, and also weaker than it was in 2012, when the coefficient was 0.574. This pattern is consistent with other work demonstrating that although economic considerations have structured partisan evaluations throughout the post-World War II era (Bartels, 2006), they were not especially or uniquely powerful in 2016 (Schaffner et al., 2018; Winter, 2018).

The thermometer-rating measure likely underestimates the impact of racial attitudes, so in Figure 10.4 I present analogous models that replaces that rating with the combination of ratings of civil rights leaders and the racial sympathy scale. This measure does a better job of assessing the full impact of racial attitudes, at the cost of less direct comparability over time and with the other measures after 1988. In these models, we observe a more robust impact of racial considerations on party evaluations, and one that increases steadily and relatively continually from the 1970s through 2016. Including this more robust racial measure decreases somewhat the estimated impact of both class and gender evaluations, though in these models both remain substantial and follow the same trajectory over time.

In sum, by 2016, Americans' evaluations of the political are rooted in considerations of gender and of race to an extent not previously seen since at least 1970. Despite this, 2016 represents the culmination of longstanding trends in which the images of the parties have been increasingly linked with gender and race, on top of their relatively steady class basis. Race-group affect, variously measured, has been an important force on party evaluations since the 1970s, with notably increasing impact since 2000. Gender-group affect came to prominence as a factor in party evaluations by the 1980s, and has remained significant ever since. And class has been a powerful force as well. In 2016, the impact of race and gender affect grew, and that of class affect fell somewhat.

CONCLUSIONS

In 2016, we observe the strongest connections since 1970 between feelings about the parties and about both racial and gendered political groups. Feelings about class-based groups loom large as well, though somewhat less in 2016 than 2012. While 2016 is extreme in this regard, it is not an aberration: rather, it represents the culmination of long-developing trends. These trends—in concert with parallel elite-level polarization—present serious challenges to policy-making in general, and to policies aimed at empowering historically excluded citizens in particular.

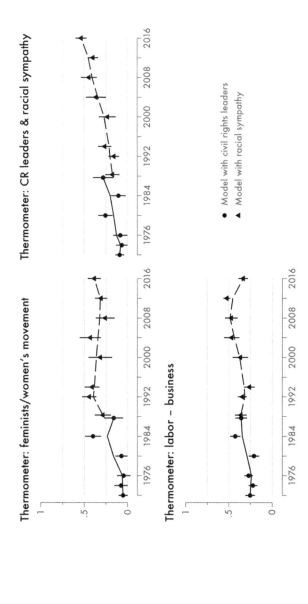

Note: OLS regression coefficients, with 95% confidence intervals; model includes controls for respondent gender and race.
Source: ANES (2018).

Figure 10.4 *Impact of group views of party thermometer rating difference (model 2)*

When parties are polarized, divided by fundamental questions of identity, and roughly evenly balanced in mass support, bipartisan action in the style of mid-century Washington is difficult or impossible. In this environment, citizens view any policy in terms of its real or symbolic impact on racial groups, on rich and poor, and on the social structure of gender. This allows polarized voices within each party to demonize their opponents, and many political leaders play to this polarization as a strategy to grow their own stature; this makes it nearly impossible to forge meaningful bipartisan reform. But 1950s-style bipartisan policy-making may not be the most likely—or even realistic—path to sustained reform of entrenched, ascriptive systems of power and hierarchy. In fact, that bipartisanship, arguably, was built on a foundation of racial (and gender) exclusion (Kalb and Kuo, 2018).

From another perspective, if we are to address entrenched hierarchies, we must first get them onto the agenda in clear terms. The increasing linkage between partisan support and views on race, gender and class allow—and even require—the parties to stake distinct positions on these issues, making it clearer where everyone stands. To be a Democrat is to be progressive with respect to questions of gender, race and class, and vice versa; my analyses imply that voters are increasingly aware of what they are going to get on these issues from each party. For a liberal egalitarian, who views systems of racial (and other) oppression as central to American political economy since the Founding, this clarification of partisanship is probably crucial to building sustained support for real change. Only if and when Democrats can claim a clear political mandate for a platform of structural change will we see major reforms to address these inequalities.[17]

If all this is true, then it means that the "space" to create public interest-based politics based on shared regard for the common good is vanishingly thin at the national level, or maybe just vanished. If so, it is all the more important to consider the Barnes/Williamson proposition in Chapter 2 of this book that it is more possible to build a politics of inclusive community at the local level that is not defined by hyper-partisan conflict, and look to local communities as the most likely place to build strong coalitions favoring community wealth building. So while the future remains uncertain, it's important to build as many positive examples of community wealth building-type initiatives as possible at local and state scales, both because they are probably easier to advance now than major federal reform and because they may prove instructive to future national reform efforts.

NOTES

1. Supplemental figures and statistical analyses for this chapter are in an online appendix, available at https://www.nicholasjgwinter.com/assets/papers/WinterCWBAppendix.pdf.
2. On the broader difficulties inherent in conceptualizing women (or men) as a coherent, cohesive political group, see Young (1994).
3. See, however, Schickler (2016), who argues that party change on civil rights began earlier and was driven by ordinary citizens and state-level party officials, not national party elites.
4. With minor variation over the years, the full question wording is "We'd like to get your feelings about some groups in American society. When I read the name of a group, we'd like you to rate it with what we call a feeling thermometer. Ratings between 50 degrees and 100 degrees mean that you feel favorably and warm toward the group; ratings between 0 and 50 degrees mean that you don't feel favorably towards the group and that you don't care too much for that group. If you don't feel particularly warm or cold toward a group you would rate them at 50 degrees. If we come to a group you don't know much about, just tell me and we'll move on to the next one."
5. This categorization is based on the standard ANES party identification question, which asks, "Generally speaking, do you usually think of yourself as a Republican, a Democrat, an Independent, or what?"
6. The wording change matters a little for evaluations of the out-party. In the years when both were asked, Democrats and Republicans are equally positive toward both co-partisans (the solid plotting symbols) and their own party itself (the hollow symbols). People 0rate the opposing *party* lower than *out-partisans* by about five points. Thus, by asking about partisans rather than the party, we observe less affective polarization. Nevertheless, both measures show the same trend of increasing polarization. It is unfortunate that the question about partisans does not appear in more recent studies, as it would be interesting to learn whether Americans continue to draw this distinction between the out-party and its partisans in this more polarized era.
7. The online appendix has tables with the numbers underlying the figures.
8. ANES cumulative file variables VCF0253 and VCF0225, respectively. The latter item asked respondents to rate "the women's liberation movement" from 1972 through 1984, and then "the women's movement" from 1986 through 2000.
9. My racial sympathy measure is simply the reverse-scored version of racial resentment.
10. This figure is analogous to the difference scores plotted at the bottom of Figure 10.1.
11. Democrats' ratings averaged 63 degrees in 1984, compared with Republicans' average of 51 degrees. The online appendix includes plots showing the average ratings by members of each party that underlie these differences.
12. In 2008, racial sympathy dropped among members of both parties, with an especially sharp decrease among Democrats. It then held steady in 2012 among Democrats, while continuing to drop among Republicans. In 2016, racial sympathy increased dramatically among Democrats and increased moderately among Republicans, leading to the largest polarization in the series.

13. Interestingly, and consistent with this interpretation, the decline in economic polarization in 2016 was driven by Republicans growing substantially warmer toward unions.
14. I use ANES items about partisans ("Democrats" and "Republicans") and about parties ("Democratic Party" and Republican Party"); in years where both were asked, I average them.
15. I average the two ratings when both are available.
16. The results are very similar in models restricted to white respondents and in models run separately among men and women. See the online appendix.
17. Many have argued that demographic destiny favors the long-run success of such a Democratic party (e.g., Judis and Teixeira, 2004). In the meantime, however, Donald Trump's success illustrates the power of backlash among those at the top of the historic hierarchies, and of Republican strategies to undermine voting rights (Hayter, this volume).

REFERENCES

Abramowitz, Alan I. and Kyle Saunders (2005), "Why can't we all just get along? The reality of a polarized America," *The Forum*, 3(2), Article 1.

Adams, Greg D. (1997), "Abortion: evidence of an issue evolution," *American Journal of Political Science*, 41(3), 718–37.

American National Election Studies (ANES) (2018), *ANES Cumulative Data File, 1948–2016*, accessed June 23, 2020 at https://electionstudies.org/data-center/ANES -time-series-cumulative-data-file/.

Andersen, Kristi (1996), *After Suffrage: Women in Partisan and Electoral Politics Before the New Deal*, Chicago, IL: University of Chicago Press.

Bartels, Larry M. (2006), "What's the matter with What's the matter with Kansas?" *Quarterly Journal of Political Science*, 1(2), 201–26.

Beauvoir, Simone de (1949 [2010]), *The Second Sex*, translated by Constance Borde and Sheila Malovany-Chevallier, New York: Alfred A. Knopf.

Bock, Jarrod, Jennifer Byrd-Craven and Melissa Burkley (2017), "The role of sexism in voting in the 2016 presidential election," *Personality and Individual Differences*, 119, 189–93.

Bracic, Ana, Mackenzie Israel-Trummel and Allyson F. Shortle (2019), "Is sexism for white people? Gender stereotypes, race, and the 2016 presidential election," *Political Behavior*, 41(2), 281–307.

Campbell, Angus, Philip E. Converse, Warren E. Miller and Donald E. Stokes (1960), "Membership in social groupings," in *The American Voter*, New York: John Wiley and Sons, pp. 295–332.

Carmines, Edward G. and James A. Stimson (1989), *Issue Evolution: Race and the Transformation of American Politics*, Princeton, NJ: Princeton University Press.

Converse, Philip E. (1964), "The nature of belief systems in mass publics," in David Ernest Apter (ed.), *Ideology and Discontent*, New York: Free Press, pp. 206–61.

Cook, Elizabeth Adell and Clyde Wilcox (1991), "Feminism and the gender gap—a second look," *Journal of Politics*, 53(4), 1111–22.

Dahl, Robert Alan (1956), *A Preface to Democratic Theory*, Chicago, IL: University of Chicago Press.

Dawson, Michael C. (1994), *Behind the Mule: Race and Class in African-American Politics*, Princeton, NJ: Princeton University Press.

Fiorina, Morris P., Samuel J. Abrams and Jeremy Pope (2006), *Culture War? The Myth of a Polarized America*, 2nd edition, New York: Pearson Longman.

Frankenberg, Ruth (1993), *White Women, Race Matters: The Social Construction of Whiteness*, Minneapolis, MN: University of Minnesota Press.

Frasure-Yokley, Lorrie (2018), "Choosing the velvet glove: women voters, ambivalent sexism, and vote choice in 2016," *The Journal of Race, Ethnicity, and Politics*, 3(1), 3–25.

Gilens, Martin (1988), "Gender and support for Reagan: a comprehensive model of presidential approval," *American Journal of Political Science*, 32(1), 19–49.

Green, Donald P., Bradley Palmquist and Eric Schickler (2002), *Partisan Hearts and Minds: Political Parties and the Social Identities of Voters*, New Haven, CT: Yale University Press.

Hetherington, Marc J. (2001), "Resurgent mass partisanship: the role of elite polarization," *The American Political Science Review*, 95(3), 619–31.

Hillygus, D. Sunshine and Todd G. Shields (2008), *The Persuadable Voter: Wedge Issues in Presidential Campaigns*, Princeton, NJ: Princeton University Press.

Iyengar, Shanto and Sean J. Westwood (2015), "Fear and loathing across party lines: new evidence on group polarization," *American Journal of Political Science*, 59(3), 690–707.

Jackman, Mary R. (1994), *The Velvet Glove: Paternalism and Conflict in Gender, Class, and Race Relations*, Berkeley and Los Angeles, CA: University of California Press.

Judis, John B. and Ruy Teixeira (2004), *The Emerging Democratic Majority*, reprint, New York: Scribner.

Kalb, Johanna and Didi Kuo (2018), "Reassessing American democracy: the enduring challenge of racial exclusion," *Michigan Law Review Online*, 117, 55–62.

Kaufmann, Karen M. (2002), "Culture wars, secular realignment, and the gender gap in party identification," *Political Behavior*, 24(3), 283–307.

Kaufmann, Karen M. and John R. Petrocik (1999), "The changing politics of American men: understanding the sources of the gender gap," *American Journal of Political Science*, 43(3), 864–87.

Kinder, Donald R. and Allison Dale-Riddle (2012), *The End of Race? Obama, 2008, and Racial Politics in America*, New Haven, CT: Yale University Press.

Kinder, Donald R. and Nathan P. Kalmoe (2017), *Neither Liberal nor Conservative: Ideological Innocence in the American Public*, Chicago, IL: University of Chicago Press.

Kinder, Donald R. and Lynn M. Sanders (1996), *Divided by Color: Racial Politics and Democratic Ideals*, Chicago, IL: University of Chicago Press.

Kinder, Donald R. and Nicholas Winter (2001), "Exploring the racial divide: blacks, whites, and opinion on national policy," *American Journal of Political Science*, 45(2), 439–56.

Ladd, Everett Carll (1997), "Media framing of the gender gap," in Pippa Norris (ed.), *Women, Media, and Politics*, New York: Oxford University Press, pp. 113–28.

Levendusky, Matthew (2013), *How Partisan Media Polarize America*, Chicago, IL: University of Chicago Press.

Madison, James (1787 [2005]), "10. James Madison, November 22, 1787. The same subject continued," in J.R. Pole (ed.), *The Federalist*, Indianapolis, IN: Hackett Publishing Company, pp. 48–54.

Mansbridge, Jane J. (1985), "Myth and reality: the ERA and the gender gap in the 1980 election," *Public Opinion Quarterly*, 49(2), 164–78.

Manza, Jeff and Clem Brooks (1998), "The gender gap in U.S. presidential elections: When? Why? Implications?" *American Journal of Sociology*, 103(5), 1235–66.

McCall, Leslie and Jeff Manza (2011), "Class differences in social and political attitudes in the United States," in George C. Edwards III, Lawrence R. Jacobs and Robert Y. Shapiro (eds), *The Oxford Handbook of American Public Opinion and the Media*, New York: Oxford University Press.

McThomas, Mary and Michael Tesler (2016), "The growing influence of gender attitudes on public support for Hillary Clinton, 2008–2012," *Politics & Gender*, 12(1), 28–49.

Mendelberg, Tali (2001), *The Race Card: Campaign Strategy, Implicit Messages, and the Norm of Equality*, Princeton, NJ: Princeton University Press.

Miller, Arthur H., Christopher Wlezien and Anne Hildreth (1991), "A reference group theory of partisan coalitions," *The Journal of Politics*, 53(4), 1134–49.

Nelson, Thomas E. and Donald R. Kinder (1996), "Issue frames and group-centrism in American public opinion," *Journal of Politics*, 58(4), 1055–78.

Petrocik, John R. (1987), "Realignment: new party coalitions and the nationalization of the South," *The Journal of Politics*, 49(2), 347–75.

Ratliff, Kate A., Liz Redford, John Conway and Colin Tucker Smith (2019), "Engendering support: hostile sexism predicts voting for Donald Trump over Hillary Clinton in the 2016 U.S. presidential election," *Group Processes & Intergroup Relations*, 22(4), 578–93.

Schaffner, Brian F., Matthew MacWilliams and Tatishe Nteta (2018), "Understanding white polarization in the 2016 vote for president: the sobering role of racism and sexism," *Political Science Quarterly*, 133(1), 9–34.

Schickler, Eric (2016), *Racial Realignment: The Transformation of American Liberalism, 1932–1965*, Princeton, NJ: Princeton University Press.

Setzler, Mark and Alixandra B. Yanus (2018), "Why did women vote for Donald Trump?" *PS: Political Science & Politics*, 51(3), 523–7.

Shapiro, Robert Y. and Harpreet Mahajan (1986), "Gender differences in policy preferences: a summary of trends from the 1960s to the 1980s," *Public Opinion Quarterly*, 50(1), 42–61.

Spruill, Marjorie J. (2008), "Gender and America's turn right," in Bruce J. Schulman and Julian E. Zelizer (eds), *Rightward Bound: Making America Conservative in the 1970s*, Cambridge, MA: Harvard University Press, pp. 71–89.

Spruill, Marjorie J. (2017), *Divided We Stand: The Battle Over Women's Rights and Family Values That Polarized American Politics*, New York: Bloomsbury Publishing USA.

Sundquist, James L. (1983), *Dynamics of the Party System: Alignment and Realignment of Political Parties in the United States*, Washington, DC: Brookings Institution Press.

Tesler, Michael and David O. Sears (2010), "President Obama and the growing polarization of partisan attachments by racial attitudes and race," presented at the Annual Meeting of the American Political Science Association.

Valentino, Nicholas, Carly Wayne and Marzia Oceno (2018), "Mobilizing sexism: the interaction of emotion and gender attitudes in the 2016 U.S. presidential election," *Public Opinion Quarterly*, 82(S1), 213–35.

Weisberg, Herbert F. and Arthur H. Miller (1980), *Evaluation of the Feeling Thermometer: A Report to the National Election Study Board Based on Data from the 1979 Pilot Survey*, technical report to the National Election Studies Board of Overseers.

Wilcox, Clyde, Lee Sigelman and Elizabeth Cook (1989), "Some like it hot: individual differences in responses to group feeling thermometers," *Public Opinion Quarterly*, 53(2), 246–57.

Winter, Nicholas J.G. (2018), "Assessing the impact of hostile and benevolent sexism in 2016: across levels of office and types of candidate," presented at the Annual Meeting of the American Political Science Association, Boston, MA.

Winter, Nicholas J.G. and Adam J. Berinsky (1999), "What's your temperature? Thermometer ratings and political analysis," presented at the Annual Meeting of the American Political Science Association, Atlanta, GA.

Young, Iris Marion (1994), "Gender as seriality: thinking about women as a social collective," *Signs*, 19(3), 713–38.

Zaller, John (1992), *The Nature and Origins of Mass Opinion*, Cambridge, UK: Cambridge University Press.

11. "Many new barriers": democracy and resistance to the Voting Rights Act of 1965[1]

Julian Maxwell Hayter

INTRODUCTION: THE VRA AND RACIAL DEMOCRACY

On August 6, 1965, President Lyndon Baines Johnson signed one of the toughest civil rights bills in United States history, the Voting Rights Act of 1965 (VRA). The VRA signified the high-water mark of American civil rights legislation—in containing both precautionary and disciplinary measures, the bill surpassed previous civil rights legislation. The VRA prohibited discriminatory tests and devices as requirements for voting in federal elections. Section 2 of the VRA forbade voting qualifications, prerequisites, and practices, such as grandfather clauses and literacy tests. The act gave federal examiners the ability to supervise and register voters in areas that were in violation of the law. Section 4 of the act established a triggering formula that froze election laws in states and political subdivisions that used voting tests on and/or after November 1, 1964. Foreseeing resistance, the act also covered states and localities that were in violation of Section 2 and suspended voting laws and/or election-based changes in states and subdivisions that fell under the triggering mechanism. Section 5 required pre-clearance (approval) from Washington—this meant that covered electoral jurisdictions were prohibited from making election-based changes without federal permission (Lawson, 1976, pp. 307–21; 1991, pp. 94–115). Johnson, Congress, the Department of Justice (DOJ), and voting rights advocates anticipated backlash. Southerners— and Washington—met the challenges of emancipation and Reconstruction by systematically denying African Americans their constitutional liberties for nearly a century. Washington designed the VRA to contend, once and for all, with the undemocratic face of Jim Crow segregation, which thrived on white political over-representation. Policy-makers failed, however, to anticipate *sustained* resistance to minority voting rights (Hayter, 2017, p. 64). By the early

2000s, the continuity of anti-VRA sentiment had compromised what Johnson called "the goddamndest, toughest voting rights bill in United States history" (Thernstrom, 1987, p. 15). In terms of race, democracy in America has often met firm resistance.

Contemporary resistance to minority voting rights and the resurgence of direct disenfranchisement has forced experts to reconsider the history of the VRA. The 1965 bill was the crowning achievement of the American civil rights movement. On the one hand, this chapter highlights the monumental achievements of black political actors following the American civil rights movement. On the other hand, the VRA did little to stem the tide of generational and systemic racism. In fact, the forces of restriction worked immediately and tirelessly to undermine the act. The erosion of minority voting rights culminated in *Shelby County* v. *Holder* (United States Supreme Court, 2013), which had long-term implications. We know now that conservatives used administrative appointments—namely, in the Civil Rights Division (CRD) of the DOJ—and federal court nominations to undermine the VRA in less traceable and visible ways (Rhodes, 2017, pp. 1–3). Yet, as African Americans racked up political victories after 1965, racial conservatives worked to weaken the VRA on the local level. Over time, the opponents of minority voting rights borrowed directly from the types of litigation strategies that civil rights organizations used during the high-water mark of the movement. While conservative appointments on the Court played a vital role in gutting the VRA, these subterranean strategies made *Shelby* much more likely.

American democracy has always been a deeply contested affair—doubly so in terms of racial politics. It is impossible to separate the evolution of the VRA from the continuation of racist trends in Southern and American politics (Hayter, 2014, p. 538). Before 1965, the South had never been a democracy. The undemocratic face of the Jim Crow era has been well documented (Kousser, 1999; Lawson, 1976; Valelly, 2004). This history not only cast a long shadow over the region's politics in the late twentieth century, it also belies the story of the civil rights movement as a triumph narrative. To be sure, voting rights upended *de jure* segregation. The freedom struggle, however, failed to eradicate deeply embedded, institutional racism from Southern life. Bigotry, despite the record number of elected minority officials after 1965, found new and continuous expression in the politics of the post-civil rights movement. Indeed, the continuity of vote dilution and the Court's decision in *Shelby* (which effectively gutted Section 4 of the VRA by prohibiting triggering mechanisms as a basis for subjecting jurisdictions to preclearance) have forced scholars to reimagine the arc of American racial progress.

The political abuses of electoral reforms have been a continuous and unfortunate feature of American political development. The United States, experts believe, often wavers between greater political access and more political restrictions (Wang, 2012, p. xiv). Periods of entrenched restriction often follow eras defined by political permissiveness. The civil rights movement, much like Reconstruction nearly a century earlier, is no exception to this rule. African American political equality heightened, rather than alleviated, white anxiety. Anti-VRA forces not only ensured that the struggle for civil rights outlived the 1960s, but conservatives also embraced a long-term strategy to weaken the VRA. Much has been made recently about how Republicans used administrative appointments—namely, in the CRD and the DOJ—and federal court nominations to undermine the VRA in less traceable and visible manners (Rhodes, 2017). We also know that the South's "reddening" and growing conservatism on the Supreme Court emboldened anti-VRA advocates. This chapter is not a delineation of that history. It does, however, demonstrate the declension of minority voting rights by highlighting several key moments on the road to *Shelby*: namely, political developments during the Nixon administration, the VRA's renewal in 1982, the *Shaw* v. *Reno* case (United States Supreme Court, 1993), and the rise of anti-VRA litigants. While these developments do not represent the entire history of the VRA's dismantling, it is my contention that they speak directly to the Court's findings in *Shelby*. In fact, *Shelby* effectively ended Washington's "close scrutiny of the state conduct of elections"—one of the most important aspects of the VRA (Bullock, Gaddie and Wert, 2016, p. xii). The VRA needed combined support from Congress, the courts, and the executive branch to thrive. Conservatives spent the better portion of the late twentieth century weakening that support. *Shelby* was the *coup de grâce*.

THE EARLY YEARS: GAINS AND RESISTANCE TO MINORITY VOTING RIGHTS

The democratic principles embodied in the VRA cannot be explained by separating black mobilization on the one hand, and federal policy directed toward race on the other. Black political will eventually gave rise to calculated white resistance. This resistance, however, does not overshadow the unprecedented rise in black registrants and black elected officials after 1965. The VRA helped shatter *de jure* segregation; by removing franchise restrictions, the act redistributed political authority along racial lines. Washington was also initially committed to the possibility of a multi-racial democracy. The Court, Congress, and the executive branch were essential to the VRA's initial effectiveness. Yet, Southerners, who had grown accustomed to one-party rule and the oligarchy it engendered, were determined to beat back the tide of racial permissiveness. The dialectic that emerged between black voters and white detractors set the stage for a new chapter in American political development. This chapter demonstrated that political improvements and political marginalization often exist at the same time.

The VRA contributed substantially to marked increases in minority electoral participation. The belief that African Americans were not active in Southern politics prior to 1965 remains a popular misconception about the Jim Crow era. By 1956, roughly one million of the South's roughly five million voting-age African Americans had registered to vote (Hayter, 2017, pp. 40–41). The struggles black Americans endured to secure the ballot inspired the creation of the VRA and led to increased black political activity, especially after 1965. Two years after the VRA's enactment, the Department of Justice estimated that 416 000 new African Americans had registered to vote throughout the South. Black registration shot up to more than 50 percent of the voting age population in every state that fell under the VRA's jurisdiction. Mississippi underwent dramatic changes—black registration rose from 6.7 to 59.8 percent of the total voting-age African American population. The rest of the Deep South underwent similar increases. In the Upper South, North Carolina's percentage of voting-age African Americans rose from 46.8 to 51.3 percent. Virginia's percentage of voting-age African Americans rose from 38.3 to 55.6. In fact, all states covered by the VRA's triggering mechanism in Section 4 saw increases in black registration. In 1966, black officials held approximately 159 public offices. That number rose to 200 by 1967 (United States Commission on Civil Rights, 1968, pp. 14–15). Between 1964 and 1972, more than 1 million new African Americans voters were registered in the seven states covered by the act. Between 1965 and 1972, the gap between white and black registrants had been reduced from roughly 44 percent to roughly 11 percent (United States Commission on Civil Rights, 1975, pp. 40–47). These developments in voting registration led to dramatic changes in electoral politics.

Southern African Americans wanted more than symbolic political victories, and with the landslide of African American registration, they had the votes to realize these ends (Hayter, 2017, pp. 67–8). The ratification of the VRA, it turned out, was the beginning of a new, more complex era in American democracy. African Americans quickly transitioned from protest to electoral politics. In the years immediately following 1965, the rise in African American voters led to a substantial increase in the number of blacks running for and winning office. By February of 1968, voters elected 156 officials—including 14 state legislators, 81 county officials, and 61 municipal officeholders—to the seven states covered by the VRA. By 1974, that number had increased to 963— including 1 U.S. congressperson, 36 state legislators, 429 county officials, and 497 municipal officeholders (United States Commission on Civil Rights, 1975, pp. 48–9). These elected officials, in keeping with Bayard Rustin's claims in his article "From Protest to Politics," "now sought advances in employment, housing, school integration, police protection, and so forth" (Rustin, 1965).

Their demands, which endeavored to address nearly a century of systematic neglect, heightened white Southerners' anxiety about growing black radicalism. Rather than embrace the politics of pluralism by sharing power, Southern powerbrokers often resolved to resist these initiatives.

Federal supervision of elections got off to a confusing, glacial start, and Southerners met black ballots with vote dilution (Moye, 2004, p. 23). By 1966, Washington assigned roughly 600 federal officials to enforce the VRA throughout the South. One year later, some 1500 federal observers attended elections in the South. Their presence may have given rise to unprecedented black political activity, but it also fanned the flames of states' rights and anti-Washington segregationists (Office of Civil Rights Evaluation, 2004, p. 5). As Washington watched African Americans transform Southern politics after 1965, whites resolved to weaken African American votes after they had been cast. Three years after Washington passed the VRA, the United States Commission on Civil Rights (USCCR) released *Political Participation* (United States Commission on Civil Rights, 1968) one of its many data-collection reports on the state of black voting (Hayter, 2017, p. 74). Of the 222 total pages in this report, more than half explained the methods Southern officials had devised to maintain political control. Local officials often camouflaged vote dilution mechanisms as color-blind urban and political reforms. They combined white and black districts, relocated polling places to white neighborhoods, threatened economic reprisals against black voters and candidates, switched to at-large election systems, and annexed predominantly white, first-ring suburbs. Apart from observers, legal oversight was slow. CRD lawyers were responsible for supervising voting rights complications. These officials also oversaw school segregation matters, instances of employment discrimination, and segregation in public accommodations. The 40 CRD lawyers were often overworked. Because of limited personnel, the DOJ and CRD concentrated most of their efforts in Alabama, Louisiana, and Mississippi—areas most commonly associated with acrimonious bigotry (United States Commission on Civil Rights, 1968, p. 169). Furthermore, the DOJ was uncertain about which electoral changes actually fell under Section 5's preclearance clause. Southern politicians often argued that changes in electoral procedures, such as annexations, denied no one the right to vote and, therefore, were not discriminatory. Local officials argued that rules such as annexations were meant to maintain cities' economic viability—especially cities trending toward majority-minority status. Washington disagreed.

Ostensibly, color-blind political machinations, for a brief moment in time, confounded federal officials. The DOJ brought only one suit against voting-related changes before the Court expanded Section 5 to cover vote dilution in *Allen* v. *the State Board of Elections* (United States Supreme Court, 1969; Hayter, 2017, p. 113). In fact, in the late 1960s and early 1970s, a deluge of cases concerning vote dilution inundated state and federal court systems. Most of these cases (including *Allen*, which involved jurisdictions in Mississippi and Virginia) were local in nature and specifically addressed the rise of structural electoral impediments (e.g., annexations) that ostensibly denied no one the right to vote (Kousser, 1999, p. 2; Parker, 1990; Valelly, 2004, pp. 213–18). Annexations accounted for 30.5 percent of the rejected changes, the highest percentage of dilution tactics recorded by the USCCR (United States Commission on Civil Rights, 1981, pp. 64–70). One thing seemed certain—as African Americans made electoral gains, white Southerners grew increasingly, yet more subtly, committed to undermining their progress.

Washington beat back vote dilution by changing the meaning of representative democracy in America. Federal officials mandated that localities implement majority-minority district systems; in doing so, policy-makers accepted the centrality of racial discourse in American politics. As white officials maneuvered to minimize the impact of black ballots, Chief Justice Warren Burger's Supreme Court recognized that resistance to the VRA might be characterized as anti-democratic. The Court eventually parlayed an employment-based affirmative action remedy known as "disparate impact analysis" (established to defend proportional representation in workplaces) to achieve equal representation. Justices held that facially neutral actions could have disproportionate and disparate impacts on minorities. In terms of voting rights, the Court applied this logic to policies that allowed blacks to vote but diluted the impact of those votes (*Griggs* v. *Duke Power Company*; see United States Supreme Court Reports, 1971). Although the Court struggled to find a standard for vote dilution, they eventually held that a "presence of factors" often made it harder for minority groups to elect preferred candidates, even though African Americans were voting in record numbers. According to historian Richard Valelly (2004, p. 215), "the Court held that an accumulation of indirect evidence [...] sufficed to show discriminatory intent. This became known as the Court's 'totality of circumstances' test." The Court eventually mandated district systems (a political jurisdiction—often made up of counties and/or precincts—that elects one officeholder to represent a region on a larger legislative body) to protect black voters and elected officials from vote dilution. As whites devised subtle strategies to weaken black ballots, Washington began to focus on electoral outcomes.

In protecting the ability of voters to elect candidates of their choice, Washington transformed voting rights from intent to effect. Covered jurisdictions submitted 30 332 potential changes to voting practices and procedures under Section 5 between 1975 and 1980, during the reapportionment revolution. In many of these cases, policy-makers made electoral changes with no discriminatory intent. In other cases, however, the DOJ issued over 700 rejections, the vast majority pertained to minority vote dilution. By the early 1990s, federal officials made hundreds of American cities and state-level jurisdictions switch from at-large to single-member district systems (Hayter, 2017, p. 153). These districts, it turned out, may have led to the election of countless local, state, and federal black officeholders, but they had ominous implications for future of representative racial democracy.

The VRA may have revolutionized representative democracy in America, but it also heightened opposition to the possibility of minority governance. During the twilight of the twentieth century, the VRA's detractors came to loathe Section 5's preclearance clause and Section 4's covering mechanism, even though their obstinance had inspired Washington to ratchet up the VRA. Leading voting rights scholars agree that the Second Reconstruction initially succeeded in large part because of jurisprudential and congressional backing. As institutional support eroded and anti-VRA sentiment gained momentum, minority voting rights were in jeopardy.

THE ROAD TO *SHELBY:* THE CONTINUITY OF ANTI-VRA SENTIMENT

In *Shelby County* v. *Holder* (United States Supreme Court Reports, 2013), the Supreme Court gutted the VRA by lifting the coverage formula in Section 4. More specifically, the Court declined to rule on the constitutionality of the VRA broadly and instead struck one of the act's most important, yet provisional sections—the triggering mechanism that made jurisdictions subject to the preclearance clause in Section 5. In fact, *Shelby* did more than strike down Section 4—the Court's decision "effectively ended close scrutiny of the conduct of state elections and, possibly, put forward the notion that states deserve 'equal sovereignty'," the notion that the federal government cannot single out states for preferential treatment (Bullock et al., 2016, p. 151). The Court argued further that, given the number of African American voters and elected officials, Section 4 and its triggering mechanism were no longer relevant to current voter discrimination. In gutting Section 4, the Court neutralized Section 5. Conservative attacks on Section 4 predate Chief Justice John Robert's Supreme Court. Attempts to "de-regionalize" the VRA's coverage formula date back to the Nixon administration. In fact, resistance to Section 4's triggering mechanism (and the politics of discriminatory intent) was decades in the making. Political scientist Jesse H. Rhodes (2017, p. 3) argues:

> Conservative elected officials who opposed the expansion of federal voting rights enforcement—but were willing to do so for fear of alienating both people of color and moderate white voters and thereby harming their party's electoral prospects—

adopted a sophisticated long-term strategy to weaken the Act while maintaining a positive public reputation on voting rights matters.

In other words, the politics of Jim Crowism gave way to a type of color-blind double-speak that detrimentally influenced minority voting rights. *Shelby* sounded the death knell for the VRA.

Richard Nixon's administration was the first to challenge regional cover- age in the VRA. By 1970, the Nixon administration and Southern delegates attempted to undermine Sections 4 and 5. To shore up the Southern Strategy, Nixon held that the triggering formula in Section 4 and preclearance clause in Section 5 should apply to all political jurisdictions in the United States or be struck from the act. Southerners, whose antipathy toward Washington dated back to Reconstruction, were of the same mind. During the Ninety-first Congress, Southern representatives attempted to "de-regionalize" the VRA by having it apply to all 50 states (Graham, 1990, pp. 360–66; Lawson, 1985, pp. 168–70). A bipartisan coalition led by Senate Minority Leader Hugh Scott (R-Pennsylvania) not only renewed a five-year extension of the VRA in its original form, but also added a provision sponsored by Senate Majority Leader Mike Mansfield (D-Montana) to enfranchise 18-year-olds. Given growing disapproval of military endeavors in Vietnam, the 18-year-olds rule tipped the scales. The House voted to accept the Senate bill by 224–183. Nixon, despite opposing constitutionally impermissible statutory enfranchisement and an amendment to the Constitution that allowed 18-year-olds to vote, signed the extended VRA for five more years on June 22, 1970 (Evans and Novak, 1971; Graham, 1990, pp. 357–65). Fatefully, the VRA not only maintained coverage over Southern states, but the renewed version also identified non-Southern jurisdictions where less than half of minority populations were registered to vote on November 1, 1968 (Graham, 1990, p. 361).

Having lost the battle over the VRA's renewal, Attorney General John Mitchell attempted to reorganize the Civil Rights Division of the DOJ. Nixon's administration continued the fight against the VRA's Section 4 during the summer of 1970. Following the creation of the CRD in the Civil Rights Act of 1957, policy-makers organized the division into sections that covered specific geographic regions. These sections were responsible for handling the full panoply of civil rights matters in their respective jurisdictions—in fact, the Southern region contained the very attorneys that suffered from limited per- sonnel. The number of attorneys in the South had been reduced in November of 1967 from 40 to 27 (United States Commission on Civil Rights, 1968, p. 169). John Mitchell reorganized these attorneys into issue-specific branches that had a nationwide focus. The departmental reorganization created branches that focused entirely on monitoring school integration, employment discrim- ination, and/or voting rights violations. Much to the chagrin of Southerners, the newly established Voting Rights Section almost exclusively covered the South. In fact, the section brought together a group of lawyers—many of them liberals left from Johnson's administration—that were specifically dedicated to enforcing Section 5 (Lawson, 1985, p. 162). Reagan's administration went further.

The Reagan administration met the challenges of Nixon's clumsiness more delicately. By the early 1980s, New Federalism and rising states' rights sentiment began to grip the nation, and policy-makers maneuvered to weaken the enforcement mechanisms in the VRA by quietly reorganizing critical departments in the CRD. William Bradford "Brad" Reynolds, assistant attorney general under Edwin Meese, re-staffed CRD with Reagan loyalists. These conservatives were given direct oversight over longstanding CRD members (many of them liberal holdovers from the Carter era). According to Rhodes (2017, pp. 106–12), these conservatives purposefully obstructed federal oversight of local elections. While Section 4 was still enforceable, the DOJ began to quietly undermine the effectiveness of the coverage formula by turning a blind eye to voting rights violations. The DOJ not only significantly slowed the litigation process, but also filed only ten suits against VRA infractions between 1982 and 1985. If the VRA initially represented an achievement in terms of federal intervention, the enforcement mechanisms were still "a reactive process" (Hardzinski, 2016). By obstructing the legal process, Reagan's CRD effectively undermined the power of the VRA. Conservatives in the CRD, however, were not simply getting marching orders from the White House. Anti-VRA sentiment at the local level began to rear its ugly head during the renewal of the VRA in 1981–82.

Local Southerners put the VRA in the proverbial crosshairs during the renewal process. Although hundreds of witnesses testified in support of the VRA during the renewal hearings of 1981, anti-VRA advocates testified against the renewal, and their criticisms, we now know, laid the road to *Shelby.* Virginians, because of their proximity to Washington (and the fact that the VRA covered the "Old Dominion," that is, the U.S. Commonwealth of Virginia), played a key role in the public hearing process. On May 20, 1981, Richmond Mayor Henry L. Marsh (D) and State Senator L. Douglas Wilder (D) spoke in front of Congress about the urgent need for voting rights mandates. They argued that Richmond's history of recent vote dilution (Richmond had annexed a portion of a predominantly white county in 1969) justified an extension of the VRA, including the extension of sections 2 and 5 (Hayter, 2017, p. 187). On the same day, Virginia's Third District congressperson and Richmond's former mayor, Thomas Bliley (R), argued in front of the same House Judiciary Sub-Committee against both the act's extension and the creation of stronger criteria, what experts called "the Senate factors." Bliley attempted not just to strike the bill down, but also in Congressperson Barney

Frank's (D) words, to "gut the bill fairly effectively" by attacking Section 2. In fact, Congress was debating whether Section 2 required proof of discriminatory intent (Congress later held that it did not, thus validating disparate impact claims) (Office of Civil Rights Evaluation, 2004, p. 4). More specifically, Bliley lobbied against the creation of stronger criteria—the "Senate factors"—for the courts to consider when assessing the "totality of circumstances" test (Boyd and Markman, 1983, p. 1378). In total, nine of Virginia's ten congresspeople voted against the VRA's extension in 1981. They had local support.

These congresspeople, with the help of Richmond Councilor George Stevenson Kemp, found like-minded allies in Richmond. The city of Richmond was not merely covered by Section 4 of the VRA, the former capital of the Confederacy also met the "totality of circumstances" criteria. In fact, Burger's Supreme Court and the DOJ mandated a district-based system in 1977 to counter the dilutive voting influence of the 1969 annexation of Chesterfield County. By 1981, Richmond had been under the authority of black majority council for roughly four years. Black elected officials met firm resistance, and whites began to argue nationally that districts represented reverse discrimination. Just prior to the renewal of the VRA, the *Richmond Times-Dispatch* (RTD) ran an editorial that summed up growing anti VRA-sentiment. The paper cited a Republican think tank's examination of the post-1965 developments in voting rights. The RTD placed a portion of the study on its editorial page. It read:

> The right to vote does not mean the right to be elected. Democracy is based on the rights of individuals, not groups. The logical conclusion concerning proportional representation in regard to the Voting Rights Act would be to establish a quota system concerning the election of minorities to office. Any quota system for elected officials will destroy a democratic government. (*Richmond Times-Dispatch*, 1981)

In August 1981, a group of white citizens traveled to Washington to demonstrate the ways in which a Richmond plan to draw new districts for city council elections discriminated against white voters. While no record exists of the conversation, the council minority's efforts were the first time in the 16-year history of the VRA that a group of white citizens made such an argument (*Richmond Afro-American & Planet*, 1981, p. 2). It would not be the last.

Nowhere was the antipathy for the VRA more evident and deeply contradictory than over the issue of racial districting and discriminatory intent. On the one hand, the compression of black voters into exclusively urban enclaves—due in large part to the continuation of segregated residential patterns—expedited the rise of the Republican South. Over time, political scientists Earl and Merle Black (2003, pp. 331–7) argue, reapportionment and redistricting for congressional districts led to almost exclusively Republican districts in the South's suburbs. Local politics, particularly in cities with size-able majority populations, had become almost exclusively Democratic. While African Americans often held district majorities in the South's urban enclaves, congressional districts in exurban and suburban areas, in effect, became safe Republican districts. Yet, at the same time that Republicans worked to undermine the VRA behind closed doors, they were also instrumental in renewing the VRA after 1965. The politics of self-interest at times eclipsed racism. Minority-majority districts may have protected African American and Democratic representation in urban areas, but they also gave rise to racially homogeneous districts—especially in the South—that began to vote almost exclusively for GOP[2] candidates in the late twentieth century. Racial redistrict-ing, it turns out, was instrumental in the reddening of the South.

By the early 1990s, however, the Court began to chip away at VRA's oversight mechanisms. *Shaw* v. *Reno* (United States Supreme Court Reports, 1993) put Section 2 of the VRA in the proverbial crosshairs and, in doing so, presaged *Shelby*. *Shaw* (United States Supreme Court Reports, 2013) too had local implications. In 1991, a group of five white North Carolinian voters tested the constitutionality of the state's new district system. These white voters claimed that the new districts tortured district lines, which they held amounted to racial gerrymandering. They also argued that the districts violated the equal protection clause of the Fourteenth Amendment. In time, Attorney General Janet Reno rejected the state's plan because it created only one majority-minority district. After the state re-submitted a second plan with two black districts (one of which was a 160-mile-long district that was often no wider than an expressway), the litigants appealed the case to the Court. *Shaw* helped undermine disparate impact claims by tightening the legal parameters for showing discriminatory intent in cases of vote dilution. In making juris-dictions prove that elections rules were purposefully discriminatory, the case required policy-makers to put forward more convincing arguments for drawing minority-majority districts. The Court went further—it also insinuated that North Carolina's whites might be harmed by increasing the number of black representatives (Hayter, 2017, p. 240). The Court also clamped down on pre-clearance by making discriminatory intent harder to prove. In *Shaw*, the Court not only failed to recognize the long history of voting discrimination, it also implied that African Americans' special treatment in Washington was ending (United States Supreme Court Reports, 1993). These types of race-neutral legal decisions and/or legal decisions that completely ignored the historical oppression against African Americans as a group set the stage for the 2000s. By the turn of the century, anti-VRA sentiment swelled at the grassroots level and migrated up to Washington (Hayter, 2017, pp. 239–41).

By the early 2000s, career litigants began to test the validity of the VRA directly in Court. Although the VRA contributed to the rise of the Republican

South, Southern states began to push back against preclearance in the 2000s. Southerners started to use the judicial process—rather than the legislative process—to challenge the VRA's bailout and preclearance formulas (Bullock et al., 2016, p. 131). Anti-VRA advocates found allies in justices John Roberts and Samuel Alito, appointed in 2005 and 2006, respectively. They also had everyday supporters—namely, a former stockbroker from Texas named Edward Blum. Blum began to subsidize and fund research that challenged the constitutionality of majority-minority districts in the 1990s. By *Shelby*, Blum had orchestrated upwards of two dozen lawsuits against affirmative action and voting rights laws (Hartocollis, 2017). In fact, Blum spent the better portion of the 1990s (particularly in *Bush* v. *Vera*; see United States Supreme Court Reports, 1996) and 2000s probing the constitutionality of the VRA generally. By the early 2000s, he had transformed into a career litigant. His Project on Fair Representation and other organizations, such as Charles Koch's Americans for Prosperity, gained significant traction following the renewal of the VRA in 2006 (Rhodes, 2017, p. 161). Blum sought out local jurisdictions that might be amenable to challenging vulnerable sections in the VRA. In 2008, he found a Texas county willing to test the constitutionality of Section 4 and Section 5. The case came to be known as *Northwest Austin Municipal Utility District Number One* [NAMUDNO] v. *Holder* (United States Supreme Court Reports, 2009). Blum inspired the NAMUDNO to seek a declaratory judgment exempting it from Section 5. The district, which had no history of discrimination, requested a bailout under Section 4 of the VRA. District representatives also alternatively argued that Section 5—given that the district had no history of discrimination—was unconstitutional. The Court (9–0) held that the VRA permits all political jurisdictions, including NAMUDNO, to seek a bailout (mandated in Section 4a) from Section 5's preclearance clause. The Court also held that since only 17 of 12 000 districts had bailed out of the VRA, Congress had no intention for the preclearance process to be difficult. While the Court agreed with Blum and the Texas district, it declined to rule on the constitutionality of Section 4. More specifically, it invoked constitutional avoidance. In ruling that the utility district had the right to seek a bailout from preclearance, the Court resolved the matter. It went further four years later.

The failure to update the triggering mechanism in Section 4 proved to be the VRA's undoing in *Shelby*. Blum sought out Shelby County, Alabama, too. In fact, he cold-called Shelby County district attorney, Frank Ellis, several years before 2013 (Hartocollis, 2017). Blum, it turned out, had been searching for covered counties that had recently struggled with preclearance. In 2010, Shelby County too sought a bailout from Section 5. The county, which was over 50 percent African American, challenged Sections 4(b)'s coverage formula and the subsequent triggering mechanism (which dated back to November 1, 1964) that made the county subject to Section 5. In 2012, the U.S. Court of Appeals upheld the coverage formula and Section 5. Blum urged the county to appeal the ruling. And it did, on the grounds that the November 1, 1964 triggering date, which stipulated that a less-than-50-percent-turnout rate in presidential elections warranted preclearance, was outdated, and no longer reflected the electoral culture of Shelby County. The Court agreed. Using voter registration statistics and the electoral achievements of minorities, Chief Justice Roberts, who delivered the opinion, held that Section 4 of the VRA imposed current burdens on political subdivisions that were no longer receptive to the current electoral conditions. More specifically, the Court (5–4) held that the formula for determining preclearance was outdated and failed to reflect nearly 50 years of racial progress. In striking down Section 4 of the VRA, the Court also struck down Section 5's preclearance clause (*Shelby County* v. *Holder*; see United States Supreme Court Reports, 2013). The enforcement mechanism of the VRA, which policy-makers designed to preclude direct disenfranchisement and stave off the emergence of vote dilution, was no more. Congress, the Court concluded, must devise a new triggering mechanism.

CONCLUSION

In relying on voting registration statistics and the number of elected minority officials alone, the Roberts Court failed to recognize the legacy of subtle machinations that followed the VRA. In the last two decades alone, the DOJ blocked over 800 discriminatory voting-related changes in the South. Despite the legacy of this backlash and efforts to repeal voting rights mandates in the early 1990s, the Roberts Court looked solely to voting statistics and the number of elected officials in the South as evidence of racial progress. Roberts held that Section 4 is premised on 40-year-old facts that have "no logical relationship to the present day." The coverage formula, the court believed, epitomized an unconstitutional imposition on the principle of "equal state sovereignty," because it singled out some localities and states for harsher treatment than others (Rhodes, 2017, p. 161). Yet, due in part to the unintended consequences of residential segregation and congressional redistricting, Republicans control all 11 Southern legislatures. In her dissent, Justice Ruth Bader Ginsberg held:

> The sad irony of today's decision lies in its utter failure to grasp why the [Voting Rights Act] has proven effective [...] Throwing out preclearance when it has worked and is continuing to work to stop discriminatory changes is like throwing away your umbrella in a rainstorm because you are not getting wet. (United States Supreme Courts Reports, 2013)

Much of the data Roberts selected were, in fact, made possible because of preclearance, not in spite of it. In ignoring the persistence of subtler machinations, such as vote dilution, and federal checks against the continuation of these devices, the Court also failed to acknowledge the recent proliferation of voter identification laws and voter purges. One thing seems clear: conservative critics of voter enforcements spent the years following the VRA institutionalizing their voting rights preferences (Rhodes, 2017, p. 186). In doing so, they effectively brought an end to the strongest piece of voting rights legislation to emerge from the civil rights revolution of the 1960s. In the end, resistance to the VRA demonstrates how important oversight is to the execution of democracy. In striking down the VRA, the Court may have ushered in another era of democratic futility. Furthermore, participatory democracy is essential to contemporary endeavors into community wealth building. The construction of economically inclusive African American communities is currently taking place on the contested terrain of inherited ongoing political bigotry. Contemporary attacks on American democracy have profound implications for the viability of future wealth-building projects.

NOTES

1.   © Portions of this chapter reprinted with permission from University Press of Kentucky, from Julian Maxwell Hayter, *The Dream Is Lost: Voting Rights and the Politics of Race in Richmond, Virginia* (Lexington, KY: University of Kentucky Press, 2017).
2.   GOP, Grand Old Party, is synonymous with the Republican Party, dating back the late nineteenth century.

REFERENCES

Black, Earl and Merle Black (2003), *The Rise of Southern Republicans*, Cambridge, MA: Belknap Press of Harvard University Press.

Boyd, Thomas M. and Stephen J. Markman (1983), "The 1982 amendments to the Voting Rights Act: a legislative history," *Washington and Lee Law Review*, 40(4), 1347–428.

Bullock, Charles S., Ronald Keith Gaddie and Justin J. Wert (2016), *The Rise and Fall of the Voting Rights Act*, Norman, OK: University of Oklahoma Press.

Evans, Rowland, Jr. and Robert D. Novak (1971), *Nixon in the White House: The Frustration of Power*, New York: Random House.

Graham, Hugh Davis (1990), *The Civil Rights Era: Origins and Development of National Policy, 1962–1972*, New York: Oxford University Press.

Hardzinski, Brian (2016), "From Selma to Shelby County, the rise and fall of the Voting Rights Act," *KGOU*, June 13, accessed January 20, 2020 at https://www.kgou.org/post/selma-shelby-county-rise-and-fall-voting-rights-act.

Hartocollis, Anemona (2017), "He took on the Voting Rights Act and won. Now he's taking on Harvard," *The New York Times*, November 19, accessed January 20, 2020 at https://www.nytimes.com/2017/11/19/us/affirmative-action-lawsuits.html.

Hayter, Julian Maxwell (2014), "From intent to effect: Richmond, Virginia and the protracted struggle for voting rights, 1965–1977," *Journal of Policy History*, 26(4), 534–67.

Hayter, Julian Maxwell (2017), *The Dream Is Lost: Voting Rights and the Politics of Race in Richmond, Virginia*, Lexington, KY: University Press of Kentucky.

Kousser, J. Morgan (1999), *Colorblind Injustice: Minority Voting Rights and the Undoing of the Second Reconstruction*, Chapel Hill, NC: University of North Carolina Press.

Lawson, Steven F. (1976), *Black Ballots: Voting Rights in the South, 1944–1969*, New York: Columbia University Press.

Lawson, Steven F. (1985), *In Pursuit of Power: Southern Blacks and Electoral Politics, 1965–1982*, New York: Columbia University Press.

Lawson, Steven F. (1991), *Running for Freedom: Civil Rights and Black Politics in America Since 1941*, Philadelphia, PA: Temple University Press.

Moye, J. Todd (2004), *Let the People Decide: Black Freedom and White Resistance in Sunflower County, Mississippi, 1945–1968*, Chapel Hill, NC: University of North Carolina Press.

Office of Civil Rights Evaluation, United States Commission on Civil Rights (2004), *Is America Ready to Vote? Election Readiness Briefing Paper*, Washington, DC: U.S. Government Printing Office.

Parker, Frank R. (1990), *Black Votes Count: Political Empowerment in Mississippi after 1965*, Chapel Hill, NC: University of North Carolina Press.

Rhodes, Jesse H. (2017), *Ballot Blocked: The Political Erosion of the Voting Rights Act*, Stanford, CA: Stanford University Press.

Richmond Afro-American & Planet (1981), August 29.

Richmond Times-Dispatch (1981), "Voting and 'rights'," July 15.

Rustin, Bayard (1965), "From protest to politics: the future of the civil rights movement," *Commentary*, February.

Thernstrom, Abigail M. (1987), *Whose Votes Count? Affirmative Action and Minority Voting Rights*, Cambridge, MA: Cambridge University Press.

United States Commission on Civil Rights (1968), *Political Participation: A Study of the Participation by Negroes in the Electoral and Political Process in 10 Southern States Since the Passage of the Voting Rights Act of 1965*, edited by John A. Hannah, J., Theodore M. Hesburgh and Robert S. Rankin et al., Washington, DC: U.S. Government Printing Office.

United States Commission on Civil Rights (1975), *The Voting Rights Act: Ten Years After*, edited by Arthur S. Flemming, Stephen Horn and Frankie M. Freeman et al., Washington, DC: U.S. Government Printing Office.

United States Commission on Civil Rights (1981), *The Voting Rights Act: Unfulfilled Goals*, edited by Arthur S. Flemming, Mary F. Berry and Stephen Horn et al., Washington, DC: U.S. Government Printing Office.

United States Supreme Court Reports (1969), *Allen* v. *State Board of Elections*, 393 U.S. 544.

United States Supreme Court Reports (1971), *Griggs* v. *Duke Power Company*, 401 U.S. 424.

United States Supreme Court Reports (1993), *Shaw* v. *Reno*, 509 U.S. 630.

United States Supreme Court Reports (1996), *Bush* v. *Vera*, 517 U.S. 952.

United States Supreme Court Reports (2009), *Northwest Austin Municipal Utility District Number One* v. *Holder*, 557 U.S. 193.

United States Supreme Court Reports (2013), *Shelby County* v. *Holder*, 570 U.S. 529.

Valelly, Richard M. (2004), *The Two Reconstructions: The Struggle for Black Enfranchisement*, Chicago, IL: University of Chicago Press.
Wang, Tova (2012), *The Politics of Voter Suppression: Defending and Expanding Americans' Right to Vote*, Ithaca, NY: Cornell University Press.

PART V

Toward a practical politics of community wealth
building

12. Targeted universalism in urban communities: racial discourse and policy rhetoric as harmony

Ravi K. Perry

INTRODUCTION: (DE)RACE, LANGUAGE, AND POLITICS

Politicians use rhetoric and language to shape public discourse around shared universal goals. How politicians then successfully package targeted policies for broad appeal amid racially diverse constituencies is a process I have described as universalizing the interests of the other as interests that matter to everyone (Perry, 2009). In urban cities, population dynamics and city histories necessitate that race plays a key role in the policy introduction and implementation efforts of politicians both as mayoral candidates seeking crossover appeal and as elected mayors seeking to maintain power. Consequently, urban mayors often engage in racial language. This racial language has historically been labeled as either explicitly racialized or deracialized. Orey and Ricks (2007) conducted the first systematic analysis of the deracialization concept using respondent data from the 2001 California Black Elected Officials Survey and found that "black elected officials are more likely to identify their political campaign as being a race-neutral or a race-moderate campaign, as opposed to a race-specific campaign" (Orey and Ricks, 2007, p. 330).

However, for many years, we have had significant evidence that minority and women candidates for public office can explicitly discuss race and racial issues and yet maintain or garner enough white support to win (Perry, 2013). The result: you don't need to run away from race to win any more. This is in direct contrast to what had been the norm for the first three decades after the civil rights movement. In Virginia, that historic norm of racial avoidance is particularly potent as the state's first black governor, Lawrence Douglas Wilder, has long been cited as having won in 1989 largely because he de-emphasized the significance of race in order to appeal to whites (Jones and Clemons, 1993). In other words, nearly all political scientists agree that Wilder ran away from race, avoiding discussing racial issues explicitly in his campaign for governor (Schexnider, 1990). At the time, the thinking was that in order for a black candidate to gain public office in a majority white jurisdiction (like every U.S. state), it was necessary to adopt a deracialization strategy to win (McCormick and Jones, 1993).

Thus, with the arrival of the twenty-first century and a new generation, a "third wave of politicians," a different type of minority politician emerged, one that was less inclined to avoid talking about race (Gillespie, 2010). As political scientist Corey Cook has described, "rather than emerge from traditional civil rights organizations or mobilizing institutions like historically black colleges or the African American church, these leaders are more connected to elite institutions" (Cook, 2013, p. 17). For political scientist Michael Dawson, Barack Obama also belongs to this "new generation," as evidenced by his campaigns for public office, whereas "then candidate Obama represented a new wave of more 'cosmopolitan' black politicians who have technocratic credentials and statewide or higher aspirations thus making them more attractive to and more interested in winning the support of non-black citizens" (Dawson, 2011, p. 112). More than just theory, quite a few studies have analyzed this new wave of black candidates and elected officials as legitimate contenders in crowded fields (Hajnal, 2007; Perry, 2009; Tate, 2010; Yon, 2010). The rhetoric employed by Barack Obama and his historic candidacy for president has been explored by many scholars, each including that his influence was extraordinary (Atwater, 2007; Dyson, 2016; Terrill, 2015). Where they and others differ in their analysis is in respect to the conclusion on what it all means. Some of my own previous work (Perry, 2009) has cited Obama's rhetoric as uniquely targeted and universal in tone, though scholars have disagreed on both the method and scope with which to study Obama's political rhetoric (Gillespie, 2019; Gillion, 2017).

In theoretical framework terms, targeted universalism is the concept employed by minority candidates and elected officials that scholars have identified can successfully appeal to whites and thereby build electoral and governing coalitions more responsive to minority interests even in nonmajority-minority jurisdictions. As defined in May 2019 by john a. powell,[1] Stephen Menendian, and Wendy Ake in the primer *Targeted Universalism: Policy & Practice* for the Haas Institute:[2]

> Targeted universalism is an alternative framework to design policies and implementation strategies to achieve policy goals. Targeted universalism is sensitive to structural and cultural dynamics in ways that often elude both targeted and universal strategies. As such, it is also a way of communicating, a vernacular to build support for inclusive policies. Despite what the term suggests, targeted universalism is more than a hybrid approach. It borrows the strengths and avoids the weaknesses of both targeted and universal approaches. Yet, it is also categorically distinct in both

conception and execution. This distinction is important since a common misconception is that the targeted universalism framework is essentially "targeting within a universal" approach—i.e., pursuing targeted strategies that respond to the urgent needs of some people, and wrapping those strategies in a universal goal that holds wide appeal. But targeted universalism is more than that. It is an entirely distinctive platform for resolving problems that are often unaddressed or exacerbated by targeted or universal policies. (powell et al., 2019, p. 7)

Thus, for powell et al. (2019), targeted universalism cannot simply be reduced to policy articulations that benefit all people and some groups to a greater degree. Rather, targeted universalism, when applied well, helps us better understand why universal goals have differential impacts on different groups of people:

Targeted universalism is based on exploring the gaps that exist between individuals, groups, and places that can benefit from a policy or program and the aspiration-establishing goal. Targeted universalism policy formulations do more than close or bridge such gaps, but ultimately clarify and reveal the barriers or impediments to achieving the universal goal for different groups of people. The focus on gaps, while important, should be measured by reference to a universal goal, not just between groups. (Ibid.)

The distinction between universal policies, targeted policies, and targeted universal policies is central to understanding how targeted universalism is meant to function and why it suffers from many misconceptions in public policy, public administration, and urban politics literature to this day. For powell et al. (2019), targeted universal policies differ in that they:

[a]spire to serve everyone by enabling different strategies based on the needs of different groups. Targeted universal policies appeal to everyone and set a goal for the general population: everyone stands to benefit by reaching the universal goal. At the same time everyone benefits from reaching the goal, different groups need different supports. Some groups also need more help because groups are situated differently with respect to the goal. Some are closer, some are further, and different groups must take different paths to get there. (Ibid., p. 31)

Universal policies apply to everyone in all groups within a candidate or elected official's jurisdiction. Universal policies, powell et al. (2019) argue, have their advantages, as American judicial precedent suggests they endure far longer as well:

By providing protections to everyone, without respect to group membership within the class, universal approaches enjoy a broader and more resilient base of political support and are less likely to be viewed as benefiting a particular group. Moreover, as legal scholars have documented, universal approaches are less likely to be construed narrowly by courts and judges. (Ibid., p. 9)

But, it is precisely the problem that these kinds of policies are not defined by the problems they are attempting to solve, but by their universal application. The challenge for universal policies is that universal access to a government good is not helpful in the same way or to the same extent to varying groups. In discussing the example of universal health care in Massachusetts, powell et al. (2019) cite how the state's program actually exasperated racial disparities in health coverage:

> The universal policy assumed that one strategy—making health insurance available—would both enable everyone to have insurance and would improve access to health care. However, for many groups, additional strategies were needed [...] For some groups, the only thing that stood between them and health care was health insurance. Groups with limited English proficiency needed health insurance, assistance with the enrollment process, and access to quality health care providers in their communities. Groups with low income needed health insurance and a cost-reduction mechanism for medical care. The universal policy, with its singular strategy, moved some to the goal, but left others behind. (Ibid., p. 10)

Although the universal approaches have their challenges, targeted policies carry significant baggage as well. Nationally, programs such as the Food Stamp Program (Supplemental Nutritional Assistance Program, or SNAP) are examples of targeted policies. Perhaps the most well-known examples of targeted policies are affirmative action policies that establish targets or soft goals (not quotas) in hiring, contracting, enrollment in education for underrepresented or historically disadvantaged groups. Hence, a major weakness of targeted policy efforts is their vulnerability to political challenge. Affirmative action, by example, remains a hot-button issue, with the Supreme Court hearing a case at the time of this writing on yet another landmark college admissions process, but this time at one of the nation's most elite institutions, Harvard University, where many current and former justices have earned their own educations.

Given these challenges to implementing targeted policies, it is no surprise then that many contemporary black politicians, for example, may increasingly no longer find explicit racial appeals appropriate for their electoral or governing goals and may instead begin to embrace targeted universalism. However, how the effort is approached and implemented determines its effectiveness. As many confuse universal, targeted, and targeted universal policies, certainly politicians can err in their articulation of similar goals. Moreover, the complexity of the universal issue in need of a targeted solution all the while meeting each community "where they are" can make the implementation of a universal solution to communities with different needs costly and complicated to explain to constituents.

For Jack Ford, the first black mayor of Toledo, Ohio, the targeted universalistic rhetoric utilized while promoting the public–private educational and training partnership, the Capacity Building Program, was increasingly unsuccessful. The program, a partnership between the city of Toledo, the University of Toledo, Associated General Contractors of Northwest Ohio, and the state of Ohio was designed to prepare local minority subcontractors to compete for city and state contracts by giving them the tools and mentorship from larger firms that are necessary to compete. But, in aggressively advocating for its continued support after mixed results, Ford's rhetoric became increasingly racialized. On one occasion he was quoted in a local black newspaper as wanting to make more black millionaires. Not surprisingly perhaps, but in a city with merely 25 percent black population, comments like these I argue resulted in the loss of white support in his re-election. Those kinds of comments may have been so inflammatory to have encouraged the neo-Nazi demonstrations led by out-of-town groups that walked on Toledo sidewalks toward the end of Ford's re-election campaign—just two weeks before the election—effectively causing a major rift between his historic re-election effort and the city's black community. Some blacks wanted Ford to ban the group from marching.

The effects of varying understandings of and implementation strategies of targeted universalism by mayors complicates the effectiveness. In many cases, the characteristic shared between politicians with successful records of implementing electoral and/or governing targeted universal strategy is that their campaigns or administrations take on the reputation of being dedicated to reform. In Providence, Rhode Island, Orr and Norlund (2013) found that the first viable (and successful) Latino candidate for mayor in 2010, Angel Tavares, won based on him running as a reform candidate in a crowded three-way race with two media-crowned frontrunners with Italian roots, a key ethnic constituency in Providence politics. For Kevin Johnson and his election as the first black mayor in Sacramento, California in 2008, his candidacy rose right at the end of a cycle of predecessors who were each historic "firsts" and thereby reform candidates who, simply by their identities alone, represented change; three of the previous four mayors were firsts—the first woman, the second woman the first Latino, and the first Asian American. Nearby, in Oakland, California, in a race versus six other candidates and featuring ranked-choice voting for the first time, Jean Quan successfully reframed herself from a familiar politician to a reform candidate by building a coalition of white liberals and minorities. Meanwhile, Quan's identity also made her candidacy historic and reformist at least symbolically. Geron (2013) has cited "her use of a universalist approach to get elected and govern Oakland while maintaining her unique identity as an Asian American woman" (p. 91) as evidence of her embrace of the unique circumstances of certain communities and the need for particular application of universal policies to fit their community needs.

Despite the varying approaches minority politicians have made in respect to articulating and implementing a targeted universal agenda, several threats remain constant. As McClerking (2013) found in a case study examining Mark Mallory's years as the first elected black mayor in Cincinnati, Ohio, and the first two-term mayor under the city's new strong mayor system. Elected in 2005, Mallory was victim to external media sources that sought to use his race to drive a wedge between black and white voters in the historically racially polarized city at the center of the underground railroad on the banks of the River Ohio. Meanwhile, Mallory was attempting to talk about the future: "Mark Mallory becomes less notably Black over time, in general, but he is portrayed as Blacker the further away you are from him. In other words, his Blackness seems to become less notable (or newsworthy) the longer he is in office, while at the same time, his race is a larger part of what seems to make him newsworthy the further the news source is from Cincinnati" (McClerking, 2013, p. 84). Also in Ohio, Chambers and Schreiber-Stainthorp (2013) write about Michael Coleman, the first black mayor of Columbus, finding that his approach was not deracialized or racialized, though nor can it be clearly defined as targeted universalism rather than perhaps, targeting within universalism:

> By pursuing moderate policies intended to benefit everyone, Coleman can sustain his own tenure while making steady, if modest, progress toward greater equality [...] For, even as Coleman appeases Columbus' wealthiest and most powerful, he does so in a manner that leverages their support to lift others. By enticing developers with profitable contracts, Coleman pleases one side. By getting them to build affordable houses, he pleases another. In the process, he ensures that the maximum possible number of people benefit. (Chambers and Schreiber-Stainthorp, 2013, p. 158)

Knowing what strategy to utilize to address universal problems that impact groups different can be difficult especially with limited resources, as Davin Phoenix (2013, p. 114) has found in respect to Denver's rise in minority coalition politics: "The shared race constituencies that constitute a significant portion of many minority mayors' support bases are often socioeconomically disadvantaged, thus preventing them from providing their mayors with the political capital they need to enact their agendas."

So, where does this leave us? We know that targeted universalism is not to be confused with deracialization as an applied theory, nor does it fit squarely with concepts of moderate politics, partisanship or ideology. We also know now that targeted universalism can become racialized by overzealous articulations by politicians or perceived as racially polarizing by the media or public.

Because people of color in urban communities see the election of one of their own as a watershed moment, which is immediately followed by overly high expectations of that incumbent leader, the rhetoric a minority politician uses to advance their agenda, especially in historically white cities, is significant insofar as how they negotiate the duality of representing one's race and the majority electorate at the same time. For Cook (2013), Mayor of Sacramento

Kevin Johnson was so concerned about this duality that he "began holding monthly meetings in the Black community to develop an actionable agenda and [to] 'take advantage of the platform and opportunity' of having the mayoralty," utilizing the National Urban League's *State of Black America Report* and its Equality Index as a template. Still, for Cook, "it is clear that this agenda is framed in universal language—creating jobs, promoting access to high quality schools, and increasing civic and political engagement" (Cook, 2013, p. 26).

Boris Ricks (2013, p. 172) cites a similar conclusion in his analysis of the election of the first Latino mayor in Los Angeles since 1972 where he finds that the then city council member Antonio Villaraigosa failed in his attempted to defeat the incumbent mayor in his first bid for the office in 2001 in part due to his "deracialized campaign" and his effort to "restore the coalition that led to the election and reelection of former Los Angeles Mayor Tom Bradley for five consecutive terms." Having learned from his attempt to employ an arguably outdated electoral strategy to build a multi-racial coalition at the turn of the century, Villaraigosa ran successfully for mayor in 2005 with a different message that at the time explicitly called attention to issues that plagued certain minority constituencies. Hence, he garnered a majority of the black vote and significant endorsements from Latinx and black notables throughout the region.

Whether Coleman in Columbus, Johnson in Sacramento, Quan in Oakland, or Villaraigosa in Los Angeles, black, Asian, and Latinx mayors, scholars have noted in each case that deracialization seems to have lost its appeal and effectiveness and has been abandoned by a new kind of minority mayor. As Elmer Eric Schattschneider (1975) has found in respect to conflict and political participation in the two-party system, "The civil rights of repressed minorities [...] becomes meaningful when we relate them to the attempt to make conflict visible. Scope is the stake in these discussions" (pp. 8–9). For Schattschneider, it is the competitive party system—not interest groups—that gives the excluded a chance for a role in the decision-making process. For Schattschneider, scope is how one can assess likely outcomes in governance, whereas conclusions are determined by the extent to which the audience becomes involved in the issue. When minority mayors explicitly acknowledge the issues of their minority constituencies in historically white communities, using a racial language of targeted universalism, they "make conflict visible" and thereby give voice to those who feel that many of their previous elected officials failed them.

NEGATIVE AND POSITIVE RACE SPEAK: UNDERSTANDING THE HISTORY OF RACIALLY EXPLICIT APPEALS

Racial language (including minority politicians' rhetorical efforts to persuade whites to support targeted policies), is as popular today as ever. The moral and ethical justification of racial language varies by time period. The predominance of racial language analysis centers on discriminatory statements directed at particular individuals or groups. Racial language encompasses more than direct interpersonal statements between people or groups. Depending on the voice and the context, racial language in contemporary politics and society can promote goodwill and harmony in addition to advocating for racism's validity and one's prejudicial or discriminatory views.

But what is "language?" Amiri Baraka implies that language itself "began in one base and spread wherever the conditions changes and is the oldest record of human life" (Baraka, 2004, p. 294). Thus, language is diverse and—put simply—much older than the people who use it. In America, such language is always an amalgamation of our complicated and difficult past. As Baraka continues, "you cannot speak an American sentence without going from Europe to Native America to Africa to Afro America" (ibid., p. 299).

So, language is powerful. As Frantz Fanon (1967) said plainly: "to speak means to be in a position to use a certain syntax to grasp the morphology of this or that language but it means above all to assume a culture to support the weight of a civilization" (pp. 16–17). Power, then, is well, everything. And power is politics. But power also plays out in a myriad of ways that can be both destructive to racial progress and helpful to its eventual achievement.

For example, one of the most pervasive features of contemporary race discourse is the denial of prejudice (Augoustinos and Every, 2007). Scholars in a variety of disciplines have deliberated about discursive textual practices in an effort to describe how some of us use words to hide our true thoughts. Since explicit racial epithets are no longer acceptable, we rephrase our subconscious word choice like unto adult animation series *Boondocks*- and *Black Dynamite*-approved off-color so-called jokes. Most researchers have found that this type of word production and speech patterns—both in the formal and informal conversation senses—have significantly increased, as it is no longer cool to be an overt racist: "[T]here is cross-disciplinary agreement that blatant forms of prejudice, commonly referred to as 'old-fashioned racism,' have been recently supplanted with a more subtle and covert variety variously known as 'modern' (McConahay, 1986), 'symbolic' (Kinder & Sears, 1981, 1985), or the 'new racism' (Barker, 1981)" (Augoustinos and Every, 2007, p. 124). The general consensus has been that majority group members—namely, whites—use a softer conceptualization of racism and racial language to convey what are really traditionally racist views and attitudes. Hence, while there is a decrease in overt race talk that is disparaging to another group, the decrease does not necessarily reflect changes in societal, political and/or social attitudes about race. This development has led to debates about what exactly constitutes discrimination, prejudicial language and racist talk. And there's really no agreement here.

And yet, perceptions of negative race talk that discriminates dominates the literature. Study after study in social linguistics, communication, political science, sociology, ethnic studies, philosophy, and related fields has argued that the prefixes to statements, such as "I'm not racist but," or "I have no problem with those Hispanic people," or "I have a lot of black friends," usually inform the direction of what comes next. It's the prefix that's the crux of the argument, not the postfix of the phrase or statement that merely seeks to qualify the prefix. Much of this literature frames the statements as discriminatory or examples of subtle or hidden racism in today's society. However, the vast majority of this literature is focused on interpersonal contact and communication. What happens in professional and political public spaces has been understudied. Those that have studied it have sought to argue that discursive language that quietly discriminates is an example of deracialized talk.

Reeves (1983) has referred to this phenomenon as the deracialization of discourse, in which racial categories are attenuated, eliminated, or substituted and racial explanations are omitted or de-emphasized. For example, even in instances where racial references are omitted, racial language is said to take place. Herein, speakers tend to replace what they use in their speech pattern as a racial code word with a word that is devoid of race. The choice of the word "urban" to describe minority communities is both strategic and convenient in that it replaces any discussion about "them" or "those people," or put more explicitly, "the blacks." This allows people to avoid race speak, justify in neutral terms their negative perceptions of the group, and avoid criticism of racism. Unlike the literature across subfields that discusses negative outgroup racism in speech, deracialized racial language can often occur within group to create divisions between subsections in communities.

Much research, such as that explored earlier, has found that many black politicians, for example, in an effort to seek what political scientists call crossover voters—would often de-emphasize the significance of race in not only their speeches, but in policy pronouncements as well—all in an effort to convince a white majority of the justificatory basis of their aim. These examples amplify the research that argues that discourse does not have to be explicitly racist to create circumstances of secondary marginalization, exclusion, discrimination and oppression—either in direct effects or indirect impact.

But it is the deracialized discourse that merits more scrutiny. If racial language can be inferred through code/word switching, then cannot every word be considered deracial in scope? Consider, for example, words perceived to be positive, such as the inscription above the doors to the U.S. Supreme Court— Equal Justice Under Law—does "equal" really refer to minority groups that have been excluded? Why is it that racial language, when perceived to be negative, can be inferred to discriminate, but racial language, when perceived to be positive, can't be inferred to support inclusion?

Political science and communication-related fields began exploring deracialization as a concept in the immediate post-civil rights era mainly as it related to African Americans. Much of that research, though, also studied so-called liberal whites, who in seeking to generate support in the black community (while not alienating blacks or whites), would walk the racial linguistic tightrope. In one community, race was central as structural and systemic conditions created disparate impacts and discriminatory effects, and in another community economics were central where a lack of progress was not tied to structural inequality but individual responsibility, individualistic politics, and limited economic opportunity as a result of fluctuations in the free market. These ideas have loosely been framed in racialized public opinion studies as debates between individualism and egalitarianism (Sears, Sidanius and Bobo, 2000).

The fact that white and black candidates for public office were found to speak differently about race to different audiences has generated several theories. Namely, though, a consensus can be argued that most of the literature argues the differences are not necessarily related to race at all—ironically, what I call deracialized utilitarianism—whereby candidates naturally speak differently to different audiences because as any novice speech maker knows, any good speech should be tailored to the audience that one should seek to win over.

But not everyone is running away from race—either in political arenas or in mass media campaigns and marketing, in say, basketball arenas. In many instances—both historically and currently—racialized talk is alive and well. Herein, racial references are deliberate and precise. Historically, racial language has been labeled many things—race talk, race speak, racialization, racialized rhetoric, discourses on race and so on—and, as referenced earlier, many of these studies argue that racial language has discriminatory effects. However racial language is more than language used *toward* someone or one group. Racial language is also inclusive of mere *references to race* in the explicit form. Hence, the language need not be directed toward any particular person or group and thus in many instances may be racial, but not racialized, and not racist. Take the following historical examples, where given the time period, word choice preferences naturally considered racial themes.

In "Fooling Our White Folks," Langston Hughes argues that:

> because our American whites are stupid in so many ways, racially speaking, and because there are many things in this U.S.A. of ours which Negros may achieve only by guile, I have great tolerance for persons of color who deliberately set out to fool our white folks […] a little daring with languages too, will often go a long way. "*Dame un boletto Pullman to Chicago*," will get you a berth in Texas when often plain English, "Give me a Pullman ticket to Chicago," will not. Negroes do not always have to change color to fool our white folks. Just change tongues. (Hughes, 1950; original emphasis)

Here, Hughes clearly uses the explicit language of race but is it necessarily negatively directed toward a particular group?

Comparatively, John O. Killens in "The Black Psyche" has written that "When I was a boy in Macon, Georgia, one of the greatest compliments a benevolent white man could give a Negro was usually found in the obituary column of the local newspaper: 'He was a black man, but he had a white heart'" (Killens, 1964, p. 37). Is Killens's statement an embodiment of anti-white language? Going back to the question raised earlier—why is it then that racial language when perceived to be negative can be inferred to discriminate and language when perceived to be positive can't be inferred to support cross-pollination?

Take another historical racialized example. James Baldwin evoked in an interview with psychologist Kenneth Clark:

> I'm delighted to know there've been many fewer lynchings in the year 1963 than there were in the year 1933, but I also have to bear in mind—I have to bear it in mind because my life depends on it—that there are a great many ways to lynch a man. The impulse in American society, as far as I can tell from my experience in it, has essentially been to ignore me when it could, and then when it couldn't, to intimidate me, and when that failed, to make concessions. (Baldwin et al., 1964)

Is Baldwin's racial language racist? Or is it just—to put in the simplest of terms—an example of "keepin' it real"? Are not our analytical deductions of historical narratives sometimes too draconian?

Those historic episodes, I argue, are clear examples of why context matters when discussing race and rhetoric in politics. In an era where race was a general everyday conversation, particularly in the lives of minorities as they negotiated what it meant to be American, cannot what some label as racial generics be nothing more than everyday talk in black communities (Anderson, Haslanger and Langton, 2012; Perry, 2011)? In other words, when does our attempt at analysis go beyond the pale of common sense?

Let's take another historical example and see if these statements meet the standard of racial language, though without being racist or racialized—albeit they may be examples of racialization:

> One hundred years of delay have passed since President Lincoln freed the slaves, yet their heirs [...] are not yet freed from the bonds of injustice [...] from social and economic oppression, and this Nation [...] will not be fully free until all its citizens are free. [...] We face, therefore, a moral crisis as a country and as a people.

The above quote by President John F. Kennedy (1963 [2000], p. 322) is an example of the first American president to ever claim publicly that segregation was a moral wrong. For Kennedy, the ethics of racial language was just in claiming how unethical was the practice of racial subjugation.

For his successor, Lyndon B. Johnson, racial language was less about making good on our nation's promissory note at our founding that "all are created equal" by advocating for the protection of individual negative liberties of all. For Johnson, racial language could be used for a broader purpose. In a speech at Howard University, he indicated that "this is the next and more profound stage of the battle for civil rights. We seek not just freedom but opportunity—not just legal equity but human ability—not just equality as a right and a theory but equality as a fact and as a result" (Johnson, 1966, p. 639). White House sources at the time argued in papers that the Howard address was the first major presidential civil rights speech conceived independently of the direct pressure of racial crisis. As Stephen Steinberg (1998 [2010], p. 23) has argued, the speech is an example of what former U.S. Senator and Assistant Secretary of Labor Daniel Patrick Moynihan calls "semantic infiltration":

> This term[3] refers to the appropriation of the language of one's political opponents for the purpose of blurring distinctions and molding it to one's own political position. In this instance Moynihan invoked the language of "equal results" only to redefine and redirect it in a politically safe direction. When semantic infiltration is done right, [argues Steinberg], it elicits the approbation even of your political opponents who, as in the case of the audience at Howard, may not fully realize that a rhetorical shill game has been played on them.

The result being, the speech was a covert ironic foretelling of the limits of the Johnson administration's commitment to civil rights despite their recent support of the Voting Rights Act. Despite Steinberg's criticism, the aforementioned language episodes of two former presidents in the civil rights era detail how the language of race can be used effectively and explicitly without it being racist, racialized, or discriminatory. Hence, as with the historic examples from black literary scholars and politicians previously discussed, we can have racial language that is not misdirected at particular groups or that only serves the purpose of masking prejudicial views, or discriminatory beliefs.

Contemporary examples of what you might consider positive racial language are manifold and are located in diverse corners of American society. What some have referenced as *slinging the new age speak*, these contemporary manifestations of racial difference are designed to bring attention to disparate conditions. From the Négritude movement of francophone black intellectuals to the Harlem Renaissance movement of American black artists to the El Movimiento of Mexican American activists to the Asian American fight for visual culture and the American Indian movement for treaty restoration, nearly every group has used the language of race to both advance their cause and protest against efforts to dismantle it.

POSITIVE USE OF RACIAL LANGUAGE: RHETORICAL ACTIONS IN PUBLIC POLICY

In describing Jack Ford's efforts as the first black mayor in Toledo, Ohio, I have previously explained how a theory of targeted universalism becomes a rhetorical strategy to influence:

> the concept of powell [2009] is a political strategy and governing approach that recognizes the need for a universal platform that is simultaneously responsive to the needs of the particular. By extension, then, targeted universalism is a rhetorical strategy and also a public policy program development strategy wherein policy output is determined in part by how a program effectively can be described as benefitting all citizens, yet with a targeted focus toward the problems of specific groups. (Perry and Owens-Jones, 2013, p. 185)

In my own work, the language of race continued to be utilized successfully by minority politicians who, in their efforts to garner white support for public policy initiatives, framed those initiatives in such a way to invite whites to view their conditioned experience as a function of and explicitly intertwined with and related to the conditioned experiences of blacks (Perry, 2011). In many cases, this effort has resulted in long-term harmony between groups historically at odds in cities where race is a dominant and often negative feature of everyday life.

The policy outcomes as a result of strategic rhetorical framing around racial language is indisputable and has significantly benefitted African, Asian, and Latino/a Americans. For example, in my study of Jack Ford, I examine how Ford's development of the Center for Capacity Building to train minority contractors was instrumental in giving them greater access and opportunity to apply for, compete for, and ultimately win city and state contracts. Ford's racially inclusive language in support of the Center, even at times quite militant, successfully secured leading white groups and individuals to support his goals—including the Republican governor of Ohio at the time, Bob Taft, who devoted millions in state resources, and the president of the University of Toledo who provided millions in in-kind contributions to make the effort work (Perry and Owens-Jones, 2013). Both key figures and a host of related white business leaders were convinced by Ford's rhetoric, where he argued it was "the right thing to do" and that "all we are asking for is a level playing field." Hence, funding for the nation's first ever effort of the sort poured in. These developments occurred because of strategic use of racial language in policy actions and program, government documents, and public speeches.

My research has found the use of racial language to be deliberate, explicit, strategic and an attempt at both redressing wrongs of the past while recognizing ongoing progress being made toward the future. As the failed re-election campaign of Jack Ford attests (Toledo remains the only major city in Ohio that has failed to re-elect a black mayor), a mayor can use his or her own misfortune to highlight racial impact. For example, in his final State of the City speech where Ford largely knew he would go on to lose re-election, Ford countered the criticisms of his personality, style, and governing approach by saying: "I have been criticized for what one pundit recently called my lumbering style. That I seem to be in perpetual hibernation and that nothing gets done or will be done." Comparatively, McLin, Dayton's first black female mayor was viewed by white business and union leaders—some of her own political party—as "wacky" and "capricious" because she used implicit racial language to seek white support for black policy initiatives in a city that was 40 percent black and 60 percent white: "When you talk about all these issues, even though I'm the mayor of color, it's across the board. There is only in the city, to your constituency, an east and a west, but to me as the mayor, they're all my constituents." The "it's across the board" was McLin's "wacky" way of saying black problems are all of our problems.

CONCLUSION

McCormick and Jones define deracialization as "conducting a campaign in a stylistic fashion that defuses the polarizing effects of race by avoiding explicit reference to race-specific issues" (1993, p. 76). While deracialization can be electoral strategy, it can also aptly describe a politician's approach toward governing (Perry, 2012). For Orey and Ricks (2007), "black elected officials who run deracialized campaigns will also support race-neutral bills. Or, more important, these officials may fail to support black-interest bills" (p. 331). As McCormick and Jones (1993) also note, a deracialized [electoral] approach "at the same time emphas[izes] those issues that are perceived as racial transcendent" (p. 76).

Some of the components of deracialization are undoubtedly present in the approach of targeted universalism but it is important not to conflate the varied concepts. For example, Corey Cook (2013) explains in "Kevin Johnson and Coalition Politics in Sacramento" how I frame the relationship between universalizing the interests of minorities in majority white cities and the concept of deracialization:

> according to Perry, the "universalizing" approach enables Black elected officials to "take the interests of Black constituents, develop particularized policy actions and program developments, and popularize them by rhetorically advocating for their interests in a way that does not deemphasize race or alienate whites" by emphasizing" "common humanity" [...] This approach is seen as distinctive from deracialization. (Cook, 2013, p. 25)

For Cook, "Johnson articulates a strikingly similar view. While he acknowledges that he '(has) to be the mayor for the whole city ...' he maintains that the 'African American community and Oak Park in particular' needs to articulate and enact an agenda for African Americans" (p. 26). As Geron (2013) has noted in respect to former mayor Jean Quan of Oakland, the city's first Asian American and woman mayor, "she has not forgotten her own ethnic roots, holding community events in Chinatown, being visible at Asian community events on a regular basis, and actively working to build ties with Pacific Rim nations, their people, and businesses" (p. 107).

Hence, the use of racial identity and language to appeal for support has always been with this country and still is today. Often employed by black mayors and other minority politicians in urban communities, racial language can be both positive and negative, constructive and destructive. What it cannot be is ignored. We are enslaved by words. "How do you become so good at math?" "Where are you from?" are questions asked daily to marginal American group members that racialize their American experience.

From the language of naming who we are—whether American, white, native ancestry, African or some other country—we've debated the use of racial rhetoric and personal and political identity. David Walker wrote in *David Walker's Appeal* in 1829 that the word "nig[g]er" was "used by the old Romans, to designate inanimate beings, which were black: such as soot, pot, wood, house, &c. Also, animals which they considered inferior to the human species, as a black horse, cow, hog, bird, dog, &c" (Walker, 1829 [1995]). Then, white Americans have applied this term to Africans. "Ella" wrote in *The Liberator* in 1831 asking "why do our friends as well as our enemies call us Negroes?" We feel it to be a term of reproach and could wish our friends would call us by some other name." A "Subscriber" in *The Liberator* also in 1831 wrote "the term colored is not a good one."

Today, there are clearly contemporary examples where if only implicitly, racial language yet occurs with potentially negative impact. In disparaging Moynihan's report[4] on the "Negro" family, psychologist William Ryan replied by arguing it was nothing more than genteel racism (Gates and Burton, 2009). A kind of racism that Sears et al. (2000) define as a coalescing of negative racial affect with the perceived violation of such traditional values—including, for example, the beliefs that discrimination no longer poses a major barrier to the advancement of blacks; that blacks should try harder to make it on their own; that they are demanding too much and that they are often given special treatment by government and other elites.

Other examples include the language discourse around the O.J. Simpson and George Zimmerman trials. In the latter, defense witness Rachel Jeantel was denigrated in black circles for having allegedly embarrassed them—and laughed at in white circles for being who she was—black. Particularly trashed throughout the media by black elites was her defense of the word "nigga" vis-à-vis "nigger." Also, her statement that "cracker," a derogatory term used for white people, was a less significant slur than "nigger" offended many whites who think otherwise.

Just think of other clearly linguistic racial episodes that caught our attention. The 1992 LA "race riots." The post 9/11 coverage of Muslim Americans. President Trump's border wall, attempt at a Muslim immigration ban, insults toward former advisor Omarosa Manigault Newman, calling her a "dog," and a "low life", and his castigating comments that majority black Baltimore was "rat and rodent infested." Note the assumed presumption of minority identity in story after story about crime and skin tone with limited information about the alleged person sought. Remember the CNN debacle of racialized assumptions as they covered the Boston Bombings. Lead politics anchor Wolf Blitzer was engaging with correspondent John King when King offered "I want to be very careful about this, because people get very sensitive when you say these things [...] I was told by one of these sources who is a law enforcement official that this is a dark-skinned male [...] There are some people who will take offense for even saying that [...] I understand that." Blitzer asked, "We can't say whether the person spoke with a foreign accent, or an American accent?" King replied "I'm making a personal judgment—forgive me, I think it's the right judgment—not to try to inflame tensions. They say it's a dark-skinned male." Still pushing it, Blitzer asked King yet again, "Who said it was a 'dark-skinned male?' A law enforcement source?" And obviously, the notorious Fox News coverage of President Obama's birth, particularly as it relates to former host

Bill O'Reilly's regular racist language attacks nearly every evening, such as his statements about Sylvia's restaurant in Harlem where he said:

> There wasn't one person in Sylvia's who was screaming, "M-Fer, I want more iced tea." You know, I mean, everybody was—it was like going into an Italian restaurant in an all-white suburb in the sense of people were sitting there, and they were order-ing and having fun. And there wasn't any kind of craziness at all.

Even CNN's Don Lemon, an African American himself has used racial lan-guage to insult members of his own group—suggesting blacks need to finish school and pull up their pants and stop having babies:

> Pull up your pants. [...] just because you can have a baby, it doesn't mean you should. Especially without planning for one or getting married first [...] Start small by not dropping trash, littering in your own communities. I've lived in several predominantly white neighborhoods in my life, I rarely, if ever, witnessed people littering. I live in Harlem now, it's an historically black neighborhood, every single day I see adults and children dropping their trash on the ground when a garbage can is just feet away [...] Sagging pants, whether Justin Bieber or No-name Derek around the way, walking around with your ass and your underwear showing is not OK [...] finish school. You want to break the cycle of poverty? Stop telling kids they're acting white because they go to school or they speak proper English.

However, racial language, discourse and rhetoric is not just individual, neg-ative speech. It is also mediated messaging through mass media. Whether it be the portrayal of black characters and black life on black networks such as OWN, Centric, and BET, or the relations expressed between black and whites in movies, such as in *Driving Miss Daisy*, in many cases black women, in particular, have been labeled as didactic pariahs to themselves, their families and own communities, thus perpetuating the longstanding racialized and sex-ualized myth of black women as dangerous. More recently, films such as *The Help* and *The Butler* have displayed racial language in period storylines that some argue engender recollections of a glorified past of false pretenses that tends to view racial context through rose-colored glasses.

These reoccurring realities suggest that what Howard Winant (1998 [2010]) calls "racial dualism" is of continuing significance. In this chapter, I attempted to argue, as he does, that:

> what racial dualism means today is that there are now, so to speak, two ways of looking at race, where previously there was only one. In the past, let's say the pre-World War II era, everyone agreed that racial subordination existed; the debate was about whether it was justified [...] But today, agreement about the continuing existence of racial subordination has vanished. The meaning of race has been deeply problematized. Indeed, the very ideas that "race matters" is something which today must be argued, something which is not self-evident. (Winant, 1998 [2010], p. 88)

Case in point: President Trump's "good people on both sides" statement from Charlottesville.

Hence, while the assertion of negative ethnonyms function as circulating objects, I also argue that the textual and contextual significations created or more commonly reproduced through these circulations—often mediated through mass media—construct a complex of set of meanings that work to enforce Winant's notion of dualism.

Repeated use of negative ethnonyms creates a cycle of marginalization and oppression that must be confronted through greater diversity in our media representations and through policy advancement that delegitimizes the practice of being an instrument of one's own oppression (as in the Lemon example cited earlier). Attending to these realities will work to embed culturally validated meanings so that it has the capacity to develop a greater number of positive examples of racial language. Such a process, though, requires us first to expand our scope of inquiry regarding racial language to focus on both positive and negative uses of race. By default, then, we will help to establish a theoretically rigorous understanding of how language, background, policy, and economic relations are constituted and related and impact policy.

Racial language is more than prejudicial statements used to harm. We're more than the ethnonyms many use to define us such as dinks, coons, chinks, Jesus killers, gringos, guidos, half-breeds, hymies, japs, niggers, sambos, sand monkeys, wetbacks, or tar babies. We can do more than study negative instances of racial language—the "some of my best friends are black" inquiries. But, what about positive uses of racial language, such as how they are framed by politicians in the context of targeted universalism? As this study explored, urban communities are the ripe locations for policy rhetoric that benefits the majority, but that also intentionally targets the least among us—the secondarily marginalized that political scientist Cathy Cohen (1997) has described as the "punks, bulldaggers, and welfare queens." Scholars' theoretical observations assert that racial language—whether used negatively to insult—or used positive to universalize black interests, can be an effective tool of communication for politicians seeking to get their ideas implemented in urban settings.

Whether we describe positive examples of racial language as excitable speech or the politics of the performative, I do believe the permanence of race in public discourse will remain. With greater attention to positive racial discourse, and on pinpointing the racial distinctiveness or targeted universalistic examples of racial language, the likelihood of eradicating the universal campaign against blackness, and efforts at maximization of a limited set of so-called American values—whatever the cost—is increased.

Threats to targeted universalism in electoral politics remain high and a bit of a gamble for politicians to readily employ. In the case study of Newark after the city's famous mayor Cory Booker was elected U.S. Senator from New Jersey, political scientist Andra Gillespie writes that "the presence of coethnic rivals in the field could split the coethnic vote" (Gillespie, 2013, p. 65). In Newark, her study found that "the deracialized candidates were not disadvantaged by the increasing presence of whites in a district but racialized candidates lost votes in districts with increasing white populations" (ibid.). Hence, whites may become a critical swing vote in situations where increasing diversity (blacks and Latinos with sizeable voting blocs) converges along racial or ethnic lines. Thus, crossover appeal remains central to minority subnational policy and program goals. With increasing diversity, perhaps no single ethnic group alone can now achieve a policy goal without first framing their community's concerns to outgroups in ways that both respect their cultural heritage and generate outside support. This suggests that targeted universalism has the potential to continue to influence our politics for years to come.

If we believe as anthropologist Raymond Williams (1977) wrote in his classic "Language," in *Marxism and Literature*, "A definition of language is always implicitly or explicitly a definition of human beings in the world" (p. 21), then we are obligated to ensure that urban political discussions, arguments and debates that engage use of racial language include equitable references to positive and negative utility in the policy formulation and implementation process.

NOTES

1. john a. powell does not capitalize his name.
2. Now renamed as the Othering & Belonging Institute.
3. For more on the meaning of semantic infiltration, see Todenhagen (1987).
4. For more context on the significance of the report in racial politics, see Geary (2015).

REFERENCES

Anderson, Luvell, Sally Haslanger and Rae Langton (2012), "Language and race," in Delia Graff Fara and Gillian Kay Russell (eds), *The Routledge Companion to Philosophy of Language*, New York: Routledge.
Atwater, Deborah F. (2007), "Senator Barack Obama: the rhetoric of hope and the American Dream," *Journal of Black Studies*, 38(2), 121–9.
Augoustinos, Martha and Danielle Every (2007), "The language of 'race' and prejudice: a discourse of denial, reason, and liberal-practical politics," *Journal of Language and Social Psychology*, 26(2), 123–41.
Baldwin, James, Nathan Glazer, Sidney Hook and Gunnar Myrdal (1964), "Liberalism and the negro: a round-table discussion," *Commentary*, 37, March, 25–42.
Baraka, Amira (2004), "Lecture," in Anner Waldman and Lisa Birman (eds), *Civil Disobediences: Poetics and Politics in Action*, Minneapolis, MN: Coffee House Press, pp. 294–300.

Barker, Martin (1981), *The New Racism*, London: Junction Books.

Chambers, Stefanie and Will Schreiber-Stainthorp (2013), "Michael Coleman: the Midwestern middleman," in Ravi K. Perry (ed.), *21st Century Urban Race Politics: Representing Minorities as Universal Interests*, Bingley, UK: Emerald Group Publishing Limited, pp. 133–62.

Cohen, Cathy (1997), "Punks, bulldaggers, and welfare queens: the radical potential of queer politics?" *GLQ*, 3(4), 437–65.

Cook, Corey (2013), "Constructing a moderate multiracial coalition in 'America's most diverse city': Kevin Johnson and coalition politics in Sacramento," in Ravi K. Perry (ed.), *21st Century Urban Race Politics: Representing Minorities as Universal Interests*, Bingley, UK: Emerald Group Publishing Limited, pp. 13–31.

Dawson, Michael C. (2011), *Not in Our Lifetimes: The Future of Black Politics*, Chicago, IL: University of Chicago Press.

Dyson, Michael Eric (2016), *The Black Presidency: Barack Obama and the Politics of Race in America*, New York: Houghton Mifflin Harcourt.

Fanon, Frantz (1967), *Black Skin, White Masks*, translated by Charles Lam Markmann, New York: Grove Press, pp 17–18.

Gates, Henry Louis and Jennifer Burton (2009), *Call and Response: Key Debates in African American Studies*, New York: W.W. Norton & Co.

Geary, Daniel (2015), "The Moynihan Report: an annotated edition," *The Atlantic*, September 14, accessed July 5, 2020 at https://www.theatlantic.com/politics/archive/2015/09/the-moynihan-report-an-annotated-edition/404632/.

Geron, Kim (2013), "Asian American politics in Oakland: the rise of Mayor Jean Quan," in Ravi K. Perry (ed.), *21st Century Urban Race Politics: Representing Minorities as Universal Interests*, Bingley, UK: Emerald Group Publishing Limited, pp. 87–109.

Gillespie, Andra (ed.) (2010), *Whose Black Politics?* New York: Routledge.

Gillespie, Andra (2013), "Beyond Booker: assessing the prospects of Black and Latino mayoral candidates in Newark, New Jersey," in Ravi K. Perry (ed.), *21st Century Urban Race Politics: Representing Minorities as Universal Interests*, Bingley, UK: Emerald Group Publishing Limited, pp. 33–68.

Gillespie, Andra (2019), *Race and the Obama Administration*, Manchester, UK: Manchester University Press.

Gillion, Daniel Q. (2017), "Obama's discussion of racial policies and citizens' racial resentment in the experimental setting," *Presidential Studies Quarterly*, 47, 517–28.

Hajnal, Zoltan L. (2007), *Changing White Attitudes Toward Black Political Leadership*, Cambridge, UK: Cambridge University Press.

Hughes, Langston (1950), "Fooling our white folks," *Negro Digest*, 8.6, April, 38–41.

Johnson, Lyndon B. (1966), "To fulfill these rights: commencement address at Howard University," *Public Papers of the Presidents of the United States: Lyndon B. Johnson, 1965. Volume II*, Washington, DC: Government Printing Office, pp. 635–40.

Jones, Charles E. and Michael L. Clemons (1993), "A model of racial crossover," in Georgia Persons (ed.), *Dilemmas of Black Politics*, New York. Harper Collins College Publishers, pp. 66–84.

Kennedy, John F. (1963 [2000]), "Civil rights: address to nation, June 11," in Fred L. Israel and Jim F. Watts (eds), *Presidential Documents: The Speeches, Proclamations, and Policies that Have Shaped the Nation from Washington to Clinton*, Routledge, pp. 320–24.

Killens, John O. (1964), "The black psyche," in *Black Man's Burden*, New York: Trident Press, pp. 3–22.

Kinder, Donald R. and David O. Sears (1981), "Prejudice and politics: symbolic racism versus racial threats to the good life," *Journal of Personality and Social Psychology*, 40, 414–31.

Kinder, Donald R. and David O. Sears (1985), "Public opinion and political action," in Gardner Lindzey and Elliot Aronson (eds), *Handbook of Social Psychology: Volume 2*, 3rd edition, New York: Random House, pp. 659–741.

McClerking, Harwood K. (2013), "'Showing his color': Mark Mallory's racial distinctiveness as seen through media representations," in Ravi K. Perry (ed.), *21st Century Urban Race Politics: Representing Minorities as Universal Interests*, Bingley, UK Emerald Group Publishing Limited, pp. 69–86.

McConahay, John B. (1986), "Modern racism, ambivalence, and the modern racism scale," in John F. Dovidio and Samuel L. Gaertner (eds), *Prejudice, Discrimination, and Racism*, New York: Academic Press, pp. 92–125.

McCormick, J.P., II and Charles E. Jones (1993), "The conceptualization of deracialization," in Georgia Persons (ed.), *Dilemmas of Black Politics*, New York: Harper Collins College Publishers, pp. 66–84.

Orey, Byron D. and Boris E. Ricks (2007), "A systematic analysis of the deracialization concept," in Georgia Persons (ed.), *National Political Science Review. Volume 11: The Expanding Boundaries of Black Politics*, New Brunswick, NJ: Transaction Publishers.

Orr, Marion and Carrie Nordlund (2013), "Political transformation in Providence: the election of Mayor Angel Taveras," in Ravi K. Perry (ed.), *21st Century Urban Race Politics: Representing Minorities as Universal Interests*, Bingley, UK: Emerald Group Publishing Limited, pp. 1–12.

Perry, Ravi K. (2009), "Black mayors in non-majority black (medium-sized) cities: universalizing the interests of blacks," *Ethnic Studies Review*, 32(1), 89–130.

Perry, Ravi K. (2011), "Kindred political rhetoric: black mayors, President Obama and the universalizing of black interests," *Journal of Urban Affairs*, 33(5), 567–90.

Perry, Ravi K. (2012), "Deval Patrick and the representation of Massachusetts' black interests," *Trotter Review*, 20(1), 9–41.

Perry, Ravi K. (ed.) (2013), *21st Century Urban Race Politics: Representing Minorities as Universal Interests*, Bingley, UK: Emerald Group Publishing Limited.

Perry, Ravi K. and Andrea Owens-Jones (2013), "Balancing act: racial empowerment and the dual expectations of Jack Ford in Toledo, Ohio," in Ravi K. Perry, *21st Century Urban Race Politics: Representing Minorities as Universal Interests*, Bingley, UK: Emerald Group Publishing Limited, pp. 181–200.

Phoenix, Davin (2013), "The mile high difference: examining the impact of institutional and political context on the electoral strategies pursued by minority mayors in Denver, and the impact of those strategies on minority communities," in Ravi K. Perry (ed.), *21st Century Urban Race Politics: Representing Minorities as Universal Interests*, Bingley, UK: Emerald Group Publishing Limited, pp. 111–32.

powell, john a., Stephen Menendian and Wendy Ake (2019), *Targeted Universalism: Policy & Practice*, Haas Institute for a Fair and Inclusive Society, University of California, Berkeley, accessed November 18, 2019 at haasinstitute.berkeley.edu/targeteduniversalism.

Reeves, F. (1983), *British Racial Discourse: A Study of British Political Discourse About Race and Race-Related Matters*, Cambridge, UK: Cambridge University Press.

Ricks, Boris E. (2013), "Antonio Villaraigosa, Los Angeles, and the politics of race," in Ravi K. Perry (ed.), *21st Century Urban Race Politics: Representing Minorities as Universal Interests*, Bingley, UK: Emerald Group Publishing Limited, pp. 163–80.

Schattschneider, Elmer Eric (1975), *The Semisovereign People*, New York: Thomson Learning, Inc.

Schexnider, Alvin J. (1990), "The politics of pragmatism: an analysis of the 1989 gubernatorial election in Virginia," *Urban Affairs Quarterly*, 23(2), 216–22.

Sears, David O., Jim Sidanius and Lawrence Bobo (eds) (2000), *Racialized Politics: The Debate About Racism in America*, Chicago, IL: University of Chicago Press.

Steinberg, Stephen (1998 [2010]), "The liberal retreat from race during the post civil rights era," in Wahneema Lubiano (ed.), *The House That Race Built: Original Essays by Toni Morrison, Angela Y. Davis, Cornel West, and Others On Black Americans and Politics in America Today*, New York: Random House, pp. 13–47.

Tate, K. (2010), *What's Going On? Political Incorporation and the Transformation of Black Public Opinion*, Washington, DC: Georgetown University Press.

Terrill, R. (2015), *Double-Consciousness and the Rhetoric of Barack Obama: The Price and Promise of Citizenship*, Columbia, SC: University of South Carolina Press.

Todenhagen, Christian (1987), "Semantic infiltration," *American Speech*, 62(2), 172–6.

Walker, David (1829 [1995]), *David Walker's Appeal: To the COLOURED CITIZENS OF THE WORLD but in particular and very expressly to those of THE UNITED STATES OF AMERICA*. New York: Hill and Wang.

Williams, Raymond (1977), *Marxism and Literature*, New York: Oxford University Press.

Winant, Howard (1998 [2010]), "Racial dualism at century's end," in Wahneema Lubiano (ed.), *The House That Race Built: Original Essays by Toni Morrison, Angela Y. Davis, Cornel West, and Others On Black Americans and Politics in America Today*, New York: Random House, pp. 87–115.

Yon, R. (2010), "The declining significance of race: Adrian Fenty and the smooth electoral transition," in Andra Gillespie (ed.), *Whose Black Politics?* New York: Routledge.

13. Identifying structural racism as a barrier to community wealth building

Risha R. Berry

Community wealth building seeks to provide a structural solution to poverty reduction by harnessing the full range of resources available in a community and establishing shared goals for sustained community change (see Barnes and Williamson in Chapter 2, and other contributions to this book).

This chapter reflects—and reflects upon—work that I was part of and helped lead in my role as a policy analyst and project manager for Richmond's Office of Community Wealth Building (OCWB) between 2014 and 2018. As noted by Barnes and Williamson, the OCWB's stated aims include: reducing the total number of persons in poverty relative to the 2013 baseline by 40 percent, and the child poverty rate relative to the 2013 baseline by 50 percent; tracking living wage attainment by hourly wages for 600 Richmond residents annually; and promoting living wage mobility and access to living wage jobs by establishing viable economic mobility pathways. I was part of the initial staff team that sought to identify and begin implementation of a broad strategy for systemic change in Richmond in order to achieve these goals (while at the same time growing or launching various programmatic initiatives). Putting a bold community wealth building strategy into place is a laudable but a deeply challenging undertaking. One of the most daunting and crucial of those challenges is promoting racial equity in wealth building.

This chapter is divided into four sections. First, I contextualize the profound racial disparities in the United States, Virginia and Richmond City's local labor market. Second, I describe the efforts of OCWB's Career Stations to redress these disparities through comprehensive workforce development services. Third, I describe an innovative effort OCWB undertook to knit together public and nonprofit service providers in a range of domains with the goal of developing a comprehensive network of services to help families move from economic crisis to thriving. Finally, in a brief concluding section, I reflect upon some of the accomplishments, limitations, and challenges involved in attempting to launch a bold new policy paradigm within an existing local government structure. It is my hope that these reflections can help inform other communities seeking to implement a community wealth building policy approach as well as future developments in Richmond.

CONTEXT: THE RACIALIZED LABOR MARKET

Moving underemployed Richmond residents into full-time, living-wage employment was identified as a top strategic priority by both the Mayor's Anti-Poverty Commission Report (2013) and the OCWB; programmatically, the city's locally funded workforce development effort has been the largest single component of OCWB's day-to-day work to date. From its inception as a pilot in 2011, the effort has steadily grown; in FY 2019 (July 2018–June 2019), OCWB Career Stations helped a total of 600 residents secure employment.

This effort is significant but has yet to transform or meaningfully dent enormous racial disparities in employment outcomes in Richmond. As this section explains, the scale of intervention in Richmond is not yet a match for the scale of the underlying disparities.

National research shows that employment discrimination, coupled with racialized jobs, segregate and disproportionately relegate high concentrations of persons of color in low-wage service jobs (Beasley, 2011). However, labor market problems such as low earnings, periods of unemployment, involuntary part-time employment, lack of flexible hours/paid sick days, also disproportionately impact individuals of color.

Structural Barriers, Racial Inequality and Demographic Shifts

Structural racism: concept and evidence

Social science scholars have developed the concept of *structural racism* to describe the systemic reproduction of profound racial inequalities over time. Structural racism is embedded in our historical, political, cultural, social, and economic systems and institutions. It works cumulatively and produces vastly adverse outcomes in racial inequity for people of color in areas such as health, wealth, career, education, infrastructure, and civic participation (Golash-Boza, 2016). Obstacles that affect a group disproportionately and perpetuate or maintain stark disparities in outcomes are *structural* barriers. Policies, practices, and other norms, left unexamined, can favor an advantaged group while systematically disadvantaging a marginalized group, thus creating structural barriers (Simms et al., 2015).

The depth and range of this work is illustrated by a literature review of scholarship on structural racism published between 2007 and 2017 conducted by a team of researchers on health disparities (Groos et al., 2018). Twenty articles met the inclusion criteria. Articles included measures of structural racism within the following domains in order of frequency: residential neighborhood/housing, perceived racism in social institutions, socioeconomic status, criminal justice, immigration and border enforcement, political participation, and workplace environment. This burgeoning body of work suggests ways to operationalize and measure structural racism. Closely related, *systemic racism theory*, a social science theory of race and racism, elucidates the foundational, enveloping and persisting structures, mechanisms and operations of racial oppression that have fundamentally shaped the United States past and present. Systemic racism theory provides empirically grounded and theoretical guidance to understand racial realities beyond the United States and in comparative perspective (Feagin and Elias, 2013).

A paradigmatic example of structural racism—and one with profound relevance for this book—is the racial wealth gap. In 2016, the net worth of a White family ($171,000) was nearly ten times greater than that of a Black family ($17,150) (McIntosh et. al., 2020). This gap is attributable not only to present-day differences in educational and career opportunities but can also be traced back to discriminatory post-World War II government mortgage policies that intentionally locked generations of Blacks and Latinx out of the primary source of wealth for America's White middle class—the housing market. This disparity leads to a persistent impact, effectively excluding many people of color. It combines with other inequities such as underperforming schools, poor access to public transit, predatory lending, and deep disproportionality in our criminal justice system (Golash-Boza, 2016).

Further dimensions of structural racism: racialized organizations
The persistence of these racial disparities, particularly in the employment context, raises fundamental questions about private sector, nonprofit sector *and* public sector employers as *organizations*. How and why are racial inequities being reproduced over time by employers?

Victor Ray has noted that organizational theory scholars typically see organizations as race-neutral bureaucratic structures, while race and ethnicity scholars have largely neglected the role of organizations in the social construction of race (Ray, 2019). Ray bridges organizational theory and race and ethnicity subfields, arguing that organizations are racial structures—made up of cognitive schemas connecting organizational rules to social and material resources. He argues that racialization theory must account for how both state policy and individual attitudes are filtered through—and changed by—organizations. He asserts that seeing race as constitutive of organizations helps us better understand stability, change, and the institutionalization of racial inequality.

Racialized exclusion

Racialized exclusion exists across economic sectors and despite matched formal credentials (Bertrand and Mullainathan, 2004; Correll, Benard and Paik, 2007), hiring discrimination, and the credential of Whiteness is part of a general organizational process (Bertrand and Mullainathan, 2004; Moss and Tilly, 2003; Pager, 2003). Job positions in the labor hierarchy become associated with racial groups and accordingly devalued (Tomaskovic-Devy, 1993) or overvalued, and racialized hierarchy is seen as a basic feature of the world as opposed to a historically constructed reality. Academic tracking stigmatizes Black students by associating Blackness with lower academic achievement (Ray, 2019).

Whiteness and interest convergence

Classical work in critical race theory argues that racial progress occurs when the interests of Whites and people of color converge (Bell, 1980). Identifying structural racism as a barrier to community wealth building assists us with the following questions that Ray (2019) posits:

- How do racialized organizations adapt in ways that support, undermine, or spur innovations in the wider racialized social system?
- What is the role of organizations in constructing group-based interest, or how organizations undermine the extension of rights?
- What racialized policies and practices did Whites who were opposed to the civil rights movement carry with them into the workplace?
- Does the naturalized and unmarked Whiteness of mainstream organizations assist in the production of racial ignorance?

An organization's role in the distribution of social resources has implications beyond employment; organizations at the local level, for example, influence community health or may spawn gentrification. From a racialized organization's perspective, organizational decision-making happens when material relations are reshuffled through human agency—not racial attitudes (abstracted) from social context (Ray, 2019). Inhabited institutions (Hallett and Ventresca, 2006) are peopled with racialized bodies that make decisions about where to locate and whom to hire. These decisions likely include a racial component. Which leads us to ponder the following questions from Ray (2019):

- How do the emotions of Whiteness shape the daily operation and distribution of resources within organizations?
- How do organizational processes contribute to the "deep stories" (Hochschild, 2016) that Whites tell regarding deservingness and merit?

- How do organizations channel and direct the "White rage" (Anderson, 2016) of backlash politics?

A Turn to the Data: Demographics and the Facts of Racialized Labor Market Disparity

These questions are of profound importance as we come to consider the implications of current demographic trends and our ongoing racial inequities in the labor market.

Demographic shift

Demographers project that by 2020 a majority of youth under 18 will be of color and that by 2030 a majority of young workers will be people of color. A mere ten years later, people of color will be a majority of the American working class (Wilson, 2016). "For the foreseeable future, Latinos and [Blacks] will remain the two largest minority groups in the U.S. By 2043, Latinos will make up 26.6 percent of the working age population, while [Blacks] will be 13.4 percent" (Wilson, 2016). This is a dramatic shift for an America that was 80 percent White as recently as the 1980s. Together, these forces—rising diversity amidst persistent racial economic exclusion—form the core challenge that America's businesses must address to compete in today's economy, and tomorrow's (Golash-Boza, 2016).

The dominant ideological framework for discussing race in the contemporary United States is that of color blindness—that is, the notion that racial inequality is best understood as deriving from individual or cultural traits as opposed to systemic racism. This ideology permeates institutions and interpersonal interactions, thus upholding racial inequality (Burke, 2016).

National labor market trends: racial disparities in earnings and poverty

In 2017, according to the Bureau of Labor Statistics, about 39.7 million people, or 12.3 percent of the nation's population, lived below the official poverty level (Bureau of Labor Statistics, 2019). Blacks or African Americans and Hispanics or Latinx were *more than twice as likely* as Whites and Asians to be among the working poor, where the working-poor rate for both was 7.9 percent, compared with 3.9 percent for Whites and 2.9 percent for Asians.

Indeed, Blacks and Hispanics generally were *more likely to be among the working poor* than were Whites and Asians *with the same educational attainment*. Among people age 25 and older, the share of the labor force with at least a high school diploma was more than 90 percent for each of Whites, Blacks, and Asians. By contrast, 75 percent of Hispanics in the labor force had attained at least a high school diploma. Asians were the most likely of the groups to have graduated from college: 61 percent of Asians in the labor force had a bachelor's degree and higher, compared with 40 percent of Whites, 30 percent of Blacks, and 20 percent of Hispanics.

Hispanics and Blacks also had *considerably lower earnings* than Whites and Asians. The median usual weekly earnings of full-time wage and salary workers in 2017 were $655 for Hispanics, $682 for Blacks, $890 for Whites, and $1043 for Asians (Bureau of Labor Statistics, 2017a).

National labor market trends: racial disparities in employment

Joblessness rates varied considerably by race and ethnicity. The notes that follow are selected trends from the Bureau of Labor Statistics report on race and ethnicity 2017 (Bureau of Labor Statistics, 2018).

American Indians and Alaska Natives (7.8 percent) and Blacks (7.5 percent) had the *highest unemployment* rates, followed by 6.7 percent for individuals of two or more races, 6.1 percent for native Hawaiians and other Pacific Islanders, and 5.1 percent for Hispanics. The jobless rates were 3.8 percent for Whites and lowest for Asians (3.4 percent).

Unemployed Blacks and Asians *experienced longer periods of unemployment* than did Whites and Hispanics. The median duration of unemployment for Blacks and Asians was 13.1 weeks and 11.5 weeks, respectively, whereas the figure for Whites was 9.3 weeks and Hispanics, 8.9 weeks. Fifty-two percent of employed Asians worked in management, professional, and related occupations—the highest paying major occupational category—compared with 41 percent of employed Whites, 31 percent of employed Blacks, and 23 percent of employed Hispanics (Bureau of Labor Statistics, 2017b).

As the next section shows, these national-level racial disparities are magnified and multiplied in Richmond, Virginia.

Labor Market Trends, Race, and Wage Inequality in United States, Virginia and Richmond, Virginia

United States

Table 13.1 shows racial differences in the United States in labor market participation and related measures. Key highlights include the following:

• Labor force participation was highest for Asians (68.6 percent), followed by Hispanic or Latinx (67.3 percent). Whites were 63.5 percent, followed by Blacks at 62.4 percent.
• The Census classifies households into ten income brackets ranging from under $10,000 to over $200,000. The highest concentration of Asians (17.4 percent) was in the $100,000–$149,999 bracket; for Whites (18.3 percent), Hispanic or Latinx (18.1 percent) and Blacks (15.7 percent), the largest percentage were located in the $50,000–$74,999 range.

- Of those concentrated in the management, business science and arts occupations, 50.1 percent were Asians, followed by Whites at 38.4 percent; 26.1 percent of Hispanics were concentrated in service locations, followed by 25.6 percent of Blacks in sales and office occupations.
- Of those who attained a bachelor's degree or higher, 51.4 percent were Asians, followed by Whites at 31.1 percent; Blacks made up 19.5 percent of those that attained a bachelor's degree or higher, followed by Hispanic or Latinx, who made up 14.3 percent.
- Of those concentrated in educational services, and healthcare and social assistance industries, 29.2 percent were Blacks and 22.7 percent were Whites; 16.9 percent of Hispanic or Latinx worked in the same domain, while 24.9 percent of Asians worked in professional, scientific and management and administrative and waste management services.
- Of those unemployed, 14.8 percent were Blacks, followed by 9.8 percent Hispanic or Latinx, 7.1 percent Whites, and 6.4 percent Asians (United States Census Bureau, 2017a).

Commonwealth of Virginia

Similar trends obtain in Virginia's labor market (see below and Table 13.2):

- Of those participating in the labor force, 76.5 percent were Hispanic or Latinx, followed by 69.9 percent of Asians, and 65.8 percent each of Blacks and Whites.
- The highest concentration of Asians (20.7 percent) was in the $100,000–$149,999 household income bracket; for Whites (17.5 percent), Hispanic or Latinx (19.6 percent) and Blacks (17.3 percent) the largest percentage were located in the $50,000–$74,999 range (United States Census Bureau, 2017a).
- Asians led the educational attainment domain with 59.3 percent holding a bachelor's degree or higher, followed by Whites at 38.6 percent, Hispanic or Latinx at 23.0 percent, and Blacks at 21.7 percent (United States Census, 2017b).
- Blacks led the educational services and healthcare and social assistance domain at 26.0 percent, followed by Whites at 21.5 percent; 22.2 percent of Asians work in the professional, scientific, and management and administrative and waste management industry; 17.2 of Hispanic or Latinx work in the construction industry.
- Blacks had the highest unemployment rate at 11.2 percent, followed by Hispanic or Latinx at 6.6 percent and Whites at 5.3 percent; Asians have the lowest unemployment rate at 4.9 percent (United States Census Bureau, 2017a).

Table 13.1   Labor market, household income, occupational participation, educational attainment, industry, and unemployment by race/ethnicity in the United States

Race/ Ethnicity	Labor Force Participation	Household Income	Occupational Participation	Educational Attainment (bachelor's degree or higher)	Industry	Unemployment
White	63.5%	18.3% $50,000–$74,999	38.4% Management, business, science, and arts occupations	31.1%	22.7% Educational services, and healthcare and social assistance	7.1%
Black	62.4%	15.7% $50,000–$74,999	25.6% Sales and office occupations	19.5%	29.2% Educational services, and healthcare and social assistance	14.8%

Race/Ethnicity	Labor Force Participation	Household Income	Occupational Participation	Educational Attainment (bachelor's degree or higher)	Industry	Unemployment
Asian	68.6%	17.4% $100,000–$149,999	50.1% Management, business science and arts	51.4%	24.9% Professional, scientific, and management and administrative and waste management services	6.4%
Hispanic or Latinx	67.3%	18.1% $50,000–$74,999	26.1% Service occupations	14.3%	16.9% Educational services, and healthcare and social assistance	9.8%

Source: United States Census Bureau (2017a, 2017b, 2017c).

Table 13.2   Labor market, household income, occupational participation, educational attainment, industry, and unemployment by race/ethnicity in the State of Virginia

Race/ Ethnicity	Labor Force Participation	Household Income	Occupational Participation	Educational Attainment	Industry	Unemployment
White	65.8%	17.5% $50,000–$74,999	45.5% Management, business, science and arts occupations	38.6%	21.5% Educational services, and healthcare, and social assistance	5.3%
Black	65.8%	17.3% $50,000–$74,999	30.9% Management, business, science and arts occupations	21.7%	26.0% Educational services, and healthcare, and social assistance	11.2%
Asian	69.9%	20.7% $100,000–$149,999	54.6% Management, business, science and arts occupations	59.3%	22.2% Professional, scientific, and management, and administrative, and waste management	4.9%
Hispanic or Latinx	76.5%	19.6% $50,000–$74,999	29.0% Service occupations	23.0%	17.2% Construction	6.6%

Source: United States Census Bureau (2017a, 2017b, 2017c).

Richmond, Virginia

These racial disparities are even more pronounced in Richmond's capital city (see below and Table 13.3). As context, in 2017, 47.0 percent of Richmond residents were African American, 40.5 percent were non-Hispanic Whites, 6.7 percent were Hispanic or Latinx, and 2.0 percent were Asian (United States Census Bureau, 2018). Trends for the city of Richmond were as follows:

- Labor force participation was highest among Hispanics at (74.2 percent), followed by Whites (70.6 percent), and lowest among Asians (61.0 percent) and Blacks (60.6 percent).
- Stunningly, more Blacks fell into the under-$10,000 household income range (18.9 percent) than in any other category; the same was true for Asians (16.9 percent). More Hispanics (21.9 percent) were in the $15,000–$24,999 range than any other group. The highest household income was among Whites (18.3 percent: $50,000–$74,999).
- Occupational participation was highest among Asians (53.2 percent) and Whites (53.1 percent) in the management, business, science, and arts occupations. Hispanics participated (31.4 percent) in the natural resources, construction, and maintenance occupations, and Blacks participated at (30.2 percent) in service occupations (United States Census Bureau, 2017a).
- Of those with bachelor's degree or higher, 66.1 percent were Asians, followed by 57.6 percent of Whites; educational attainment was lowest among Blacks (13.7 percent) and Hispanics (13.0 percent), among those wo have a bachelor's degree or higher (United States Census Bureau, 2017b).
- Among the employed, Hispanics are more likely to work in construction (28.6 percent), and arts, entertainment, and recreation and accommodation and food services (17.7 percent).
- Employed Blacks are more likely to work in retail trade (12.7 percent), transportation and warehousing (6.4 percent), and public administration (6.5 percent). Employed Asians are more likely to work in educational services (33.4 percent), and finance, insurance and real estate (10.5 percent) industries. Whites are more likely to work in professional, scientific and management, and administrative and waste management services (15.4 percent), information (2.2 percent), and wholesale trade (1.9 percent).
- Blacks have the highest unemployment rate (15.6 percent) followed by Asians (8.2 percent), Hispanics (7.2 percent) and Whites (5.2 percent).

Future Top Job Industries

Projected employment trends suggest that racialized disparities in the employment sector are likely to continue for the foreseeable future. Virginia Commonwealth University's Center for Urban and Regional Analysis

Table 13.3   *Labor market, household income, occupational participation, educational attainment, industry, and unemployment by race/ethnicity in Richmond, Virginia*

Race/ethnicity	Labor Force Participation	Household Income	Occupational Participation	Educational Attainment (bachelor's degree or higher)	Industry	Unemployment
Hispanics	74.2%	21.9% $15,000–$24,999	31.4% Natural resources, construction, and maintenance occupations	13.0%	Construction (28.6%) Arts and entertainment, recreation, accommodation, and food services (17.7%)	7.2%
Whites	70.6%	18.3% $50,000–$74,999	53.1% Management, business, science, and arts occupations	57.6%	Professional, scientific and management, and administrative and waste management services (15.4%), information (2.2%), and wholesale trade (1.9%)	5.2%

Race/ ethnicity	Labor Force Participation	Household Income	Occupational Participation	Educational Attainment (bachelor's degree or higher)	Industry	Unemployment
Blacks	60.6%	18.9% Less than $10,000	30.2% Service occupations	13.7%	Retail trade (12.7%), transportation and warehousing (6.4%), and Public administration (6.5%)	15.6%
Asian	61.0%	16.9% Less than $10,000	53.2%	66.1%	Educational services (33.4%) and finance, insurance and real estate (10.5%) industries	8.2%

Source: United States Census Bureau (2017a, 2017b, 2017c).

(Accordino et al., 2016) projected that Virginia's future top job industries are accommodation and food services (19 percent); healthcare and social assistance (16 percent); retail trade (16 percent); professional, scientific, and technical services (11 percent); and administrative support and waste management and remediation services (9 percent). Hispanics are more likely to fill vacancies in accommodation and food services (average full-time salary of $29,810). Asians are more likely to fill vacancies in healthcare and social assistance (average full-time salary of $35,853). Blacks are more likely to fill vacancies in retail trade (average full-time salary of $31,653). Whites are more likely to fill vacancies in professional, scientific, and technical services (average full-time salary of $59,996) as well as administrative support and waste management and remediation services (average full-time salary of $30,100).

ENTER COMMUNITY WEALTH BUILDING: OCWB CAREER STATIONS

These data indicate that Blacks in Richmond are specifically disadvantaged in every measure of labor market success: full-time employment, sector, and earnings. To counter this disparity, Richmond city government launched a locally funded workforce initiative in 2011 (now overseen by OCWB) that seeks to identify growth sectors and employers with employment needs, then prepare and connect underemployed residents to such opportunities through training, courses, case management, and other strategies. Importantly, OCWB also seeks to work with program participants holistically to address needs and barriers beyond the employment sphere.

OCWB currently oversees four Career Stations that specialize in workforce readiness. In 2018, the Career Stations reported weekly seeing over 300 persons seeking employment per week, based on 1000 visits per month (City of Richmond, 2018). As shown in Figure 13.1, these heads of households report facing an array of labor market problems in their journey to economic stability that mimic national unemployment trends: unemployment (15 weeks or longer), job loss, discouragement, and marginal attachment to the workforce (the "marginally attached" include persons who currently are neither working nor looking for work, but indicate that they want and are available for a job and have looked for work sometime in the past 12 months). Participants also report wanting and being available for full-time work, but settling for temporary jobs, part-time jobs, and shift work while searching for full time employment.

Census data indicate there are about 30,000 adults in poverty in Richmond who are not working full-time; about one-half of these are employed part-time. To meet the bold goals of cutting poverty 40 percent by 2030, it is estimated that about 10,000 of these adults *net* (and their children) must gain incomes above the poverty line (City of Richmond, 2018).

Unemployed Job Seekers

Part of this challenge has to do with the nature of unemployment itself. The Bureau of Labor Statistics studies alternative measures of labor underutilization. This category includes persons who may be:

- unemployed 15 weeks or longer;
- experiencing long-term unemployment (those jobless for 27 weeks or more);
- have lost their jobs or completed temporary jobs;
- are marginally attached to the labor force (as defined above);
- are "discouraged" (have given a job market-related reason for not currently looking for work, or believe that no jobs are available for them, or had not searched for work for reasons such as school attendance or family responsibilities);
- are involuntary part-time workers (employed part-time for economic reasons—those who want and are available for full-time work but have to settle for a part-time schedule); they would have preferred full-time employment, were working part-time because their hours had been cut back or because they were unable to find a full-time job).

OCWB's Career Stations are intended to provide support to residents in any of these categories, but especially residents with deeper challenges whose needs are not being adequately served by existing workforce programs in the region. Specifically, OCWB Career Stations clients are primarily concentrated at the unemployed job seekers level. They serve clients who are transitioning back into the workforce, based upon these categories, as well as those that are returning citizens from incarceration. They do have the capability to serve other clients, but their niche and primary client base is in this domain (unemployed job seekers).

Wage Mobility (The Ladder)

The "living wage" as described by Massachusetts Institute of Technology (MIT, 2018) is the minimum subsistence wage for persons living in the United States. Tracking living wages, along with occupational mobility trends emerged as key strategy undertaken by the OCWB. Prior to the formal creation of the office, Career Stations have informally tracked occupational change and mobility among unemployed job seekers.

Powers, Livermore and Davis (2013), examined employment barriers, social support, and informal employment of persons leaving public assistance—a group of people facing challenges similar to many low-income Richmond residents. They studied job seekers (excluding the small number of self-employed, unpaid family workers, and inactive people who search for a job). Job seekers they studied were categorized as working age (men and women ages 16–64) who (1) were looking for paid employment; (2) have looked for work in the last four weeks; and (3) mentioned at least one method of job search. Figure 13.1 illustrates OCWB's adaptation of this study.

Employed Job Seekers and Mobility

The Powers et al. (2013) study cited above discovered that *already employed* job seekers have numerous advantages in the labor market. They are more likely to move into occupations paying higher than average wages relative to their previous occupation; more likely to move from relatively low ranking occupations (such as sales and customer service or elementary occupations) into higher-ranking occupations (such as professionals, associate professional and technical); and more likely to exhibit upward occupational mobility (Powers et al., 2013).

According to their study, employed job seekers tend to move away from occupations such as sales and customer service, and elementary occupations, and into occupations such as professionals, associate professional and technical, and administrative and secretarial. Employed job seekers' occupational change may reflect career progression, with advancement into higher wage occupations (or higher wage growth). Employed job seekers were much more likely than unemployed job seekers to experience upward mobility and much less likely to experience downward mobility.

Unemployment and Mobility

Alternatively, Powers et al. found that unemployed job seekers tend to exhibit downward mobility, defined as job seekers who (1) change occupation and (2) move to an occupation with a mean wage at least 10 percent lower than the mean wage in their previous occupation. Unemployed job seekers are much more likely to accept jobs in an occupation with a lower mean wage. While occupational change is more likely to be an opportunity for employed job seekers, it seems to be a constraint for unemployed job seekers.

This suggests that the scarring effects of unemployment exceed the immediate impacts on wages and have longer-term career consequences. Indeed, the evidence suggests that employed and unemployed job seekers operate in

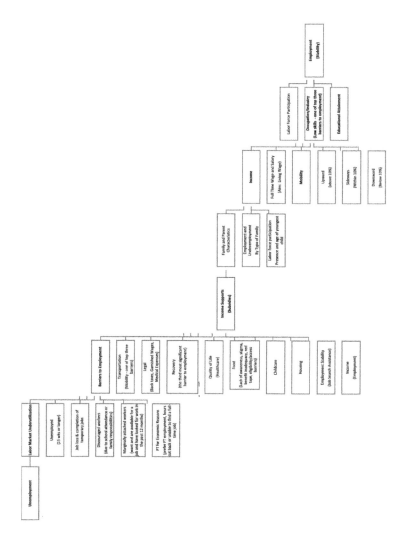

Figure 13.1 Unemployment and mobility

different labor markets. For the unemployed, a change in occupation is likely to have a negative impact on future wages.

All these data indicate the degree to which the deck is stacked against underemployed Richmond residents seeking to obtain employment, move to living wage employment, and establish a stable career path allowing for economic stability and thriving. Further, these racialized disparities in the labor market are multiplied by equally profound racial inequalities in education and housing.

TOWARDS CHANGE IN MULTIPLE SECTORS: THE NETWORK FOCUS GROUP INITIATIVE

According to the Aspen Institute (2016), structural racism refers to "a system in which public policies, institutional practices, cultural representations and other norms work in various often reinforcing ways to perpetuate racial group inequity." This lens allows us to understand the way that historically accumulated White leadership, dominance and privilege have preserved the gaps between White Americans and Americans of color. Changes in multiple sectors, they maintain, will be required to make sustainable progress towards racial equity in labor markets.

Systems thinking can help people to understand why, and can help identify both entry points for change and links among those entry points. Richmond's OCWB convened a series of nine network focus group meetings in 2017 marking the establishment of a bold way of aligning community-based assets to build a coherent ladder out of poverty. The network focus group meetings (Figure 13.2) were designed to identify and categorize service providers who support job seekers moving through the self-sufficiency continuum and identify structural barriers in economic mobility.

This task was undertaken to identify the feasibility of connecting citywide networks along the domains of the self-sufficiency matrix. The short-term goal was twofold: to document service providers in each domain, and identify potential access gaps and barriers to service delivery. Ultimately, the long-term goal was to identify strategies to alleviate systemic and structural barriers to economic stability so that 1000 citizens each year are able to move from crisis to a thriving level of economic stability.

During a series of meetings, service providers from employment, income, mobility, childcare, housing, quality of life (ex. healthcare, mental health, physical health), food, legal and recovery sectors were asked to identify the services and supports they delivered and rank them according to the self-sufficiency scale, where (1) was in crisis; (2) at risk; (3) safe; (4) stable; and (5) is thriving.

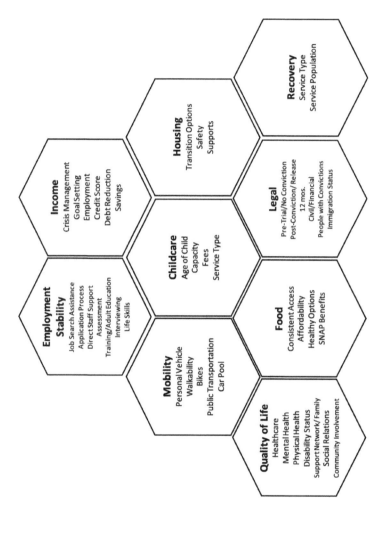

Figure 13.2   Community wealth building focus group domains

Almost all network focus group meetings were facilitated by OCWB's workforce administrator, who asked providers to identify supports and interventions that they believed had the greatest impact in removing structural barriers that prevent individuals from finding navigable pathways to financial well-being. (In my capacity as an OCWB project management analyst, I attended and documented each of these meetings and subsequently analyzed the resultant data.) Meeting participants were asked to specifically identify strategies that preclude heads of households who were in the categories of in crisis (1) or at risk (2).

Findings revealed that while agencies served residents across the self-sufficiency continuum, they primarily served residents in the following order: first, level 3 (safe), second, level 2 (at risk), third, level 4 (stable), and finally, level 1 (in crisis). Agencies revealed that residents in crisis were the hardest to serve, noting that perhaps they weren't ready for services, for many reasons. They also revealed that residents in crisis weren't a target population per se, because there weren't "quick" wins associated with their interventions.

They also reported that clients at level 1 were harder to track with regard to their mobility. While level 2 (at risk) clients also required more resources, they were identified as having a greater level of readiness for services than in crisis (level 1) clients.

Level 3 clients (safe) were associated with being easier to serve, and therefore capable of gaining quicker wins with successful interventions. Agencies reported being spread too thin, and did report that they attempted to serve all categories, across all domains. They also reported that while referrals to other agencies took place, they were not sure if they worked—if they happened to see the client again, they would ask, but otherwise they weren't sure.

Agencies reported that it was difficult to track services across domains. There was not a way, for instance, to ensure whether services were efficient, or if resources were being deployed in a redundant manner. For example, many providers reported distributing bus passes.

It was also reported that there was no way to find out if a client dropped out of the pipeline, or caseload. The responsibility they reported, resided with the client seeking services to follow up with their case manager on their progress, making it hard to apply wraparound support. The following summary represents highlights of the focus groups and participant recommendations in the income category.

Income

The income focus group discussed topics, programs and best practices that have had or would have the greatest impact in removing the systemic and structural barriers that, at this point, preclude levels 1 (in crisis—no income) and 2 (at risk—inadequate income to meet basic needs) from economic mobility. Structurally, they noted that incomes, particularly of people classified as low income—had not kept pace with inflation. This, coupled with a federal minimum wage that had not seen an increase since 2009, had serious long-term impact on movement towards economic stability, ultimately threatening the individual personally, and the local economy holistically.

Low Wages

Traditional low wages associated with entry-level positions coupled with the systematic regulations that drastically cut benefits and subsidies (known as the "Cliff Effect") were noted as having had an adverse effect on moving individuals toward economic stability. Increasing wages by supporting a living wage or an increase in the federal minimum wage and requesting waivers or eliminating dramatic subsidy reduction can help citizens find navigable pathways to financial well-being.

Income focus group recommendations for interventions included continuing to develop a living wage certification program, called the Richmond Area Living Wage Certification Program. This was established in 2018 as a joint program of the Richmond Chapter of the Virginia Interfaith Center for Public Policy and the City of Richmond's OCWB. The program would recognize employers who are currently paying a living wage or making strides to pay better wages. Strategies recommended included piloting a program that trained volunteers to help with identifying businesses who are eligible for recognition.

Additional policy recommendations included:

- supporting changes in policy or regulations that provide for a transition period or a sliding scale to ease the Cliff Effect on participants working toward economic stability;
- standardizing a one-on-one, financial planning model based on the Virginia Local Initiatives Support Corporation Financial Opportunity Center programs;
- establishing partnerships, guided by Memorandums of Understanding to increase capacity of groups with demonstrated success in supporting economic stability of targeted populations;
- working with financial institutions to explore options for creative savings programs, that is, Saving Sharing Programs, and Child Savings Accounts.

Taken as a whole, this process generated a robust range of policy recommendations that continue to inform action and advocacy undertaken by OCWB, the City of Richmond, and numerous partner organizations. Clearly, there is potential and necessity for a comprehensive, ongoing advocacy effort aimed at continuously identifying and removing structural barriers to upward mobility impacting low-income African American residents in Richmond.

IMPLICATIONS

Community wealth building strategies aimed at creating a more equitable and secure future, must move away from public policies that fuel and exacerbate racial disparities in wealth building. The impact of labor markets, housing, and education on the wealth gap between White, Black, and Latinx households is well-documented. The U.S. racial wealth gap is substantial and driven by public policy decisions that sustain racial disparities in income, and wealth return on income, which impacts homeownership (rates and returns) and college graduation (rates and return).

Improving the economic returns that households gain requires confronting and changing the deeply entrenched structures that inhibit the ability of households seeking economic stability to build assets. Policies that successfully address disparities in returns to income are likely to be the most effective in reducing the racial wealth gap. The charge to policy-makers that seek to promote racial equity in community wealth building strategies must act with precision to challenge the deeply rooted structures of inequality that create barriers to access and achievement, and that ultimately reproduce disproportionate advantages for White households.

REFERENCES

Accordino, John, Fabrizio Fasulo, Ivan Suen and Sarin Adhikari (2016), *Commonwealth of Virginia, Virginia Workforce Development Survey*, accessed January 27, 2020 at https://cura.vcu.edu/media/cura/pdfs/cura-documents/VEC2016_FINALE_June20.pdf.

Anderson, Carol (2016), *White Rage: The Unspoken Truth of Our Racial Divide*, New York: Bloomsbury.

Aspen Institute (2016), "11 terms you should know to better understand structural racism," July 11, accessed July 7, 2020 at https://www.aspeninstitute.org/blog-posts/structural-racism-definition/.

Beasley, Maya A. (2011), "Black professionals in racialized and community-oriented occupations: the role of equal opportunity protections and affirmative action in maintaining the status quo," *Race/Ethnicity: Multidisciplinary Global Contexts*, 4(2), 285–301.

Bell, Derrick (1980), "*Brown v. Board of Education* and the interest-convergence dilemma," *Harvard Law Review*, 93(3), 518–33.

Bertrand, Marianne and Sendhil Mullainathan (2004), "Are Emily and Greg more employable than Lakisha and Jamal? A field experiment on labor market discrimination," *American Economic Review*, 94(4), 991–1013.

Bureau of Labor Statistics (2017a). "Earnings," accessed January 27, 2020 at https://www.bls.gov/opub/reports/race-and-ethnicity/2017/home.htm.

Bureau of Labor Statistics (2017b). "Educational attainment," accessed January 27, 2020 at https://www.bls.gov/opub/reports/race-and-ethnicity/2017/home.htm.

Bureau of Labor Statistics (2018), *Labor Force Characteristics by Race and Ethnicity, 2017* (BLS Report No. 1076), U.S. Department of Labor, accessed September 2020 at https://www.bls.gov/opub/reports/race-and-ethnicity/2017/home.htm#:~:text=The%20employment%E2%80%93population%20ratios%20for,and%2055.6%20percent%20for%20Whites.

Bureau of Labor Statistics (2019), *A Profile of the Working Poor, 2017* (BLS Report No. 1079), U.S. Department of Labor, accessed September 2020 at https://www.bls.gov/opub/reports/working-poor/2017/pdf/home.pdf.

Burke, Meghan A. (2016). "New frontiers in the study of color-blind racism: a materialist approach," *Social Currents*, 3(2), 103–9.

City of Richmond (2018), *Office of Community Wealth Building Annual Report*, accessed January 27, 2020 at http://www.richmondgov.com/CommunityWealthBuilding/documents/2018-CWB-Final-Annual-Report-Mayors-Signature-App-A-B.pdf.

Correll, Shelley J., Stephen Benard and In Paik (2007). "Getting a job: is there a motherhood penalty?" *American Journal of Sociology*, 112(5), 1297–339.

Feagin, Joe and Sean Elias (2013), "Rethinking racial formation theory: a systemic racism critique," *Ethnic and Racial Studies*, 36(6), 931–60.

Golash-Boza, Tanya (2016), "A critical and comprehensive sociological theory of race and racism," *Sociology of Race and Ethnicity*, 2(2), 129–41.

Groos, Maya, Maeve Wallace, Rachel Hardeman and Katherine P. Theall (2018), "Measuring inequality: a systematic review of methods used to quantify structural racism," *Journal of Heath Disparities Research and Practice*, 11(2).

Hallett, Tim and Marc J. Ventresca (2006), "Inhabited institutions: social interactions and organizational forms in Gouldner's *Patterns of Industrial Bureaucracy*," *Theory and Society*, 35(2), 213–36.

Hochschild, Arlie Russell (2016), *Strangers in Their Own Land: Anger and Mourning on the American Right*, New York: The New Press.

Mayor's Anti-Poverty Commission (2013), Mayor's Anti-Poverty Commission Report to Dwight C. Jones, Mayor of City of Richmond, January 18, accessed July 2020 at http://www.richmondgov.com/CommissionAntiPoverty/documents/Antipovertycommissionfinal1_17_2013c--printready.pdf.

McIntosh, K., E. Moss, R. Nunn and J. Shambaugh (2020), "Examining the Black-White wealth gap," (February 27), Brookings Institution website, accessed September 2020 at https://www.brookings.edu/blog/up-front/2020/02/27/examining-the-black-white-wealth-gap/.

MIT (2018), "About the Living Wage Calculator," accessed February 3, 2020 at http://livingwage.mit.edu/pages/about.

Moss, Philip and Chris Tilly (2003), *Stories Employers Tell: Race, Skill and Hiring in America*, New York: Russell Sage Foundation.

Pager, Devah (2003), "The mark of a criminal record," *American Journal of Sociology*, 108(5), 937–75.

Powers, Rebecca S., Michelle M. Livermore and Belinda Creel Davis (2013), "The complex lives of disconnected welfare leavers: examining employment barriers, social support and informal employment," *Journal of Poverty*, 17(4), 394–413.

Ray, Victor (2019), "A theory of racialized organizations," *American Sociological Review*, 84(1), 26–53.

Simms, Margaret, Marla McDaniel, Saunji D. Fyffe and Christopher Lowenstein (2015), "Structural barriers to racial equity in Pittsburgh: expanding economic opportunity for African American men and boys," Washington, DC: Urban Institute, accessed January 27, 2020 at https://www.urban.org/research/publication/structural-barriers -racial-equity-pittsburgh-expanding-economic-opportunity-african-american-men -and-boys.

Tomaskovic-Devey, Donald (1993), *Gender and Race Inequality at Work: The Sources and Consequences of Job Segregation*, Ithaca, NY: ILR Press.

United States Census Bureau (2017a), American Community Survey: "Table DP02: Selected economic characteristics, 2011–15," accessed January 27, 2020 at American FactFinder [data now available at https://data.census.gov/cedsci/].

United States Census Bureau (2017b), American Community Survey: "Table DP03: Selected social characteristics, 2011–15," January 27, 2020 at American FactFinder [data now available at https://data.census.gov/cedsci/].

United States Census Bureau (2017c), American Community Survey: "Table B15002: Sex by educational attainment for the population 25 years and over, 2011–15," September 2020 at American FactFinder [data now available at https://data.census .gov/cedsci/].

United States Census Bureau (2018), American Community Survey: "Table CP05: Comparative demographic estimates," accessed July 7, 2020 at https://data.census .gov/cedsci/.

Wilson, Valerie (2016), "People of color will be a majority of the American working class in 2032," Economic Policy Institute, June 9, accessed July 7, 2020 at https:// www.epi.org/publication/the-changing-demographics-of-americas-working-class/.

14. The university as anchor institution in community wealth building: snapshots from two Virginia universities

Barbara Brown Wilson and Meghan Z. Gough

INTRODUCTION

Despite considerable attention placed by university administrations on con-tributing positively to their surrounding communities, universities continue to exacerbate instead of remediate inequity. As large, tax-exempt anchor organizations with global footprints, universities do not fully acknowledge the local impacts they impose on their surrounding communities; for instance, universities influence regional housing markets, transportation infrastructure, and often the quality of jobs and wages in the region.

Universities are a particularly important example of *anchor institutions*. Anchor institutions are nonprofit entities that have a substantial stake in their surrounding community, typically due to landownership and mission. Because anchor institutions have important economic impacts on communities through employment, revenue garnering, and spending, they play a vital role in their local communities and economies. And because universities and other anchor institutions have a broader mission than profit-maximizing corporations, they have greater potential to harness this impact in more intentional ways to benefit local communities.

Increasingly, the public are asking anchor institutions to do more in their communities and become active civic participants in improving their local surroundings. Across the nation, local and regional organizations are engaging anchor institutions as important partners to advance equitable growth and create opportunities for disadvantaged residents in local communities to be the workers and leaders helping to advance the economy (Schildt and Rubin, 2015).

The idea that universities play a vital economic and social role as anchor institutions is not new. Many research universities were established with a civic mission to prepare students to take an active role in a diverse, democratic society and to develop knowledge that might improve communities (Cohen and Kisker, 2010; Kezar, Chambers and Burkhardt, 2015). During the civil rights movement, universities served as important sites for political mobilization and demonstration. Students demanded that universities no longer ignore the needs of their surrounding neighborhoods, and many universities responded by building infrastructure for community liaisons and new academic programs focused on multicultural studies (Harold, 2018).

The social contract expanded again in the 1980s with the Campus Compact, created to use community service and service learning as methods to teach students the values and skills of citizenship. But this "service" orientation can often perpetuate a dehumanizing subjectification of local residents. Instead of being honored as partners with deep local knowledge, students can be tacitly taught to understand local community members as lesser beings in need of charity (Kendall, 1990; O'Grady, 2000).

Universities are unique anchor institutions because they aspire to leverage their knowledge-generating abilities and partnerships to improve the community conditions (Cantor, Englot and Higgins, 2013). Today, many "engaged" university campuses seek to use this knowledge-generating capacity for application to the wider community, and they do so by partnering with community and residents who possess local knowledge about the broader community goals and needs (Holland, 2001). As more universities started to integrate the anchoring role into their mission, policies, and curriculum, national associations were established to account for and assess these civic renewal efforts. By 2010, over 300 colleges and universities received the Carnegie Foundation Community Engagement Classification,[1] recognizing significant involvement, commitment, and potential impact on community.

Despite these efforts, university-based towns continue to be some of the most inequitable communities in the country. They are marked by higher education gaps (Gleibermann, 2017), as well as higher income and occupational segregation (Florida and Gaetani, 2018). Universities often use their local surroundings as a site of study, positioning residents as appropriate subjects for research investigations and teaching demonstrations. This othering, and the corresponding loss of autonomy, becomes exponentially harmful when compounded with previous injustices.

In response to the provocation "How should universities claim their responsibility as democratic actors in this moment of American history?" we offer the position that universities must expand their global focus on discovery to include a local focus on reparative and equitable practices that may advance goals of building community wealth. To advance this argument, we examine select current efforts at two public research universities through the conceptual frame of community wealth building and consider the opportunities and challenges in these cases toward sharpening the university role as an anchor institution toward the redress of inequity. Building off the wisdom espoused in this collection of chapters, we suggest that the inclusive co-creation and adherence to bold equity metrics in the service of building community wealth might help orient universities toward a version of what Balfour refers to in Chapter 3 of this book as reparations as a "framework for thinking." Further, a rebalancing of power in research and education is needed to approximate Walker's vision for a deep democracy built on respect for local knowledge (Chapter 4).

ANCHOR INSTITUTIONS IN BUILDING COMMUNITY WEALTH

City governments, nonprofit organizations, students, and local residents are increasingly turning to their anchor educational institutions to influence local community and economic development through community wealth building (Dubb and Howard, 2012). Community wealth building is a multifaceted framework employed by many U.S. localities to simultaneously address multiple deep-rooted, interrelated economic and social challenges that perpetuate the cycle of neighborhood and individual instability and poverty.

A community wealth building approach recognizes the obduracy of structural racism and calls upon existing local capacities and institutions to strengthen underutilized local assets and lift whole communities, both economically and socially (The Democracy Collaborative, n.d.). Focusing on the systemic manifestations of racism is critical to disrupting cycles of intergenerational poverty. Legal scholar john a. powell[2] (2007, p. 796) asserts, "Structural racism shifts our attention from the single, intra-institutional setting to inter-institutional arrangements and interactions. Efforts to identify causation at a particular moment of decision within a specific domain understate the cumulative impact of discrimination." When looking at individual-level actions, we overlook patterns with disproportionate impact that prevent us from fully redressing inequities under the guise of fairness. powell points out that the built world is a vehicle through which structural racism manifests, where "racially isolated and economically poor neighborhoods restrict employment options for young people, contribute to poor health, expose children to extremely high rates of crime and violence, and house some of the lowest-performing schools" (ibid., p. 804). To reverse these patterns, one approach is to view racial equity and neighborhood-level capacity building as essential components to making change (Lawrence et al., 2004). The community wealth building approach is system focused and requires stakeholders to work collaboratively to develop place-based assets that form an inclusive, sustainable economy built on broadly held ownership (Kelly, McKinley and Duncan, 2016), thus leading to economic democracy (Dubb, 2016).

Bold Equity Goals and Metrics

Barnes and Williamson (Chapter 2) characterize the establishment of shared goals and metrics as a cornerstone of community wealth building. While bold equity goals may be established at the scale of a city to support community wealth building, it is critical that the strategic goals of community organizations and institutions are aligned with this larger-scale goal. This is important because community wealth building employs strategies that locate and build on the existing assets in a community—including the resources and abilities of a city's anchor institutions. Shared equity goals may result in a commitment to inclusive, local hiring and procurement as a way to build resident employment and local business or a commitment to place-based investment that will increase housing affordability and reduce displacement.

Inclusive Participation

Barnes and Williamson (Chapter 2) also cite inclusive participation as a key feature in community wealth building because of the "relational foundation" such generative partnerships produce. Inclusive participation is important not only because of the trust engendered from traditionally unheard residents when they are a part of decision-making processes, but also because these balanced partnerships are less likely to fall into the patterns of pathologizing underserved communities and obscuring underlying structural inequities. Instead, inclusive participation often takes an asset-based approach to community development, focuses on action that reduces inequities, recognizes and corrects power imbalances, and fosters long-term, mutually beneficial partnerships.

PLACE-BASED ANALYSIS: UVA AND VCU

Although constituents of research universities are increasingly interested in conducting community-engaged scholarship that is driven by community needs, the infrastructure required to build viable, mutually beneficial partnerships is often insufficient. And, their historical relationships with community frequently complicate university attempts to build partnerships; anchor institutions commonly exacerbate local inequities, compounding existing trauma and distrust of higher education. For example, universities often engage with communities only for the duration of a funded research project. The community, which typically does not benefit from the knowledge generated from the project, often feel used and betrayed.

If community wealth building requires bold equity goals and metrics and inclusive participation, anchor institutions aspiring to contribute to such work must measure the impacts of their contributions with this lens in mind. How does this look in practice? This question requires a place-based analysis, as each locality has different socio-economic contexts, political and cultural norms, and historic legacies with which they must contend as they define measures for success, as well as identifying what qualifies as inclusive participation in this work. In what follows we consider this question as it applies to two public universities, both located in the state of Virginia (and thus both necessarily grappling with the legacies of slavery that are so deep in the state's history), but operating in very different socio-economic and political contexts.

University of Virginia (UVA)

The University of Virginia's purpose is "to serve the Commonwealth of Virginia, the nation, and the world by developing responsible citizen leaders and professionals; advancing, preserving, and disseminating knowledge; and providing world-class patient care" (University of Virginia, 2014). But it was also built and operated with the labor of enslaved people until the end of the American Civil War. Further, it did not accept African American students until the 1950s and women were not permitted to enroll until the 1970s. In the past decade, UVA has tried to grapple with its participation in the chattel slave system and in the structural racism that has marked our economic system since then. In 2007, UVA created the University and Community Action for Racial Equity (UCARE), whose mission is to help "the University of Virginia and the Charlottesville communities work together to understand the University's role in slavery, racial segregation, and discrimination and to find ways to address and repair the legacy of those harms, particularly as they relate to present day disparities" (University of Virginia, n.d.). Supporting the Charlottesville Office of Human Rights Dialogues on Race and the UVA President's Commission on Slavery and the University, UCARE helped to correct the narrative regarding the roles of enslaved laborers at the university, assisted with the design of a remarkable Memorial to Enslaved Laborers that opened in the spring of 2020, and began the discussions about truth and reconciliation between university and community relations.

However, because the university has not addressed the current inequities it perpetuates, the university–community relationship remains very strained. Charlottesville is a city burdened with social, economic, and political inequities. Forty-seven percent of black families living in Charlottesville make under $35 000/year. Eighteen percent of residents live with food insecurity, compared to 12 percent statewide. The racial disparities around public health, incarceration, and educational outcomes are nationally significant. Charlottesville's social mobility rate for poor residents is among the worst in the country. Some local residents still refer to UVA as "the plantation," because of the legacy of slavery they see perpetuated in community–university relations today.

In August 2017, the long history of structural racism played out in a deadly white supremacist rally—one that forced many stakeholders at the institution to think hard about past and present inequities and about what a resilient, forward-looking anchor institution might look like in the former slave-holding South. On Friday, August 11, white nationalist's marched on the University and assaulted anti-racist student protestors with torches. Two of the coordinators of this rally were UVA alumni. The events the next day ended with a white nationalist terrorist driving an automobile into a crowd—killing counter-protester Heather Heyer and injuring many more. In the year after, the university formed a follow-up commission on UVA in the Age of Segregation, but many faculty, students, and community partners sought out much more profound and direct action.

Virginia Commonwealth University

The 1967 Wayne Commission Report endorsed the creation of an "urban-oriented state university" that concentrates on meeting the needs of an urban population living and working in an urban environment for the Commonwealth's capital city. The report recommended the formation of Virginia Commonwealth University (VCU) by merging the Richmond Professional Institute and the Medical College of Virginia, noting that "the urban environment offers the university great resources" but also stating that the urban university has an obligation to participate in the solution of urban problems.

VCU is located in Richmond, the former capital of the Confederacy and a major port for the slave trade. Richmond continues to suffer from deep racial divisions, but it also celebrates many "firsts" in African American leadership, such as being the first city to host a bank chartered by African Americans and being the birthplace of the first African American governor of any U.S. state since Reconstruction. This complicated history creates challenges and opportunities for community wealth building. In 2011, in response to the city's exceedingly high poverty rates that were concentrated among African American residents, Mayor Dwight C. Jones established an Anti-Poverty Commission made up of community advocates, academics, business representatives, and other stakeholders committed to building community wealth. In 2014, the city of Richmond launched the country's first Office of Community Wealth Building (OCWB).

VCU exists at the center of this city with a complicated history—and has contributed to this narrative in various ways around land acquisition and its infringement on sacred burial grounds and neighborhood identity. The university's mission and strategic plan reflect roles and responsibilities symbolic of a university anchor institution dedicated to community wealth building; the most recent strategic plan seeks to advance "[i]nterdisciplinary collaborations and community partnerships that advance innovation, enhance cultural and economic vitality, and solve society's most complex challenges" (Virginia Commonwealth University, 2019). Despite these intentions, just a few blocks away from Virginia's premier urban public research university are neighborhoods with the lowest life expectancy because of factors like poverty, substandard housing, and lack of access to health care.

FROM ANCHOR INSTITUTION TO ANCHOR INSTITUTION MISSION

Hodges and Dubb (2012) differentiate between universities that are anchor institutions (by definition) and universities with an anchor institutional *mission* that "consciously and strategically apply their long-term, placed-based economic power, in combination with their human and intellectual resources, to better the welfare of the communities in which they reside" (pp. xix–xx). Over the last decade, VCU has taken intentional steps toward transitioning from an anchor institution to a university with an anchor institutional mission.

More than a decade ago, VCU set a strategic goal to become a national model for community engagement. To support this goal, VCU established a Division of Community Engagement led by a vice-provost, signaling a commitment to strengthen the connections between VCU and Richmond in addressing community-identified needs. Then VCU sought elective classification to publicly affirm institutional commitment to community engagement and became one of the first universities to receive the Carnegie designation as a community-engaged campus. Today, VCU is a national model for community-engaged research and is one of only 54 universities with both a "Very High Research Activity" and a "Community Engaged" designation from the Carnegie Foundation.

Infrastructure dedicated to an anchor mission ensures that there is a unit with a lens on the anchor mission, charged to consider the impact of the gestalt of the university. What are the positive and negative impacts of academic programs and ancillary services, such as student housing, athletics, procurement, and real estate development on the community? VCU's Division of Community Engagement provides programming, support, and reward systems to prepare faculty and students with the knowledge and skills to establish mutually beneficial partnerships with the community for research, teaching, and service purposes. However, to capture the impact of this work, VCU must commit to indicators that measure local wealth and develop a more robust infrastructure that links institutional investments to more equitable communities.

Measuring Institutional Impact

In 2014, the VCU Division of Community Engagement and the Office of Planning and Decision Management initiated a process to evaluate and assess VCU's institutional impact on the Richmond region. The following year, The Democracy Collaborative (TDC), a think tank and advocacy group for equitable, sustainable local economies, invited VCU to be one of six universities to participate in an Anchor Dashboard Learning Cohort (Sladek, 2017). The purpose of this multi-year process was to pilot metrics to track anchor mission impact, assess baseline data, and help create a framework that will put the anchor mission into practice more widely.

The learning cohort was an opportunity for VCU to evaluate more effectively the long-term and place-based impact of its activities on low-income communities (Dubb, McKinley and Howard, 2013). As part of this process, universities were encouraged to develop an anchor mission goal, which is a university's commitment to intentionally commit its place-based economic power and human capital to improve the well-being of the community. VCU's anchor mission alignment is measured by two discrete indicators. (1) Is the anchor mission articulated in the strategic plan? (2) Is the anchor mission reflected in the structure of the institution (i.e., hierarchy of the lead community-engagement staff person in the organizational chart)?

Although the pilot was an experiment to understand the broad impacts in the community, it provided the traction to further refine VCU's overall approach. After participation in the Democracy Collective Anchor Dashboard Learning Cohort, VCU transitioned to developing place-based metrics that focus on impact. In 2016, VCU President Michael Rao commissioned a study to investigate the economic impact that VCU has on Richmond, the metropolitan area, and the state. A report titled *VCU's Impact on the Region: Talent, Innovation, Collaboration* (Accordino et al., 2016) found VCU's economic impact within the city of Richmond is $1.5 billion, including about 18 000 jobs. In the metropolitan area, the impact is $4 billion and 47 000 jobs.

Higher education is now emphasizing the institutionalization of the anchor mission. The Coalition of Urban and Metropolitan Universities (CUMU) recently partnered with The Democracy Collaborative to establish the Anchor Learning Network (ALN) (CUMU, 2017) as a tool to facilitate quicker implementation of the anchor mission by more universities. ALN participants commit to making significant strides toward institutionalizing the anchor mission, reporting annual data, and involving internal and external stakeholders in the process.

Underlying measurements of institutional impact is a process by which the university and community jointly set goals and align resources to address those goals. VCU continues to refine metrics to better capture the strengths of the university and leverage the pre-existing investments (i.e., areas in which VCU has robust research output or momentum) and match them to community-identified needs. VCU is tracking data that fit within the broad categories of indicators established by The Democracy Collaborative, in addition to indicators especially relevant to the Richmond region. However, much of the data exist in dozens of units across the university and within the community, creating burdens for groups with little knowledge of the data purpose or its relationship to community wealth building. The co-creation of goals is critical for building commitment from partners around long-term data tracking; absent this robust process, many indicators remain unreported and listed as unavailable in the VCU tracking instruments.

For VCU, the early commitment to measuring institutional impact is helping the university transition from an anchor institution to a university with an anchor institutional mission. In addition to tracking data, VCU has used its measurement systems to target and modify its own behavior in ways that will support the local economy and promote changes in practice that can have immediate local impact. Most recently, a new procurement data system was implemented to allow VCU to localize sources and types of vendors as a means to increase procurement from local small businesses. However, to better claim its agency and responsibility in democratizing knowledge, VCU needs to better communicate the mutual benefit of tracking institutional impact across the institution and with community partners.

Ensuring Inclusive Participation

As UVA reflects on both the positive and negative legacies of its first 200 years, it is moving to reclaim its status as a local anchor institution, committed to the premise that "in order to be a great university, we must also be good" (Ryan, 2018). In his inaugural fall as UVA president, James Ryan convened a University-Community Working Group (UCWG), on which one of the authors served as a member, and asked that it "assess UVA's collaborations with the community and determine the highest-priority issues for consideration, which might include wages, housing, education, health care, and other matters" (University-Community Working Group, 2019, p. 10). The group was "charged to identify the issues but not to solve them, and also to think about the best long-term structure for developing solutions, possibly through the establishment of a more permanent council or board" (ibid.). The UCWG leadership included one faculty member and two community leaders from different parts of Charlottesville, and the UCWG membership was diverse in terms of race, class, age, and professional orientation.

The UCWG went through decades of community-based reports and research to identify seven key areas of focus for partnership in the next five years.

Several members also drew from their knowledge of structural racism gleaned from lived experience, growing up as part of the local underserved resident community. The top seven areas of focus included: affordable housing, institutional accountability, jobs/wages, law enforcement/criminal justice reform, public health care, transportation, and youth/education. Recognizing the power in ranking these priorities, the UCWG implemented a multi-faceted engagement approach that included an electronic survey distributed through various channels, including an online survey, interviews, focus groups, and in-person intercept conversations at five large public gatherings. The UCWG prioritized the recruitment of low-income resident survey respondents, who are also disproportionately racial and ethnic minorities and experience the worse community outcomes in every identified quality-of-life area. The UCWG held focus groups with the University Staff Senate, as well as staff working in recycling, landscaping, housekeeping and contract employees from across the university. The UCWG also coordinated with the Albemarle-Charlottesville Regional Jail to implement the survey with a random sampling of 100 currently incarcerated community members. Over a three-week period, more than 3000 community residents responded to the priority-ranking survey via one of the means described above. The survey was designed to be simple and quick and result in a ranked list of priority areas from respondents. It was available in English, Spanish, and Arabic. The survey achieved a representative sample for the region in terms of race, but it passively over-sampled higher-income populations. The results were then weighted to reflect the demographic make-up of the Charlottesville Metropolitan Statistical Area. All demographic groups agreed on the top four priorities: (1) jobs/wages; (2) affordable housing; (3) public health care; (4) youth/education.

On February 25, 2019, the UCWG sent its report to President Ryan and the UVA Board of Visitors (University-Community Working Group, 2019). The report included the ranking of four top priorities and suggestions for structures that would ensure ongoing institutional accountability related to this work. A week later, the university president publicly announced that UVA was raising the base wage from $12.75 to $15.00 per hour for all university employees; he then successfully negotiated agreements with contractors to extend the same $15 commitment to contract employees by the fall of 2019 (Ryan, 2019).

Of course, this important policy shift to raise the base wage was not the result of any singular internal effort. For over 20 years, students at UVA, in collaboration with the nonpartisan advocacy group Virginia Organizing, have been actively pushing for the university to pay a living wage to its employees (Harold, 2018). Former Charlottesville City Council member and Vice-Mayor Kristin Szakos sees higher wages as the "most justice-oriented" way the university can be a better neighbor, because the university really sets the wage for the entire town as the major employer; but she also sees the alleviation of the "downward pressure" the university applies to the local housing market and to the public infrastructure as important unmet responsibilities of the university as the primary anchor institution in this smaller city.

Aspiring for an infrastructure of institutional accountability that includes both bold equity goals and metrics and inclusive participation, the University's Office of the President recently reconstituted the UCWG as the President's Council on UVA–Community Partnerships to oversee the next few years of partnership development and project implementation around these four priorities. Members of this group had already built rapport with one another, so the decision to retain the membership was one of efficiency. Further, the council voted to elect its own leadership—two community leaders who meet with the president to drive the agenda of the council each quarter, centering all decision-making around the principles of shared power and co-creation. The council worked with the Office of the President to collaboratively craft new policies to ensure compensation for all non-university members of the council for costs incurred through participation. The council, which is forming community–university working groups around each of the four priority areas, will first define criteria for success in each area and then will draft action plans to achieve and measure progress towards those goals.

Another priority expressed in the UCWG report is the deep need for an infusion of accountability into the university's research, educational, and service footprints in the communities in which it engages. Several community-driven platforms, piloted with support from the newly formed UVA Democracy Initiative Center for the Redress of Inequity, are intended to ensure that the community-engaged university activities are done in partnership and with mutual benefit as a key driver for the work. For example, the Charlottesville's Public Housing Association of Residents (PHAR) developed a community-based research review board (CRRB) to ensure that low-income residents review the goals and methods of research aspiring to engage them as subjects and ensure any such research is crafted so as to benefit the residents—whether conducted by senior faculty, students, or independent researchers. The team drew from models of indigenous research partnerships, where the sovereign entity has full powers of self-determination over any research conducted (e.g. Claw et al., 2018). The eventual goal is to create an administrative infrastructure in and outside the university that facilitates co-production at every stage of a community-based research process or community development investment, including goal-setting, implementation planning, data collection, analysis, and results dissemination (Beier et al., 2016; Coutts, 2019; Howell and Wilson, 2018). As a part of these coalition-building efforts, city and county leaders are also discussing the possibility of entering into a three-party memorandum of understanding that would further articulate how these commitments all relate to one another across the region.

For UVA, the orientation towards community wealth building is new and its goals of institutional accountability yet unrealized, but the socio-political infrastructure being built to ensure inclusive participation under this new administration has the potential to be transformative for the region, if paired with a bold vision for partnership toward the redress of inequity.

DISCUSSION AND IMPLICATIONS

This case study analysis illustrates the tremendous potential for universities to function as anchor institutions in regional efforts to build community wealth, but it also leaves us with more questions than answers. As public universities reorient themselves toward their social charge, what infrastructure is needed to ensure institutional accountability? Under what conditions can universities best contribute to community wealth building in their region? And what is the role of public discourse in this work?

There is no one way for universities to leverage their resources to generate community wealth—the socio-economic context, political norms, historic harms that require redressing, as well as the governing format of the local, state, and university governments all factor into the most effective strategies an anchor institution can take to make positive change in its community. In January 2019, The Democracy Collaborative launched the Anchor Collaborative Network (ACN), under the premise that while individual anchor institutions hold significant influence within their geographic communities, *networks* of anchor institutions hold significant potential for making large-scale change (Porter, Fisher-Bruns and Pham, 2019). VCU has been an active contributor to The Democracy Collaborative and is poised to help it model best practices in the next phase of its work. In Richmond, VCU is one of several anchor employers, and thus the Anchor Collaborative Network approach is essential to its operations. In the case of Charlottesville, there is an oppressive history to repair and a local economy that is highly dependent on UVA as the primary educational institution and health care provider whose actions drive wages, housing markets, and infrastructure investments. Partnerships are essential to the work, and transparency and power sharing are paramount, but structures for institutional accountability must also be upheld by UVA internally to function well.

Our preliminary analysis suggests that for legitimate community wealth to be built, regardless of the size of the community, a few essential preconditions are required. First, anchor institutions must take a systems change approach to building community wealth that centers racial equity if they hope to spur community investments that redress systemic inequities. Such change demands that anchor institutions invest in building mutually beneficial partnerships with local community-based and grassroots organizations, which have established relationships and a history of working directly with the marginalized residents and businesses that should be at the center of wealth-building initiatives. Second, for anchor institutions to effectively weave community wealth building commitments into their decision-making processes, they must start with a strategic plan that prioritizes equity. These goals should be aligned with clear metrics that work toward *impact* on community wealth. This shift in thinking about the purpose and value of data points will help move anchor institutions away from collecting metrics that only seem to build on longitudinal datasets about investments made, and toward tracking progress in the larger vision of redressing inequity.

Finally, administrative commitment and shared governance are key to ensuring that equity-based community wealth building becomes institutionalized into the fabric of the university's actions and investments. Although institutional leadership is important to initiating priorities and crafting strategic plans, for community wealth building investments to redress inequity, they need to be animated by an intentional governance structure that values local knowledge by fostering shared, horizontal agenda-setting, decision-making, and implementation. Central to this process is the constant application of grassroots political pressure from both within and outside the network to combat the gravity of entrenched structural racism. Shared accountability provides stability for community wealth building initiatives that can weather changes in leadership at the university and help universities become active, consistent contributors to local equity goals.

NOTES

1. In 1970, the Carnegie Commission on Higher Education developed a classification of colleges and universities.
2. john a. powell does not capitalize his name.

REFERENCES

Accordino, John, Fabrizio Fasulo and Mike McKenzie et al. (2016), *VCU's Impact on the Region: Talent, Innovation, Collaboration*, Center for Urban and Regional Analysis at VCU, accessed June 26, 2020 at https://president.vcu.edu/media/president/assets/pdfs/initiatives-and-reports/CURA_EI_Report.pdf.

Beier, Paul, Lara J. Hansen, Lynn Helbrecht and David Behar (2016), "A how-to guide for coproduction of actionable science," *Conservation Letters*, 10(3), 288–96.

Cantor, Nancy, Peter Englot and Marilyn Higgins (2013), "Making the work of anchor institutions stick: building coalitions and collective expertise," *Journal of Higher Education Outreach and Engagement*, 17(3), 17–46.

Claw, Katrina G., Matthew Z. Anderson and Rene L. Begay et al. (2018), "A framework for enhancing ethical genomic research with indigenous communities," *Nature Communications*, 9(2957), 1–7.

Coalition of Urban and Metropolitan Universities (CUMU) (2017), "Anchor Learning Network," accessed May 21, 2019 at http://www.cumuonline.org/what-we-do/anchor-mission-initiative/#Mission.

Cohen, Arthur M. and Carrie B. Kisker (2010), *The Shaping of American Higher Education: Emergence and Growth of the Contemporary System*, San Francisco, CA: John Wiley & Sons.

Coutts, Pippa (2019), *The Many Shades of Co-produced Evidence*, report by the Carnegie UK Trust, accessed June 26, 2020 at https://d1ssu070pg2v9i.cloudfront.net/pex/carnegie_uk_trust/2019/02/06161920/The-many-shades-of-co-produced-evidence-final.pdf.

Dubb, Steve (2016), "Community wealth building forms: what they are and how to use them at the local level," *Academy of Management Perspectives*, 30(2), 141–52.

Dubb, Steve and Ted Howard (2012), "Leveraging anchor institutions for local job creation and wealth building," The Democracy Collaborative at the University of Maryland, accessed February 10, 2020 at https://democracycollaborative.org/sites/default/files/downloads/paper-dubb-howard.pdf.

Dubb, Steve, Sarah McKinley and Ted Howard (2013), "The Anchor Dashboard: aligning institutional practice to meet low-income community needs," The Democracy Collaborative at the University of Maryland, accessed February 10, 2020 at https://community-wealth.org/content/anchor-dashboard-aligning-institutional-practice-meet-low-income-community-needs.

Florida, Richard and Ruben Gaetani (2018), "The university's Janus face: the innovation–inequality nexus," *Managerial and Decision Economics*, 1–16, accessed February 10, 2020 at https://doi.org/10.1002/mde.2938.

Gleibermann, Erik (2017), "The college–town achievement gap: persistent inequality plagues the places some prestigious universities call home. Are the higher-education institutions to blame?" *The Atlantic*, accessed June 27, 2019 at https://www.theatlantic.com/education/archive/2017/06/the-college-town-achievement-gap/526305/.

Harold, Claudrena N. (2018), "No ordinary sacrifice: the struggle for racial justice at the University of Virginia in the post-civil rights era," in Louis P. Nelson and Claudrena N. Harold (eds) (2018), *Charlottesville 2017: The Legacy of Race and Inequity*, Charlottesville, VA: University of Virginia Press.

Hodges, Rita A. and Steve Dubb (2012), *The Road Half Traveled: University Engagement at a Crossroads*, East Lansing, MI: Michigan State University Press.

Holland, Barbara A. (2001), "Toward a definition and characterization of the engaged campus: six cases," *Metropolitan Universities*, 12(3), 20–29.

Howell, Kathryn and Barbara Brown Wilson (2018), "Preserving community through radical collaboration: affordable housing preservation networks in Chicago, Washington, DC, and Denver," *Housing, Theory, and Society*, 36(3), 319–37.

Kelly, Marjorie, Sarah McKinley and Violeta Duncan (2016), "Community wealth building: America's emerging asset-based approach to city economic development," *Renewal*, 24(2), 51–69.

Kendall, Jane C. (ed.) (1990), *Combining Service and Learning: A Resource Book for Community and Public Service*, Raleigh, NC: National Society for Internships and Experiential Education.

Kezar, Adrianna, Anthony C. Chambers and John C. Burkhardt (eds) (2015), *Higher Education for the Public Good: Emerging Voices from a National Movement*, San Francisco, CA: John Wiley & Sons.

Lawrence, Keith, Stacey Sutton and Anne Kubisch et al. (2004), *Structural Racism and Community Building*, Washington, DC: The Aspen Institute.

O'Grady, Carolyn R. (ed.) (2000), "Integrating service learning and multicultural education: an overview," in *Integrating Service Learning and Multicultural Education in Colleges and Universities*, Mahwah, NJ: Erlbaum, pp. 1–19.

Porter, Justine, Danny Fisher-Bruns and Bih Ha Pham (2019), *Anchor Collaboratives: Building Bridges with Place-Based Partnerships and Anchor Institutions,*" The Democracy Collaborative at the University of Maryland, accessed May 21, 2019 at https://democracycollaborative.org/content/anchor-collaboratives-building-bridges -place-based-partnerships-and-anchor-institutions.

powell, john a. (2007), "Structural racism: building upon the insights of John Calmore," *North Carolina Law Review*, 86, 791–816.

Ryan, James (2018), "Faith in the unfinished project," Inaugural Address, October 18, accessed July 6, 2020 at https://news.virginia.edu/content/read-president-jim-ryans -inaugural-address-faith-unfinished-project.

Ryan, James (2019), "Living wage," UVA Community Working Group, accessed May 21, 2019 at https://communityworkinggroup.virginia.edu/updates/living-wage.

Schildt, Chris and Victor Rubin (2015), "Leveraging anchor institutions for economic inclusion," *PolicyLink*, accessed February 10, 2020 at https://www.policylink.org/sites/default/files/pl_brief_anchor_012315_a.pdf.

Sladek, Emily (2017), "Higher education's anchor mission: measuring place-based engagement," The Democracy Collaborative at the University of Maryland, accessed February 10, 2020 at https://democracycollaborative.org/higher-ed-anchor-mission.

The Democracy Collaborative (n.d.), "Community-wealth.org," accessed May 21, 2019 at https://community-wealth.org/.

University-Community Working Group (2019), *Report to University of Virginia President James E. Ryan*, February 15, accessed February 7, 2020 at https://bov.virginia.edu/system/files/public/meetings/UVA-Community%20Working %20Group%20Final%20Report.pdf.

University of Virginia (n.d.), "Race and repair at the University of Virginia: engage," accessed February 7, 2020 at https://uvaraceandrepair.wordpress.com/engage/.

University of Virginia (2014), "University code of ethics and mission statement," accessed February 7, 2020 at https://www.virginia.edu/statementofpurpose.

Virginia Commonwealth University (2019), "Quest 2025: together we transform," accessed February 7, 2020 https://quest.vcu.edu/.

Wayne Commission Report (1967), *Report of the Commission to Plan for the Establishment of a Proposed State-supported University in the Richmond Metropolitan Area*, accessed February 10, 2020 at https://scholarscompass.vcu.edu/cgi/viewcontent.cgi?article=1004&context=vcu_books.

15. Conclusion: the promise of 21st-century democratic renewal

Corey D.B. Walker and Thad M. Williamson

The question of the future of democracy in America is generally framed by considerations of policy or procedure. Unasked and unanswered are the more substantive issues involving democracy's reconstruction. This book takes up the issue of how American democracy might be reconstructed, in fact and not just rhetoric. In this closing chapter we consider how the community wealth building paradigm might develop from a promising idea to a full-fledged social and political movement capable of delivering structural reform of American democracy.

A fully developed account of social, political and economic transformation must address the following urgent questions:

- What are the underlying moral principles of this transformation?
- What are the political goals of this transformation (i.e., racial equality, gender equality, economic empowerment and stability, ecological sustainability, democratic accountability, personal freedom, respect for all persons)?
- What specific structural reforms are required to achieve those goals, in a given specific context?
- How can coalitions be built in support of such reforms, at different scales and in different political contexts?
- How can a process of change be established that is self-sustaining, that gathers increasing momentum over time, that utilizes different forms of leadership but is not dependent on any particular leader or small sets of leaders, that engages political power and the electoral process without being fully defined by it?
- How can such a movement interact with formal political leadership? How can the movement interact with other forms of civic and social organization?

Community wealth building as laid out by Barnes and Williamson (Chapter 2) is envisioned as both a process for initiating bold transformations at the local level, and as a paradigm impacting American governance and democracy as a whole. In particular, it posits that the substance of on-the-ground radical change must be steered by local-level democracy, but that local-level democracy needs significant support and resources from higher levels of government. It posits that the needed levers of structural reform are both in Washington, DC and in local communities and states. And it posits that the lines between the local and the national are porous: what happens in local communities drives national conversations and national policy, and vice versa.

What makes this new and different? Here we can cite at least four key elements. First, the locus of change for community wealth building is inclusive participation at the local level: grassroots political engagement and problem-solving, not (in the first instance) national policy or bureaucratic reform. The traditional New Deal vision focuses heavily on using and expanding the tools of the federal government and using federal rules to compel states and localities in desired directions. While important and pivotal to rescue American democracy in the 1930s, such an approach fails to activate more substantive and robust democratization throughout American society. Community wealth building begins with movements rooted in local communities, then calls on state and federal resources (including programs originating in the New Deal and the Great Society) to support such efforts. It moves the center of action closer to the ground where citizens can see, touch, participate in, and influence what actually happens.

Second, community wealth building places front and center bold, locally determined goals for achieving equity. The point is not simply to offer or expand a program, but to actually achieve measurable goals (such as poverty reduction) that significantly impact residents' daily lives.

Third, whereas traditional liberal approaches take the distribution of wealth as given and seek to promote equity through taxation, community wealth building aims to expand who owns wealth directly by promoting collective forms of wealth and other measures aimed at broadening ownership of land and economic enterprise, using a holistic approach. This focus on wealth is important for its own sake and because wealth and political influence are deeply connected; the lopsided distribution of wealth characterizing American society today inevitably distorts and biases our political processes in ways favorable to the wealthy.

Fourth, the vision is pluralistic. Community wealth building in Richmond, Virginia may have common principles and goals with what community wealth building will look like in Seattle or Boston, but the specifics can and generally should vary from place to place, according to local needs and what local residents choose to prioritize. In Richmond, programmatically it has made sense to focus first on establishing and bolstering a holistic model of workforce development as the lead initiative while continuing to work on transportation, education, housing, and social enterprise development; other communities might prioritize initiatives differently and properly so. While community wealth building focuses on establishing democratic processes, norms of inclusive participation, and strong equity commitments, the specific resulting initiatives will and should vary from place to place.

In this, way advocates for community wealth building contend that it is a paradigm that will bring both the key policy decisions that shape localities and the tangible results of government action closer to the ground, closer to where people actually live. Importantly, advocates for community wealth building contend that this shift will permit bolder rather than more cautious commitments to equity. In a place like Richmond, very few people are in fact satisfied with the status quo; it's possible to have a quite open discussion (and of course, much debate and disagreement) about what direction change needs to take. Rather than promote a cookie-cutter approach to building local change, the community wealth building paradigm allows and encourages localities to follow a multitude of paths towards change.

This book deepens the intellectual grounding for the community wealth building paradigm while also raising further questions. In different ways, Lawrie Balfour (Chapter 3) and Corey D.B. Walker (Chapter 4) each demonstrate why community wealth building cannot be "neutral" on numerous fundamental questions: from our collective obligation to name and tackle the legacies of white supremacy and structural racism to the notion that a compelling public philosophy should name and claim the idea of citizens having a positive obligation to do justice upon one another in a spirit of love, echoing Martin Luther King, Jr.'s conception of the Beloved Community. This boldness of purposes contrasts to both philosophical views (often associated with John Rawls) that regard neutrality about contested issues as a requirement of building an overlapping consensus in favor of social justice, and political analyses that argue that the best way for progressives to win elections is to drop or downplay claims of racial justice and focus narrowly on the concerns of (white) swing voters. Instead, community wealth building recognizes there can be no serious conversation about economic justice in the United States that is not also a conversation about racial justice, and also recognizes that achieving a just society will require groups to be able to think beyond narrow self-interest and instead embrace the justice claims of other citizens as worthy of solidarity and support.

Community wealth building as a paradigm, by design, throws open a much-needed conversation about the future of American capitalism. Isabel Sawhill (Chapter 5) persuasively critiques the dominant neoliberal free market mold as the cause of numerous failures and discontents, then lays out several alternative views. The editors believe that "community wealth building" should be considered a plausible alternative view as well, insofar as it explicitly prioritizes the needs of communities and the norms of inclusive participation over market imperatives, and aims at systemic change in the structure of opportunity and the ownership of wealth.

More ambitiously, community wealth building implies that the "capitalism vs socialism" debate as it is commonly (and somewhat archaically) waged itself poses a false dichotomy. The Barnes-Williamson vision of community wealth building points in the direction of a mixed economy with a robust public sector, a robust nonprofit and community sector, and a robust private sector that also includes employee-owned firms, cooperatives, and other wealth-broadening firms alongside traditional private capital. This variety of wealth-holding forms are seen as operating in a market regulated by democratic norms so as to achieve social goals from equity to ecological sustainability. As Margaret Kohn (Chapter 6) reminds us, community wealth building is an established practice in Italy through its impressive and long-standing cooperative sector. The Italian cooperatives illuminate one possible pathway that community wealth building efforts in the United States might take, a pathway informed not by a priori ideology but the practical demand to create viable, growing forms of wealth and enterprise that can both deliver the goods and share them more equitably.

The chapters on politics and government in this book underscore the deep challenges community wealth building—or any other candidate new paradigm—faces in healing our polity and re-establishing trust and confidence in government (and politics) as institutions. There are several dimensions of this challenge. As Julian Maxwell Hayter (Chapter 11) reminds us, the basic concept of equal voting rights and meaningful political influence for all groups has activated an all-too-effective opposition. As Nicholas J.G. Winter observes (Chapter 10), the increasing correlation between party identification and feelings about race and gender groups opens the door for fear or resentment of certain groups to be utilized as a political weapon—and also makes it harder to forge compromises and advance governance. Kenneth P. Ruscio (Chapter 8) outlines the existing framework for holding executive authority accountability—and raises questions about its fragility and effectiveness. J.S. Maloy (Chapter 9) shows that there is room and necessity for improvement in the conduct of both elections and policy deliberation at the local level. Not addressed explicitly in the chapters but lurking in the background is the role of wealth inequality and unconstrained campaign contributions in shaping both elections and governance.

While better national political leadership can address some of these matters, we are not optimistic about the possibility of dramatic changes in the status quo over the next decade. Indeed, we anticipate ongoing fundamental conflict on matters of national identity as well as broad policy: are we or are we not committed to being a racially diverse, inclusive democracy? Are we or are we not capable of making a genuine effort to tackle climate change? Are we or are we not committed to establishing a baseline of economic inclusion and equal opportunity so that all can share in the nation's prosperity?

We certainly agree with many analysts and political actors that political and social mobilization—including but not limited to electoral campaigns—on a massive scale will ultimately be needed to tilt the national conversation on these matters in a progressive direction. But we also believe that local communities in need of urgent change now cannot and should not wait for this "Cold Civil War" to play itself out before taking up the work of addressing equity goals and other local community needs (Barnes and Williamson, 2019). On the contrary, we believe that effective work and progress initiated at the community level can illuminate the path forward, not only for other communities but ultimately for the nation as a whole. Work at the local level for bold change is incredibly difficult and complex—a matter that we turn to in the next section—but it still holds open the prospect that public governance can in fact help solve problems and address people's needs. National-level polarization and dysfunction have led some to conclude that the public work of democracy inevitably disappoints or fails; bold community-driven action can (and has) demonstrated the opposite.

To this end, numerous chapters in this volume have addressed the possibilities and challenges of implementing a community wealth building vision in practice. Richard Dagger's analysis (Chapter 7) of homelessness from a civic republican perspective shows how any community committed to equal civic voice must commit to provide housing first rather than follow a more traditional social services model of trying to "fix" a person before they can be "ready" for housing. This chapter is important because it shows how the internal logic of democracy and a robust commitment to community can yield a persuasive demand for specific material goods to be provided as a matter of policy (namely, decent housing). This argument is highly relevant to Richmond and communities throughout the United States wrestling with homelessness and affordable housing crises. Also in a hopeful vein, Ravi K. Perry (Chapter 12) on "targeted universalism" lays out a compelling strategy by which local leaders can articulate truly bold equity goals while also building and sustaining winning political coalitions in favor of change. Leaders concerned with advancing community wealth building, to the degree they embrace truly bold equity concerns, certainly face political constraints, but they are not without power to significantly influence and alleviate those constraints provided they act strategically and communicate their intent and goals clearly. This insight is critical because, in practice, community wealth building on the Barnes/Williamson model will require local political leaders to frequently undertake initiatives and risks that have not been previously taken in their specific communities.

The insightful chapters by Risha R. Berry (Chapter 13) and the team of Barbara Brown Wilson and Meghan Z. Gough (Chapter 14) shed further light on challenges of implementing community wealth building in practice, in both cases in the setting of central Virginia. Berry's chapter shows how the seemingly straightforward charge of helping underemployed Richmond residents find better jobs through targeted workforce development necessarily collides with structural obstacles at the intersection of race and poverty. This realization has led Richmond's Office of Community Wealth Building (OCWB) to promote both local systemic change and formulate policy advocacy strategies naming and tackling structural racism in various aspects of policy and institutional practice. In this way, the Richmond OCWB model aims not just at a traditional workforce development or service delivery model but also to push upwards for policy change (and greater resources), drawing on new knowledge generated by the very work of seeking to fulfill its mission of cutting poverty in Richmond dramatically. Gough and Wilson describe the challenges and contradictions involved in efforts by both Virginia Commonwealth University (in Richmond) and the University of Virginia to redefine university social responsibility and act as progressive anchor institutions committed to using their respective resources to benefit local residents. Universities—especially public research universities—are major forms of community wealth and must be key players in community wealth building coalitions; as Gough and Wilson show, however, that moral imperative exists side-by-side with and at times in tension with other organizational imperatives and goals, and sometimes simply institutional habits that need to be challenged.

REMAINING QUESTIONS

This book is a timely and unique contribution to both the emerging understanding of community wealth building in the United States and to the ongoing conversation among scholars and the broader public concerning democracy's future. Quite obviously, many critical questions remain to be taken up, building on the work here and a growing body of related work by practitioners and theorists in the U.S. and elsewhere. In this final section, we point towards the future by laying out how we believe the community wealth building paradigm can (and should) impact both the theory and practice of American democracy at four levels: national politics, local politics, social movement organizing, and academic discussion.

National Politics

While an explicit community wealth building agenda has not emerged in national politics, several leading contenders in the 2020 presidential campaign have presented visions that include key aspects of the community wealth building paradigm. Public conversation on broadening the ownership of wealth along with the intense focus on race and inequality is motivating candidates to work to assemble a broad and diverse electoral coalition. Indeed, the prospects of a Democratic president portends a receptiveness to embracing the idea of bottom-up, locally steered change aimed at fundamental issues as a component part of the governing strategy. The community wealth building paradigm can serve as an umbrella for a broad policy agenda that is targeted and structured in community-driven ways.

Community wealth building is a viable policy paradigm. Given the polarities in American political life, the work of governance itself may force national candidates in this direction. However, progress would be made much faster by a president undertaking a commitment to community wealth building with intentionality. We could imagine a White House Office of Community Wealth Building charged with promoting and supporting best practices across local communities while also undertaking the difficult work of re-orienting and aligning existing federal programs in a coherent, community-sustaining direction—an effort that would necessarily involve multiple crucial federal agencies. Certainly, one can imagine in the near future a progressive federal administration taking the following steps:

- providing matching grants to communities that establish and institutionalize bold equity goals, rewarding not just established players but also communities seeking to tackle equity issues in a serious way for the first time;
- promoting and incentivizing best practices at the local level for equitable economic development, housing, education, transportation, and more, that mirror community wealth building principles such as inclusive participation, with particular focus on localities seeking to challenge entrenched local patterns;
- identifying policy tools available to broaden community-based wealth ownership, from housing to employee-owned firms to public procurement policies;
- enhancing the scale of resources available to support local communities and integrating such support with other federal policies aimed at impacting the structure of opportunity and broadening the distribution of income and wealth;
- committing the federal government itself to bold equity goals (national level) with a place-based component (no place left behind!).

Local and State Politics

There is much that state and localities as well as ordinary citizens can do to promote a community wealth building paradigm. This does not entail following a simple series of cookie-cutter steps or reducing the paradigm to a simple formula applicable to all localities. But there is at least one thing any city interested in community wealth building must do: build local political support to establish bold, transformational equity goals, then make that goal the focal point for public communications and policy-making.

States can encourage localities that take that initial step through matching grant programs (as in Virginia) and technical assistance. Numerous organizations already are building networks of connected cities pursuing this work to promote best practices and peer learning, while accumulating a body of practical expertise on how to get things done. We believe more cities and localities will continue to go down this route because there are few other appealing options for tackling fundamental issues of equity and justice; and because even if there are major new federal programs to expand the safety net, improve health care, raise wages, and other elements of "structural change," such welcome changes still would not be enough to overcome entrenched local inequities.

Community wealth building is deliberately a capacious concept, and in practice, disagreements—even heated disagreements—about how best in practice to advance bold equity goals are inevitable. So too is political competition. That's why it's important in local arenas for the community wealth building paradigm to build broad and inclusive community-level support and to avoid unnecessary partisanship that can come with being excessively tied to a single political figure.

While we do not claim community wealth building as a paradigm that brings an end to conflict and disagreement within urban politics or local politics more generally, what is most important is that it features processes of deliberation as a key component to allow for inclusive participation and the fullest possible discussion, review and vetting of major ideas and proposals at the front end of any major initiative. Here is one of the places in which the aspirations of community wealth building and the practice of democracy are mutually reinforcing. If communities are unable to engage in a deliberative process and work through difficult questions, then prospects for local community wealth building may appear more idealistic than realistic.

Social Movement Organizing

While we are hopeful that many cities and localities can take a lead role in adopting a community wealth building approach, that hope comes with three important amendments. First, in any locality there are likely to be powerful entrenched interests that might resist bold steps to build community wealth. Second, it is probably not realistic that all cities and localities will have political leadership with sufficient vision and courage to take bold actions in advance of equity goals. Third, communities and cities will need to learn from one another as this work unfolds.

All those emendations lead to this important observation: it is critically important that local community wealth building efforts tap into and draw upon the energy, organization, and power of larger-scale social movements—social movements that transcend specific places. In recent years, Black Lives Matter, #MeToo, climate change activism, gun control activism, and more have sparked national conversations and mobilized citizens across communities. New movements for economic justice such as Fight for $15 have garnered momentum, alongside traditional labor organizing. Numerous organizations and advocacy groups are focused on political reform, criminal justice reform, drug law reform, and more.

There are also a variety of robust policy-making networks linking together cities interested in pursuing bold, progressive change and advancing equity agendas: organizations in this space include the National League of Cities, PolicyLink, The Democracy Collaborative, The Aspen Institute, foundations, university research centers, and private consulting firms. Those networks act to circulate and cross-pollinate promising ideas across cities and allow municipal leaders and advocates to learn from one another.

But the question remains, "How can local community wealth building efforts tap into vibrant social movement energy while also calling attention to novel local solutions that social movement activists might advocate for?" This challenging question has no easy answer other than to acknowledge: (1) it will require a lot of mutual translation between the worlds of policy-makers and officials and social movements; (2) it will be complicated and requires committed effort; and (3) it will require risk taking on behalf of all parties involved – for instance, the risk that local knowledge or locally generated alternatives are diminished when brought into conversation with "expert knowledge" from other communities. Governance, including taking responsibility for difficult decisions in constrained circumstances, is different than protest or advocacy, yet robust democracies should have a healthy tension between these modes of democratic engagement.

We suspect there will be need, sooner than later, for multiple new national networks and organizations specifically dedicated to spreading knowledge and information about community wealth building strategies, showing how they are a natural extension of the demands made by prominent social movements, and connecting policy-maker and activists across localities. These networks might be national in scope, or they might be regional. Some may be directly connected to a political party or organization, some may be independent. What is essential, however, is that knowledge and policy content, in considerable substance, be shared and made available to communities at low or no cost, as well as toolkits on how to learn about and participate effectively in local government. The goal should be not only to promote activism and engagement, but also deeply informed activism and engagement that has the potential to be truly effective.

Academic Discourse and the Reconstruction of Democracy

The last several years have seen an explosion of academic discourse concerning the future of democracy, largely but not completely fueled by the 2016 election of Donald Trump. This literature has generated substantial insights, this discourse typically has been stronger on providing analysis and diagnosis of what's gone wrong rather than providing realistic or persuasive prescriptions for change.

What would it take to significantly reform and improve the system of American governance, to address American democracy's fundamental flaws and restore a measure of confidence in the efficacy of popular self-government? That's the crucial question facing not only scholars of democracy, but all of us in our capacities as citizens. We think that any serious investigation of that question in the American context must focus on local, state and national levels simultaneously and be critically attentive to the ways in which local government has the capacity to create deep democracy based on the working through of common, fundamental problems.

The dominant image of American democracy is that of the voter going to the poll to cast a ballot. That act will always be important, but for defining and understanding of what democracy requires it is far too thin. A more robust image is that of citizens attending a public meeting focused on shared concerns that will be influenced by their perspectives, or even better a group of citizens organizing to advance a shared goal.

The low-intensity version of American democracy-as-just-voting is insufficient to deal with the deep and intertwined histories of inequality and inequity that divides the American polity. Community wealth building offers an alternative vision of American democracy as robust and inclusive participation and organization, not simply for organizing's sake, but in order to advance core equity goals reflecting our commitments to one another as citizens and as humans. That's the version—and vision—of American democracy that can inspire dedication and action as we move deeper into the 21st century.

REFERENCE

Barnes, Melody and Thad Williamson (2019), "Winning the 'Cold Civil War'," *Democracy: A Journal of Ideas*, No. 51, Winter.

Index

'How do we address housing, community development, environmental pollution, public education, crime, and other issues facing U.S. cities? Inspired by "community wealth building" taking place in Richmond, Virginia, the editors and contributors of this path-breaking book explore the theoretical and empirical realities of 21st century American democracy. To make democracy really work we need creative approaches, fresh ideas, and new voices. Melody C. Barnes, Corey D.B. Walker, and Thad M. Williamson have gathered in one work a rich collection of chapters covering social movements, racial justice, voting and ballot access, leadership capacity, and more. Increased political polarization and widening economic inequality have many Americans asking if democratic reform is possible. This welcomed and remarkable book highlights "community wealth building" as a policy paradigm that could provide some answers. This is an important book for anyone interested in the possibilities of making democracy work for everyone in the United States.'
Marion Orr, Frederick Lippitt Professor of Public Policy and Professor of Political Science, Brown University, USA
Editor, *Transforming the City: Community Organizing and the Challenge of Political Change*

'I underlined, asterisked, and cheered at almost every page of Community Wealth Building and the Reconstruction of American Democracy: Can We Make American Democracy Work? It is a book and a practice that could not be more timely or essential for what America and every community within it needs right now. Finally, a framework that combines elements of New Deal liberalism with federalism and localism, recognizing that only at the community level can Americans achieve the inclusion and participation we need to rebuild trust, democracy, and lasting prosperity for all.'
Anne-Marie Slaughter, CEO, New America

'We don't need to wait for overturning capitalism and the racial injustice it inflicts. We don't need to argue for a Black Capitalism that relied on a Neo-colonial critique. Instead, real change to combat the racial inequities of contemporary American capitalism is possible right now starting at the local level. This work edited by Melody C. Barnes, Corey D.B. Walker, and Thad M. Williamson brings together a strong group of scholars who provide insightful theoretical perspectives and pertinent empirical information, illuminating how the community wealth building approach can show us how racial progress is indeed possible and achievable. Moving well beyond the despair that can overwhelm us today, this book provides much needed hope in dark times.'
Sanford Schram, Professor of Political Science , Hunter College and the Graduate Center, CUNY, USA
Co-author of *Hard White: The Mainstreaming of Racism in American Politics*

'This book's unyielding focus on community wealth building is provocative and timely. The strategies offered here are actionable at multiple layers of our republic and are simultaneously practical and profound. This is a necessary antidote to the growing disparities that divide our country, erode our democracy and impair the potential of individuals and communities.'
Bruce Katz, Founding Director Nowak Metro Finance Lab, Drexel University, USA